**Men'sJournal**

# The
# Great Life

A MAN'S GUIDE

TO

SPORTS,

SKILLS,

FITNESS,

AND

FUN

**Men'sJournal**

# The Great Life

Edited by Sid Evans

Foreword by P.J. O'Rourke

PENGUIN BOOKS

PENGUIN BOOKS
Published by the Penguin Group
Penguin Putnam Inc., 375 Hudson Street,
New York, New York 10014, U.S.A.
Penguin Books Ltd, 27 Wrights Lane,
London W8 5TZ, England
Penguin Books Australia Ltd, Ringwood,
Victoria, Australia
Penguin Books Canada Ltd, 10 Alcorn Avenue,
Toronto, Ontario, Canada M4V 3B2
Penguin Books (N.Z.) Ltd, 182–190 Wairau Road,
Auckland 10, New Zealand

Penguin Books Ltd, Registered Offices:
Harmondsworth, Middlesex, England

First published in Penguin Books 2000

1  3  5  7  9  10  8  6  4  2

A Rolling Stone Press Book
Editor: Holly George-Warren
Associate Editor: Kathy Huck
Assistant Editors: Ann Abel and Wendy Mitchell
Editorial Assistant: Andrew Simon

Some of the selections in this volume first appeared
in issues of *Men's Journal*.

LIBRARY OF CONGRESS CATALOGING-IN-PUBLICATION DATA
The great life : a man's guide to sports, skills, fitness, and serious fun /
forward by P.J. O'Rourke ; introduction by Sid Evans
p.  cm.
At head of title: Men's journal
Includes index.
ISBN 0-14-029626-3
1. Men—Recreation—Handbooks, manuals, etc. 2. Men—Conduct of life—
Handbooks, manuals, etc.
3. Sports—Handbooks, manuals, etc. 4. Physical fitness—Handbooks, manuals,
etc. 5. Leisure—Handbooks,
manuals, etc. I. Men's journal (New York, N.Y.)

GV174.G74 2000
305.31—dc21                                            00–033634

Printed in the United States of America
This book was set in Weiss
Designed by Jennifer Ann Daddio

# CONTENTS

## Adventure

# Competitive Sports

# Fitness and Health

# Women

# Skills

# Vices

# Who Needs Adventure?

## BY P.J. O'ROURKE

THIS BOOK is too much for me. The "Ice-Climbing" article, for example—I've been ice-climbing for years, and there's no over-estimating the skill and courage required to get the station wagon up my driveway when I've forgotten to put on the snow tires. But here is someone ice-climbing on slopes even steeper than those of the Mount Pleasant neighborhood where I live in Washington, D.C., and doing it without the benefit of driveway salt, or even a driveway, and instead of being inside a car he's dangling from a rope. I am amazed. Also perplexed. What is a "crampon"? Has anyone thought to register it as a trademark? It's an excellent name for a feminine-hygiene product to provide relief during the difficult time of the month that, it occurs to me, the target audience for this book never has. Nor do I. I'm past menopause. Plus I'm a guy.

Being a postmenopausal guy, this book isn't targeted at me either. Men my age are not much for wielding ice axes unless the automatic cube dispenser on the Frigidaire jams. And we aren't inter-ested in kayaking Niagara Falls, magma boarding in active volcano cones, taking unicycle tours of the Andes, or butt-skiing the Great Pyramid of Khufu. Not that we're adverse to facing danger in the outdoors. Just last year a friend of mine dropped dead of a heart attack while mowing the lawn. But what's the point of my risking life and limb when both will be useless soon? It's more fun to risk money. Preferably other people's. You, the reader of this book, want to fly an airplane. I, the writer of this introduction, want to raise venture capital for a start-up pharmaceutical company—principal asset, the Crampon trademark—float an IPO, cash in the stock options, and buy a Gulfstream jet.

That G-5 I'm getting is another reason this book is too much for me. Look at the piece "Crash Course." The information is sound, the advice is intelligent, but none of it applies in my case. Once a fellow is into the colorectal-cancer-exam years, the way to deal with plane crashes is by making a list: back taxes owed, alimony due, yard chores outstanding, amount of school tuition to be paid next year, net loss when Crampon Inc. went into chapter 11, date of next scheduled colonoscopy, etc. Then, if the plane gets into trouble, I pull out this piece of paper and die smiling. What's with the adventure-travel trend anyway? You want excitement and risk on your vacation? Go anywhere with a beach or pool, and tell your wife she looks fat in her bathing suit.

*Huh?* I'm getting a little deaf in this ear. Old draft-dodging injury. *What's that?* Ah, it's the Voice of Youth saying, if I'm not mistaken, "Shut up." Yes. Good point. Who wants to hear one more ex–bong-sucker in pinstripes choke on his Pepcid AC over what's the matter with kids today? I shall mock no more the generation of

*Cubicle workspace, calf tattoos*
*Itty-bitty phones, and great big shoes.*

Especially since you with the ore-freighters on your feet are supposed to purchase this book— thereby making ex–bong-suckers a bunch of money. Which reminds me of another business-opportunity idea. (I understand that many—if not most—book buyers in your age cohort have a billion dollars from founding websites. No doubt you are looking to diversify your investment portfolio.) It's a national franchise chain of mall-based cosmetic surgeons specializing in laser tat removal and invisible closure of body-piercing holes. The retired bookkeeper who runs the bake sale at our

church has a tongue stud and a four-inch-wide American Indian thingy permanently inked around her biceps, so the hip phase of this trend is over.

But where was I? I think I was saying that this book contains too much stuff about achieving physical fitness and improving sexual per-formance and not enough about raising money to fight Alzheimer's. I envision a dramatic national campaign. Slogan: "Alzheimer's— Fergedaboutdit!"

Come to think of it, I wasn't saying anything about Alzheimer's. Of course, a fund-raising campaign would accomplish tremendous good. Although a little late for me. Actually, I was saying that I have to stop making fun of your generation for fear of hurting book sales, getting fired, and so on. But it's not just that. Consider what *The Great Life* would be if it were, indeed, written for my generation instead of yours. Imagine the chapter headings:

PLAID SHORTS, PLAID SHIRTS,
BLACK SOCKS, AND WINGTIPS
Not Just for Dress-Down
Fridays Anymore?

HOW TO OPEN THOSE
PESKY CD CASES
When the Grand Funk Railroad LP
Is Hopelessly Scratched

3-DAY SOLO SURVIVAL COURSE
Finding Food, Clothing, and the TV
Remote While Your Wife Visits
Her Sister in Atlanta

I BET I DIE
Everything That's Ever Been Printed or
Said About Life Insurance

Plus the artwork would be color photographs of Christie Todd Whitman in her underwear and other age-appropriate illustrations.

No, this is a better book, even if it is full of advice on sit-ups instead of excuses to sit down. You have no business sitting down anyhow. You're not tired yet. Plus a workout will add zipper noises to your private life because you can still get bulges in your clothing that interest women—other than the bulge in the right hip pocket.

The bulge that pops the top two buttons on my cardigan sweater doesn't seem as effective. Although the vagaries of fashion may bring pudge into style. Perhaps one day I'll be walking down the street and major babes will holler, "Yo, Budweiser Balcony, you're looking . . ." Looking, no doubt, like this book makes me feel—superannuated, out-of-shape, and green with envy.

Not that I haven't enjoyed every page of *The Great Life*. And envy is the key. I hate you for being young and fit, of course. But don't mind me. Read everything in here and take it to heart. I'll be home beside the lava lamp listening to Grand Funk Railroad and smiling with the secret knowledge that if your generation actually goes on every adventure listed in this book, plays each of the sports, does the whole program of exercises, and practices all the recommended sexual techniques, you're going to kill yourselves.

# No Regrets

## BY SID EVANS

*You only live once, but if you work it right, once is enough.*

— JOE E. LOUIS

THIS BOOK is about the things a man can do to live a more adventurous life. Recently I tried one of those things, whitewater kayaking, when I was visiting *Men's Journal* contributor Reggie Crist in Sun Valley, Idaho. Reggie is a former Olympic skier and a world-class kayaker who likes to run six miles in the mountains before breakfast. For years he and his family have kayaked the North Fork of the Payette River near Stanley, which is famous for having some of the most difficult whitewater in North America. We were going to be paddling the Cabarton, just above the North Fork, which Reggie assured me was "not as serious."

On the drive from Sun Valley we stopped at a small alpine lake where Reggie's sister Danielle, a winner of the Survival of the Fittest contest and the owner of a kayak school, spent an hour teaching me how to do an Eskimo roll—*lean to the opposite side of the boat, get your paddle out of the water, flick your hips, and stroke*—how to steer, and how to "exit" the boat if I was unable to roll. I told Danielle and Reggie I was nervous about the idea of going through rapids upside down.

"All you have to do is lean forward and keep paddling hard," Reggie told me. "Especially when we get to the Plunge." "The Plunge?" I asked. Reggie just laughed.

By noon the next day we were stroking toward the first stretch of rapids on the Cabarton, known as the Cocaine Wave. I could see up ahead where the river narrowed into a canyon and the clear green water turned to white foam. As we got closer, I could hear the crashing of the waves, a sound that until this moment I had always considered pleasant. Wearing a wet suit, a plastic helmet, and a life vest, I was flanked by Reggie, Danielle, and several of their superathletic friends, but I was still not convinced that I would survive the day. When the first big waves started tossing around my 40-pound kayak, I heard Reggie shouting something, but before I could figure out what it was, I was underwater.

It had crossed my mind on the drive up to Stanley that whitewater kayaking was not my kind of sport. A longtime fly-fisherman, I had spent the majority of my river time on the surface, breathing oxygen. Now, as my kayak was being whisked through the Cocaine Wave, I was gaining an entirely new perspective. If a rapid looks wild when you are paddling into it, then it is ten times as wild on the other side. Clouds of air bubbles are swirling all around you, strong currents are pushing and pulling you in different directions at the same time, and, of course, there is no oxygen. Add to this the fact that it's somewhat difficult to "exit" a kayak—pull off the spray skirt, push with both hands to free your butt from the seat, slide your legs out—and being upside down in a rapid becomes an intensely urgent situation. If you can perform an Eskimo roll in mid-rapid—what kayakers call a "combat roll"—you right your boat and keep paddling downriver; if not, then getting out of that boat quickly becomes the most important thing you've ever done. Bagging the idea of an Eskimo roll almost immediately, I focused, made my exit, came gasping to the surface, and rode out the rapid on my back. Reggie and Danielle and the others were whooping and clapping when I finally crawled out of the river. As if I'd been kayaking for years, Reggie said, "Hey, man, what happened to the roll?"

Adventure, of course, is all about experience—in some cases, years of experience—but if you turn to pages 8-9, you'll find a short piece about whitewater kayaking that tells you how to perform an Eskimo roll and how to exit your boat in a rapid, should the need arise. (It will.) It also tells you a little bit about what to expect on the river, what sort of gear you might want to buy (I strongly recommend nose clips), and what kinds of skills are required to become proficient in the sport. Like a lot of what's in this book, this information won't do you much good until you've bought it in your first big rapid. There is nothing like a dose of terror to speed up the learning process. But just as we try to do in *Men's Journal*, our goal for *The Great Life* was to give men a kind of road map to an interesting life. You pick a route and take your chances; how much territory you cover is up to you.

You can't learn much about tantric sex or mountain climbing or catching a six-pound trout by reading about them, either. Especially tantric sex. But we've gone to the absolute experts in all of these areas—and a lot more—to try to create a comprehensive guide to a modern man's active life. Some people will tell you that the great life is all about making more money, buying a nicer house, driving a faster car, drinking expensive wine, and having the right cuffs on your shirt. There's nothing wrong with any of that, but we think that men are looking for something a little bigger, more surprising, more fun. We think that men want adventure in the natural world, where life is stripped to its purest forms; they want to excel in sports that make them feel strong; they want to know how to take care of their bodies; and they want to travel to interesting places and be ready for anything when they get there. This can become complicated when you get in over your head—literally—but at the end of the day it's all about having as many experiences as possible.

There are six sections in this book, each one covering an important part of a man's life: adventure, sports, fitness and health, women, skills, and vices. We've compiled some of our favorite articles that have appeared in *Men's Journal* since the magazine was founded in 1992, and we've also included lots of new material that goes into greater detail than what the magazine usually covers. We've tried to pack every section, every chapter, and every sidebar with the kind of information that a man can really use, the secrets you learn over a lifetime.

I spent most of my day on the Cabarton going down the rapids upside down. I learned to exit my boat quickly, and after my second or third swim I felt completely comfortable in the river. When we reached the Plunge, we pulled into an eddy to strategize. About 100 yards down, I could see where the river disappeared over a ledge into a cloud of mist. "Just remember, lean forward and paddle hard and you'll be fine," Reggie said. "And try not to freak out when you see it." He was laughing—that same maniacal Idaho laugh—as he said this, and then he stroked downstream and was gone.

Every time I think about going over that water-fall—head down, paddling hard—I wonder how I could have lived so long without learning how to kayak. I remember the free fall of descending that seven-foot drop, riding the big tongue of water that exploded into the deep hole below, and the way my breathing stopped before I'd even gone under. It was a foregone conclusion that I was going to wipe out at the bottom, and wipe out I did—mightily. Maybe if I'd read about kayaking in a book like this one, I would have known that almost no one pulls off a combat roll on their first trip. It might have made me feel better about the thrashing I took. But here is the image that stays with me: I think about flushing through the Plunge upside down, throwing my paddle into position, flicking my hips and stroking hard for the combat roll. In my mind's eye I nail it every time.

# Adventure

THE TRUTH about adventure is that it usually happens when you aren't looking for it—when you forget your $50-a-pair long underwear, when the canoe flips in the Class V rapid and your gear isn't strapped down, when the helicopter that was supposed to lift you out of the Alaskan backcountry doesn't show up, when the grizzly bear you were stalking with your camera suddenly winds you—and charges. During such moments, as the grizzly is swatting you playfully down the side of the mountain, you might wonder why you ever left your couch. You might wonder why, with hundreds of adventure websites, adventure books, and adventure television shows in the world—not to mention adventure magazines—you didn't stay home where it's safe, warm, and grizzly-free.

Well, forget the grizzly for a moment. You went to the wilderness to play because that's where you feel the most alive. It's where the rules change and where you feel part of a world that's bigger than your living room, your gym, and certainly your office. So we've tried to fill this section with smart pieces that will tell you how to be competent when you're out there and how to take on outdoor sports that test your physical and mental abilities, whether you want to kayak, ski, rock-climb, surf, or just hang out in the mountains. You won't become an expert reading about these sports, but hopefully there's enough here to get you started or perhaps to inspire you to pick up a sport you've left behind.

As for the grizzly, you'll also find some advice in this chapter that's partly generated from a regular *Men's Journal* column called "Trouble." This is one of the most popular columns in the magazine, probably because getting into trouble is something men have always been good at and getting out of it is one of the things they pride themselves on the most. There is not a piece in here about exactly what to do if a grizzly is rolling you down the side of a mountain, but what are the chances of *that* happening? Besides, we thought we'd leave the best adventures up to you.

# Get Vertical

LEARNING TO rock-climb is one of those good-news, bad-news propositions. The good news is that getting started is easier than you think. With a few hours of solid instruction—and climbing is definitely too high stakes for a trial-and-error education—you will probably have ascended vertical terrain as hard as 5.7, which is halfway up the difficulty scale to its current limit, 5.14. You will have earned the right to stride away with the muscles in your shoulders throbbing and a fine little glow in your head. The bad news is that you will know fear.

Fear of heights is surprisingly universal. Psychologists have placed newborns two hours old onto a glass table and noticed how they recoil from the perceived drop. The bolder ones (psychologists, that is) have gone so far as to suggest that fear of heights might be an instinct. I see this fear all the time while teaching climbing classes, before we even touch stone. No one wants to bring it up; each is sure he's the Lone Ranger. So I talk about my own fear. Like being able to look down the 2,000-foot face of Yosemite's Half Dome only by lying on my belly and just peering over the edge.

Climbing is strong medicine, equal parts exhilaration and humility. If you keep it up—and

## ESSENTIALS

Don't worry about it. Rent shoes; your instructor or the gym will provide everything else. Soon enough you can buy a pair of shoes and a harness. You won't need your own rope until much later, when you know how to set up an anchor safely.

I'll tell you flat-out that it's addictive—the alchemy of hesitation and afterglow will stick with you. Even the countless falls will become reassuring; they will drill into the reptilian part of your brain where the fear resides and prove that the rope and your climbing partner can actually stop you in mid-plummet. Climbing makes me feel more alive—humble before the forces of nature but lighter and more playful among men; a little more nimble in thought, with a broader perspective on the world and my place in it. You know that feeling in your body after a good workout? Climb-ing amplifies the sensation, especially in your head—thanks to the challenge factor, that dose of fear. This wonderfully clear-eyed elation is the closest I often get to what Rimbaud called "supernaturally sober."

## First

Most people begin with instruction at one of the country's 350 climbing gyms. Inexpensive basic courses last a few hours. But go outside. That's where they keep the real rock, and playing on it will make you a better climber. You will get less vertical initially than you would in a gym, but the advantage, even when starting on a 40-degree slab, is that your footwork and balance will be better right from the start. Two hours outside will put your footwork ahead of two months in the gym. If you want to get more for your money, more detailed programs run one to several days. The American Mountain Guides Association will give you a list of certified guides and accredited schools.

### Next

Eventually, you may aspire to be at the "sharp" end of the rope—leading, or being the first up the rock, trailing the rope behind you for others to follow. My mentor, Chuck Pratt, flatly states that "leading is climbing," though it's not for everyone. It takes a rack of protection hardware, which you attach to the rock to shorten a possible fall—and, of course, balls. But the crucial skill is judgment, which you build up slowly only after spending lots of time moving over stone.

—DOUG ROBINSON

# Ride the Trail

RIDING SINCE the age of three when I borrowed my next-door neighbor's Big Wheel, I soon graduated to a Raleigh ten-speed, which took me far away from my high school on those days I was supposedly (cough, cough) out sick. This prepared me for my first job in Manhattan, as a bike messenger, weaving in and out of congested Park Avenue traffic and blowing my whistle like a crazed lifeguard. So, a decade ago, when a friend asked me to try this newfangled bike with fat wheels in the woods of New Hampshire's White Mountains, I was game.

For the first three miles, riding on dirt roads, I was starting to feel comfortable—with automobile and exhaust fumes being replaced by the sweet smell of balsam and fir. We took a left at a grassy snowmobile trail, snaking our way into a thick forest. Finally, we made it to the base of a steep hiking trail, which my buddy immediately started to climb.

"Are you out of your @#$&* mind?"

"No, this is killer singletrack. Follow me!"

I tried, but failed miserably. The narrow trail sliced up and down the mountain over rocks, roots, and shallow streams. I was off the saddle, carrying my bike more than I was pedaling. On the way down, I slid over sheets of rock, got whipped by branches that were impossible to avoid, and flew over my handlebars when my bike got stuck in a mud bog. I reached the bottom caked in sweat and dirt, wanting desperately to put my fist through my pal's ear-to-ear grin, but I couldn't lift my arm. I vowed never to try this insane sport again.

Reggie Crist carries his
bike through the waters of
Adams Gulch, Idaho.

ANDY ANDERSON

Well, I did, and now I'm hooked. But I quickly learned that mountain biking is more like downhill skiing than road biking. You can't just jump on a bike and climb a mountain without risking all that wonderful orthodontic work. You have to start slow on the beginner greens (rolling dirt roads) before making your way to the double diamonds (technical singletracks).

## First

Go to a reputable bike store and find a frame that fits your body perfectly. Ideally, your leg should be slightly bent when your pedal crank is at six o'clock. Your tires should feel firm when you squeeze them but not rock-hard, ensuring that the tire is soft enough to absorb any shock. Find a decent helmet and a backpack-style hydration system called a CamelBak, which can hold upwards of 100 ounces of water. Mountain biking, with its frequent slowing and accelerating, is an excellent workout and thus requires far more water than a road biker's bottle.

Start with a hilly gravel road or grassy double-track that lets you test your balance. Good riders know how to find their sweet spot (where your weight is perfectly distributed). On ascents, your body should be crouched and slightly forward, your butt touching the tip of the seat. For descents, move behind the seat, almost grazing the rear wheel, and feather the brakes to avoid sliding. You should also be looking ahead for changes in terrain to anticipate gear shifts. Most neophytes shift way too late on an approaching hill and often find themselves walking their bike. For riding over small logs or rocks, lift the front tire and then shift your weight forward to allow the rear tire to follow smoothly.

## Next

Advance to singletrack riding by taking a mountain-biking course. Dirt Camp offers a series of weekend camps across the country. You'll learn how to jump logs in the middle of the trail by doing the bunny hop.

Crouch real low on the bike and spring up before the log by lifting your handlebars. At the same time, you lift the rear of the bike by pulling up with your feet. To do a water crossing, speed up before you hit the stream and steer away from the dark spots, where the water is deep.

Soon you'll be able to pick a line on a sweeping single-track and conquer every obstacle. The immediacy of this type of riding—where every ten yards or so you face another challenge—replaces the mundane worries of modernity. You get caught in the web of the woods, a Zen-like groove where your only thoughts are jumping, jerking, slowing down, and speeding up.

—STEVE JERMANOK

## CITY BIKING

# Hit the Streets

I am often asked by people who have seen me bicycling around New York City why on earth I do such a thing. They assume that it is dangerous and certainly inelegant, as if the streets should be left to the messengers and the delivery boys. In fact, those who bicycle in the city tend to become somewhat smug about what they do. Bicycling is nowhere near as a dangerous as it appears, and almost invariably one can get to one's destination, certainly in rush hours, quicker than by car. As for inelegance, that is surely in the eye of the beholder. After all, I once estimated that by not taking the subway, buses, or especially taxis, I have saved $79,000 over the twenty years I've been bicycling around New York City. True, I don't know where that bundle is, haven't put my hands on it, but it's a comforting thought.

I ride a ten-speed bike, which cost me about $200. There are many choices, of course. For $500 one can buy a bicycle that folds up and you can take it into your office or whatever rather than leaving it on the street where it can be removed by the bicycle thieves. But talk about inelegance, to stride down an office corridor carrying a briefcase and a bicycle.

Whatever the model, the gear shifters should be on the handlebars, and also the brakes. A foot brake, effected by standing down on the back foot, is a bit slower than what you can do with the hands, and thus unacceptable, I think, in the cities. Some riders have bells on the handlebars to warn pedestrians they are coming their way. Worked with the thumb, bells don't make much a noise in the city bedlam, and besides, I would rather have my fingers free to work the hand brakes. The messengers, who are the true artisans at getting through traffic at speed, often carry whistles in their mouths. My own preference is the shout. "Watch it!" is a common usage, and in the milliseconds before a possible collision a sharply delivered "Huh!" or "Hey!" or even "Ho!" is generally useful. Another term in one's vocabulary is "Sorry," which means you haven't had time to say "Watch it!" or the other, shorter alternatives.

A basket on the handlebars is a sensible appliance. Straw baskets have a certain aesthetic value but generally will not survive more than two or three rainstorms: they gently disintegrate off the handlebars. It is best to get a large wire basket, the kind that delivery boys use on the front of their bikes. True, there is a certain loss of dignity riding down Park Avenue wearing a dinner jacket, say, on a bicycle with a wire basket; on appearance one would seem to be returning from delivering a pizza. But no matter. The basket is especially useful on hot muggy days in summer when a luncheon appointment is forthcoming: one can fold one's coat into the basket, even a tie, and arrive at the restaurant without being sweat-soaked.

Now, a few words on the dangers.

One of the most alarming sights in the city is to be riding along peacefully enough with the traffic flow and suddenly spotting a bicyclist barreling down the avenue the wrong way with two shopping bags dangling from his handlebars and a package of pizzas in his basket — a delivery boy! They are a bigger problem than the messengers, who tend to keep to the middle of the streets, weaving in and out of traffic like skiers on a wooded slope. The delivery boys keep to the bicycling lanes, but they seem to prefer going the wrong way. I don't know why this is . . . perhaps to get a little suspense in their lives. They are usually on clunky-looking mountain bikes, invariably with the seats lowered, so that their faces, often wide-eyed with anxiety, seem to peer above the basket rims like woodchucks peeking out of a burrow. The solution to their approach is to crowd to the curb and let them pass.

A peculiar danger of the street is to be "crocodiled," which occurs when the back door of a car, or more likely a cab, is opened to let out a passenger just as a bicyclist is sailing by between the cab and the curb. If the timing is just right, the bicyclist can be engulfed right into the taxi itself, the bicycle a heap on the pavement behind him. The key to avoiding the "jaws" of a taxi is to peer through the back window to try to gauge the situation within . . . if someone appears to be getting out.

At a stoplight it is not a good idea to put a hand out and steady oneself on a car with a driver in it. The car, being an extension of the body inside, is figuratively as sensitive as a thigh, and touching it can result in (1) an ugly look, (2) a fistfight, (3) a gunshot, or (4) all of the above.

In New York a constant danger is that your bicycle is going to be stolen off the light pole or wherever it has been moored. If this happens whatever the protective device, a small but comforting thought is that you can instantly buy another bicycle and amortize its cost within a week or so. I once moored my bicycle in front of the Sherry Netherlands Hotel on Fifth Avenue using one of the poles that support the awning. When I came out from lunch, I discovered my bicycle was missing. Furious, and at the same time rather admiring the gall of a bicycle thief able to make off with one from the front of a prestigious hotel on Fifth Avenue, I rushed off to the nearest bicycle shop to buy another. Subsequently, I found out that the hotel staff had removed my bicycle (it was blocking the entrance) by unscrewing the base of the awning support, and it was in their basement. I got it back. I had two bicycles. I gave one to a friend. He wheeled it into a hardware store to buy a wrench. While he had his back turned, it was stolen.

But he'd had such fun riding the bicycle around the city during the two days he had it, he bought another. I wasn't surprised.

—GEORGE PLIMPTON

# Conquer the Rapids

ONE OF THE greatest rushes in sports is traveling down a fast-moving river in an 8-foot-long, 40-pound plastic kayak as it threads between boulders the size of cars and rushes over 4-foot drops. Whitewater never rests. Imagine if those conveyor belts at the airport sped up to 30 miles per hour and were constantly rising and falling and throwing themselves from side to side, trying to suck you into their machinery. That's something akin to whitewater kayaking, though drier.

ANDY ANDERSON

## First

I felt as if I had been stuffed into a floating toilet bowl the first time I climbed into a kayak, but the crafts are actually quite maneuverable—as long as you, the engine, are pulling hard and, most importantly, true. If you can't paddle in a straight line, you won't be able to dart to an eddy for safety or choose one shoot over another; the river will control you. So to venture into Class I through III rapids, you'll need to learn a few basic paddling techniques, including forward and

Grant Amaral does an endo on the Payette River in Idaho.

backward strokes, sweeps (leaning forward, extending your paddle, for more severe turns), sculling moves (just kissing the top of the water with your paddle), and bracing (planting the paddle for balance, as if it were a giant hand extended into the water to keep you from flipping).

Start on flat water—if you can't move in a straight line there, you're not ready for whitewater. You'll also need to master the wet exit—squeezing your way out of the cockpit after you've capsized and getting to shore with your kayak and paddle. Unfortunately, this requires lots of practice in fast water. Hey, gotta pay your dues.

Find a good teacher through a local kayaking club; or, if you can, take a week and go to a whitewater school, where you'll learn more quickly.

---

### Next

To attempt Class IV or V rapids, you'll need to know how to Eskimo roll, restoring your boat to its right-side-up position while staying in the cockpit. The most important thing is to quell panic. Stay calm, move your paddle perpendicular to the boat, flick your hips, and pull toward the surface. The best place to learn (and practice) rolling is in a pool. The water is generally warmer, there's no current to drag you downriver, and you can even wear a face mask at first to keep water from forcing its way up your nose.

—JON BOWERMASTER

---

**SEA-KAYAKING**

# Stroke Surf

B Y THE TIME I caught them, it was too late. Deep in the heart of Alaska's Prince William Sound, on Day Six of a 10-day sea-kayak trip, the rest of the group had paddled too far ahead, mesmerized by the towering Harriman Glacier. They were smart enough to stay clear of the calving ice. The ensuing waves, however, were another matter. When I reached them and reprimanded them for straying too close, a seven-story chunk crashed into the water, sending a tsunami straight toward us. We responded the only way possible: letting out a unified yell. Then, keeping our sea-kayaks together and pointed toward the wave, we rode it out, letting its giant undulations pass beneath our hulls. Such is the nature of sea-kayaking. With more than 2,000 years of design history behind them, the boats are so stable and sleek, they lull you into pressing onward. And they are so user-friendly that even beginners can take them deep into the wilderness, sometimes a little *too* deep.

### First

To get started, attend one of several sea-kayak symposiums scattered throughout the country. Attended by manufacturers, reps, instructors, and consumers, these gatherings let you try out boats and accessories in a controlled environment, under the watchful eyes of experts. Here you can sample different hulls to tell firsthand the difference between primary and secondary stability, and you can assess the performance characteristics between singles and tandems, and plastic and fiberglass. If you don't like the confined nature of conventional decked boats, where you're sealed inside a cockpit with a spray skirt, try a sit-on-top that, as its name implies, lets you sit on top of the hull in depressions for your buttocks and legs. These have a simple advantage over their cockpitted cousins: If you

tip over, you simply flip the boat back upright and climb aboard. The craft can also be used for diving, snorkeling, and surfing.

No matter which option you choose, be prepared to make time. Where their whitewater counterparts leave squiggly wakes, touring kayaks track as straight as a harpoon. Turning them, in fact—especially longer, tandem models—often requires the use of rudders controlled with foot pedals.

### Next

To really see what sea-kayaks are capable of, head out on an overnight trip, either with an outfitter or on your own. This will let you in on a secret known only to other trippers: A sea-kayak is both a vehicle and a backpack. And since the water carries the weight instead of your back, meals don't have to be restricted to Top Ramen; feel free to cart along everything from a Dutch oven to your favorite Chardonnay to go with fresh salmon. With storage hatches fore and aft, gear can be packed for weeks on end. If you want control of your own destiny, take a single, where you alone are engine and captain. For a more social ride—and better power-to-weight ratio—try a double. These are steered from the rear, with the bowman responsible for power.

**—EUGENE BUCHANAN**

# Get Altitude

FAUST SOLD his soul for a very few things. The ability to fly was one of them. Flying is one of the most primitive dreams of the human imagination, but it's rarely a reality. Why? The physical act of piloting an airplane is no harder than driving a car while talking on the phone—and it's less dangerous. The truth is, most people don't learn to fly because it's scary.

My first solo flight went like this: I had about six official hours in my logbook. I was practicing landings in a Cessna 150 at a lonely little field in northern Illinois when my instructor hollered, "Pull over and leave the engine running!" Then he got out, shouting above the engine, "Take it around and come back here! Have a good time!" And he slammed the door.

I sat petrified for a moment, then thought, *Well, do I really want to be a pilot, or am I just bullshitting myself?* I pushed the throttle forward, turned the plane around, and took off. And there I was, all alone, watching the world dissolve in a summer haze beneath my feet. Less than a minute after takeoff I was lost. *I'll circle aimlessly*, I thought, *until I run out of fuel and crash.*

I eventually landed safely and went on to earn my license. But that flight in Illinois was the first time I

> ## All things considered, there are only two kinds of men in the world: those that stay at home and those that do not.
> ### — RUDYARD KIPLING

understood what it meant to put my life into my own hands. I could scream and cry into the radio or pull out my hair, but only my hands and my skill would bring me back to earth. Most of us never take this kind of responsibility for ourselves. There's always a back door. If we sink our boat or get stranded on a mountain, we can call for rescue—and in either case it'll be a pilot who comes for us.

## First

To fly a single-engine plane in the United States, you must earn a private pilot's license from the Federal Aviation Administration. The training for this could cost $6,000 to $8,000, depending on how many hours you fly. The minimum of flight training required by law is 40 hours—20 with a certified flight instructor and 20 solo. But the instructor decides when you're ready; the national average is 65 hours. There is also classroom time to study such subjects as weather, navigation, aerodynamics, and federal aviation regulations. You must pass a written, an oral, and a practical exam—meaning you fly with a representative of the FAA and demonstrate that you can, among other things, hold a course at a certain altitude, read charts, use electronic-navigation aids, and find your way home. If you fly well and answer well, the examiner shakes your hand, signs a form, and from that day forward you are a pilot.

### Next

A private license is really just a learner's permit, and you will need some additional training to become a truly proficient—and safe—pilot. An instrument rating equips you to fly "blind," or solely with reference to the plane's instruments, so you can fly in the clouds and when there is poor visibility. It also enables you to file an instrument flight plan with the FAA: This makes trips much easier, since you are in constant contact with an air-traffic controller, who monitors you on his radar screen the whole way. (Non–instrument-rated pilots out on a weekend jaunt don't get this kind of assistance.) An instrument rating—which requires another 125 hours of flight time and costs another $3,000 to $4,000—is not a prerequisite to becoming a pilot, but flying without one is the equivalent of driving a car and not being allowed on the interstate.

Every pilot also should know how to control the airplane in all possible attitudes—right side up is only one of them. Light planes can (and do) stall, spin, loop, and roll upside down. To learn to cope with such situations, you need aerobatics training, during which you practice rolling the plane back to its wheels-down position. Such courses cost as much as a couple of hundred dollars per hour, but they're the best insurance you can have. Ten hours of training is sufficient for most pilots.

—LAURENCE GONZALES

> ### GEAR
>
> Unless you are planning to buy your own plane, you'll need little in the way of gear at first: a navigational plotter, charts, cool sunglasses, a white scarf, and earplugs to wear on the tarmac so you don't lose any of your hearing.

## SKYDIVING

# Lose Altitude (Fast)

THE MOST TENSION-filled part of skydiving isn't the jump. After all, you have to fly 15 or 20 minutes to get up to 12,500 feet to make the jump, which is a lot of time to worry about everything that can go wrong. Of course, all that is forgotten the sec-

## ESSENTIALS

Parachuting has come a long way since the World War II movie *The Longest Day*, when John Wayne hooked his chute to a static line and ribboned out of the airplane. Today the equipment is easier to use, safer, and much less bulky. Unfortunately, the equipment is also expensive, even used gear. You'll need a harness with a backpack, which holds your main and reserve chutes, as well as a jumpsuit, helmet, and goggles. Optional is an auto activation device, which automatically opens the reserve chute if the main chute fails (something all novices use in the AFF program). Many drop zones rent or sell equipment, and there are also a number of reputable mail-order companies like PD Source. You can find used equipment at some drop zones and through listings in the USPA's magazine, *Parachute*.

ond you step out of the plane and start 2,000 feet of free fall for 45 seconds. As the sky rushes past you in a way you never thought possible, it's amazing how everything that seemed so important just a couple of minutes earlier isn't. The change in perspective is as refreshing as it is exhilarating, which may explain why such an expensive sport—it can cost as much as a few thousand dollars to get started—has such committed adherents.

## First

One of the most efficient ways to learn to jump is through the United States Parachute Association's (USPA) Accelerated Freefall program, or AFF. You can learn the basics in a single, eight-hour day and jump at the end of it—the first stage of the seven-stage program. AFF, taught by a USPA-certified jumpmaster, combines classroom instruction—how to pull the ripcord, how to be aware of altitude—with jumps that get more difficult as one improves. On your first try, two jumpmasters stay with you until the parachute opens; by stage seven, you're soloing, performing back loops and barrel rolls. AFF is

taught at USPA-sanctioned drop zones. Expect to pay up to two hundred dollars for your first AFF jump, which includes equipment and training. The cost goes down by thirds as you move through the program, since only one instructor jumps with you after the first couple of times. Nonstudent jumps, incidentally, cost less than $20 each. This doesn't seem like much until you consider it's possible to make a half-dozen jumps in one day.

## Next

You can compete—there are innumerable local, regional, national, and world competitions, from solo to formation events. Someone like Sergeant Scott Rhodes, who jumps with the U.S. Army's elite Golden Knights team, has made more than 11,000 jumps in 13 years and has won nearly two dozen national and world titles. You can also get your USPA license, which entitles you to teach. There are four levels, A through D, with D being the most expert. Reaching D isn't easy—one-half of the applicants who apply for it wash out.

—JEFF SIEGEL

# Take the Plunge

THE FIRST GREAT diver I ever saw was Jarrod Jablonski, who was my cavern-diving instructor. During our first class, he talked about the modified flutter kick, the shuffle kick, and a few other propulsion techniques. Then we dove into Ginnie Spring, a popular site in central Florida, and he performed them. That's the way I still remember it—as a performance. He seemed to hang in placid free fall wherever he wanted to be, and then he would simply shape-shift to another place, the way a gibbon sort of pours itself from tree to tree.

To see him stride about on the cavern ceiling—upside down on just his fin tips, fingers folded casually across his belly—was to witness a kind of ballroom dancing in water, and it relieved me at once of the illusion that I was a good diver.

Since then I've made progress, I hope. In the warm waters of the Bahamas, I've stepped off the edge of the world and descended the walls of colossal coral canyons, a human mite among organic gargoyles. In the cold and surging currents of the Galápagos Islands, I've drifted among hundreds of hammerhead sharks and kept my heartbeat down to a gentle canter. I've mastered those propulsion techniques and have even gotten to the point where I can softly dribble myself on my head across sandy sea floors, just watching the garden eels garden and the urchins crawl.

---

## First

Most of the world's true wilderness is now underwater, and all you need to know to dive it has been summed up thusly: Breathe in, breathe out, and don't hold your breath. Oh, yeah, and beware of decompression sickness (DCS)—it can kill you. Indeed, DCS is the rub that makes taking a scuba-certification class an absolute necessity.

A basic open-water diving course (about nine hours of lectures, six hours in a pool, and four dives) can be knocked out in a couple of weekends. Most dive shops also schedule night classes during the week. You'll

## ESSENTIALS

While scuba equipment is usually provided by the instructor for the duration of a course, you'll need to show up with personal snorkeling gear: a mask, fins, and booties. Certified divers can scuba around the world using decent rental gear, but since the equipment is beautiful, functional, long-lasting, and reliable, few can resist buying their own. For a small investment, you can do yourself proud with a regulator and a buoyancy-compensator device (which doubles as a backpack, for carrying your cylinder).

learn a little about physics and physiology and a lot about underwater safety.

## Next

It's not unusual to complete a basic course without attaining much skill. Good instructors will tell you that a C-card is just your license to begin to learn. Then you should master true neutrality—buoyancy control at any depth—which makes for the difference between flying and floundering. Your scuba instructor will teach you to match the downward drag of the weight belt with the upward lift of the wet suit and to make small adjustments by letting air in and out of your buoyancy compensator. But true neutrality is achieved with the diaphragm and the ribs, holding on to liquid space the way a snake grips the earth. Steady, even breaths suspend you. Take a big, chest-expanding draw on the regulator and you cast off for slow ascents; a long exhalation and you steadily descend—mammal as bathysphere.

Ready to explore, you position yourself with good trim, the perfect balancing of flotation and weight that allows for a horizontal posture. Orient yourself like a fish, relax, and see what happens. Most likely your fins will sink as your torso rises. Then you'll need to make adjustments, not in the amount of weight you carry but in how and where you wear it. Once you feel the rightness of good trim, you'll never forget it: the pivot point across your navel, a balance as delicate as a postal scale's and—like any point—infinitely refinable.

–BUCKY McMAHON

SURFING

# Catch a Huge Wave

SURFING TAKES place in the ever-changing margins between two primordial forces: the radiant, surging energy of ocean waves and the downward pull of gravity. Flirting elegantly with the pair, playing one against the other, you try to catch a wave as it crests an instant prior to breaking, then slide down and across its face—edging and releasing, climbing and dropping, maneuvering to stay just ahead of the breaking curl. This act will become a strong enough addiction, detaching you from such concerns as work, taxes, and stress, that the hunt for the perfect wave may become your highest priority. Among the brethren, this condition is known as "surf fever." Then again, you may not need to search at all. Phil Edwards, one of surfing's most respected elders, claims that his first wave was the best of his life.

### First

Surf shops are the sport's cultural centers. Survey a handful of surfers on the beach to locate a good one, then take a few lessons; private or group, it doesn't matter. Surfing is the combination of two skills: handling a board and understanding the tendencies and dynamics of waves. After a few lessons, it's mostly a matter of trial and error. Taste a variety of breaks. Each offers a different ride and a unique education.

There are also hundreds of surf schools around the country, as well as learn-to-surf programs at YMCAs and recreation departments in beach towns throughout the United States. If you're bucks-up, fly to Oahu and learn from one of the Waikiki beach boys who set up shop in front of the hotels and give lessons on the world's best beginner waves.

### Next

Eventually, you'll progress to surfing "green-water waves" (waves that haven't yet broken). But first you'll have to get out to them. Study the surf,

noting where and how often it breaks (no two days are the same). Practice picking a path between waves in a set, and keep your board pointed either out to sea or toward shore—if a wave hits you broadside, it'll roll you. Paddle hard, and as the whitewater hits, raise yourself up with your arms and let the wave sweep between you and the board.

—STEVE PEZMAN

## WINDSURFING

# Ride With the Wind

BE PREPARED for a large dose of humble pie if you opt to take up windsurfing. My serving came in Australia when, trying to impress a bikini-clad local, I took a large beginner board out. I got up and going okay, but the wind had me at its mercy, carrying me far from shore, toward sharkville. After wrestling with the sail for the umpteenth time, I glanced up to see my knight in shining bikini bear-

You can only rent a board so long, and even the best of friends hesitate to make lifetime loaners of their quiver. To truly improve, you'll need to make the big purchase. Although you'll outgrow it rather quickly, you can get started with the new WindGlider, an inflatable windsurfer. For more performance, you can get a new beginner board and sail, which can be expensive. Your best bet, however, is to go with a used package, which you can secure for about half the price of a new set. Other gear includes a wet suit for cold water sailing, wet-suit booties, a harness, and helmet.

ing down on me in a rescue boat, readying to haul me back to shore. I was saved, but humbled.

## First

Swallow your pride and get on the biggest board you can find—one that will float you and your anvil collection at a complete standstill. Before attempting to pull the sail out of the water, take a bearing on the wind; you want it at your back. Once your vertebrae are back in place and the sail is up, place your feet behind the mast, grab the boom with both hands, and hold on. To head upwind (a wise choice so you can be blown back home), tilt the mast back, toward the stern. When your momentum stalls, quickly walk around the mast to the other side, letting the board spin beneath you. Congratulations. If you're not swimming, you just completed your first tack. To head downwind, tilt the mast forward, toward the bow. When you've stalled and are ready to jibe, whip the mast around on its axis and grab the boom on the opposite side. Another version is a duck jibe, where you turn your board downwind with your feet and duck your head under the boom. Jibes are the more difficult of the two maneuvers, but they're also the most common; you'll rarely see an expert tack after zipping across a bay.

To save face, sign up for a lesson before venturing out on your own. Many windsurfing schools have sailboards specially designed for dryland training, which lets you get a feel for the board and its response to wind without the consequences. When you invariably mess up, simply step off onto the sand instead of falling into the water.

## Next

To further progress in the sport, you'll have to learn how to waterstart. Akin to an Eskimo roll in kayaking, a waterstart gives you another chance when things go awry. Instead of standing on the board and hoisting the sail, which is next to impossible in strong winds, stay in the water and let the wind do the work. Position the board so the wind is at your back, place your feet on the deck, and hang on. With the right technique, the wind will fill your sail, pulling you out of the water and sending you on your way. If you're in winds requiring a waterstart, you'll want a harness, which takes the strain off your arms and places it on webbing hooked to the boom. This lets you sit back Cadillac style, placing the craft on cruise control.

—EUGENE BUCHANAN

# Catch More Fish

JASON SCHNEIDER

THE FASTEST WAY to catch more fish is to cover more water more effectively while presenting the fly accurately and naturally where the trout hang out. And in angling, as in life's lesser pursuits, you sometimes get the edge just by being different.

Fishing the edge where deep water meets shallow often yields the largest fish. The deep water offers refuge to trout, the shallow stuff furnishes bugs, and the edge provides the action. So important are the shallows as food producers that trout stick close by whenever they can remain concealed.

## Fish the Edges

Knowing where to fish, particularly in the cold, high, sometimes-off-color water of the early season, is a bit like theology—you must use the visible to infer the unseen. Your best bet is seeking out areas of contrast, difference, and change; that is, fishing at the edges of things. The edge, or seam, where currents of different speeds run side by side, often holds good numbers of trout, which wait in the slower water for lunch to be delivered by the faster flow. Any obstruction—a rock, a shoal, or a bed of vegetation—will form a seam, and even the smallest one can be productive.

## Add a Trailing Fly

Though fly-fishing can be a sport of finesse and subtlety, sometimes the direct approach works best: Use more flies to catch more fish. The "trailing fly" arrangement, for years an underground technique among Western guides, has filtered into the general angling ranks. With good reason—trailing flies set up easily, cast well, and offer superb flexibility. "Even relatively unskilled clients catch more fish with this rig," says Deschutes River guide Jim Schollmeyer. "It's tremendously productive, especially in riffled water."

*A hobby is a defiance of the contemporary.*

— ALDO LEOPOLD, *A SAND COUNTY ALMANAC*

# SECRET WEAPONS FOR THE STREAM

Of course, all is for naught without the right flies. These four lesser-known flies are considered by such top guides as Schollmeyer to be secret weapons in the early season, when fewer insects hatch and what you tie onto your tippet is most crucial. They may be different from what the local fly shop is pushing—but that's the point.

- **DEER HAIR CADDIS:** Its dark body makes it a good imitation of the small adult stoneflies common in the spring in both the East and the West.
- **MARCH BROWN SOFT HACKLE:** Fish this one swinging on a tight line as a searching pattern, or use it as an emerger for the spring hatches of larger mayflies.
- **GREEN ROCKWORM:** Work this caddis-larva pattern on the bottom or below riffles.
- **HARROP'S BIOT MIDGE/CADDIS EMERGER:** Stick with small sizes, for early-season rises and difficult-to-see bugs.

Tie on a fly as usual. Take a separate length (30 inches or so) of tippet and clinch-knot one end to the hook bend; tie a second fly on the other end. To really boost your odds, attach a third fly to the bend of the second hook. Serving up a smorgasbord like this is perhaps the most effective way to search water when no fish are visible. But check local regulations; the use of multiple flies is restricted on some waters.

During a hatch, try the life-cycle approach: Use a pattern to match the floating adult as the first fly, an emerger as the second, and a nymph as the third. Three well-placed casts will present a trout with all phases of the hatch, saving you a lot of trial-and-error fly changes.

## Learn the Slack-Line Cast

Effective fly-fishing is about presenting an artificial fly attached to a line as though it were a free-floating insect. The biggest obstacle to achieving this kind of unencumbered drift is "drag," which is created when the line on the water travels faster than the fly, pulling it in a decidedly unnatural way that can instantly activate a trout's bullshit detector. One of the most useful techniques to counter drag is the slack-line cast—"the ultimate in drag-free, fly-first presentation," says Schollmeyer. "It's my cast of choice for tough fish or tough conditions, and it works equally well with nymphs or dry flies."

Standing upstream (and slightly to one side, if you like) of a rising fish or a promising spot, execute a conventional overhead cast, but with an overpowered forward stroke. As the line straightens out, simply tug the rod toward you. The combination of excess power and rod tug springs the line, leader, and fly back upstream, landing them on the water in a series of S-curves. This not only sends the fly drifting into the trout's window of vision before the line or leader—a huge advantage on glassy water or with wary fish—but it also extends the length of the drag-free float; you spend more time fishing your fly and less time casting it.

# THE CAST EVERY FLY-FISHERMAN SHOULD KNOW

Those individuals who bring to their fly-fishing the same tolerance for ineptness that allows some skiers never to graduate beyond the stem-christie turn have no reason to learn how to double-haul cast—but everyone else should. The double-haul speeds up the line as it travels through the air on both the back cast and the forward cast, and good line-speed results not only in more distance when you need it but quickness of presentation and better accuracy in any wind at all. It is a skill without which your casting cannot help but be limited. Though I have known a few expert fly-anglers who could not double-haul, they had become expert in freaky defiance of their handicap, rather like a 5'8" player in the NBA.

A double-haul cast is one during which the casting hand performs as in a normal cast, but the line hand pulls, or "hauls," the line two separate times. Many people are put off learning how to double-haul by two misconceptions: that to do so is difficult, and that the only fruit of the skill is added casting distance, which many freshwater anglers, particularly trout fishermen, feel they don't need. In truth, the double-haul can be thoroughly learned, if not mastered, in less than 15 minutes by any reasonably coordinated person. What's more, it will improve your casting at any distance greater than 20 or 30 feet.

Until you internalize its rhythm, practice the double-haul to a short rod stroke between 10 and 2 on the clock, and keep the two hauls snappy and short—about a foot each.

Start with 20 to 30 feet of line out beyond the rod tip, with your casting hand and line hand held close together at about chin height. Say "one, two, three" to yourself, timing it with a watch, until the saying of it consistently occupies one second—that's your rhythmic control, your metronome. You will use an initial one-two-three count for your backcast, and a second one for your forward cast. Start your backcast on the first "one," stop it on "two," and let the line straighten out behind you on "three." Then begin your forward cast on the second "one," stop it on "two," and let the line straighten in front of you on "three." Do this with the same length of line and with no help from your noncasting hand, saying "one, two, three; one, two, three" as you cast, until you own the rhythm. Now introduce the hauls.

Tug the line briskly about a foot down and away from your casting hand on the count of the first "one," then let your line hand drift back up to join the casting hand, so that the two meet again just off your cheek at the count of the first "three." At the count of the second "one," tug the line, again about a foot, as your casting hand starts forward. Then release it on "two" when your casting hand stops the rod. Once you've memorized the motion, start to lengthen your line and your rhythm. That's it. You're double-hauling. —CHARLES GAINES

Producing the slack is easy, but managing it takes some skill—too little causes the fly to drag; too much prevents a solid hook-set when a fish strikes. As the current begins to straighten the curves, lower the rod tip and wiggle it up and down or from side to side to shake out additional line and extend the drift.

—TED LEESON

# Take to the Sea

A S A MOUNTAIN-GROWN kid from Colorado, I felt oddly conspicuous at the TransPac Awards ceremony in Honolulu's Ilikai Hotel. Here were sailing's elite, having just raced 2,250 miles across the Pacific from San Francisco, and try as I might, I just didn't blend in. Where they had Top-Siders, I had Birkenstocks. Where they had experience that would turn Captain Bligh into a deckhand, I was a land-locked Gilligan.

My introduction to their world came by signing up to help crew the *Notorious* back to her home berth in Santa Cruz. As I later discovered, this was all upwind, precisely why our captain solicited the help of greenhorns: Anyone with experience knew better. Visions of Jimmy Buffett barbecues on the aft deck vanished with the first ice-cold wave over the deck. Still, it was an indoctrination I wouldn't trade for all the Dramamine in the world. Rotating 3-hour watch duty every 6 hours until we arrived 20 days later, I learned the basics in a 40-foot nutshell, from how to dodge a Pacific High—a high-pressure system that can keep a boat stuck in the same place for days—to throwing up on the windward side of the boat. And despite all the hardships—the puking, the wetness, the con-finement, and the dreaded knock on the door signaling a 3 A.M. watch duty—I fell prey to the sport's addiction, signing on the next year to sail upwind from La Paz, Mexico, to Los Angeles, California.

## First

There's a better way. You needn't practice sleep deprivation and staying in polypro for three weeks to get a grasp on sailing. Your best bet is to take a lesson. The following schools can teach you everything you need to know: J World (sailing schools throughout the country); Annapolis Sailing School; American Sailing Association; and Offshore Sailing School. Sign up for a multi-day course to get the most out of your investment; there's a lot to learn. And don't be afraid to ask questions no matter how stupid they may seem. Not

## ESSENTIALS

Unless your pockets are as deep as the Pacific, hold off on buying a yacht until your stock options mature. Your best bet is to look at a number of affordable small-boat options, starting as low as a couple hundred dollars for a nine-foot polyethylene sailboat. A Sunfish can run about a few thousand dollars, and a 21-foot Hobie Sport Cruiser catamaran costs over ten thousand dollars. No matter how small your boat, if you own it, take part in the age-old art of bestowing it with a name. It will be with you for a while. Other items to add include life jackets for everyone on board, a boat trailer, and of course, seasickness drugs.

everyone is born knowing the difference between shrouds and backstays.

---

## Next

Get your feet wet on a small body of water. Familiarize yourself with the basics by renting a Laser, Sunfish, or another small boat and taking it out on a local waterway. Sailboats as small as 12 feet can get you on your way to appreciating the America's Cup.

First, of course, you have to understand the wind. Take it out in a light breeze and tack upwind. Look at telltales to ensure that the sails are working to their capacity. Steer as high into the wind as possible without sloughing the sail; then tack to the other side without losing ground. (Remember to duck the boom.) Practice a broad reach by putting the wind at your side and then run downwind and practice a few jibes.

Another piece of advice: Practice your knots. Know the difference between a clove hitch and a bowline and learn how to cleat a rope before the captain asks you to secure the boat to the dock.

—EUGENE BUCHANAN

---

ICE-CLIMBING

# Hug the Ice

A WATERFALL ROARS over this band of cliffs three seasons of the year, but now a steep pillar of ice stands in its place. I grasp the handle of one of my ice axes and swing it into the ice above my head. *Chunk, chunk.* I kick my crampons (spikes strapped to the bottom of my rigid boots) into the ice and stand up on the metal front points beneath my toes.

I wiggle my left ax loose and plant it higher. *Thunk.* Then again my right one. I climb 20 feet in this familiar ice-climbing rhythm. Here, I twist an ice screw (an eight-inch-long, one-and-a-half-inch-in-diameter threaded hollow tube) into a patch of solid ice and attach the rope that joins my partner and me to the screw with aluminum snap links (carabiners). The "protection" of this ice screw setup will shorten the length of any fall I might take.

From here, at the top of a 70-degree skirt, a ribbon of ice rears up and coats vertical rock beneath. The ice ribbon is only five inches thick, a pane of glass. I gently tap in my ice axes. I move up again and again, content with every six inches of progress. My forearm muscles are ablaze, my calves scream. A few feet above, the ribbon ends, and the angle lessens. I crane my head back to examine the ice above the ribbon. It looks more substantial, but I can't tell for sure. I plan a swing for what I hope is the thickest, most solid ice. I pull back my right ax; my right arm a spring. I swing, and—*thunk!* The pick of my ax sinks into thick, solid ice.

Welcome to the wild world of ice-climbing—a long, slow adrenaline burn, fully radical but totally unlike the cannon-shot jolts of thrill sports. If you want to be good at ice-climbing, you've got to earn it, and it will take a lifetime to master. You don't need Popeye's massive forearms to ice-climb, and to start, you certainly don't need to be strong— your strength will grow with practice. Technique, thoughtfulness, and smooth, efficient move- 0ments do much more than brute strength. Of course, strength helps, but the best ice climbers blend both power and finesse. One of the great attractions of the sport is the ice itself. It is a fascinating, ever-changing medium. Even on the same climb, it is never exactly the same twice. As you learn to "read" the ice, you'll learn the characteristics of blue ice, white ice, gray ice, translucent ice, chandelier ice, aerated ice, and black ice.

but the best place to learn the basics is at the Ouray Ice Park in Ouray, Colorado. There, water diverted from a nearby aqueduct runs over a shady canyon wall, freezes, and forms an incredible concentration of quality climbs—all within a few hundred yards of town.

## Next

Learn to "lead climb" once you have a good feel for the axes and crampons and a solid knowledge of the fundamentals like knots, belays, anchors, and protection. "Second" a more experienced friend who can lead you at first so you can learn how the lead-climbing system works and gain an appreciation for its risks. Then simulate a lead climb for practice: While a partner belays you with a top-rope, tie another rope to your harness and drag it up below you while you climb, placing the ice screws you would need for protection and clipping the rope to the screws with quickdraws—just like you would if you were really leading. The top rope above will allow you to sort out the hassles of placing ice screws for protection without facing the real risk of taking a lead fall. Once you've rehearsed a couple of leads and feel confident, do it for real. But when you do actually lead an ice climb, stay in control and do not fall. It is NOT okay to fall while leading an ice climb— you will probably get hurt. The risks of leading ice are greater, but so are the rewards. Climb on!

—GREGORY CROUCH

> ## GEAR
>
> Ice climbers need a good winter clothing system; multiple layers work best. As for ice axes, boots, and crampons, at first, borrow them. If you hire a guide, he'll help you out. Try as many different types of gear as you can before you buy. When you do drop the big dime, buy a set of two ice axes, crampons, helmet, rope, ice screws, and quickdraws. These are expensive, but so are lift tickets. And always wear a helmet.

## First

Make sure to learn with someone truly competent, a professional guide or an experienced friend. Beware of friends who may not be as able as they advertise. To locate a certified guide or accredited climbing school, call the American Mountain Guides Association (AMGA). Hotbeds of ice-climbing activity are found in California, the Cascades, Utah, Colorado, Wyoming, Montana, Alaska, and New England—anywhere it's cold. The current state of the art is in the Canadian Rockies,

# Learn the Turn

SKIING BEGAN as mere transportation: In fourteenth-century Scandinavia there was no better way to get around. But once it took hold in the bigger, steeper mountains of the Alps, skiing became sport, and mankind has since skied on every continent. Today there are 50 million people around the world who ski. That leaves about 48 million who aren't doing it *right*.

Too many weekend warriors ski like the shape of paper clips: a herky-jerky mix of straight lines with sudden, jarring turns. They can get down the mountain, but the less said about their form, the better. They would enjoy the sport so much more if they only remembered one crucial detail: Skiing takes place on a form of precipitation. The key to playing on the heaven-sent frozen water vapor called snow is to stay fluid.

## First

If you've ever heard a Winter Olympics broadcaster praise a racer for being "over his skis," you can comprehend the benefits of a low, forward-leaning stance. When you stand over your skis, you're coiled to absorb shock. You're quick—almost literally on your toes—and you can adjust on the fly to sudden stimuli, such as trees or wayward snowboarders. As the Austrian expatriate instructors used to tell students in the early days of American skiing, "Bend ze knees, five dollars pleez." The knees part is sound advice, but there's more. Position the hips directly above the feet and bend only slightly at the waist. Like a good dancer, face straight ahead and try not to look at your feet. Keep your shoulders square and perpendicular to the slope. Hand position cannot be overestimated: The trailing hand is the main reason many intermediates struggle to advance. Because their hands

### ESSENTIALS

**BOOTS:** Boots are a skier's most valued tool because they determine how you drive the ski—indeed, how you're attached to it. Buy a boot with a "bi-injected" shell: The use of two different densities of plastic, bi-injection makes boots both more comfortable and more precise.
**SKIS:** The most versatile ski is a shaped, all-mountain mid-fat: basically, a wood-cored ski whose geometry (roughly 105mm wide at the tip, 70mm at the waist, and 95mm at the tail) encourages medium-radius turns.
**CLOTHING:** The first rule is to layer with a moisture-wicking material like Capilene or Thermax near the skin, fleece insulation on the torso, and on the outside, something waterproof and porous, with lots of pockets and zipper vents. While leather gloves look good, keep in mind that they're lousy in deep snow because they dry out about as quickly as the Mississippi Delta.   – R. S.

Reggie Crist takes a run down on the Pioneer Mountains, Idaho.

ANDY ANDERSON

der width. The day you keep your hands in front is the day you start making aesthetic, sinuous curves—and stop making paper clips.

---

## Next

It's said that Eskimos have 200 ways of saying the word *snow.* Skiers understand: They, too, deal with white stuff in all its permutations. You officially "rip" when you can tailor your skiing on the following conditions.

**MOGULS.** Ski the bumps by letting your knees rise and fall to absorb them. Stay out of the deepest part of the ruts, which are narrow and grabby.

**POWDER.** Deep snow makes for dream skiing, but at first it's difficult. Instincts and bad skiers tell you to lean back, but ignore them. What you're really trying to do is not sink one ski, so keep your weight more evenly balanced between the two, thereby providing better flotation.

**HARD SNOW.** To maintain control, make sure one edge on each ski is biting into the snow. If you don't, you're riding what's called a flat ski, which will accelerate till the edge sinks. Or you sink.

lag behind the rest of their body, they're late for every turn. So punch your hands forward and hold them out in front of you a little wider than shoul-

---

GO BIG

## THE ART OF THE TAKEOFF

"You have to know how to jump," says Doug Coombs, the two-time World Extreme Skiing Champion and a man who, at 42, still likes to hurl off a cornice. "Otherwise, the world of skiing, or boarding, just isn't yours." Before launching, Coombs advises, loosen up, build your comfort with the snow, and scout the landing area to be sure it's steep, not flat, and free of cliffs, rocks, and slow-moving midwesterners. Ready? Just before takeoff, bend your knees to lower your center of gravity, and at the moment of truth, push off from the center of your skis or board. In the air, throw whatever tricks you like. But just before landing, get yourself back into the same fundamentally sound position you'd use on the snow. Finally, think through before you jump what your runout line is going to be. "Any doubt and you'll blow the landing," Coombs says. Get it right, though, and transcendence is yours: "When a big-mountain jump clicks, it's one big Zen package."

—JON GLUCK

**ICE.** The most difficult surface for any skier, ice demands an even stronger emphasis on edging. As with driving on ice, avoid sudden acceleration or deceleration.

**CRUD.** Any type of sunbaked, cut-up, or rain-crusted snow that's more chunky than soft, crud is ever unpredictable. And it's some of the most diffi-cult snow on which to ski. The best strategy is to stay forward enough to adjust to crud's vagaries. Make frequent, speed-checking turns, keeping your skis light and on top of the snowpack. But if crud won't let you turn, don't fight it. Crud wins most fights.

—ROB STORY

# Surf the White Stuff

AS SNOWBOARDING continues to take the world, the Olympics, and Mountain Dew ad execs by storm, more of its devotees are finding great gobs of joy in the backcountry. You get to etch your signature into a place where it can be erased only by new snow-fall or nonhibernating rodents, and the board-on-snow sound changes from a fin-gernails-on-Styrofoam scratch to the most seductive hiss since Michelle Pfeiffer wore Catwoman's leathers. Plus, resorts quickly run out of the fresh stuff, so it pays to know how to get o.b. (out-of-bounds) and surf the goods. You may need only to strap your board to a backpack and hike a few hun-dred yards from the chairlift in your snow-boarding boots. On more remote journeys, boarders have historically used snowshoes, which work well with snowboarding boots and are small enough to store in a pack.

## GEAR

Buy or rent a "free-ride" board, which can handle a variety of backcountry conditions. Step-in bindings, which connect to a cleat in the sole of the boot, elim-inate the hassle of adjusting straps and can be much easier to escape from should you find yourself upside down in deep snow. An option that eliminates the need for snowshoes is the split board, which sepa-rates lengthwise into two pieces. You attach climb-ing skins to each and rotate the bindings; at the top of the run, lock the two halves back together, rotate the bindings again, and surf down. Soft boots look like a combination of galoshes and L.L. Bean duck shoes, but their leather uppers and sufficient ankle freedom make them more comfortable and forgiving of mistakes.

### First

A solid in-bounds snowboarder should perform capably out of bounds: Balance is more important than precise carving, but the kinetics are basically the same. Still, the backcountry is no place for rookies to venture alone; fear of avalanche drives everything you do there. A good way to get started is to go on a resort's tour of unpatrolled terrain. Telluride, Colorado, for example, offers guided excursions to wild San Juan Mountain slopes just outside its ski-area boundary.

### Next

For more intensive instruction, consider a backcountry-skills course. Alpine Skills International, near Lake Tahoe, offers a two-day program that includes sorties into the Sierras. Several state avalanche-forecasting services offer classes that teach not only how to use backcountry equipment but also how to read snow.

**—ROB STORY**

SURVIVAL

# Three Days to Live or Die

A SURVIVAL RULE of thumb: 72 hours are all that separate the lost, the adrift, and the snowed-in from the Stygian shore. Unless you are subjected to extremes of heat or cold or are grievously injured, the human body, in most situations, can function for approximately three days without water and for weeks without food. Do nothing but avoid exposure—no small task, of course—and you'll probably be alive three days down the line. Three days that give search-and-rescue teams much-needed time to locate you.

Wilderness survival today means staying uninjured, keeping hydrated, and staving off hypothermia or heat exhaustion. You should know how to find water or draw it, how to signal for help, and how to do these things with common materials.

### Lost at Sea

The outboard dies 32 miles from the coast. You have no cell phone, and the VHF is on the fritz. You told no one where you were going. You have a cooler packed with a sub sandwich, a 16-ounce soft drink, four beers, and three refreezable cooler packs. There's a light wind from the west.

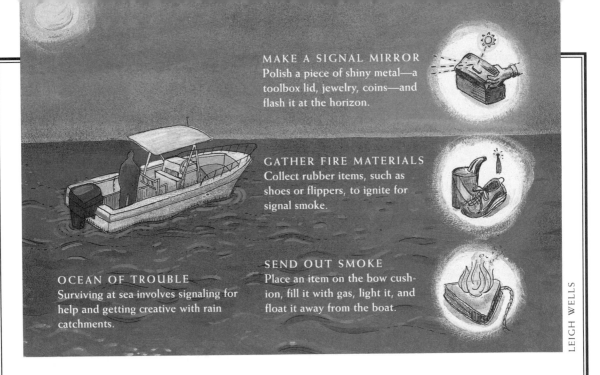

**MAKE A SIGNAL MIRROR**
Polish a piece of shiny metal—a toolbox lid, jewelry, coins—and flash it at the horizon.

**GATHER FIRE MATERIALS**
Collect rubber items, such as shoes or flippers, to ignite for signal smoke.

**SEND OUT SMOKE**
Place an item on the bow cushion, fill it with gas, light it, and float it away from the boat.

**OCEAN OF TROUBLE**
Surviving at sea involves signaling for help and getting creative with rain catchments.

LEIGH WELLS

**DAY ONE.** To get smoke in the air, snap out the bow cushion, tie a 10-foot line to one corner, and tether it to a downwind cleat so it will float away from the boat. Next, rummage around for something made of rubber—for thick black smoke—and fill one item with siphoned gas. Balance the board on the cushion, stand back, and light your signal fire. Shove the cushion off with an oar to prevent flare-ups on the boat.

At a half-pint of water per day, you can make it for two days on the soft drink alone. Don't touch the beer; alcohol will only dehydrate you. If you don't have a seawater-to-freshwater pump,

lay your unzipped jacket on the bow platform so it will funnel water into the cooler in case it rains.

**DAY TWO.** Your stomach is growling, but hold off on the sandwich—digestion requires fluids, and you don't have much to spare. Using a fishhook as an awl and fishing line as thread, fashion a Bimini top by stitching together extra clothing, garbage bags, a canvas tote. The shade will prevent sunburn, save your eyesight, and conserve water by lessening your body's need to sweat. Torch an occasional smoke signal. Find a piece of shiny metal for a makeshift signal mirror.

---

### SEAWATER

Collect as much rain as possible with rain gear, tarps, plastic bags—anything that will channel water into a basin. Catch fish, too, if you have the equipment. Their eyes are full of liquid, and you can break their vertebrae to lap up spinal fluid, which will help replace electrolytes. Blood, however, is salty and requires additional body fluids to digest. And *never* drink salt water. It takes the body two quarts of liquid to flush out the salt from one quart of seawater.

One wonder product is a hand-operated reverse-osmosis seawater-to-freshwater pump. It sucks the salt out of seawater at the rate of one ounce every two minutes. That's not exactly a gushing mountain stream, but it'll keep you alive.

**DAY THREE.** At sunrise, perfect aiming your mirror, and signal toward the empty sweep of blue, even though there are no vessels in sight. The reflection can be seen for up to 100 miles. Every five to ten minutes, flash the horizon.

If even the most distant speck of white appears, leap into action. Light another sneaker full of gas; then use the mirror to signal SOS—three short flashes, three long, three short. If you're lucky, the speck will turn into a gleaming 40-foot sportfishing boat coming to investigate.

## Stuck in the Woods

You're five miles in when something draws your eye. Elk. You want a closer look, so you shimmy over a log in rubber pac boots. Just before your left foot skids across skim ice, your bad knee pops, and in you go. It was to be a day in the woods, with only a daypack, so you brought just a few essentials: pocketknife, lighter, water bottle, and six strips of jerky wrapped in foil. Now you're soaked, you won't be able to travel any distance, there's a storm front headed your way, and all that matters is building a fire.

**DAY ONE.** Hobble into the closest evergreen copse, where dead understory limbs will provide wood in all sizes. Snap away twigs no thicker than pencil lead. With these dry needles and thin chips of bark, construct a tepee; then light the fire. Shed some clothing and dry them beside it while feeding the blaze the bigger branches.

Darkness will fall before you know it, so you'll have to settle for a rough bivouac. Break down evergreen boughs and use them to weave a roof and

SET UP A SHELTER
Before nightfall, build a lean-to from available tree boughs and grasses.

STAY WARM
Construct a fire bed to lie on by digging a shallow trench, lighting a blaze, then covering the embers with a few inches of dirt.

SIGNAL TO SEARCH PLANES
Create a large X on the ground or in the snow, preferably next to a creek or a river, since rescue craft often follow waterways

LEIGH WELLS

walls. To help raise your body's core temperature, heat stones in the fire; then put them in your water bottle, filled from the nearby stream (purify with tablets first if you have them), and drink up.

**DAY TWO.** Build up the fire; then fashion a leg splint with two pieces of green wood and webbing cut from your pack so you can get around easier. Move away from the dark timber to signal so any rescue craft flying above can spot you. The creek offers the best site: It's an open slash through the forest, and aircraft frequently follow watercourses on search missions. With your injury, it will take hours of limping around to construct a large X near the creek—using downed branches, rocks, and evergreen boughs, anchoring a bit of foil in the middle—but do it anyway. Then feed the fire and stockpile wet reeds to throw on the flames in case an airplane appears close enough to signal with smoke. By midafternoon, start creating a more weathertight shelter for the approaching storm front.

Follow survival instructor Ron Hood's two-four-eight rule to build a fire bed that will keep you alive. Between a pair of large rocks, scrape out an eight-inch-deep trench and build a blaze in it. Gather more boughs for a lean-to cover as you let the trench fire burn for two hours into embers. Spread them evenly through the trench and cover them with four inches of dirt, tamping it down softly with your boots. Fashion a low lean-to across the rocks, sheathing it with boughs, bark, even sod. You'll need four to five inches of insulation.

## HIGH-COUNTRY H$_2$O

Finding water in mountain environments is often as simple as heading downhill, but in high, arid country—or for anyone injured—constructing transpiration or vegetation bags is a good way to supplement meager water supplies. These bags condense the water vapor transpired by plants and other leafy vegetation.

Slip a large, transparent plastic bag around a live shrub or a leafy tree branch. After placing a small stone in the bag, blow it full of air, then tie it off, plugging the hole with paper or cloth if you have it. Gingerly work the stone into the lowest point of the bag so that the water condensing inside will pool in one corner, making it easy to pour into your mouth. With direct sunlight and ample vegetation, this method can yield up to two quarts of water a day.

A vegetation bag is even easier to construct. Stuff a large, transparent plastic bag up to three-quarters full with (nonpoisonous) green leaves and grasses. Place a small stone in the bag and fill with air; then tie it off. Lay the bag on a slope in full sunlight, knotted side facing downhill, and work the stone into its lowest point.

**DAY THREE.** The snows came in the dark, adding another layer of insulation to your shelter but covering your signals. You'll need to shift strategies—stamp out a large X in the snow and fill it with green boughs. Embers from the fire bed can be used to spark a new blaze. You hear geese coursing down the river; the sound grows more distinct. Dogs. Shout with all of your energy and shovel the grass and boughs onto the fire to create smoke. When the first bloodhound bursts into the small clearing and throws back his head and bays, you can relax. Your name won't be in the obits after all.

## Breakdown in the Desert

Twenty miles up the national park road, your rental truck gives out. The air temperature hovers at around 115 degrees Fahrenheit; the ground surface may be pushing 130. You have a quart of water in a

**DEALING WITH THE DESERT**
The key to survival is water and shade. Do whatever you must—rip apart your vehicle's interior, even—to make it.

LEIGH WELLS

**INDICATE TROUBLE**
Use bright-colored clothing to signify the situation.

**PREPARE A SIGNAL FIRE**
Have materials ready to light at a moment's notice.

**KEEP COOL**
Unbolt your car seat and rig an awning to it for shade.

plastic bottle and two beers floating in a handful of hotel ice.

**DAY ONE.** In the desert, you're dead in a day and a half without water. So immediately signal for help by raising the truck hood and tying a brightly colored cloth to the radio aerial. Break off the rearview mirror to use as a signaling device.

Tending a signal fire will waste too much energy, but it's critical to have one ready to light. Shred maps and newspapers for tinder. If you can find mesquite, stack it for kindling. Next, shimmy under the truck with a hubcap and fill it with oil. It goes beside the firewood, along with two rubber floor mats from the truck.

During the night, the truck can serve as a shelter, but come morning, it will heat up like a microwave. Spend the cool hours of night cutting out upholstery; then lash the pieces together with dental floss or yucca leaves to make a tarp for shade. The inside of your vehicle has much of what you need to survive; don't be afraid to carve it up.

**DAY TWO.** Empty your water bottle in three gulps; current desert-survival strategy looks down on rationing. "The water in your stomach saves you, not the water in your canteen," says David

---

### WATER FROM SAND

Vegetation and transpiration bags are a good method if you have access to a plastic bag and leaf-bearing plants. If your vehicle is still running, David Alloway suggests tying a plastic bag around the air-condenser drip outlet, which can gain you a pint of liquid in four to six hours.

Search for water during the cooler hours of the day by looking in cracks and pockets in rocks, and dig into seep springs in side gullies. Converging animal trails—wild or domestic— often mean that a water source is at the end of the path. Truly desperate measures include wiping dew off a poncho or a car hood.

Alloway, a Texas Parks desert-survival instructor. But you're going to need extra water—more than the bit pooled in your cooler. Your best chance lies in making a vegetation or transpiration bag.

In the meantime, get out of the sun and off the ground. Putting yourself just a foot or so above the hot desert sand can make a 10-to-20-degree temperature difference. Unbolt a car seat and place it on the ground near the truck; then wedge one end of your makeshift tarp into the truck door and attach the other to the seat back, to jury-rig an awning for shade.

Don't move far from your truck; people who wander in the desert looking for a way out usually don't make it. Midafternoon, finish off the remain-ing water from the cooler and replace it with the greenish liquid from the bag. It won't be much, but it will keep you going a bit longer. As the sun begins to set, use the rearview mirror to reflect your truck's headlights toward the horizon.

**DAY THREE.** The buzz of an insect tugs at your brain, a distant whine that morphs into a mechanical drone—an airplane! Fire up the truck's cigarette lighter and torch your carefully hoarded tinder. Throw in a handful of finger-thick mesquite, the floor mats, and finally, the oil. Let the smoke billow. A wiggle of the search plane's wings means you're home free. Grab a beer—115 degrees never tasted so good.

—T. EDWARD NICKENS

SURVIVAL

# Animal Attacks

NATURE AT ITS best is beautiful and untainted, but it is also raw and untamed. When encountering some of its less friendly creatures, it is important to follow some guidelines that will enable you to steer clear of trouble.

## Bear Trouble

Twenty-two-year-old Bayne French was scouting for elk one bright day in the Cabinet Mountains of northwestern Montana when he heard an animal crashing toward him in the thick brush.

At the first sound, French drew his can of pep-per spray. Then he saw the grizzly. The bear was only a few yards away when French fired the spray directly in the animal's face. The grizzly skidded to a halt—so close French's legs were showered with dirt—then turned and ran.

Grizzly bears generally roam the north-south corridor from Yellowstone National Park through British Columbia and the Yukon Territory into Alaska; black bears inhabit just about any wild area from California to Minnesota to New Jersey. Although summer may be the season when the greatest number of people wander into bear country, autumn has some serious bear concerns of its own, for both grizzlies and black bears sleep little and forage nearly around the clock, consuming up to 20,000 calories a day while laying on fat reserves for the long, sleepful winter. All of which means there's no time like autumn for hikers, mountain-bikers, campers, hunters, and fishermen to brush up on how to peacefully coexist with the beasts.

## FIRST CONTACT

You can generally avoid encountering a bear by following the traditional guidelines: Steer clear of high-risk zones, make noise if you hear a bear and do so well before you see it, travel in groups of three or more, hang or store food and supplies properly, and keep a clean camp.

Unfortunately, these guidelines are not always clear and simple. Take the old saw about making noise: It can be a good idea when bears aren't too close. But if you see a sow grizzly with cubs coming down the trail or hillside 100 yards away, it's better to move away, unseen, as quietly as you can. But if there's no way to back out or to climb a tree before the bear spots you, then you *should* alert the bear to your presence as early as possible, hopefully while it's still beyond the "critical distance," the point at which it feels impelled to charge. Critical distances vary from a few yards (with "socialized" brown bears along Alaska streams) to as many as 150 yards (with cub-protecting sows in Glacier and Yellowstone parks).

One thing all experts agree on is that you should never run from a bear. Running triggers aggression; it's tantamount to asking for an attack. Climb a tree for safety only when you have seen an approaching bear that has not yet detected you or when there is no better avenue of escape.

## UP CLOSE AND PERSONAL

Should you come face to face with a bear, don't "play dead" too soon. The best rule of thumb is to screw up your courage and *stand your ground* even if the bear

charges. If you have pepper spray, use it when the bear comes into range.

During a standoff, look down and to the side while watching the animal peripherally. (Staring at the bear can be seen as an act of aggression.) Such leading bear authorities as Charles Jonkel believe that talking calmly and sensibly to a nearby bear ("It's okay, bear, I don't want trouble") also helps; it imparts nonthreatening messages the creature can perceive.

## UNDER ATTACK

If a grizzly does make contact, then it's time to hit the dirt. The best position is not fetal; rather, lie flat on your belly, hands and arms gripped over your head. (Bears tend to bite most actively on the face and head; this position also protects your vital organs.) The good news: Few bears continue the attack very long. The bad news: It's important that you not thrash or scream, that you lie completely still and stay that way even after the bear has started to leave. In dozens of instances, retreating bears returned for a second assault when the victims stirred or called out too soon.

It's generally argued that you should never play dead with black bears; that fighting back—with pepper spray, any other kind of weapon, or even with only shouts and fists—is the best way to stop or prevent black-bear maulings. Any bear—black or grizzly—that comes into camp at night should be faced aggressively, as well. Bang pans or yell; throw stones, cans, or sticks; use pepper spray; and if you're in a group, team up in an attempt to intimidate the animal. Faced with such tactics, most camp invaders will scoot.

—ANTHONY ACERRANO

## Snake Smarts

While fly-fishing California's San Gabriel River, David Bosman saw a large western diamondback rattlesnake rustling through the streamside boulders near him. He dropped back a few steps, waited 15 minutes, then reached down for a tackle bag. That's when the snake struck, and a single fang grazed Bosman's right forefinger. "You hear the old cowboy stories about sucking out the poison," he recalled, "so that's what I did." Before long, the civil engineer was in dire straits. By the time he reached his truck minutes later, his eyes had started to twitch, and he was having trouble breathing. Bosman made it 10 miles down a road and stumbled upon a ranger on patrol. He spent the next 11 days in the hospital.

## BITE BASICS

Thankfully, only two families of poisonous snakes are found in North America: the Crotalidae (rattlesnakes, cottonmouths, copperheads) and the Elapidae (coral snakes). The eastern coral snake makes up a tiny fraction of the country's 11,000 to 12,000 snake incidents each year, but rattlesnakes, which inhabit almost every region of the United States, account for 60 percent of the cases and most of the 6 to 12 annual fatalities.

Stay out of their way by practicing good snake sense. If mice, chipmunks, and any other rodents inhabit an area, it's a good bet that snakes do as well. Watch where you place your hands and feet—many victims fall prey when they're scrambling over boulders or otherwise reaching into areas they cannot see. Be particularly vigilant on warm spring and fall days, when the coldblooded reptiles will be basking on rock piles, logs, and sunny trails. And use a trekking pole or a stick to poke around deadfalls (a favorite hideout) for firewood. Be especially wary of snakes that have triangular heads (a common trait of crotaloids) or the coral snake's black, red, and yellow bands.

If you're bitten, take heart in the fact that no venom is injected in 20 percent to 30 percent of cases, and even without treatment most victims survive. But quick and proper action can head off snakebite's most dangerous side effect: major soft-tissue damage caused by massive swelling, which can lead to permanently decreased function and even amputation.

If you ever feel the fangs, here's the game plan:

• **Do *not* suck on the bite site (the venom just works its way into your bloodstream via tiny cuts in the lining of your mouth) or use a tourniquet (which can worsen swelling).**
• **Apply suction from a Sawyer Extractor. Quick removal of bite-site venom will drastically reduce soft-tissue death.**
• **If you can rule out a bite by a coral snake, forget about trying to identify the species. One antivenin is used for bites from all other North American snakes.**
• **Most importantly, get to a hospital. The majority of victims have about 90 minutes before they face a serious systemic crash, so use that time wisely. If you can't self-evacuate, move to a location and send a companion for help. If you are alone and unable to reach medical facilities, find shelter, put out signaling devices, and gather water, food, and firewood. It's going to be a long night, but you should still be around come morning.**

—T. EDWARD NICKENS

## Attack Cat

It was a typical evening jog for Moses Street, a 48-year-old photographer from Estes Park, Colorado—until a mountain lion began tailing him. Street had been running near Grand Lake in Rocky Mountain National Park when he looked over his shoulder to find a *Felis concolor*—the Western Hemisphere's very own lion—gaining on him fast and "coming up for the neck bite that kills." Street stopped, waved his arms, and yelled; the beast backed off. After picking up a stick and swiping it at the animal, the photographer then retreated toward an abandoned cabin and climbed up its wall and into a pine tree. Park rangers found him at 2:00 A.M.

Mountain lions are not, to be sure, a common killer, but they can be seen roaming the woodlands of most of the western and northeastern United States, and their presence has also been felt in more populated regions. "These animals are out there," says Steve Torres of the Wildlife Management Division of the California Department of Fish and Game. "Attacks are rare events, but they do occur."

So be prepared. If you're in mountain-lion country, never travel alone and always keep a careful watch on the area around you. Experts also recommend that you carry a sizable walking stick or a can of pepper spray. If you encounter a lion, "your chances of injury are small if you demonstrate that you're in charge," says Raymond Skiles, a wildlife specialist with the National Park Service. The most important rule is: Don't run. Running tells the lion that you're prey, making an attack more likely. Stand your ground. Wave your arms. If there are two or more of you, gather together and create a big silhouette. And don't turn your back on the animal, either. If the cat does attack, fight back—spray, gouge, kick, yell. But don't play dead. Play dead and you're lunch.

As for Moses Street, he says that his own unusually persistent pursuer "made being in the mountains a lot more interesting." But he adds, "I don't go out alone anymore."

—ANTHONY BRANDT

# Surviving Whitewater

SCOTT WOOD knew plenty about North Carolina's Roanoke River. Every spring, he fishes the waterway twice a week. But when his friend's 25-horsepower outboard engine died in the middle of the river, roiling spring runoff swept their johnboat into a downed tree along the riverbank. Wood's buddy stood up and grabbed the branches hanging overhead, causing the weight in the boat to shift. "I yelled for him to sit down," recalls Wood, "but the upriver gunwale slipped underwater, and it was over just that quick."

The two men and $10,000 worth of fishing equipment were plunged into a muddy torrent that was roaring at 30,000 cubic feet per second over massive boulders and along a bank strewed with treacherous fallen trees, called strainers. (The force behind water running through submerged branches can trap a person indefinitely.)

> *Talents are best nurtured in solitude; character is best formed in the stormy billows of the world.*
>
> **—GOETHE**

REELED IN:
A rafter gets pulled from the Skykomish
River near Index, Washington.

Grasping a floating cooler, Wood ferried himself across the current to the middle of the river, then drifted several hundred yards before finding a spot on the bank that was clear enough to allow him to claw his way out. Upstream, his friend had been squashed into a strainer. Luckily, he was able to free himself, and he survived—with a badly bruised chest and a yearlong disinterest in river fishing.

Wood's spring-melt fandango illustrates how you don't have to be kayaking a Class V glory rapid to suddenly find yourself neck-deep in a raging river. You could slip while wading through big trout water. You could take a dunk while backpacking across a log bridge. Or you could be bumped out of a raft by a boulder during a guided whitewater joy ride. What you do in the moments immediately afterward could determine whether you make it safely to shore or wake up on the far side of the river Styx.

## On the Defense

If you are thrown from a boat, assess all your appendages right away to make sure that your arms, legs, and feet are free of any rope that might tether you to the vessel. Next, even if you're already wearing a personal flotation device, take hold of anything else that will help you float—coolers, cushions, spare life vests—and get upstream of your craft as quickly as possible. Unmanned canoes and kayaks are little more than battering rams with fancy decals.

Assume a defensive swimming posture. Float on your back with your feet pointed downstream, and keep your butt as high in the water as possible—few things are more painful than crushing your pelvis against a boulder. Use your feet to push yourself away from exposed rocks and any other obstacles.

If you can't avoid a strainer or a debris dam, get aggressive. "You don't want to wash into it passively," says Hugh Bailey, a whitewater instructor in North Carolina. "Roll over onto your chest and approach it head-on. Try to go up and over by climbing or by grabbing limbs. Just get out of the river's flow, and never try to swim under [the obstruction]. You don't know what's down there."

Once you're out of the danger zone, roll onto your back again and thrash toward safe water.

This can be a hairy ride. Keep calm. Swim strategically all the way to the riverbank. With luck, you'll be clutching the beer cooler. Once on dry land, you'll have plenty of reasons to celebrate.

—T. EDWARD NICKENS

## SURVIVAL

# Avalanche!

AN HOUR IS a long time to be buried alive. Just ask Todd Ludeman, who was sure he was going to die. Trapped under four feet of cement-hard snow after an avalanche, Ludeman couldn't move his arms or legs, and with only a small air pocket in front of his face, he could barely breathe. After about 40 minutes, he began drifting in and out of consciousness.

He had been snowmobiling with two neighbors when a 60-yard swath of snow broke free and roared toward them. Trying in vain to remain on top of the snowslide, he was hit in the back by a snowmobile and packed into the drift like a fish stick. "I always thought I'd be able to claw my way out, but you can't move a bit," he said later. "Toward the end, I was really gasping. I could hardly breathe." Then he felt a poke in the leg as a searcher's probe hit him. Within ten minutes he was extricated, unhurt; he soon recovered enough to eat lunch and ride his snowmobile back to the trailhead.

As more and more recreationists—especially snowmobilers, climbers, and skiers—leave the groomed slopes and trails to head deeper into the backcountry, such incidents are becoming more and more common. Every year in the United States, close to 100 people are caught in avalanches, and 15 to 25 of them die. According to Bruce Tremper, codirector of the Utah Avalanche Forecast Center, most victims are 16-to-35-year-old men who, although adept at their sports, don't know enough to avoid triggering avalanches.

## Steering Clear

Avalanche workers control slides at ski areas and along highways and mountain-transportation corridors, but there are no such niceties in the backcountry, where you must be able to recognize trouble yourself.

The most dangerous terrain is any relatively open snowfield on a 30-to-45-degree decline. The prime pitch for accidents is 38 degrees (slightly steeper than the average expert ski slope). Though there are exceptions, on milder pitches the snow stays put; on steeper ones, it sloughs off too much to build any depth. A convex slope is more hazardous than a dished-out bowl. Avalanches can start in sparse stands of trees, but thick woods or copious boulders help anchor snow and usually indicate low-risk zones. Watch for evidence of previous slides, such as chutes where trees have been broken, uprooted, or scoured clean. And always beware of ravines and draws; their steepness and deep snow make them potential deathtraps.

Simply heeding local weather reports can also reduce the threat of being caught in a slide. Nearly 90 percent of avalanches occur during or just after significant storms. New snow, especially if it accumulates at a rate of one inch or more per hour, adds weight and instability to an existing snowpack, as does rain in any substantial quantity. Also be conscious of any dramatic change in temperature. Finally, check the snow. Anything that cracks or shifts audibly beneath you is unsafe.

## If You're Caught

If you find yourself in the midst of an avalanche, calm, quick thinking could save your life. First, try to get away from the moving snow slab by angling off to the side or grabbing a tree and lifting yourself above the slide. If you can't get out of the way, toss your poles, skis, or snowboard (or jump away from your snowmobile), then "swim" to stay atop the snow. If you're buried when the avalanche stops, punch out an air pocket in front of your face with one hand while thrusting your other toward the surface. Hopefully, it will poke through so that searchers can locate you quickly. Avalanche snow tends to set up concrete-hard, so you probably won't be able to dig yourself out; generally, you're at the mercy of rescuers.

Most victims are not as lucky as Todd Ludeman. After 30 minutes beneath the snow, odds of survival plummet. That doesn't mean you should abandon all hope if you do get trapped: One Colorado miner survived for 22 hours under a slide. Still, by being aware of the factors that create avalanche trouble, chances are you'll never see one—at least not from the bottom up.

—ANTHONY ACERRANO

# Fire in the Sky

THE STORM RIPPED in fast, as storms in mountain country often do. On an 8,000-foot peak, Ray Risho, 52, and his son Ephraim, 19, worried as the lightning bolts moved toward them. The two men took shelter in a crevasse and waited. Although it was July, snow and ice began to fall, and the temperature plummeted; father and son, dressed lightly for a summer hike, started to shiver. An hour later, on the verge of hypothermia and with no sign of the storm's abating, they decided to chance hiking out. About 30 yards down the rocky peak, Risho says, he heard "a funny, crackling sound" and then felt as if somebody "had dropped a boulder on my head." Both men were thrown to the ground, unconscious.

When they regained consciousness, it was to a smell reminiscent of burned hair. "We realized we'd been struck by lightning," says Risho. "We also realized we needed to get out of there—fast." The descent was long, terrifying, and difficult, but they eventually made it to their van, exhausted but otherwise uninjured.

## Danger Zone

Since a lightning bolt can carry an electrical charge of more than 100 million volts, it's amazing that

---

### THE SQUAT

If you're caught in the open when a lightning storm blasts in, the best tactic is to drop into a deep squat, resting on the balls of your feet only, with your feet together. In the case of an indirect ground strike, the current will follow the path of least resistance, "bumping over" your feet and reentering the ground. If there's space between your feet, the current may course up one leg, into your body, then down the other leg. Members of a group should spread widely apart before assuming the squat position.

anyone survives contact with one. But of the roughly 1,500 people who are hit by lightning each year in the United States, more than 70 percent live. Still, that 30 percent level of fatality makes lightning America's most dangerous natural disaster.

There are several ways to be hurt by lightning. First, and most brutal, is the direct hit, in which the current flows straight through the victim—generally someone who is standing in the open during a storm, wearing or carrying anything made of metal or graphite. Many victims literally have their socks and shoes blown off.

Indirect lightning strikes are also common. Here the current jumps or spreads outward from the original contact point, traveling through any conductive medium until it finds a victim. This phenomenon accounts for most cases in which several people are struck simultaneously. A common scenario: A bolt hits a tall tree, causing electricity to spiral down the trunk and jolt any-

one who has foolishly taken refuge around its base.

The best way to protect yourself is to take thunderstorms seriously. Some topographies put you at greater risk than others: golf courses (you're carrying metal clubs in an open area), bodies of water (an extremely transmissive medium), and high country (which is closer to the clouds). But whenever you're one of the highest objects in the vicinity of a storm—or if you're standing near one of the highest objects—you're a target. Move to safe cover (a ditch, a ravine, a copse of *low* trees) or, if none exists, pick a clear area and drop into a squat.

But don't follow the example of famed golfer Lee Trevino, who, after having been struck once before, tempted fate during a thunderstorm by running onto a green and waving a metal club high. Later, he explained himself by saying, "Even God can't hit a 1-iron."

**—ANTHONY ACERRANO**

# The Lowdown on Altitude Sickness

A
S THE FIRST whiff of steam from the bowl of *tsampa* hit me, I felt a tide of nausea rising. Now my headache had some-

thing to keep it company. My friend Carey and I sat in the two best chairs in a dark mud-brick house. We were hunkered down on central

China's Tibetan-Qinghai Plateau—a wind-blasted, treeless land of giant dogs, smallish horses, and "blue sheep," the wild goat-sheep that we had come to see. The altitude was 15,000 feet above sea level.

Our Tibetan hosts gave us bowls of their traditional heated beverage—salty tea mixed with roasted barley and about a quarter-pound of half-melted yak butter. Carey tossed his down straight off, much to the delight of the Tibetans—while it was all I could do to keep from tossing, period. This was not the fault of the *tsampa*. It was the onset of acute mountain sickness (AMS), something Carey, the swine, would be spared.

## Thin Air

Anyone—no matter how fit or seasoned at altitude—can experience AMS. Scott A. Gallagher, a physician in the emergency room at Colorado's Aspen Valley Hospital, sees an average of five AMS cases per week, and a 1998 survey found that 24 percent of travelers who venture rapidly from sea level to 10,000 feet suffer from the condition.

AMS—which normally occurs at 8,000 feet and upward and usually strikes within 6 to 48 hours of arrival at elevation—is caused by hypoxia, a lack of oxygen in the blood. At high altitudes, the barometric pressure is too low to push enough air through a person's lungs to maintain normal measures of blood oxygen. Although the disorder chooses its victims capriciously, the most common trigger is going too high too fast. I had invited it, two days before, by traveling via 4x4 nonstop from an elevation of 7,000 feet to this remote, officially very high altitude camp.

Symptoms of AMS almost always include shortness of breath, headache, and nausea; they may also run the gamut from loss of appetite, swelling of the hands and the face, cyanosis (blue fingernails and lips), lethargy, and malaise all the way to Cheyne-Stokes respiration, a benign death rattle that occurs during sleep.

There is no sure-fire method for preventing AMS. The young and the fit are often struck first, since they normally travel the fastest, so training is no prophylaxis. What may help is staged ascent (progressing no more than 1,000 feet per day above 8,000 feet); a "climb high, sleep low" strategy (descending below 8,000 feet at night); and taking certain drugs. (Besides analgesics, such as aspirin, doctors recommend Diamox, which increases the respiratory rate.) Also, keep hydrated (drink extra water; avoid caffeine and alcohol), eat light, and go easy on the salt.

If you do come down with AMS, the only definite cure is to head back below 8,000 feet. If you want to wait it out, don't overexert yourself; give yourself time to acclimate before going any higher. If your condition doesn't improve or actually worsens, get down quickly.

## Breathing Easy

A few days later, back at 7,000 feet (after which my symptoms cleared up), we enter Xining, the capital of Qinghai Province. At a side-street restaurant, Carey, our interpreter, our driver, and I surrounded a washtub-sized wok roiling with a spicy broth aswim with noodles, vegetables, mushrooms, tofu, beef, pork, fish, fish heads, chicken, and chicken heads. Farther west on the Silk Road, the driver told us, are 20,000-foot-high mountains with mega-sheep, the argali, whose horns can spiral more than five feet.

He asked me with his nod, *Would you go that much higher to see something as wondrous as an argali, the wild sheep of Marco Polo?*

I shrugged, then nodded. Of course. Just let me catch my breath.

—THOMAS McINTYRE

# Crash Course

THERE ARE a frightening number of reasons why a small plane can fall from the sky—an engine malfunction, bad weather, a midair collision, an inexperienced pilot. True examples: A single-engine plane on a tour over the Grand Canyon gets lost in fog, runs out of fuel, and crashes. A pilot eats a sandwich, succumbs to food poisoning, and plummets to his death. A carbon-monoxide leak asphyxiates a pilot and his passenger, who die in the ensuing crash.

The National Transportation Safety Board, which investigates aircraft accidents, has recorded more than 39,000 such incidents involving small planes (those with fewer than 30 seats) since 1983. But according to Brian Horner, a survival instructor in Anchorage, Alaska, who specializes in aviation emergencies, the majority of these disasters are actually survivable. Small aircraft have less mass, weight, and speed than the big jets do, and thus produce less impact force and flying debris during a crash. They also have less interior space to become trapped in, so they can be more easily evacuated. All of which could mean fewer injuries and deaths among the more than 3 million people who fly aboard small aircraft each year.

## Proper Posture

Contact injury—the most common danger during impact—occurs when your body slams into a bulkhead or another seat or when a piece of the aircraft hits you. A typical result is broken legs: When you are in a normal seated position, the impact of a crash shoots your lower legs upward, smashing them into the metal base of the seat in front of you and cracking your bones. If, however, prior to impact, you move your feet back past the vertical position, so that they are flat on the floor beneath your own seat, you can greatly reduce the odds of this kind of injury.

If there is a seat in front of you, another way of protecting yourself is to lean forward at the waist, which puts your head closer to that seat. With less distance to travel, your head will pick up less speed before striking the seat. Also, be sure to guard your neck. Using one arm, reach across your body and grab your shoulder, burrow your chin into your bent elbow, and lean forward, making your upper body as level as possible. Wrap your other arm around this makeshift cervical collar to brace it.

## Water Landing

According to Horner, water crashes kill more people than those that happen on land. Yet 75 percent of water-crash victims are virtually uninjured by the impact. They drown, usually while trapped inside the plane, so knowing how to escape is crucial. If the plane is sinking or fully submerged, the pressure of the water outside the cabin virtually seals the doors. Wait until the interior is partially filled with water, the pressure has equalized, and inrushing water is not a danger before you attempt to open an exit. Once the water in the cabin is waist-deep, stay put for a slow count to five, then release your seat belt and pull yourself out through the exit.

Even Horner admits that no matter how prepared you are for an emergency situation, whether or not you survive is sometimes beyond your control. "In most plane crashes," he says, "it's either gonna hurt like hell, or it ain't gonna hurt at all."

—ANTHONY ACERRANO

# Test Yourself
## 20 QUESTIONS FOR OUTDOORSMEN

FOR TRUE OUTDOORSMEN, comfort and survival in the wilderness are synonymous. Both come through a combination of knowledge, skill, and attitude. This quiz, designed to test all three elements, was developed with the assistance of Tom Brown Jr., the author of *Tom Brown's Field Guide to Wilderness Survival,* and Dr. William Forgey, the author of *Wilderness Medicine.* If you read the essays within this section, a lot of these should come easy to you.

**1** Here are four essentials for survival in the wild. Assuming none is at your immediate disposal during a crisis, which should you try to arrange for first?

    A. Shelter
    B. Water
    C. Food
    D. Fire

**2** You've got no water and are near no obvious water sources. Describe three options for slaking your thirst.

**3** Of the following, which is probably your safest source of water?

    A. River
    B. Stream
    C. Lake
    D. Pond

**4** Ground-to-air visual signals are used to attract the attention of pilots and can be made using branches, strips of cloth, or even footprints tramped in the snow. In such instances, what does the signal "V" represent?

**5** True or false: A good way to test the edibility of a plant is to eat a minuscule amount of it and wait two hours to see if any symptoms occur.

**6** In two words, describe how to quickly fashion a knife from a rock.

**7** Describe three survival uses for a plastic trash bag.

**8** When building a tent or a survival hut, it's best to situate the entrance so that it's facing in which direction?
- A. North
- B. South
- C. East
- D. West

**9** Match the shelter with the phrase that best describes it.
I. Hogan      A. Sturdy, cemented
II. Debris hut      B. Instant protection
III. Snow burrow      C. Simple and versatile
IV. Lean-to      D. Improvised and warm

**10** What's the difference between tinder and kindling?

**11** As a man, are you more likely or less likely to survive a wilderness crisis than a female in the same situation?

**12** Which best describes the reason experts advise looking over your shoulder frequently when hiking?
- A. It alerts you to the presence of wild animals.
- B. It lets you know what the trail looks like in reverse.

**13** Which serve(s) as a good natural insect repellent?
- A. Mud
- B. Cedar
- C. Frog saliva
- D. Pine tar

**14** Which is the paramount concern when sheltering yourself in a snow cave?
- A. Freezing to death
- B. Bear attack
- C. Suffocation
- D. Dehydration

**15** The main difference between feline tracks (those of mountain lions, bobcats, etc.) and canine tracks (those of foxes, coyotes, wolves) is:
- A. Canine tracks have five toes; feline tracks, four.
- B. Feline tracks show claw marks; canine tracks are rounded.
- C. Feline tracks are rounded; canine tracks show claw marks.
- D. To the untrained eye, there is no difference.

**16** Define "reflector," in its fire-building sense.

**17** Which is not true about bears?
- A. They can tear apart a car.
- B. They can run as fast as horses for short distances.
- C. They can climb trees.
- D. They will not attack unless obviously threatened.

**18** True or false: Your level of physical fitness affects how susceptible you are to altitude sickness.

**19** You sprain your ankle on a hike. All of the following are sensible responses except:
- A. Soaking the foot in an icy stream
- B. Urinating on a cloth compress and wrapping it around the injury
- C. Tightening the laces on your hiking boot
- D. Soaking the foot in fire-heated water

**20** You're shivering, but you have no extra clothing and you're two hours from the trailhead. In your pocket is a box of matches. You're surrounded by dry leaves and twigs but few branches. What should you do?

---

## Answers

**1. A.** The majority of wilderness casualties result from exposure either to extreme cold or extreme heat.

**2. a.** Use a cloth to soak up morning dew from rocks and nonpoisonous plants (like most grasses); then wring it out into a container or your mouth.

**b.** If you have a plastic trash bag, build a solar still: Dig a hole three feet deep and four feet in diameter, place a container at its bottom, and arrange the bag in the hole with a rock at its center, secured around the edges by more rocks so that one corner of it is about three inches above the receptacle. Heated by the sun, the soil in the hole will produce moisture that will condense on the underside of the plastic sheet and collect in the container.

**c.** Go the plant-and-tree route: Use a knife to carve a notch about a half-inch into a hardwood or a sycamore tree, then use a hollow reed to slowly tap the fluid; slice the bottom off a grapevine; or crush the fruit of a prickly pear cactus after skinning it and removing the spines.

**3. B.** A clear, fast-running stream is generally safest. The higher its elevation, the less the chance that you'll encounter chemical pollution from farm or factory runoff or biological pollutants from humans and animals. But you should always filter water into a container through cloth and then purify it with an iodine tablet or by boiling it.

**4.** Seen from above, a "V" indicates that assistance is required.

**5. False.** Some plants can be toxic even in small amounts. It's best to positively identify a plant before digging in. Become familiar with the characteristics of grasses, cattails, pines, and acorns—four plant groups that are almost always safe for consumption.

**6.** Break it.

**7.** Here are six: a. raincoat; b. rescue flag; c. insulated coat or sleeping bag (when filled with dead leaves, pine needles, etc.); d. rainwater catch; e. solar still; f. lean-to cover.

**8. C.** Situating the entrance to the east allows you to catch the morning sun, crucial for heat. Also, since most North American weather patterns move from west to east, you'll be minimizing the chance that wind or rain will blow into your shelter.

**9. I-A; II-D; III-B; IV-C.** A *hogan* is essentially a log or rock cabin, with a well-kneaded mixture of mud and grass forming the durable mortar. A *debris hut* uses a rib cage of triangularly placed branches; multiple layers of soft debris (such as leaves, grass, brush, and moss) are piled around this frame to create amazingly effective insulation. A *snow burrow*—formed by cannonballing into a safe snowbank and settling in backward—can provide instant shelter during a blizzard. A *lean-to* can be constructed just about anywhere with dead leaves, some branches, and a couple of poles.

**10.** Thin strands of dry fibers (culled from grass, reeds, or the inner bark of dead trees) that require only a few sparks to ignite are *tinder.* Small, dry twigs of wood that catch and amplify the incipient flames of tinder are *kindling.*

**11. Less likely.** Research studies and anecdotal evidence both support the notion that testosterone is a liability in the wilderness. One guy, for instance, broke his leg and crawled back to civilization on the power of his upper-body muscles. In the process, he dragged his legs through snow puddles and got frostbite in both of them, leading to a double amputation. A woman in the same situation would probably have used a branch as a cane.

**12. B.** Trails look dramatically different in reverse, so looking over your shoulder is an excellent measure against getting lost. For the record, animal attacks in the wilderness are exceedingly rare.

**13. B and D.** Cedar contains insect-repelling tannic resins. The pitch, or tar, of pine trees is also an excellent, if gooey, form of insect repellent.

**14. C.** To avoid suffocation, use a stick to create an air vent in the wall. During a blizzard, check the hole frequently to make sure that snowfall hasn't obscured it. Incidentally, your body heat can warm a snow cave to 40 degrees Fahrenheit even as the outside temperature hovers just below zero.

**15. C.**

**16.** A reflector is a U-shaped wall of rocks, usually about two feet high by three feet wide, that helps concentrate the warmth of a fire.

**17. D.** Bears are entirely unpredictable in their behavior toward humans, so you should always consider them to be dangerous.

**18. False.** On the other hand, adequate hydration, consumption of carbohydrate-rich foods, avoiding overexertion, and gradual acclimatization have all proved to forestall altitude sickness, which usually strikes at above 8,000 feet.

**19. D.** Soaking a recent sprain in warm water will increase internal bleeding, leading to inflammation and pain. Snow, ice, or cold water combined with tighter compression around the joint will prevent or slow swelling. As a last resort, a urine-soaked compress will cool during evaporation and provide some relief.

**20.** Tuck your shirt into your jeans and your jeans into your socks; then stuff as many dried leaves into your clothes as possible, for insulation. Start for the trailhead at a moderate clip and you may even work up a sweat.

## Scoring

Give yourself 5 points for each correct answer.

**100:** You can enter the woods naked and come out dressed, fed, and possibly inebriated.

**80 TO 95:** Take along a knife, some clothes, and a plastic bag.

**65 TO 75:** Add to that food, water, a flashlight, a first-aid kit, a whistle, and a compass.

**BELOW 65:** Add to that a cell phone, a global positioning system, and cab fare.

—TED G. RAND

# Competitive Sports

WITHIN THE world of sports, certain images stand out in your mind: Muhammad Ali standing over the crumpled Sonny Liston in 1964, baring his teeth and flexing his biceps; Pete Sampras puking his guts out in the quarterfinals of the 1996 U.S. Open, then coming back to win the set, the match, the tournament; Tiger Woods striding up to the eighteenth green at the 1997 Masters with a 12-stroke lead; John Elway raising the Super Bowl trophy over his head not once but twice; Michael Jordan doing anything at all. These are the images that make you want to compete. They make you want to raise your game—whatever it may be—to an absolute ass-kicking level of competence. Who cares if you're only playing in a friendly Sunday-night basketball league at the gym? These guys make you want to pummel your opponents into oblivion.

And so they should. Every time a man plays a competitive sport, his pride is on the line. Basketball, golf, tennis, boxing, pool, squash, softball, flag football—it doesn't matter what you're into; you absolutely have to learn the tricks and moves that will help you dominate the game. Or, if it's individual sports you're into, like running or cycling, you have to learn how to beat yourself, how to push the boundaries of what you can do. You have to win that Sunday-night game—otherwise it's going to be a very long week.

To make sure you never lose, we have talked to some of the best athletes in the world. This is not much different than talking to Ernest Hemingway about writing; some things you have to figure out for yourself. But try thinking like Stephon Marbury (page 53) the next time you have to make a jump shot or like Jerome Bettis (page 57) the next time you're playing flag football, and you might become aware of a whole new level of intensity— that is the secret. And that's why we've also included the secrets of the mental game (next page), the tricks that can make you tougher, harder to beat. At the end of the day, it's all in your head.

# I. Will. Win.

WHEN TROY TANNER experienced a string of bad events on the professional beach-volleyball circuit a few years back, it started to cast ugly karma over the entire season. "I was doubting myself for the first time in my life," says the 1988 Olympic men's volleyball gold medalist. "Mentally, I was all messed up." So he had his inner athlete analyzed by Kenneth Baum, a San Juan Capistrano, California, sports-performance consultant and the author of *The Mental Edge*. Baum gave him motiva-

> *Every man believes he has a greater possibility.*
>
> —RALPH WALDO EMERSON

tional tapes and taught him how to banish negative thoughts. Every night, Tanner would listen to the tapes, then, lying in bed, do visualization exercises, imagining himself making 100 perfect serves. Soon enough, his serve went where he sent it, and he leapt to a top-10 ranking.

Tanner has discovered a secret long known to Asian and former Iron Curtain competitors: Training the mind works. Winning athletic teams, from high school girls' field-hockey squads to the National Football League, use sports psychologists, who mon-

---

## SEE YOUR WAY TO WINNING

Kenneth Baum says: Grab a piece of sports equipment you use—a baseball, a golf club, or a basketball, for example. Scrutinize its size, shape, color, smell, the way it feels, how it sounds when it bounces or connects with a ball. Close your eyes and conjure up its image. Study the object in your mind's eye, zooming in so it looks larger and sharper. Make the image as clear and detailed as possible.

Now picture the object in its sports environment. Envision the dugout, the goalposts, the flag flapping on the tenth green. See yourself using the object flawlessly in competition. Employ all of your senses: Feel the wind on your face; smell the chlorine in the pool. Make sure you are fully "in" the movie—it has to be happening to you to be effective, says Baum. Now feel yourself making perfect contact with the tennis ball or sinking the jump shot.

itor their heart rates, blood pressure, stress hormones, and brain waves to help them identify peak-performance modes and access those states with their bodies. Stars like tennis player Chris Evert, speed skater Dan Jansen, and elite pole-vaulter Dean Starkey claim sports psychologists have helped their game. Powerlifter Ed Coan and golf great Jack Nicklaus utilize visualization methods. (Nicklaus calls the technique "going to the movies." In his legendary pregame preparation, he vividly "plays" every hole in his head and then attempts to replicate the strokes he envisions.)

Anyone who's ever choked on a simple putt or missed an easy layup knows the toll that emotions can take on performance. "When we feel anger or fear mobilizing, we're really feeling this very powerful shift in physiology and neurochemistry, neurologically as well as throughout the body," says James Loehr, Ed.D., the director of LGE Performance Systems, in Orlando, Florida, and the author of The New Toughness Training for Sports. "The same is true [in a positive way] when you're in what we call an ideal performance state. When you study videotapes of Michael Jordan and he misses five or six shots in a row, you'll see absolutely no indication that he missed those shots: no slumping shoulders, no head drooping down. The Michael Jordans are very careful not to show any negative emotions because it begins to unravel their sense of control, their sense that they can regulate this delicate process of keeping fear at bay, staying aggressive, and keeping this ideal performance state within reach."

A growing number of scientific studies support the idea of mental training. One study at New York City's Hunter College looked at the mind's effect on the performance of basketball players from eight universities. It turned out that players who used relaxation and visualization techniques before practice sessions increased their free-throw accuracy by 7 percent over that of players who didn't use such methods.

"There are only two ways to control the physiology of peak performance," Loehr says. "Control what you're thinking and act with the physical body."

Here are some specific approaches you can take:

**1. SHOOT YOUR INNER CRITIC.** Statements like "I won't make this shot" and "That guy's huge!" aren't helpful. Substitute "I can do this!" and "I'm faster than him!" Says Jerry Lynch, Ph.D., a Santa Cruz, California, sports psychologist who works with top NCAA basketball teams and elite marathoners, "Negative self-talk and images create anxiety and tension, both of which block your efforts to perform up to your capabilities."

**2. COP A BUZZ.** Think back to one moment of transcendent athletic glory—when you turned a pivotal double play in softball or defeated that A-league opponent in tennis. Recall everything you can about that moment as vividly as possible—feel the excitement, hear the cheers. Then "hook" that feeling of success to a buzzword or a performance cue. "The word can be something like 'excellence' or 'explode' and the gesture a slap on the knee or the touch of a glove," says Baum. When you master this, he says, you can summon a peak-performance state instantly.

**3. ACT TOUGH.** Acting like a winner plays a big role in your becoming one. Studies of actors showed that those who most effectively connect with audiences actually experience the emotions they portray onstage. Athletes can take advantage of this physiological phenomenon: By playacting—that is, looking confident, strong, and invincible on the playing field—they can "genuinely move their chemistry to target peak-performance emotions," Loehr says.

**4. PUT IT IN WRITING.** Write affirmations such as "I deserve to represent my country in the Olympics" on index cards. Then put the cards where you'll see them throughout the day. "When I walk into a locker room at Duke University to do a pregame meditation-visualization with the basketball team, I'm just in awe of all these affirmations," says Lynch. "It's 'We are the 1999 National Champions!' all over the walls." Affirmations are commitments, he says.

"This is not New Age stuff at all," says Baum of these techniques. Still, he says, some athletes resist mental training, thinking it's a sign of weakness.

That's fine by Tanner: "I would much rather not have my opponents do it."

—STEPHEN RAE

BASKETBALL

# Own the Court
## TWO UNSTOPPABLE PLAYS
## FROM THE MASTERS

NBA LEGENDS Michael Jordan and Karl Malone have always seemed to have a preternatural sense about how best to shake their defenders, in large part because of their titanic athletic ability. Both players were also beneficiaries of offensive systems employed by their teams that enabled them to be in position for all of those rim-rattling dunks in the first place, such as Malone's Utah Jazz using the old standby "pick-and-roll" and Jordan's Chicago Bulls the more complex "triangle offense."

"I don't want to sound like I know what I'm talking about," says the infamously self-effacing Jazz coach Jerry Sloan, "but I know that good things happen for us whenever [we] pick-and-roll." Learning these pro sets from the gurus themselves—Sloan and Tex Winter, the legendary Bulls assistant who invented the triangle offense—doesn't mean you'll be able to perform them exactly like Jordan and Malone. But it's safe to say that with these proven schemes under your belt, good things will happen to you and your rec team the next time you take the floor. Take it from the man himself: "The triangle offense has innovated the game of basketball," says Jordan.

## The Triangle Offense

The idea is to overload one side of the floor, forming an equilateral (more or less) triangle. "This offense is predicated on countering the defense," says Winter, who designed the system back in 1947, when he was an assistant coach at Kansas State. "It creates opportunities for players that they couldn't create on their own."

The three points of the triangle are created when the player who brings the rock up the floor passes it to a wingman, who has positioned himself on the three-point arc at or near the level of the free-throw line (point 1). The passer then runs toward the corner and sets up on the 3-point stripe closer to the base line (point 2). A third player posts on that same side of the lane, about midway between the base line and the free-throw line, completing the triangle (point 3).

The other two men on the floor position themselves on the weak side of the court, one posting on the opposite wing (point 4), the other at the top of the key (point 5). Spacing is crucial: Winter advises that on a pro-sized court, players should be 15 to 18 feet apart; adjust accordingly for the size of your gym.

## Plan A

The first priority is for the wingman to feed the ball to the strong-side post. From there, you have three main options. The first is for the post man to try to create a shot for himself by driving or just shooting. The second and third depend on the man in the corner: The wing player who passed in to the post should run toward the corner to set a pick for the corner man, who can either (a) fake toward the base line and head out to the wing for a jumper or (b) fake up and then drive to the basket along the base line, hoping for a backdoor bounce pass from the post. If neither of those possibilities looks viable—or if the defense is sagging on your post man, blocking the entry pass—throw back out to the top of the key for a new set of options.

## Plan B

At this point, you want to utilize the weak-side wingman, perhaps the most important player in this offense, according to Winter. Not surprisingly, that is where the Bulls often used Jordan. The key is for the weak-side wing to get himself in position to receive a pass in what Winter calls the pinch-post, a post position at the spot where the free-throw line intersects with the side of the lane. Then you have the choice of letting your pinch-post man get the ball for what is called an isolation, which is taking his defender one-on-one to the hoop (perfect for Jordan or your team's best ball handler), or you can work the play made famous in Utah. . . .

## The Pick-and-Roll

Since the days when James Naismith, the game's inventor, had his YMCA teams shooting into peach baskets before the turn of the last century, the pick-and-roll has been the quintessential, fundamental-yet-hard-to-defend play.

The basic purpose of the pick-and-roll is to create a mismatch for one of your bigger players by forcing the defense to switch defenders. For instance, Sloan often uses the six-foot-nine

# STEPHON MARBURY

To the rest of us, the hallowed hardwood of Madison Square Garden is a reminder that everything we've ever done on a basketball court is, after all, chump change, even meaningless. To New Jersey Nets point guard Stephon Marbury, the storied court is a canvas he intends to paint, no, tattoo, with his impression. He has given some insight on what separates the 348 NBA players in the world from the rest of us.

The best pickup players played in college, maybe Division I. "In college, I could tell who could play in the NBA, and it wasn't many," Marbury says, referring to his one-year sojourn at Georgia Tech. "I mean, in the pros there's no zone defense, and so even the big guys have to move. Everybody has to be strong, and you have to know how to shoot." He isn't talking about the kind of studied jumpers we let fly in gyms, though. "You only got a split second—less than that. You have to have such a quick release to get off a shot—or a pass. And you have to make decisions right away. And it better be the right one, know what I'm saying? All real quick"—he snaps his fingers—"like that."

On a more encouraging note, Marbury says, the first step is having an all-around game. Make sure you can handle the ball with both hands, nail the 15-foot jumper, box out, snap a crisp pass. More and more, he notes, distinctions between positions are breaking down. "It's just spots on the floor—1, 2, 3, 4, 5—now," says Marbury. "I mean I play point, but I post up." The result, Marbury notes, is that "at this level, it doesn't matter how tall you are, you have to be able to do everything—even if you never have to in a game." Still, he says, the most important thing is to play your game; if, say, you're a big man who plays better on the perimeter, do it. To illustrate this, he points to his former teammate on the Minnesota Timberwolves, Kevin Garnett, a seven-foot-tall "small" forward who is deadly facing the basket and putting the ball on the floor. Play like Garnett, huh? So much for encouraging.

Marbury spent the summer of 1998 lifting weights rep for rep with a former NFL defensive lineman, and like most NBA players he lifts between five and seven times a week. But endurance is key. "You need to be as quick in the forty-eighth minute as at tipoff," he says. "Guys in a gym start out quick, but a half-hour later people don't notice but they've slowed down by like a third. In the pros you got great players 1 through 12—slow down and a guy off the bench with fresh legs *will* go right around you," he adds. "I play against another Stephon Marbury every night, someone who's just as good as me, so I need to have my edge every minute of every game." Then, he adds, "See, even if you're a great gym player, there's no competition, no way to get better."

So would he lace 'em up with some solid gym ballplayers to, you know, help them develop? "Nope, I won't ever run ball with guys in a gym." Marbury adds, "They're so much slower and so clumsy I could get hurt. Seriously."

—ALEX BHATTACHARJI

Pro set: Michael and company run the triangle against the Pacers in the '98 playoffs.

Malone to set a pick for six-foot-one guard John Stockton, who is usually covered by another player of similar height. When Stockton brings the ball up the court, Sloan often has Malone set up near the foul line (though the play can be run from anywhere on the court). Stockton dribbles straight past Malone, making sure his path draws his defender smack into Malone's huge frame. "We just want Karl to headhunt on the pick," says Sloan, emphasizing the importance of making the pick impenetrable to contact from the defender. When Stockton's defender runs into Malone's pick, the player guarding Malone will usually be forced to

switch and pick up the suddenly unguarded Stockton. As he does, Malone spins off the pick and toward the basket, most often chased by a much smaller defender, who is already a step behind. Presto, monster jam. (In your case, a layup will suffice.)

Don't be frustrated if it takes some practice to get the plays down. Even the Bulls needed half a season before they felt comfortable running a triangle offense. "They were getting sick of my whistle," says Winter.

**—JULIAN RUBINSTEIN**

# Dominate the Sand Lot

OVER THE LAST few years, NFL defenses, and defenders, have become so big and strong—and fast—that they've been able to dictate the flow of games with such innovative schemes as the quarterback-terrorizing zone blitz. The result has been that signal-callers who hope to make an impact and avoid injury have been forced to find something in their own arsenal that, if executed, is sure to trump even the most diabolical of defenses. For the San Francisco 49ers' star Steve Young, it's been a special play that gives him a run or pass option. The Dallas Cowboys' Troy Aikman has perfected the simple but glorious bomb. Fortunately for us, both plans are also perfect for the schoolyard Turkey Day game. Take a knee, men.

## The Steve Young Thanksgiving Special

Line up two wide receivers to your right, put a fullback and a halfback in the backfield in the T-formation (fullback, left; halfback, right), and place your tight end on the left side of the ball. "We designed this play for me to roll left," says Young, a lefty, "but you can flip it and run it to the right."

When you take the snap, pivot to the right and fake a handoff to the fullback, who comes across the field and heads into the right flat. The two wideouts serve as decoys and should both run deep patterns. Young says that the combination of the formation, the play-action fake to the fullback, and the receivers on the right going deep "will get the defense flowing to the right. Then you turn and sprint out to the left."

The tight end and halfback are your primary targets. The tight end should run a zigzag pattern, slanting in about 10 yards and then angling back out to the left. The halfback runs a fly pattern straight up the left hash marks. In man-to-man defense, the halfback should be able to beat his defender up the left side of the field, since the cover man will have drifted right a bit. If the tight end runs a sharp pattern, he'll also get a step on his man when he cuts back across the grain. (Think Brent Jones rumbling across the field waving his "I'm open" arm.)

*The test of any man lies in action.*

**— PINDAR**

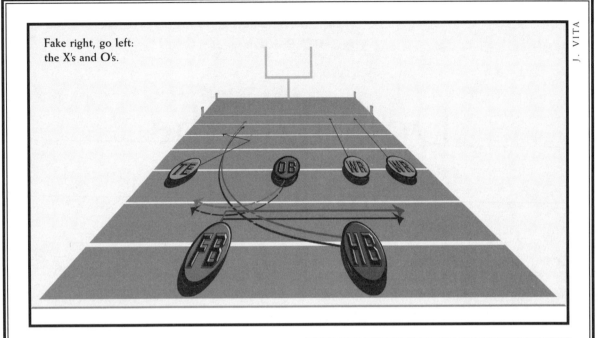

Fake right, go left: the X's and O's.

Against a zone defense, one of the two main receivers is usually open because their patterns are designed so that both players pass simultaneously through the same area. "By flooding that part of the field, inevitably one of them has room," says Young.

However, if both of them are well covered, you may find yourself all alone in the left flat with a defensive end bearing down on you. This, says the fleet-footed Young, is not necessarily a bad thing. If you can freeze the onrushing defender with a pump fake, he says, "you may see some serious daylight ahead."

## Troy Aikman's ICBM Attack

For this play, Aikman prefers to align his troops in the standard pro set formation: a receiver on each side of the ball and a tight end lined up on the same side as your primary receiver. Against a zone defense, "the tight end should run right up the hash to hold the safety," Aikman says. "I just kind of stare at him or maybe make a quick pump fake

### IMPROVE YOUR PASS

If you want to increase your passing range, Aikman recommends lifting—and lots of it. "Not just upper body," Aikman says. "Legs and hips are as important as anything. A lot of people talk about arm strength, but legs and hips provide the power."

In terms of the mechanics of the throwing motion, the Cowboys' quarterbacks coach, Buddy Geis, says it's simple: "Be sure your back foot is planted solid, and once you're ready to throw, your left shoulder [for a right-hander] becomes like a telescope. It should be pointed right at your target, especially for a deep pass. Then step in the direction you're throwing, and as you follow through, you should feel your weight shift from the back foot to the front." —J.R.

# JEROME BETTIS

Jerome Bettis, the Pittsburgh Steelers' four-time Pro Bowl running back, perks up and looks out from under his eyebrows. "'What does it take for you to play with the big boys?'" he says, repeating my question. "Okay, well, run a 4.3 in the 40.

"You see," he explains to me, "if you're 5 feet 11 and 180 pounds, like you are, that's a prerequisite." Bettis, also 5 feet 11, but a rippling 250 pounds, runs a 4.56 himself.

Next, Bettis explains, size does matter. "Guys who are defensive end–sized for high school had better be track stars too, because at 6 feet 2 and 225 pounds, they're looking at playing safety in the pros." I see what he means: Bigger is better; bigger and faster better still.

"You get drafted on being an athlete, you play when you get skills," he says. He goes on to recall the early- to mid-'80s when a number of Olympic sprinters were drafted as wide receivers, only to flop because they couldn't run precise routes or work free at the line of scrimmage, much less catch the ball. He talks about the need to know the finer points of club moves, seal blocks, jamming a receiver, and how to throw a fade pattern a full second before the receiver makes his cut.

But what he says next seems more important. "An NFL player's reaction," he says. "It was the one thing that stuck out to me coming out of college. Ever wonder why a misdirection or a play-action fake works? It's 'cause the defensive players have already covered 10 yards towards the flow of the play. Read, react, and go 10 yards in a second and a half. It's pretty incredible. Check out how many tests at the [NFL predraft] combine have to do with quick reaction times and you see—it's huge.

"Then there's a lot of premium put on being versatile and having multiple talents," he adds. Even though there are only a few two-way players in the NFL, most play on one or another special-teams assignment besides their position. And of course, Bettis reminds me, most positions require having more than one forte. "Take me at running back—tailback really—I gotta pass-protect, catch the ball, block for the other backs sometime, *and* rush the football," Bettis says. "At this level, in this league there aren't any one-trick ponies." Then he adds, "Well, except maybe kickers. You don't kick, do you?"

—ALEX BHATTACHARJI

to him." Against a man-to-man, use your tight end to clear out the side you plan to throw to by getting him to run a slant or a down-and-in away from the ball.

As for your primary receiver, Aikman says not to even waste time having him run anything other than a straight fly—unless you've noticed that the defense has been overplaying your down-and-out route. "Then you can go with the down-out-and-go," he says.

The biggest key to executing the bomb, according to Aikman, is how your receiver runs his route. Even a lot of NFL receivers, Aikman says, make the mistake of veering toward the sideline once they get past their defender. "That's exactly what the corner wants," he says. "The sideline becomes like an extra defender, and the quarterback has no place to put the ball where it can't be intercepted."

The solution? When your receiver runs up on the corner, he should straighten out his route, establishing a 10-yard-wide lane between himself and the sideline and pinning the defender to the inside. "Then the throw should go to the outside shoulder so the receiver can fade off to the ball away from the defender," he says. This way, regardless of whether or not your man has beaten his defender, he should have room to catch the pass.

The key for the quarterback, Aikman says, is twofold. First, don't hold the ball too long: "Quarterbacks sometimes feel like they need to see the receiver go by the defender before they throw it. If you wait that long, more times than not you're going to underthrow the route." Better, Aikman says, to take a five-step drop hitch and just chuck it.

Second, he says, it's important to put enough arc on the ball so that the receiver has enough time to adjust his position while the ball is in the air. "If you throw the ball too flat, your margin of error is a lot smaller," he says.

You may be thinking, *Sure, easy for Aikman to say.* But the two-time Super Bowl champ insists there is one very good reason that this play is worth practicing: "If the receiver runs the route correctly and the ball is delivered on target, the defender, no matter how good he is, can't defend it."

—JULIAN RUBINSTEIN

GOLF

# The Short Game

I N THE AGE of Tiger Woods and titanium, everybody's trying to hit the long ball. It seems that if you're not driving it 275 yards, you might as well stay home. But no matter how far you hit off the tee, golf's oldest adage remains true: Drive for show, putt for dough. It's on and around the green where you have the best opportunity to drop your score. So put down the Big Bertha for a minute and plug into these tips on putting, chipping, and getting out of the sand. Your titanium driver won't help you here unless, of course, you're Tiger Woods.

## Putting

"It's a proven fact that if your ball doesn't reach the hole, it can't go in," says Greg Lecker, the teaching pro at Canoe Brook Country Club in Summit, New Jersey. That's why he advises hitting all your putts—both in practice and while playing—so that they roll past the hole.

It's also why he touts the pendulum theory of putting. As most golfers know, this stroke requires a few basic mechanics. Keep your shoulders, elbows, wrists, and hands locked throughout the stroke. Take the club back at the same speed you plan to bring it forward. Follow through.

The last step sounds the simplest but actually requires the most finesse, according to Lecker. "The important thing is not to allow the club face to get in front of your left hand until the club head is at least a foot past the point of impact," he says. This may be hard to picture in your head, but if you stand up and try it, you'll see that it forces you to take a longer swing and to keep the putter closer to the ground. The result is better rotation on the ball and longer, smoother putts.

## Chipping

Some of the most difficult chip shots are the ones in which your ball is sitting just off the green. You can't go to the putter just yet, and a wedge shot seems treacherous at best. The solution might just be your 7-iron.

"You want to get the ball on the green as fast as possible and let it roll," says Dale Ray Akridge, the head pro at Southshore Golf Club in Henderson, Nevada's Lake Las Vegas Resort. A highly lofted club like a wedge would do just the opposite, sending the ball high in the air with relatively little roll once it lands. A 7-iron, however, creates a low-trajectory shot that clears the tall grass in one quick hop and then rolls across the green.

You hit the shot, says Akridge, with a slightly open stance, your weight on your left foot and the club angled slightly forward. "Once I get the club set, I try to imagine my hands are in casts so that my wrists can't move," says Akridge. "Then it's a nice easy swing with the arms and shoulders." If you can make the ball land one-quarter of the way to the hole, it should roll the rest of the way. So if you have a 40-foot chip, you should try to make the ball land 10 feet away, and that spot, not the hole, should be your target.

## Sand

"They've gone overboard with the directions," says Bobby Eldridge, who runs the Bobby Eldridge Golf School at the Pointe Hilton Tapitio Cliffs in Phoenix, Arizona. He's talking about the way TV talking heads have caused many golfers to exaggerate unnecessarily the motions of the standard sand shot.

The trick, then, is to get back to the basics. With a slightly open stance, place 60 percent of your weight on your left foot and place the ball forward in your stance. Take your arms back as if you're going to make your regular swing, but don't turn your body all the way. "You want the back swing to be 80 percent arms and 20 percent body," points out Eldridge. As you come down, make sure to hit "safely" (two to four inches) behind the ball and follow through. Aim slightly left of the hole and take the same swing no matter how far you're trying to hit the ball. You can adjust for distance by opening or closing the face of the club—the more open, the shorter the ball will fly.

If the ball is buried, move back in your stance, put 80 percent of your weight on your left foot, square the face, and take a steeper swing, "as if you're trying to pound in a tent stake," says Eldridge.

—JIM GORANT

# Develop a Powerful Punch

POWER TENNIS is alive and flourishing, and though pummeling an opponent with a smoking forehand or a clean ace is a worthy end unto itself, there are other benefits to be derived from having a big shot.

"It creates a threat, inspires fear in your opponent," says Allen Fox, Ph.D., former pro-circuit player and author of *Think to Win*, "and in the process, forces him to hit tougher shots that aren't necessarily in his repertoire." Honing an aggressive shot can also reconfigure your on-court MO. "Players with a big shot develop a sense of aggressiveness that carries into all aspects of their game," says Jim Loehr, a sports psychologist who works with tennis star Sergi Bruguera. "If you don't have a knockout punch, you're forced into a passive role."

How do you build a big shot? This three-pronged strategy requires adjustments in your technique, fitness level, and court strategy. Don't shrink from the task if your first forehand and serve scatter like birdshot. Developing a weapon takes patience and enough courage to risk looking—at least temporarily—like a beginner.

## The Serve

### Technique: Tune the Toss

In a three-set match, a big server like Pete Sampras can win 35 to 40 points strictly on service winners. That's 9 to 10 games; sure, you say, but he's hitting them in excess of 120 miles per hour.

Don't sell yourself short. Teaching pro Vic Braden believes recreational players who typically serve in the 70-mph range can crank up the velocity into the 90s. The key is to groove the toss and accentuate the wrist snap. "As the toss climbs to its apex, your power is also reaching its climax," says Braden. "Most players short-circuit that power by tossing the ball too close to their body, breaking the kinetic chain [the power that is generated by the legs, transferred through the midsection, and delivered to the shoulder and arm]."

To maximize power, toss the ball two or three feet into the court in the direction of the right net post (if you are right-handed). The toss should be only as high as your racket can reach; any higher and you'll find yourself pausing,

## THE SERVE

# USE YOUR LEGS

Your legs produce most of the power on the serve. "You can't deliver a powerful serve if your legs aren't strong enough," says Pat Etcheberry, who trained Sampras and Courier throughout the '90s. Squats, side lunges, leg extensions, and leg curls (three sets of 8 to 10 twice a week) can give you a solid foundation. Crunches (including twisting crunches) and trunk twists (three sets of 20 to 25 each two to three times a week) will build strong abdominals, which facilitate the transfer of power.

Since your shoulder is a critical link in the kinetic chain, you'll need to build it up as well. One study found that strengthening the back of the shoulder (specifically the external rotator) could improve service velocity by 25 percent. External rotations (three sets, 10 repetitions, twice a week) with five-pound dumbbells should do it.

One of Etcheberry's favorite drills is throwing a tennis ball at a backboard from about 15 feet away and catching it on the fly. Throw the ball at 80 percent to 90 percent of your full power for 20 to 30 seconds. Do four or five sets twice a week. A solid throwing motion will work the muscles needed for a powerful serve, and the catching element will teach you to keep your feet moving after you've hit your serve. "It's easy to just stand there and admire a big serve," says Braden. "But you've got to be ready to jump on the return."

thereby slowing the acceleration you've generated. A right-hander should hit the serve at about two o'clock on a watch face (assuming the center line of the court corresponds to twelve o'clock). As you hit the ball, be sure to squeeze the racket handle firmly and snap your wrist; this will add more power to your delivery. Braden says the snap should be like shaking down the mercury in a thermometer. Once you've hit the ball, don't stop short. Let the momentum carry you into the court so you can pounce on a weak return or hit an approach shot and move in for a volley.

### How to Use It: Smart Bombing

Now that you know how to hit the big serve, use it selectively. Though the hardest-serving pros usually opt for power on their first serve, we mortals would do better with a mix-and-match strategy—changing spins, pace, and direction. Some players have an easier time returning a big, flat serve (using the pace to block the ball back) than handling a briskly hit spin serve aimed at or away from their body.

Use a high-paced flat serve when taking a chance on a point you can afford to lose, when you are up, say, 30- or 40-love. If you are a consistent server—routinely getting in 65 percent to 70 percent of your first serves—go for the ace from time to time. Flat servers such as Boris Becker generally hit down the middle of the court because the net is at its lowest point and they have less chance of netting their delivery.

# QUICK POWER

Because so much of the power of the forehand comes from the legs, Etcheberry recommends two sets of leg presses (15 to 20 repetitions per set), lunges (8 to 15 reps per set), and step-ups (also 8 to 15 reps) twice a week. (*Note:* If you're already doing some of these exercises for your serve, skip them.) "You're not trying to be Mr. America," he says. "But you are trying to build your legs into pistonlike springs. Tennis is a sport with lots of stops and starts. It's those first couple of steps that make the difference. If you can't get to the ball quickly, you won't be in a position to hit it with power." Etcheberry favors 10 to 20 minutes of comfortably fast sprints (taking a minute or more of rest between sprints) twice a week, preferably on a soft surface to protect your joints.

Strengthening and stretching the forearm muscles, which grow tighter with every shot you hit, will ensure a powerful stroke while reducing your risk of injury. Wrist curls (two sets of 10 reps each) with two 5-pound dumbbells or squeezing a tennis ball for five seconds (10 hard reps with each hand) will build them up.

## The Forehand

### Technique: The Coil

Converting the forehand into a topspin weapon requires a technique that helps build and unleash power. The key is coiling—making sure your shoulders turn when you set up to hit the ball. As you move forward to strike it, rotate your hips, turning your shoulders toward the net at the absolute tail end of the stroke. "People think those big forehands are hit strictly with the arm," says sports scientist Jack Groppel, Ph.D. "That's how they get hurt. It's the legs that are doing the work. The more you use your legs and hips, the more powerful a shot you'll hit. Your arm just comes along for the ride." To develop topspin, don't think of brushing the ball with the racket strings as much as generating a long low-to-high motion. Try to maintain contact with the ball as if you were sweeping it across a long table. This will prevent you from pulling off the ball too soon.

### How to Use It: Advertise the Weapon

Establish your forehand as a weapon in the early stages of a match. Like a quarterback throwing an early bomb, you want to open up the defense. Whip a service return crosscourt or gun one down the line. Even if you miss, you'll be alerting your opponent to the strength of your shot.

A classic setup is opening up the court with some solid crosscourt forehands—the higher and deeper, the better. As your opponent's shots land shorter, close in and rip a forehand down the line to his backhand (if he's a right-hander). If he returns it at all, it will be weak, allowing you to knock off the next shot for a winner.

Another strategy is to run around medium-paced shots to your backhand, then blast a forehand either down the line or crosscourt. The trick here is to make sure you crack the shot so that you elicit a weak response from your opponent. If you don't, your court position—deep into your back-hand corner—will possibly leave you vulnerable to *his* big shot.

—JOEL DRUCKER

# Hit a Fast Pitch

FOR 10 DAYS in August 1996, Colin Abbott found the most hallowed place in sports: the Zone. It was the World Fastpitch Tournament, the World Series of fastpitch softball, and the 26-year-old outfielder for the All Car Roadrunners of Green Bay, Wisconsin, felt "like I could hit anything." He very nearly did. By the end of his team's 12 games, the 6-foot-3, 225-pound Abbott had swung himself into the record books of the International Softball Congress (ISC), for the most hits (17), RBIs (14), and home runs (5) in a single World Tournament. That's in 49 years of play.

If you think that hitting a fastpitch softball is about as challenging as swatting a lobbed water-melon, you're thinking of the wrong game. Sure, slowpitch softballs arc high and slow (and you can clobber them with half a keg in you), but fastpitch, the original game, is a hard-core version of the sport that rivals what pro baseball players do.

Games, each seven innings long, are played in a compact, frenetic arena. The bases are only 60 feet apart, and the home-run fence is as short as 250 feet out. The ball hurtles from the mound to the batter at speeds of more than 90 miles per hour over a distance of 46 feet—which is especially rip-ping when you consider that while a major-league fastball might top 100 mph, it travels 60 feet 6 inches, making its relative speed slower than that of a fastpitch ball. And because a fastpitch soft-ball is thrown underhand from a level mound, it usually rises as it moves toward the plate. (Fast-pitch legend Eddie Feigner, whose summer softball show has been touring for over fifty years, struck out many major-leaguers, including Willie Mays and Roberto Clemente.)

All of which makes Abbott's performance in the '96 World Fastpitch Tournament even more impressive. "You watch an athlete like Abbott play," says ISC executive director Milt Stark, "and you wonder why he's not playing Major League Baseball."

"I did play baseball once," responds Abbott. "But it seemed too slow."

Herewith Abbott's slugging secrets.

## The Stance

Most coaches recommend a square stance—feet shoulder-width apart along a line running parallel to home plate, with an equal amount of weight on each leg. But Abbott favors a closed stance (his front foot significantly nearer to the plate than his back one), and he places roughly 85 percent of his weight on his back foot, which, he says, "helps me stride into the ball with more power." The closed stance helps him keep his head down and his chin tucked into his right shoulder (he bats left-handed). That's crucial, he says: The urge to jerk your head out of place is overwhelming, and if your head turns, your body turns with it, pulling you out of position.

As for your grip, the manuals advise lining up your middle knuckles to facilitate a level swing and to generate maximum bat speed, but Abbott believes that's getting way too nit-picky—"just one more thing to distract you," he says. He prefers a more natural approach: "I don't try to position my hands. I just pick the bat up like a broomstick." To give himself as much time as possible in which to see the ball and react to it, Abbott stands as deep in the batter's box as he can. "I put my foot right on the back of the line, and sometimes even over it. If you're only out by a couple of inches, most umpires won't say anything."

## The Stride

The stride is the little step that batters take just prior to swinging, generally at the moment the pitcher lets go of the ball. But Abbott starts his stride an instant *before* the ball is released. Wait longer, he says, and you're already too late. A caveat: Even though you take a step to start the swing, your hands and your head should stay immobile. Discipline yourself to keep them where they are. "If they come forward too early," says Abbott, "your timing will be totally off."

## The Swing

Your initial motion with your hands should be straight ahead. "People have lots of problems with their swing because their hands move up or down first. Instead, your first move should be forward, with no unnecessary motion in other directions," says Abbott. Start straight and level, and your hands will get to the ball in plenty of time, he says. If you raise or drop them first, you'll be wasting motion and hitting air.

Next, Abbott transfers most of his weight to his front leg, rotates his hips and shoulders, and extends his arms. "That's where my power comes from." As Abbott continues his swing, his left shoulder (since he's a lefty) winds up under his chin, mainly because his torso, not his head, moved. Even as Abbott follows through, he keeps his head down. "When people get into slumps, it's almost always because they're turning their head up and away," he notes.

## The Focus

Ultimately, says Abbott, even perfect swing mechanics will take you only so far. Mental focus is just as important. "My concentration level is high. When things are going well, I can see the ball clearer than life." That's what the Zone is all about: a higher state of consciousness. This is an awareness you develop through practice and experience, he says.

Once you've smacked the snot out of the ball, the one thing that's left to do is to run like hell. "When you're as big as I am," says Abbott, "that's when your problems start."

**—CARL HOFFMAN**

# Throw. Hit. Catch. No Problem.

**B**ASEBALL IS a simple game," said Skip Riggins, the manager in the classic film *Bull Durham*. "You throw the ball. You hit the ball. You catch the ball." The problem, of course, is that players often make the game harder than it needs to be. And this is especially true for those who made their last trip to the diamond in a company softball game and not a double-header against the Boston Red Sox. To ensure that you don't look like a bush leaguer the next time you play hardball, follow this sound advice from a former major-leaguer.

## Pitching

"Babe Ruth is dead. Throw strikes." That is what every pitching coach worth his chaw tells his starters. And it's especially good advice for amateur players, according to Ken Sanders, former American League Fireman of the Year and now a coach at the Milwaukee Brewers Fantasy Camp. "From Little League on up to the major leagues, there's a shortage of pitchers," he says, "and a bigger shortage of good pitchers, guys who can get the ball over the plate." How do you get to be a good pitcher? Start slowly. Until you develop your arm strength and control, Sanders suggests starting out by throwing from 40 feet—moving home plate closer so you're still throwing from the mound—and then moving the plate back gradually as you get stronger.

Sanders also suggests having your catcher set a target in the middle of the plate and aiming for his mitt. If you're not trying to get fancy, you're less likely to plunk a hitter—remember, this is supposed to be fun—or cross up your catcher. Your bread-and-butter pitch should be a basic four-seam fastball, thrown from a simple, no-frills motion. Leave the fancy contortions to El Duque. Instead, simply throw the ball, using the same basic body position and arm angle as you would if you were throwing from the outfield.

Once you've got your fastball humming, the next pitch to add to your arsenal is the slider. It can be thrown from the same motion as the fastball; just give the ball a little football-style spiral. It's easy on the arm, and it's effective, dipping just a few inches at the last second, turning good cuts into ground-ball outs. What about Uncle Charley? "I pitched ten years in the big leagues, and I never threw a curveball," says Sanders. Which means that you don't have to either.

## Hitting

At the plate, the "keep it simple, stupid" rule still applies. Start from a basic, balanced stance and make sure you don't overstride, if you even stride at all. Keep your swing as clean and simple as possible. If you're going to emulate a big-leaguer, choose some-

# TIM McCARVER

"Because of all the variables involved, hitting a baseball *is* the hardest thing to do in sports," says Tim McCarver. To hear Tim McCarver dispense baseball wisdom—without the interruptions of a game in progress, his words unfettered—is to remember that there are students of the game and then there are the professors. His dissertation topic du jour is built on the maxim "Pitchers are born and hitters are made." But people often misunderstand that statement, the 21-year major-league catcher turned broadcaster notes: The making of a hitter is no mean feat.

"People say, 'Well, what about hitting a golf ball? You've got to play your foul balls,'" McCarver continues. "But golfers don't have fielders out in the fairway catching balls that are well hit either." Hitting, he says, is more than making contact or putting bat to ball; it is a skill used adversarially. "Putting the ball into play isn't enough. You need to put it into play on your terms. That's what pitchers strive to do, too—have hitters put it into play on the pitcher's terms," he says. "And right there that's pretty much the crux of the whole game and clearly the most intense tête-à-tête in sports."

Physical ability is only part of the equation, McCarver posits. "There's a toughness that most people don't have—and probably don't fathom—and a stick-to-itiveness. That's concentration. Every pitch, every at-bat, every game—remember, now, there are one hundred sixty-two of them."

When it comes to hitting, talent is hard to define, but two things stand out: judgment and bat speed. "People measure the amount of time you have to decide on whether to swing at a pitch in terms of nanoseconds." But "It's not just the vision of the hitter, it's the acuity of the hitter," McCarver says. "Acuity is picking up the ball with a background, figuring its speed and its spin. Then, too, you have to calculate the arm angle." And then there's the swing, which comes down to bat speed, a skill that combines "strength, flexibility, explosiveness. If you don't have those traits, you're not going to get the bat through the strike zone in a hurry," he says.

Finally, McCarver begins to wax more philosophical. "Think about it: Results are the ultimate measure in baseball, and no one has ever hit 1.000 over a season in the majors. No one ever will, either, despite the fact mathematicians insist it will happen." As he presents his conclusions, McCarver's professorial tone lightens. "So there's no such thing as a perfect swing," he says, breaking into a laugh. "So you might as well keep trying, kid." —ALEX BHATTACHARJI

one with a simple, minimalist swing like Mariners first baseman John Olerud rather than the baroque stylings of Blue Jays shortstop Tony Batista.

Tactically, you should also take a page from the pros. "Don't swing unless the pitch is in the strike zone," says Sanders. Don't laugh; Greg Maddux has built a Hall of Fame career on getting hitters to swing at ball three. Swinging for the fences is counterproductive, too. "Look at Derek Jeter, the way he uses the whole field," says Sanders. "Just try to hit the ball back through the middle." Trying to pull the ball causes your hips to fly open prematurely, and if that happens, you'll end up looking like Randy Johnson. Randy Johnson the hitter, that is.

---

## Fielding

Before you can catch the ball, you've got to get to it. And since you probably don't run like Kenny Lofton or Omar Vizquel, positioning is more than half the battle. Know who's at the plate and where he's likely to hit it—and remember that at this level hitters can't always pull the ball. It's also smart to play deep because it's much easier to run in for a ball than have to backpedal for a hot smash. "As the ball approaches, get into a crouch and wait for it to come to you," says Sanders. If it takes a bad hop, you'll at least be able to keep the ball in front of you. If you do bobble the ball—and eventually you will—don't compound the error. Sometimes the smartest thing to do is just hold the ball instead of rushing and throwing wildly. On pop-ups, forget the snatch catch and squeeze the ball with two hands. And one safety note: Remember to call for the ball and to listen when your teammate yells, "I got it." Failure to observe this basic rule has led to more than one trip to the orthopedic surgeon.

The mental side of fielding is one of the places where you can emulate a big leaguer. "Be a better player by being a better thinker," says Sanders. That means keeping on top of the situation. Knowing how many outs, which base you'll be throwing to, how fast the hitter and the runners are, and when you should be the cutoff man and when you should cover third base. You may not be Bernie Williams, but at least you won't go trotting off the field when there are two outs.

—ALLEN ST. JOHN

# Ride Right

OF COURSE, riding a bicycle isn't as difficult as, say, hitting a major-league fastball or playing Bach's *Goldberg Variations*. But there's a world of difference between merely being able to stay upright while turning the pedals and being a real rider. Just follow these few simple, universal tips from top riders and you can be efficient, comfortable, and yes, even elegant both on the road and on the trail.

---

## Perfect Pedaling

The good news: You learned how to pedal on your tricycle when you were three. The bad news: You're still pedaling the same way now. Take a look at your

Endurance Test:
A serious cyclist in the
California desert.

MARC JOSEPH

turned pro mountain-biker. Concentrate on pushing forward and pulling back at the top (between eleven and two o'clock) and the bottom (between four and seven o'clock) of the circle, almost as if you were scraping dirt off the bottom of your shoe. Make sure, of course, that the soles of your shoes are grippy enough that your foot doesn't really slip. If you've got toe clips or clipless pedals, Dunlap suggests trying to pedal in a full circle, pulling up with one foot while pushing down with the other. One of the best places to practice your pedaling, away from the distractions of school buses, unleashed dogs, and your neighbor's new BMW, is the gym. Practice on a stationary bike, or better yet, a studio cycling class, is the perfect place to smooth out your pedal stroke.

## Cornering Quickly

There's no bigger thrill in cycling than laying your bike over, fast and smooth, like Alberto Tomba carving a turn. And it's an important skill because scrubbing off speed in a turn means you'll have to expend more energy when the

chainring and pretend for a minute that it's a Rolex Daytona. Most riders simply stomp on the pedals between two o'clock and four o'clock. You don't have to be an exercise physiologist to understand that there's a better way. "You need to pedal all the way through the top and bottom of the stroke," says Alison Dunlap, a former Olympic road cyclist

road straightens out. The first key to effective cornering: Stop pedaling. "If you hit your pedal on the ground, you're going to launch yourself," says Dunlap. Again, pretend your chainring is the face of a clock and put your inside pedal at the twelve o'clock position and your outside pedal at six o'clock. Dunlap's second rule: Brake first; then turn. "If you hit your brakes in the middle of the turn, it can sometimes shift your weight to the front wheel just enough so that the back wheel gets loose." Which means a one-way ticket to Road Rash City. Strange as it may seem, the real secret to effective cornering is to turn your handlebars as little as possible and instead lean the bike over. To help move your center of gravity into the turn, Dunlap suggests bending your arms extra deep and pointing your inside knee toward the inside of the turn. The final key is line judgment. You want to straighten out the turn as much as possible by starting wide and ending wide and laying a straight line across the apex of the turn, just like Michael Andretti on a road course.

---

## Climbing Higher

When that long, steep hill begins to look like something from *Into Thin Air,* smart riders get out of the saddle. It not only gives you a psychological break; it also lets you recover by enlisting different muscle groups. *If* you do it right. "A lot of riders climb like they're on a StairMaster," says Cindy Whitehead, a former road and mountain-bike racer who teaches mountain-bike clinics. "Their body weight is doing most of the work." Needless to say, this stomp-stomp-stomp style of climbing is inefficient. Instead, Whitehead suggests actively rocking the bike back and forth, using the brake hoods or the bar ends for leverage: "It's like being in the gym and doing a biceps curl." This motion gets the strong muscles of your shoulders and your chest into the action, allowing you to push a bigger gear. Which means getting to the top faster. And that's what we all want, isn't it?

—ALLEN ST. JOHN

---

RUNNING

# Go the Distance

RUNNING MORE won't make you faster. Research shows you've got to train smart to improve your 10K or marathon times. The word now is less mileage, more intensity. According to exercise physiologist Ken Sparks, Ph.D., author of *How They Train,* it's much more effective to run at the speed at which you want to race. Sparks, who clocks marathons in the low 2:30s when he's not lecturing on cardiovascular disease at Cleveland State University, says intense, shorter-distance training has worked for him and a growing number of elite runners, including such household names as Rodgers, Salazar, and Shorter.

# TWO WEEKS OF SMART RUNNING

If you can't train without a program, here's one that will give you the three qualities needed to reach optimum times. Alternate high-mileage and low-mileage weeks. Long runs on low-mileage weeks should stay around 13. On high-mileage weeks, build the runs 1 mile at a time, to a max of 24. For 10K runners, top out at 15. If you are a marathoner and have the luxury of time and reserves of discipline, do it for 16 weeks or longer.

## HIGH MILEAGE/
## LOW INTENSITY

**MONDAY** Off.

**TUESDAY** Marathon: 7 to 10 miles steady-state pace at 75 percent to 80 percent maximum heart rate (MHR). 10K: 4 to 5 miles steady-state pace.

**WEDNESDAY** Marathon: (1) One mile at marathon-goal pace, plus 40 seconds; recover with a 440-yard jog. (2) Repeat step one. (3) One mile at marathon goal pace, minus 40 seconds; same recovery as step one. (4) One mile at 5K pace (85 percent to 90 percent MHR). 10K: Ten to twelve 440-yard laps at 5 seconds per lap faster than 10K race pace (90 percent to 95 percent MHR); recover between each with a 220-yard jog.

**THURSDAY** Same as Tuesday.

**FRIDAY** Off.

**SATURDAY** Marathon and 10K: Fifteen-minute anaerobic threshold (AT), meaning you're barely able to take in enough air, at 80 percent to 85 percent MHR, or run a mile at 10K pace, plus 20 seconds.

**SUNDAY** Marathon: 20 to 24 miles. 10K: 10 to 15 miles.

## LOW MILEAGE/
## HIGH INTENSITY

**MONDAY** Off.

**TUESDAY** Same as previous week.

**WEDNESDAY** Marathon and 10K: Twelve 440-yard laps at 10K pace, plus five seconds per lap, or 90 percent to 95 percent MHR; recover between each with a 220-yard jog.

**THURSDAY** Same as Tuesday.

**FRIDAY** Off.

**SATURDAY** Marathon: Planned marathon pace run, 5 to 10 miles (add 1 mile every two weeks) at 75 percent to 80 percent MHR. 10K: Race pace, or 15 to 20 minutes AT. (See previous week.)

**SUNDAY** Marathon and 10K: 12 to 13 miles.

Sparks's genetic gifts aside, it's a principle all of us can use to achieve better race times. If you're fortunate enough to squeeze in 20 miles during a week, putting some of that time into faster workouts will make you a better runner—and racer—than just piling on a few more miles at the same old pace. Yes, high-gear training feels a little tougher, but it consumes less time with greater results.

Use the training and race tips (along with the day-by-day training program) on this page and the next two. Figure on six weeks to improve your 10K times, assuming you're already logging weekly mileage somewhere in the 20s. Figure on three to four months for the marathon, which will require an eventual weekly mileage goal of 50 or more.

But why choose one or the other race now? Unless you think you can win the Mercedes at the next New York City Marathon, you can have it both ways. Train for a 10K early in the season for strength and speed, run a couple of races as benchmarks, then add more miles to the longest run of the week if you decide to go for a marathon later on and need more endurance. "The 10K is a great prep for the marathon," says coach Tom Fleming. He thinks most of us are too caught up in the training secrets of the famous. "We live in a world of specialization," says Fleming, "where you're either a 10K runner or a marathoner." Only if you're a world-class runner does that become a major concern. If that's not the case, you should use the opportunity to maximize your training so you can run your best in both races.

## Alternate Long/Short Weeks

"No pain, no gain" is for no-brainers. Today "the most important element of training is allowing your body to recover," says Bob Williams, a private coach and former all-American in the 3,000-meter steeplechase.

That means two "vigorous" training sessions each week—never back to back—and long runs (which for marathoners can be 20 miles or more) every other week.

## Planned Marathon Pace

Called PMP, the planned marathon pace is simplicity itself: If you want to run a marathon (or a 10K, for that matter) at a certain pace, do a lot of your training miles at that exact pace. Marathoners should do a PMP run every second week. This training strategy applies to 10Kers as well. According to Williams, who pioneered the PMP, those running a 10K should finish two races as rehearsals before the big one. In race one, do the first three miles at an easy, comfortable pace and the remaining miles at goal speed. During the second race, do the first two easy and the last four at goal pace. Finally, in race three—the big one—you should go for the brass ring right from the gun.

## Fluid Dynamics

"It isn't just hydration anymore; it's *energy* and hydration," says Roy Benson, an Atlanta-based coach and exercise physiologist. A good sport drink supplements the limited supply of energy stored in your muscles, increasing endurance. Although endurance isn't a major concern for 10K runners, it's crucial for marathoners. On especially long runs, "make sure you have 8 or 10 ounces of Gatorade or your favorite sport drink salted away every three miles along the course," advises Benson. Prerace and pretraining hydration is critical. Clear urine is the best indication that you've gotten enough water for the workout ahead. If not, keep drinking. On marathon day, don't rely on aid-station cups. "Run with the smallest water bottle you can find," says Benson. "At every stop, quickly dump in eight ounces of energy drink, snap the lid back on, open the spigot, and take off, drinking as you run." But practice first. Not all drinks agree with all runners. Avoid any containing fructose, cautions Williams, since it takes too long to break down. And be sure to drink 12 ounces or so within 20 minutes at the end of every hard workout, because muscles replenish glycogen fastest within that post-training time window.

## Taper, Taper, Taper

Don't train hard leading up to the last minute. "There's a bigger chance you'll be fried than out of shape by race day," says Benson. A marathoner's final long run should be about a 15-miler in a 40-mile week, three weeks before the race. Two weeks before the race, a 9-miler in a 30-mile week is plenty. And finally, avoid running more than 12 to 15 miles *total* in the week leading up to race day. A 10K runner can wait until race week, then trim weekly mileage anywhere from 25 percent to 50 percent, making the cuts mostly in the last three days before the race The more you've done, the more you have to cut. Drop a 20-mile week to 15 percent or 25 percent. But chop a 45-miler down to 25—a 50 percent reduction in round numbers.

–JOHN DELVES

BOXING

# Punch Harder

EVER SINCE the night Tommy Fahey was knocked out cold in a restaurant parking lot by a skinny kid half his size, I have believed myself to be sliding through life by the grace of God. Tommy Fahey couldn't fight. And neither could I.

Tommy had stepped into a domestic quarrel that night—he could not bear to see a man pushing a woman around—and he assumed that his sheer size would be all the deterrent needed to end the bullying. It was not. In a flash it was over, and even now I remember feeling the weight of Tommy's indignity as we slung him like a sack of grain onto the bed of our pickup truck.

Which is why I not long ago became a disciple of Martin Snow, who was at the time a boxing trainer at Gleason's Gym in New York City. The walls at Gleason's—which bills itself as the Most Famous Boxing Gym in the World—tell a triumphant story. Many of the gym's 109 world champions are pictured there, along with photographs of other famous fearless men, and women, like Jersey Joe Walcott, Riddick Bowe, and Guardian Angel Lisa Sliwa. I asked Martin to show me a few essential strategies, and thus began, as we bobbed and weaved, Gleason's *Cliff Notes* on preparing a defense.

## The Defensive Stance

There are four vulnerable spots to protect—or aim for—that run vertically down the body: the temple, the chin, the Adam's apple, and the solar plexus. So keep your chin down and hold your fists, palms, and forearms facing one another, in front of your body. Look out over the tops of your fists. Now that you've shielded most of those susceptible areas, it's less likely you'll go down on the first punch. Sure, this stance makes you resemble a daguerreotype of John L. Sullivan, but as Martin pointed out, "You're ready to buffer any punch that comes in."

Your eyes matter, too: Watch the action. "Once the fists go up, the first thing everybody does is look down at the floor," Martin said. "I don't know why. It's the toughest instinct to break in people. But you've got to keep looking up at what's happening."

## Don't Present a Big Target

Never stand square, full front, before an opponent. Here's why: "First, you're wide open, offering the other guy all those areas to hit. Second, you're off balance; one push and you'll fall backward. Third, a punch thrown from that position won't have anything in it. Instead, stand *sideways* to the guy, and if you're right-handed, put your right foot behind you. Now when you throw the punch, your whole weight and power will naturally follow it."

A moving target is harder to hit, so float like a butterfly. "Don't just stand there," Martin

instructed as I stood in front of him, apparently looking like a wooden Indian. "A lot of fights end with one guy in a headlock and the two of them wrestling on the floor. That's because it's easy to lunge at and grab someone who's not moving. So be an unpredictable target. Sidestep left or right, feet shoulder-width apart." (One note of caution on footwork: In 1977, during a Golden Gloves bout, witnesses said that a fighter named Harvey Gartley "danced himself into exhaustion and fell to the canvas" in the first 47 seconds of the first round. Proof that you can overdo a good thing.)

## Punch the Body

"They never expect it, *ever,*" Martin said. "Everybody goes for the head. The body, if you can get a clear shot, is bigger and easier to hurt. And if you connect, he'll instinctively drop his hands. *That's* when you give him a shot to the head."

Watch your technique. Perhaps because people look at their shoes when the dukes go up, the punch they deliver most often is a blind, wide roundhouse right. Trainers say that if you do this and your opponent does nothing more than throw up his left arm the instant you draw your fist, he'll probably carry the day. Instead, throw your punch straight ahead. Turn your wrist at the end of the stroke so that your knuckles are up and your palm is facing down.

Don't stop there. Blitz your foe. "People often throw just one punch and then stand there admiring their handiwork," Martin said, dropping his hands to his sides in demonstration and offering me targets of opportunity. "Chances are your first punch won't be any good, so hit him three or four times. Don't stop punching him until he goes down. And again, the first shot to the body"—his hands drop—"then *BOOM* to the head."

BILLIARDS

# Make the Shot

DECEMBER 1999 marks a full decade since the night George "Ginky" SanSouci, then an 18-year-old high-school dropout working part-time in a doughnut shop, first darkened the doors of a New York City pool hall. There SanSouci stumbled onto a money match between two old-timers whose control over the geometry of the game seemed almost supernatural. "I fell asleep on a table watching them," SanSouci recalls. "At that point, I realized I loved pool."

SanSouci, who got his nickname as a baby, not as a pool shark, soon became a regular. "Within a year, I was practicing 4 days a week for 6 to 10 hours a day," he says. "I would watch money matches between good players. There would be, like, 10 going on—and the lowest one was for $500." Before long, the youngster was joining in. "I never hustled. I never turned down a match, but I never played somebody who could not hold a stick. I just wanted to be the best."

And now he just might be. In April 1999, SanSouci captured first place in the prestigious National Straight Pool Championships. At one point, the nine-ball aficionado sank 120 successive balls without relinquishing the table.

According to SanSouci, while winning at pool undoubtedly requires talent, luck, nerve, and an innate sense of geometry, it's also about learning certain fundamentals. Herewith some advice from him on bringing your own game up to speed.

## The Games

Eight ball, or solids and stripes, is the most common beginner's game because it's also the easiest: It gives the shooter the most balls to aim at per turn. Plus, if you play in bars, where the table keeps the balls as you sink them, it's the only cost-effective game. But if you plan to get serious, you've got to learn nine ball, the most popular game in pool halls. It is more complicated and a greater test of skill, since you have to pocket the balls in numbered order instead of taking the best available shot. Straight pool, where players call every shot, even off the break, is the most difficult game—the billiards equivalent of chess.

## The Stance

One of the first maxims you hear in virtually every sport is "Bend your knees." Not so in billiards. Pool, like marksmanship, is about steady aim. And you can't accomplish that, says SanSouci, if your knees are wobbling even slightly. Stand at an angle to the table, your legs shoulder-width apart. Lock your knees for stability, bend from the waist, and settle your free hand on the table.

## The Grip

To find the proper grip, SanSouci suggests, first balance your stick horizontally in one hand. Having pinpointed the center of balance, slide your hand back toward the butt about 6 to 10 inches, keeping in mind that it will take some experimenting to locate the best spot. Ideally, when you bend over to shoot, the arm powering the stick should hang straight down, like a plumb bob, from the elbow and should be positioned roughly over your rear foot. If you manage all this, your forearm will swing smoothly, like a pendulum, when you shoot.

How you hold the stick matters just as much as where you hold it. For the best results, encircle the grip point loosely with your thumb, index finger, and middle finger; allow your ring finger and your pinky to relax. Keep your wrist as loose as your forearm. When you pull back for that pendulum-swing stroke, your wrist should bend, too. Your objective is a smooth, level stroke.

## The Bridge

The position of the hand that is guiding the tip of the cue—in pool patois, the "bridge"—is also extremely important. There are basically two kinds of bridges: the closed bridge, with the index finger curled over the cue, and the open bridge, with the cue resting in the V formed by pinching your thumb against the upper segment of your index finger. Many novices believe that bridging is simply a matter of preference. Wrong, says SanSouci. Use a closed bridge whenever it's possible. "Closed bridging prevents you from lifting the stick, which is what causes people to miss the shot," he says.

## Putting a Spin on Things

Although the term *English* is widely used to describe any kind of spin placed on the cue ball, serious pool players know only *left English* and *right English*. Topspin is not English—it's *follow*. Backspin is *draw*. There are specific reasons for applying each type of spin to the cue ball.

Generally speaking, English is used to make shots. The idea is to transfer the spin from the cue ball to the object ball, thereby increasing ("throwing") or decreasing ("cutting") the angle at which the object ball scoots away. Follow and draw also play a role in sinking a shot—to prevent scratching, for example—but they're typically used to influence your "leave," the way you're set up for the next shot. Good players use English, follow, and draw in different combinations.

You put spin on the cue ball by hitting it at any point other than dead center. Picture the cue ball in cross section as a clock: Striking it at twelve o'clock creates follow, which keeps the cue ball moving directly forward after contact with the object ball. Conversely, hitting the cue ball at six o'clock imparts draw, which brings the cue ball back toward you after it has smacked the object ball. Striking at three o'clock creates right English, which initiates left-hand spin in the object ball; striking at nine o'clock has precisely the opposite effect. Any other point on the clock combines the effect: A hit at one-thirty, for example, uses follow and right English.

## Breaking the Rules

The one shot in which all bets are off is the break, which, says SanSouci, "defies the textbook fundamentals." So feel free to bend your knees, crack the balls as hard as you can, and follow through by rising up from your shot to get more power.

Unless you're playing straight pool, SanSouci observes, you're not calling your shots off the break—you're simply trying to scatter the balls, hoping that at least one of them drops into a pocket. The key, then, is power. Drive the cue ball directly into the point of the rack as hard as you can: "You want to transfer all the force from the cue ball to the object balls." If you're not dead-on, he says, "you're not going to transfer the maximum amount of energy."

—LAMAR GRAHAM

# Get Wired Up

I F YOU WANT to get good in sports, head straight for the neurological system," says trainer Randy Smythe. "That's the mother lode."

Smythe and an emerging cadre of fellow speed, agility, and quickness (SAQ) gurus see a basketball game or a tennis match as a universe so random, it would befuddle Einstein; a pandemonium where lightning-fast anticipation and reflexes are the keys to victory. In this unpredictable world—where high levels of strength, power, and cardiovascular endurance are a given—traditional attributes are less critical than are explosive acceleration, Porsche-like deceleration and change of direction, and computer-like quickness to read the chaos and respond to another player or the ball, all strung together in intense bursts.

"Even a weekend pickup-basketball game is an endless series of split-second responses," says Smythe, a former University of California at Berkeley football player and sprinter whose SAQ clients have included the Dallas Cowboys and the Chicago Bears. "You could get in shape by jogging around Central Park for days, and it wouldn't make you a better basketball player. But if you play that old hand-slapping game that kids play, your hands will get quicker and maybe you can steal the ball."

## Repatterning Your Brain

Getting "wired up," as SAQ trainers call it, is a matter of goosing the neuromuscular system to fire faster and more efficiently. It can be as simple as learning the proper biomechanics of running or as complex as performing weird coordination drills, like running while twirling a Hula-Hoop with one foot and dribbling a tennis ball with a racket.

Usually, some combination of both methods is necessary to elicit the all-important progression from proper biomechanical technique to programmed agility to the peak of athletic performance—random dexterity amid high states of disorder.

"What we're after is brain patterning," says Josh Katz, a Cincinnati-based trainer whose company, Prep Performance, runs SAQ clinics and camps for a raft of NCAA and high school teams. "Most people have never been taught to run properly, for instance, and they've perfected bad movement. It's ingrained in their nervous systems. But sprinting, decelerating, cutting—they all require specific skills and techniques, and we want to repattern you correctly." Learn to move correctly and you'll do it more efficiently and faster every time, with greater force.

Beyond basic biomechanics, SAQ calls for "more macaroni," as Mark Verstegen, the director of the International Performance Institute in Bradenton, Florida, puts it. Running fast and in various patterns through ladders laid on the ground or playing tennis with asymmetrical "wobble balls," all in a sequence of increasing difficulty, wreaks havoc on the central nervous system, forcing it to adapt. "I make professional basketball players dribble an asymmetrical ball off a wall with their feet for three minutes, and they hate it," says Smythe. "When you're wearing size-17 Air Jordans, it makes your feet feel like cement." Adds Katz: "It's really challenging to athletes because they have to step out of their comfort zones." After a 30-minute

*Winning is everything. The only ones who remember you when you come in second are your wife and your dog.*

**—DAMON HILL, ENGLISH MOTOR-RACING DRIVER**

SAQ workout, you might not be panting, but you should be exhausted.

## Whatever a Spider Can

What Verstegen did to Boston Red Sox shortstop Nomar Garciaparra is enough to make your head spin—or your whole body, for that matter. "It's more like what didn't we do," says Verstegen, who has worked with Garciaparra on everything from fielding to batting and whose all-star client list also includes Mary Pierce, Kobe Bryant, and Eddie George. First, he had Garciaparra work on the fundamental biomechanics of being a shortstop—accelerating efficiently on his first step, crossing over the infield, sprinting. When Garciaparra had mastered those basic movements, he advanced to what Verstegen calls "more chaotic preplanned work," or programmed agility: Garciaparra fielded balls in predetermined patterns at gradually increasing speed. Then he went to "assisted work": doing the same with bungee cords attached to his belt for added resistance. From there Garciaparra gradually progressed to the epitome of SAQ training, higher and higher states of randomness, ultimately with resistance: fielding various types of balls—from baseballs to tennis balls to asymmetrical balls—on uneven or rough surfaces, while attached to bungee cords, all while Verstegen made sure the shortstop kept to his new, efficient body movements.

Did it work? In 1997 Garciaparra hit 30

home runs, improved his ability to hustle the ball so much that he's now called Spiderman, and became the American League's 1997 Rookie of the Year. "Obviously, no one can take credit for Nomar's success but Nomar himself," Verstegen says. "But he has certainly made phenomenal strides in bat speed and defensive range."

All of which isn't to suggest that you should throw away that set of weights or desist with the long runs. Strength, power, and endurance form the foundation upon which speed, agility, and quickness rest. "There is a progression," cautions Chicago Bulls strength coach Al Vermeil, "and too many people do all these cutesy things before they build core strength in their legs and midsection."

That said, it's never a bad time to mess with your nerves a bit. "The aim of SAQ isn't to get strong or buff," reminds Smythe. "It's to win. If two NBA players who represent the ultimate in human performance can be differentiated by SAQ training, think about you and me in a weekend game. If I can work on SAQ, then maybe I can steal the ball from you. All it takes is one little thing, and maybe I can kick the crap out of you."

## The SAQ Regimen

These drills get you to maintain the proper posture and train you to amp up the force you apply to each movement, for explosive acceleration. All of the biomechanics drills should be done leaning against a wall at a 30-to-40-degree angle. Do 3 sets of 10 reps with each leg, with 30 seconds of rest between each set.

### Biomechanics

**LEG SWINGS.** Primarily a warm-up. Stand sideways to the wall, leaning on your inside hand. Swing your inside leg forward and back. Keep your toes up and swing from the hips.

**SCISSORS.** Another warm-up. Face the wall, leaning on either hand for support, and swing the opposite leg straight across the other, through a full range of hip movement.

**UPWARD EXPLOSION.** Lean on both hands, facing the wall, with your weight on the balls of your feet. A straight line should run from your ankles up through your ears. Explode off the ball of one foot, driving that knee up in front of you. Bring your foot back down and repeat.

**DOWNWARD EXPLOSION.** Lean on both hands, facing the wall, with your weight on the ball of one foot and the other knee in the "up" position, your heel close to your butt. Explosively drive the leg down like a piston, striking the ball of the foot on the floor. (Remember, you're leaning forward, so the foot should strike behind your hip.) The force should be enough to propel your body up off the ground.

**UPWARD/DOWNWARD EXPLOSION.** Maintain the downward-explosion position and perform a complete cycle with one leg. Start with one knee up and actually paw the ground with your foot like a horse; then pop it into the up position again.

**SKIPPING.** Beginning in the upward-explosion position, perform quick skips.

**RUNNING.** Maintain the upward-explosion position and run, focusing on driving the balls of your feet into the ground with every step and on keeping your knees and toes up as you explode off the ground. Count a new rep each time your right foot hits the ground.

The SAQ drills should take 10 seconds or less and should be done in sets of 3 (unless otherwise noted), with 25 seconds rest in between every set.

### Speed

**LET-GO'S.** Have a workout partner stand in front of you with his hands on your shoulders. As he holds you back, accelerate forward as fast as you can. (Your partner should be trying to slow you down but not stop you completely.) After you've gone about five yards, your partner should let go and step aside—at which point you should explode free for another five yards. Do the drill backward and then sideways; three reps forward, three backward, and three to each side.

**PUSH-UPS.** Assume a push-up position, arms extended, and imagine that your body is an arrow. Explode forward for five yards, trying to maintain that low, horizontal arrow position by driving your feet into the ground.

## Agility

**BALL DROPS.** Stand a few feet in front of a partner, facing him. When he drops a "wobble ball," try to catch it after just one bounce, as if you were playing jacks. After 10 reps, stand with your back to your partner. When he drops the ball and says, "Turn," spin around and try to snatch it. Repeat.

**WALL BALL.** Stand a few feet away from a wall and try to dribble a wobble ball against the wall with your feet—letting it bounce once before hitting it back again—in sets of 10.

## Quickness

**QUICK-FOOT LADDER.** Do these drills through a rope ladder laid on the ground. Run the length of the ladder as fast as you can, staying on the balls of your feet, which should pop off the ground with every step.

While running forward, touch each box (the space between the rungs) once with alternating feet.

Run forward, touching each box twice, once with each foot.

Skip through the ladder, with each foot touching each box twice.

Run forward, with one foot landing outside the ladder and the other inside each successive box; then switch sides.

Run sideways, alternately stepping in a box once and outside the ladder twice.

Run sideways, with one foot landing inside a box and one outside, alternating which foot is in and which foot is out.

**SIDE STEPS.** Do this drill through a rope ladder laid on the ground. Run the length of the ladder as fast as you can, staying on the balls of your feet, touching inside each box with one foot. Then run it again, touching each box with both feet.

—CARL HOFFMAN

## SPORT-SPECIFIC DIETS

# Eat to Win

KEEP YOUR DIET low in fat and high in carbohydrates and you'll be fine" is the canned line many sports nutritionists pass out to any athlete willing to listen. But the truth is, if you want to get serious about it, you can effectively match your diet to your sport. "Every sport makes individual energy demands that require specific dietary plans for prime performance," says Bonnie Worthington-Roberts, Ph.D., coauthor of *Food for Sport*.

The usefulness of sport-specific diets has never been more evident than in the past two decades. Every year, more and more world records fall in various sports. For example, since the late '60s, when carbohydrate loading was first being investigated, the marathon world record has fallen numerous times. Researchers attribute these improvements not only to better training techniques but also to improvements in sports nutrition. "There's no doubt about it, carbo loading lets endurance athletes maintain an optimal effort for longer periods of time," says Melvin Williams, Ph.D., author of *Beyond Training*.

The case of Bruce Smith is typical. After his first few years of self-described "mediocrity," the [then] Pro Bowl defensive end for the Buffalo Bills realized his diet contained too much fat and protein. So he replaced his steaks and fried foods with skinless chicken, broiled fish, and vegetables—and dropped from a sluggish 310 pounds to a lean and quick 275. Of his metamorphosis, Smith says, "I'm a totally different player. [My diet] turned me around."

In general, an athlete should get 65 percent of his calories from carbohydrates, 15 percent from protein, and 20 percent from fat. To maximize your performance in a particular sport, though, you need to make some modifications.

Listed below are five categories of sports, ranging from running to weight lifting to tennis. While the percentages of recommended nutrients may differ by only 5 percent to 10 percent from sport to sport, this can be a significant change when you're eating 3,000 to 4,000 calories per day. To determine how many calories you need daily, calculate the number of calories you're burning (listed below) and add this to your basic daily requirements—which can be determined by multiplying your weight by 15.

For each sport, you'll also find tips to help you structure your diet. When making changes, start small and progress in steps until your diet falls into the recommended range. For example, if you're a bit too high in fat, switching from whole milk to low-fat milk or simply removing the skin from your chicken may be all that you need to do. "Make small changes and then recalculate your percentages every three or four weeks to see where you are," says Ellen Coleman, iron-man veteran and sports nutritionist at the Sports Clinic in Riverside, California.

Also keep in mind that the percentages given are for an entire day's worth of food; each meal you eat doesn't have to meet these standards. "Since athletes need more calories than the average guy, they have more room to splurge and still meet their nutritional needs," says Coleman.

## Running

Calories burned per hour (8.5-minute miles): 905

Fat: 15–20%

Protein: 15%

Carbohydrates: 65–70%

**PUMP IRON.** More than any other athletes, runners can lose a significant amount of iron during their workouts. Besides losing trace amounts through sweating, studies have shown, runners can lose iron through gastrointestinal bleeding caused by the constant pounding. More recent research has suggested that runners lose additional iron through "foot-strike hemolysis"—the destruction of red blood cells that also results from the pounding of running. To ensure maximum performance, runners need 10 to 15 milligrams of iron per day. Good low-

# A DIET BY THE NUMBERS

Figuring out the composition of your diet is simple, but to do so you may need to keep a food log that records the number of calories and the number of grams of fat, protein, and carbohydrates in all the food you eat in a given day. If this information isn't readily available on the food label, check your local bookstore for nutritional guides.

To keep an accurate log of your food intake, you'll need to measure your food portions with a kitchen scale or a measuring cup. Although this may seem a bit painstaking at first, don't worry—the whole process shouldn't last long. "It takes most people only a few days before they see a consistent pattern in their diet," says Coleman.

At the end of the day, tally up the total number of calories you've eaten as well as the number of grams of fat, protein, and carbohydrates. To find the percentage of calories in your diet coming from fat, start by multiplying the total number of grams of fat you've eaten by nine (the number of calories in one gram of fat) and divide the result by the total number of calories you've eaten that day. Multiply this number by 100 to determine the percentage of calories you got from fat that day. To figure out the percentage of calories you're getting from protein or carbohydrates, follow the same procedure as described above, but replace the nine in the first step with four. (Both protein and carbohydrates supply only four calories per gram.) For example, say you've eaten 3,000 total calories on a particular day, including 111 grams of fat, 150 grams of protein, and 350 grams of carbohydrates. Your arithmetic would be as follows:

## FAT
111 grams x 9 calories per gram = 999 calories
999 fat calories/3,000 total calories = 0.33
0.33 x 100 = 33% of total calories from fat

## PROTEIN
150 grams x 4 calories per gram = 600 calories
600 protein calories/3,000 total calories = 0.20
0.20 x 100 = 20% of total calories from protein

## CARBOHYDRATES
350 grams x 4 calories per gram = 1,400 calories
1,400 carbohydrate calories/3,000 total calories = 0.47
0.47 x 100 = 47% of total calories from carbohydrates

To check your arithmetic, add up your final percentages. If the three numbers equal 100, you did everything right.

fat sources of iron include lean red meat, skinless turkey, tuna, fresh spinach, dried apricots or prunes, fortified cereals, wheat germ, and beans.

**WATCH YOUR CALORIES.** Every extra pound of body fat a runner carries adds two to five seconds per mile. If you have a few extra pounds to spare, cut 100 calories out of your daily diet and see where that leaves you after two weeks. Cutting back more can sap you of energy.

**DRINK UP.** To avoid dehydration, runners need to drink lots of water or sports drinks. "Because they're so high in sugar, fruit juices and sodas actually delay the body's absorption of fluid," says Dr. Jay Kenney, nutrition research specialist at the Pritikin Longevity Center in Santa Monica, California.

## Swimming

Calories burned per hour: 700

Fat: 20–25%

Protein: 10–15%

Carbohydrates: 60–70%

**BEWARE OF OXYGEN'S EFFECTS.** In endurance sports like running, biking, and swimming, unstable molecules called free radicals are produced, a result of the body's oxygen-burning process. These molecules can damage cells in the body and actually slow your postworkout recovery. Researchers have found that vitamins A, C, and E—collectively known as the antioxidant vitamins—may help reduce the production of free radicals and speed recovery. Nutritionists recommend including the following foods in a training diet: carrots, squash, broccoli, orange juice, green peppers, almonds, and spinach.

**EAT BEFORE YOU SWIM.** The idea that swimmers are overly prone to cramping if they eat before a workout is an old wives' tale. "Any athlete who eats too much before a workout is going to get cramps," says Kenney. "There's nothing special about swimming." In fact, a small high-carbohydrate meal eaten about 30 minutes before a workout helps to provide a strong, steady flow of energy.

**FAT IS GOOD.** Unlike other athletes, swimmers can actually benefit from a small amount of fat in their diet, which increases buoyancy. Thus, swimmers can have a bit more fat in their diet than can other endurance athletes—to a point. "Once a swimmer's body fat exceeds 15 percent, the extra drag created from the increased surface area outweighs the benefits of the added buoyancy," says Kenney.

## Weight Lifting

Calories burned per hour: 360

Fat: 10–15%

Protein: 10–15%

Carbohydrates: 70–80%

**AVOID PROTEIN OVERKILL.** Bodybuilders and weight lifters have long labored under the misconception that they need to eat huge amounts of protein to increase their strength or muscle mass. "Only 20 to 25 percent of a muscle is made up of protein, so you need 90 to 100 grams of protein to synthesize a pound of muscle," says Kenney. And since the average man already eats enough protein to synthesize an additional four pounds of muscle a week, there's no need to eat more. "Even if you're on anabolic steroids, you'd be lucky to gain three pounds of muscle a week," he adds.

**POLISH OFF SOME CHROMIUM.** Recent studies suggest that the mineral chromium may actually help weight lifters build muscle by stimulating their bodies to utilize more protein.

According to nutritionists, the average man gets far less than his fair share of the mineral—which may slow weight-lifting gains. However, since the safety and efficacy of chromium supplements are still unknown, nutritionists suggest that weight lifters stick to more chromium-rich foods, including prunes, shredded wheat, low-fat American cheese, peas, corn, and brewer's yeast.

**MAGNESIUM FOR MUSCLE.** In a recent study involving two groups of weight lifters, researchers found that the lifters who got enough magnesium in their diets experienced greater strength gains than those who didn't. At the end of seven weeks of controlled research, the magnesium-deficient group experienced an 11 percent increase in strength, while the magnesium-rich group experienced a 26 percent increase. Researchers theorize that inadequate magnesium levels may compromise protein synthesis in the body. High-magnesium foods include tofu, pumpkin seeds, wheat germ, spinach, pasta, almonds, halibut, and sunflower seeds.

**EAT CARBS, QUICK.** Since weight lifting involves repeated high-intensity efforts over short periods of time, weight lifters rely primarily on fast-burning carbohydrates stored in their muscles for fuel. These energy stores are depleted quickly—weight lifting is 18 times less energy-efficient than endurance activities. Because carbohydrates are depleted so quickly, weight lifters need to eat high-carbohydrate foods, like dried fruit, bread, pasta, and fruit juices, immediately after they work out. "Studies have shown that during the first 30 minutes after a workout the body is primed to replenish its carbohydrate stores," says Coleman.

## Cycling

Calories burned per hour (13 mph): 712

Fat: 20%

Protein: 15%

Carbohydrates: 65%

**CHOW DOWN.** Since their workouts tend to last longer than those of most other athletes,

cyclists need to be especially vigilant about getting enough calories to support their activity. "Since fat is so high in calories, having a small amount of it in their diet will help cyclists get the extra calories they need to power through long workouts," says Kenney.

**PACK A LUNCH.** Because they don't experience the jarring that runners do, cyclists are usually able to tolerate solid food while working out. "Eating or drinking 50 grams of carbohydrates for every 30 to 60 minutes of cycling can be another big endurance booster," says Coleman.

**POWER WITH PROTEIN.** During a workout lasting more than an hour, endurance athletes can get 10 percent or more of their energy from burning protein. "Skinny cyclists need a higher proportion of protein in their diet than do bulky weight lifters," says Kenney. Good low-fat sources of protein include skinless poultry, lean red meat, tuna, cottage cheese, low-fat yogurt, egg whites, and beans.

## Tennis/Basketball/Volleyball

Calories burned per hour: 646

Fat: 15–20%

Protein: 10–15%

Carbohydrates: 65–75%

**COVER ALL FRONTS.** From a nutritional standpoint, court sports are among the most complex because they combine the demands of an endurance sport like running with the demands of an explosive, high-intensity activity like weight lifting. For endurance purposes, court athletes need to make sure that they eat enough calories to keep them energized through long workouts. In addition, the explosive nature of these sports can be a real drain on the body's stores of carbohydrates, so be sure to refuel with carbohydrates immediately following each workout, suggests Kenney. Good postworkout foods are bread, pasta, cereal, rice, potatoes, dried fruit, beans, energy bars, sports drinks, fruit juices, fruit yogurt, and wheat germ.

**BOTTOMS UP.** Since court athletes typically play in hot, stuffy gyms, they have a tendency to lose a tremendous amount of fluid and are constantly at risk for dehydration—especially when playing several games in a row. "These athletes would do well to keep water or a sports drink on the sidelines to keep them hydrated," says Ann Grandjean, Ed.D., chief nutrition consultant to the U.S. Olympic Committee and executive director of the International Center for Sports Nutrition in Omaha, Nebraska.

**GO FOR CARBOHYDRATES.** Since court sports involve so much running and jarring, many athletes find it difficult to eat right before a hard workout. So prepare yourself by eating a small meal loaded with carbohydrates—like bread, cereal, or a sports-energy bar—two to three hours before your game, says Grandjean. Also avoid fiber-rich foods before playing, since they increase your chances of experiencing intestinal problems.

—DAN BENSIMHON

P.S. MUELLER

The Evolution of Extreme Sports

# Fitness and Health

MARC JOSEPH

YOU ALWAYS have to be smart when you work out. People should never look for a quick solution. . . . All the fad diets, all the shortcuts, all the rubber belts that make you sweat around your waist, all the quick diet pills, the secret machines . . . all are nonsense. The thing you must understand is that fitness is like eating and sleeping—it will be around until you die." Arnold Schwarzenegger said that in an issue of *Men's Journal,* and you can interpret his declaration in one of two ways: Make fitness a part of your life, or make fitness a part of your life. You don't really have a choice.

With that in mind, we've put together some of the best workouts for a man who truly *wants* to get fit, whether you're in your twenties, thirties, forties, or fifties. There are no rubber belts or secret machines here—just smart, challenging exercises that a busy man can do to look good and feel even better. Run faster, get stronger, improve your balance, even tighten up the much-ballyhooed abs. It's not going to be easy, but we've always found, as Arnold has, that the gritty approach works best.

The other half of this chapter is devoted to good health, which is of course a big part of the program. You won't find a medical reference book there, but what you will find is smart reporting and expert advice on some of the male health issues you're most likely to face: impotence, heart problems, testicular cancer—a whole list of pleasantries. Some of the *Men's Journal* writers have even experimented on themselves in a search for the truth, and they've found it. Of course, staying healthy doesn't always have to be so heavy. There are pieces about some of our favorite things—eating and relaxing—not to mention a few tips on how to have sex into your seventies. Words for the wise.

# Get Fit in 12 Weeks

TO BE "IN SHAPE" is an utterly fundamental yet surprisingly squirrelly concept. Try this definition, for instance: "being able to do your normal daily activities as well as activities that require extraordinary efforts, such as running to catch a bus, with a minimal degree of disruption of physiologic processes or stress to the cardiovascular or musculoskeletal systems." That's Dr. Barry Franklin, the director of cardiac rehabilitation at Beaumont Hospital in Royal Oak, Michigan. But . . . to catch a *bus?* That's the highest aspiration of fitness? Such a definition reeks of the same scaled-back counsel so famously flogged by the American College of Sports Medicine: that to achieve serious gains, all we've got to do is walk around the block for 30 minutes a day—in three 10-minute sessions if doing it all at once is too overwhelming.

But that's not the *Men's Journal* definition of fitness, and it certainly doesn't describe being in the *shape of your life.* Within every man's personal definition of perfect fitness resides an image of spur-of-the-moment athletic transcendence: the diving stab during softball in the park; the hop-on-your-bike century ride; the huff-free, 20-point, full-court pickup game. And to achieve that kind of shape, as you'll see here, you'll need to start with good posture. Then you'll need a thorough grounding in the tenets of cardiovascular training, strength training, nutrition, and flexibility. You'll need a self-test for each to see where you stand and to set goals for improvement. And you'll need a solid 5-day-a-week regimen guaranteed to deliver a new body at the end of 12 weeks.

# Stand Up Straight!

A BODY, PERHAPS, like the one that decorates the next page—that guy has achieved the goal, right? *That's* the living embodiment of "shape of your life." Right?

Well, actually, wrong. Our heroic ideal of the chiseled physique stands, in fact, as a (nude) model of the supreme lack of balance in most bodies—particularly when that body has been retooled and case-hardened to look aesthetically pleasing head-on (which is, admit it, the default approach of most men who bother to work out with weights). This man, in other words, is overly developed in an anterior direction. Out of whack. Front-heavy.

We are, of course, looking at an extreme case. But trust us when we tell you that you're almost certainly out of whack, too. Or don't trust us; trust Bob Shaw. When Shaw, a certified physical trainer, opened his mid-town-Manhattan gym, he named it Physical Structure—a bow to the elemental idea that a well-constructed foundation will keep the building from falling in on itself. "As I started examining more and more clients," Shaw says, "I found that most people have bad posture, whether they have worked out a lot or they never work out. They get these tight upper-back muscles. Their shoulder blades move the wrong way. And bad posture, because it has a slow, cumulative effect, can be as bad for you as falling down a flight of stairs."

An even more important Shaw truism holds that once the average out-of-whack guy launches himself into a standard bench-press, shoulder-press, crunch-heavy self-improvement regimen, he's just going to make matters worse. To be in truly great shape, your body's foundation has to be in balance. Using our model as an annotated example of What Went Wrong, here, then, is how to get it right.

Abs, as the covers of various fitness mags remind us monthly, are the second most important signifier of a man's manhood. In the rush for the six-pack, though, the upper abs have been crunched into iron, while the more functionally important lower abs have largely been forgotten. "The upper abdominals make you look good," Shaw says. "But they don't do much for you structurally. The lower abs, on the other hand, support your spine. They give your pelvic girdle stability." Which is why you—along with our model, whose lower back shows a bit too much of an arch—need to balance your crunches with just as many sets of reverse crunches, which develop the lower abs.

JOHN HUET

## Reverse Crunches

Lie on your back with your feet in the air, your legs almost vertical, and your knees slightly bent. Your hands should be at your sides in a relaxed position, palms down. Push your lower back down so that it's flat to the mat. Contract your lower abdominal muscles and lift your butt an inch or two off the mat, holding it there for a second. Then return to the starting position and immediately repeat.

Note the way these hands, in their relaxed position, wave at anyone who walks behind this guy. "With proper posture, when you have strength and endurance in your external shoulder rotators, your palms should face directly in toward your body," says Shaw. "When they're facing back, there's too much internal rotation in your shoulder joints." The culprit here: excessive time at the pec deck doing flies and on the bench hoisting barbells. The solution: Balance those front-of-the-body exercises with work on the external shoulder rotators.

## External Shoulder Rotations

Lie on your side on a mat, with your head supported either by your bottom arm or, preferably, by a rolled-up mat or a pillow, so that your spine stays straight. Grasp a three-to-five-pound dumbbell in your top hand, with your elbow at a 90-degree angle and held firmly to your side. Start with the weight down against your body and rotate it up until your forearm points toward the ceiling, all without taking your elbow from your side. Lower and repeat to the prescribed number of reps; then switch sides.

Hold your arms straight out in front of you and clap your hands. That movement is called horizontal shoulder adduction, and you can do it because you've got chest and front-shoulder muscles (or, in the physiologist's parlance, pectorals and anterior deltoids). Our man has great pecs and front delts. But his shoulders are rounded forward; this indicates that he's weak in the posterior delts—the rear-shoulder muscles, which allow the shoulders to rotate backward. The exercise that develops these is the reverse fly.

## Reverse Fly

Lie facedown on a bench with your chin hanging off the end. Holding a dumbbell in each hand, with your elbows rotated up away from the body, raise the weights to about shoulder height without moving them toward your legs or your head. Your shoulder blades should not squeeze together, and your thumbs should not rotate toward the ceiling (a sign that your external shoulder rotators are engaged). Lower the weight and repeat.

In the average out-of-balance body, the shoulder blades start to float away from each other over time and stick out, contributing to that round-back look. This is a signal that the rhomboid muscles (down the center of the upper back) and the medial fibers of the trapezius (in the same area) are flabby. The best way to correct this is with seated rows. To do them right, you've got to learn to squeeze your shoulder blades.

## Seated Rows

Sit up straight, chin up, shoulders back, at a seated-row machine, with the pad against your chest. Your head shouldn't lean forward, and your back shouldn't arch beyond its natural curve. Stretch forward to grasp the handles. Before you even move your elbows, pull your shoulder blades in toward each other; that retraction is what puts the stress of the exercise on your rhomboids and medial traps. Then pull the handles back by bending your elbows, squeezing your shoulder blades even closer together. Stop the handles in front of your chest, return to the starting position, and repeat. It's important not to elevate or shrug your shoulders, which will involve your already overdeveloped upper traps.

This guy's been doing quite a few sets of heavy shrugs, which accounts for his well-developed upper back. Unfortunately, those upper trapezius muscles completely overwhelm the rest of his back, particularly the lats and lower trapezius, which are practically nonexistent. The solution is an exercise that is a staple of many weight routines, and that is almost always done wrong: the lat pull-down.

## Lat Pull-Down

Sit up straight at a lat-pull machine and grasp the bar at the point where it bends. With your arms locked, pull your shoulder blades down and hold them in that position for the rest of the exercise. (This is what most people *don't* do.) By bending your elbows, pull the bar down to just below your chin; then slowly raise it until your arms are straight—but don't elevate your shoulder blades. Repeat.

—MARK JANNOT

# Work for Your Heart

LOOKING FOR A REASON to run? A Finnish study found that elite high-endurance athletes live more than four years longer than their sedentary peers. Another major study determined that lack of exercise is as bad for you as smoking is—being a slug nearly triples the risk of an early visit by the Reaper. But here's the odd paradox: Put highly fit men and couch potatoes through the same battery of tests. Though you'll likely find *some* differences in their physiologies, these differences are often subtle or inconsistent. Take blood pressure, for instance. About half of all men who work out regularly and vigorously do see clinically significant reductions in their readings; the other half see no changes at all. Evidence also suggests that exercise can sometimes help people slightly enhance their immunity, elevate protective HDL levels, combat depression and stress, sleep better, keep blood-sugar levels in check, perform better sexually, and garner a host of other rewards.

But to be honest, when you focus on individual aspects of cardiovascular physiology, aerobic exercise yields mixed "sort of, sometimes" results that, taken by themselves, are often underwhelming. "The reason aerobic exercise has such an *overall* beneficial effect is that these subtle effects do add together and reinforce each other in such a way as to make you 'robust,'" says Dr. Geoffrey Moore, the director of cardiac rehab at the University of Pittsburgh Medical Center. "And if you want to become robust, the only way to do it is by exercise. No medicine or magic food will make you tougher and stronger."

The second surprise about aerobic exercise is how little of it you need to do to harvest the lion's share of the health and longevity benefits it has to offer. Researchers at the Cooper Institute for Aerobics Research in Dallas have found that you need to burn just 1,000 calories a week through moderate activity. Most guys can probably do this by integrating more physical activity into daily life, says Dr. Jody Wilkinson, the institute's medical director. Try to work in 30 minutes of walking most days of the week. Take the stairs at work. Hide the remote so you have to do a sit-up with every channel surf.

But let's face it—there's health and then there's Golden Boy, chick-magnetizing, slam-dunking magnificence. If you're hoping for the latter, you need to do some work. "People ask me why I continue to run 15 miles a week at 66 years of age," says aerobics pioneer Dr. Kenneth Cooper. On his yearly ski trips to Colorado, Cooper explains, he spends a week skiing six hours a day. The bottom line: Getting in top aerobic shape means never having to say no to fun.

"Aerobically fit men become tuned like Ferraris," says Moore. "Their bodies simply become better suited to high performance."

If your body performs more like a used Yugo, don't despair—you can trade up. Here are some guidelines to follow on the road to aerobic fitness:

• **If you're not in top shape now, give yourself plenty of time to build stamina. A smart rule of thumb: Start**

## TEST YOURSELF: THE 1.5-MILE RUN

VO$_2$max is the maximum rate at which your muscles can process oxygen—the higher the rate, the fitter your heart, lungs, and muscles. You can get a good estimate of your VO$_2$max on your own by taking the following 1.5-mile-run test. The test requires a near-maximal effort, so if you're over forty, haven't worked out in more than a year, or ever have chest pain, check with your doctor first. Jog a mile to warm up, then time how long it takes you to run 1.5 miles. At the end of the run, note your heart rate for later use. Plot your time on the curved line on the graph at right; then look below to find your fitness score (which roughly equals your VO$_2$MAX). Once you have that, check the table to see your current fitness level based on your age.

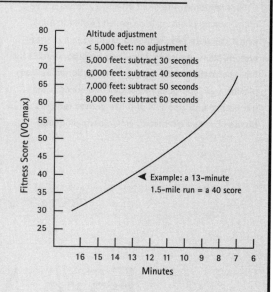

Altitude adjustment
< 5,000 feet: no adjustment
5,000 feet: subtract 30 seconds
6,000 feet: subtract 40 seconds
7,000 feet: subtract 50 seconds
8,000 feet: subtract 60 seconds

◄ Example: a 13-minute
1.5-mile run = a 40 score

### HOW DID YOU DO?

| Age | 20–29 | 30–39 | 40–49 | 50–59 | 60+ |
|---|---|---|---|---|---|
| EXCELLENT | 50+ | 47+ | 44+ | 41+ | 38+ |
| GOOD | 44–49 | 42–46 | 40–43 | 37–40 | 34–37 |
| AVERAGE | 41–43 | 39–41 | 37–39 | 34–36 | 30–33 |
| BELOW AVERAGE | ≤40 | ≤38 | ≤36 | ≤33 | ≤29 |

—DAN BENSIMHON

off slowly and increase your aerobic-exercise load by no more than 10 percent a week. If you see signs of overtraining—anything from fatigue to overuse injuries—back off.

• Pick a goal and design your training around it. For most men, cross-training keeps aerobic exercise fun, lowers the risk of injuries, and provides great overall conditioning. But if you want to excel in a particular sport, realize that training in activities that don't use the same muscles in the same ways won't help. Swimming a lot makes you a better swimmer; it does next to nothing to improve your running.

• Exercise five to seven days a week, but exercise "hard" on only two of those days. "Hard" can mean either a long workout at moderate intensity or a shorter workout at higher intensity. Make sure your two hard days are not consecutive.

• Do interval training. A study of distance runners compared men who ran long distances at a steady pace with men who alternated high-intensity intervals with slower jogs or rests. Though researchers could not find any physiological differences between the two groups, the interval trainers proved to be much better racers at distances up to 10K—most likely because they had trained their bodies in both endurance and speed.

• When interval training, follow a 1-to-1 or 1-to-2 ratio of activity to rest. For example, run hard for a minute;

then jog slowly for one or two minutes before repeating.

• **Think randomly.** The most effective interval training, many coaches believe, is so-called Fartlek training, which staggers easy and hard exercise in a random pattern. Many stationary bikes can be programmed for this approach; you can also get the randomness from playing such sports as basketball and soccer, since the normal ebb and flow of these games requires bursts of speed alternating with steady plodding.

• **Be wary of surging, hill-climbing, and other forms of "resistance" training.** Though these drills can help you increase strength, says Moore, the odds of developing an overuse injury in the process are very high.

• **Get a coach.** Most Master's teams have one. True, you can become pretty magnificent on your own. But if you reach the point where mere magnificence is not enough, a knowledgeable coach is your best guide to the next level.

—JIM THORNTON

# Earn Muscle

THE BODY IS such an incredible mechanism that you can take Mort Meek and, with the proper training, make him a different man," says Dwight Galt. The director of strength and conditioning for the University of Maryland's 24 varsity athletic teams isn't just talking about turning 96-pound weaklings into showy Schwarzeneggers. He's talking about pumping iron to improve your performance in soccer, tennis—even golf. "Your ability to hit a golf ball is based on speed and fine-motor skills," says Galt, "and a properly done strength program will enhance both."

To understand how lifting weights can make you not only stronger but quicker and more coordinated, you need to know a little about your muscular and nervous systems. Muscles are composed of hairlike fibers whose principal building blocks are two proteins: actin and myosin. The motion and ever-increasing resistance of weight lifting slightly tears the muscle fibers and stimulates the production of the two proteins; as the fibers heal and more actin and myosin is created, your muscles hypertrophy—or thicken—and you get stronger.

That alone is a good thing. Increasing your strength also increases your lean body mass, which helps your body burn fat more efficiently, even when you're sitting down. More important, from the age of 30 on, men lose about 1 percent of their muscle mass every year, or about 10 percent every decade. Bones, too, tend to lose their density with age. Pumping iron helps restore muscle mass and bone density even as aging inevitably chips away at them. And, put simply, increasing your strength improves your performance on the court or the playing field. "We took a golfer and put him on a basic strength routine," says Dr. Wayne Wescott, the fitness research director at the South Shore YMCA in Boston and an advisor to the National Strength Professionals Association. "After two months, his club-head speed had increased 6 percent."

But increasing raw strength is only half the story. Indeed, it's the efficiency and speed with which your body can use the muscle fibers that really counts. "Look at Michael Jordan," says Galt. "There are a million guys who are the same height and weight who can jump as high, but Jordan can do it quicker than anyone else on the court because he has an incredible nervous system." When you start bench-pressing for the first time, your nervous system doesn't have a clue which and how many muscle fibers to use; you push the bar up unevenly, you tire quickly, you're an uncoordinated mess. But keep at it and very soon your nervous system sorts out which fibers to fire and when to fire them. Suddenly you

can lift more weight. "In the first month of a weight program, probably 80 percent of your gain in lifting capacity will be neural," says Wescott, "and only 20 percent will be from larger muscle fibers."

Strength trainers and physiologists are unanimous on the fundamentals of weight work: Focus on compound, multijoint exercises—such as bench presses, lat pull-downs, and squats—that work all the major muscles in a given area. Combine low weight with high reps to build muscular endurance and shape, high weight and low reps for muscle strength. Although conventional wisdom has long held that at least three sets are necessary, four different studies by Michael Pollock, Ph.D., the director of the University of Florida's Center for Exercise Science, suggest that that advice has little scientific merit. "Our studies have been very consistent," says Pollock. "One set to your maximum ability will give

## TEST YOURSELF: PUSH-UPS

Sure, push-ups are more a measure of muscular endurance than of pure strength. But if we sat you in a leg-press machine and asked you to lift hundreds of pounds just once, we'd be sending the ill-prepped to the emergency room and spending the next decade in litigation. Thus, push-ups will have to suffice, on the imperfect assumption that a man with good muscular endurance has good muscle strength, and vice versa.

Assume the standard push-up position—hands and toes on the floor, hands shoulder-width apart, back in a straight line with your head. Starting in the "up" position, keep your back straight as you lower yourself until your chest just touches the floor. Press yourself up—do not bounce—until your elbows are almost locked. Do as many as you can in one minute without having your form fall apart. You can pause for a rest at the top of any rep, but once you put your knees on the ground, the test is over. Compare your score with the table below.

### HOW DID YOU DO?

| Age | 20–29 | 30–39 | 40–49 | 50–59 | 60+ |
|---|---|---|---|---|---|
| EXCELLENT | 36+ | 30+ | 22+ | 21+ | 18+ |
| GOOD | 29–35 | 22–29 | 17–21 | 13–20 | 11–17 |
| AVERAGE | 22–28 | 17–21 | 13–16 | 10–12 | 8–10 |
| BELOW AVERAGE | ≤ 21 | ≤ 16 | ≤ 12 | ≤ 9 | ≤ 7 |

—DAN BENSIMHON

system adapt so quickly that one set isn't enough to completely shock conditioned muscles. In any event, every-one agrees that the time-pressed can get *some* results with a single set.

Rest and recovery time between workouts is critical. Indeed, pumping iron merely stimulates your muscles; the actual growth takes place over the next 48 to 72 hours as the muscle fibers heal and their cells generate actin and myosin. Train too often and you inhibit the body's ability to grow stronger.

While everyone's body is different, at the end of 12 weeks a 35-year-old man should be able to bench-press his weight 10 times and squat 1½ times his weight 10 times. And don't miss

your muscles the same stimulus as three sets." Other experts, including Eric Lawson, the strength and conditioning physiologist for the U.S. Ol-ympic Committee, point out that muscles and the nervous even one workout. "In 12 weeks, you've got maybe 36 workouts," says Galt, "and consistency is critical."

—CARL HOFFMAN

## NUTRITION

# Eat Like an Athlete

WHETHER YOU'RE A weekend cyclist or a marathon man, food provides the fuel that powers performance. It's the energy for working muscles and the raw material that rebuilds battered cells after a grueling workout. Plenty of eat-right, get-fit gurus out there want to make feeding the tiger in your tank sound like rocket science. (What better way, after all, to look like an expert?) Best-selling diet plans feature long lists of good foods and bad foods, complex schedules for what to eat when, and rickety scientific explanations to prop up zoned-out theories about nutrition.

Don't buy the hype. "People are always looking for some magic formula, especially athletes," says David Nieman, a professor of Health and Exercise Science at Appalachian State University in North Carolina and the author of *Fitness and Your Health*, one of the most highly regarded textbooks on sports nutrition. "The best diet for fitness is the same as that for overall good health, with a little fine-tuning for elite-level performance. And the basics are simple."

**1. TAILOR YOUR DIET TO YOUR WORKOUT.** Whatever else they may argue about, sports nutritionists agree that carbohydrates are the main fuel for athletic performance. Carbs are converted into glycogen, a polysaccharide that is stored in muscles and then converted into energy. Protein and fat can also be tapped for energy, but usually only after glycogen is depleted; neither figures much in athletic performance.

How much is enough? If you're exercising no more than 90 minutes a day, the basic dietary recommendations are fine: Make sure 55 percent of your daily calories are in the form of carbohydrates, 30 percent maximum from fat, and 15 percent in the form of protein. Crank up the intensity and duration of your workouts and you'll need to increase your carb intake. Nieman suggests that high-performance athletes get 70 percent of their calories from carbohydrates, 15 percent from fat, and 15 percent from protein.

**2. CHOOSE HIGH-OCTANE FOODS.** Almost any form of carbohydrate you put in your mouth—unless it's some sugarless, calorie-free chemist's concoction—provides energy. The trick is to make sure you're getting more than just energy: A candy bar can power a workout, but a handful of raisins or a glass of orange juice also packs all sorts of antioxidants that may help stop free-radical damage to muscles and tendons. And that's not all. Over the past

decade, researchers have found that fruits, vegetables, and grains contain phytochemicals that block carcinogens, clear out clogged arteries, and may even slow the aging process. Broccoli and other cruciferous veggies (cauliflower, cabbage, Brussels sprouts) are loaded with cancer fighters. Garlic and onions help lower cholesterol. Grapes and raisins have both artery-clearing and cancer-fighting substances.

**3. TOP OFF YOUR TANK.** An hour or two before you set out on a long run or an arduous ride, load up on carbohydrates. In a University of Massachusetts study, high school athletes who ate 200 to 280 calories' worth of fat-free fig bars before bicycling and sprinting finished an average of 12 seconds ahead of those who didn't. Replenishing carbs after working out may be just as important. When a group of 22-year-old weight trainers consumed carbs immediately after doing heavy resistance work and then again an hour later, researchers recently reported, they suffered significantly less muscle-protein breakdown than those who ate nothing.

**4. GO FOR GOOD FATS.** Fats have gotten a bad rap. Sure, saturated fat (the kind found in meat and dairy products) leads to artery-clogging cholesterol and a higher risk of heart attack. But plant-based mono- and polyunsaturated fats actually lower total cholesterol and improve the body's ratio of good to bad cholesterol. The vaunted Mediterranean diet, for instance, is actually very high in fat: almost 40 percent of calories, which is way over the American Heart Association's recommendation. But virtually all of that fat comes from olive oil, which is monounsaturated. That's probably the reason, many researchers say, why heart-disease rates have traditionally been almost zero in many Mediterranean countries. The best advice: Go easy on saturated animal fat and cook with such plant oils as olive and canola instead.

**5. DRINK DEEP.** Sweat out a heart-popping workout, and you'll lose at least a liter and a half of water an hour. In hot weather, some athletes pour out as much as three liters of sweat. Here's the problem: The stomach can release to your body only about one liter of water per hour. Sweat more than a liter and a half, and your blood begins to thicken, your heart rate accelerates, and performance takes a dive. The remedy's a no-brainer: Drink plenty of water

# TEST YOURSELF: FAT PERCENTAGE

Body composition is a measure of what percentage of your body weight is fat and what's not. The more fat you have, the worse your shape and the greater your risk for heart disease, high blood pressure, and stroke.

Partly because of hormonal changes and decreases in metabolic rate and level of activity, the average man starts replacing muscle with fat around the age of 25. But men who follow a regular program of resistance and aerobic training can cut the age-related body-fat increase in half and stay lean.

Exercise physiologists typically use underwater weighing or caliper-measured skin-fold tests to calculate a person's body composition. But based on hundreds of these tests, experts at the University of Texas have come up with a simple chart to help you determine your body composition without being dunked or pinched.

To use the table, locate your body weight on the scale on the right and draw a line from there to your waist size, also found on the scale. Your body-fat percentage is the point at which the drawn line intersects the diagonal scale in the middle of the chart.

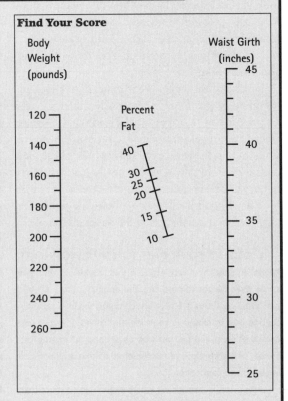

**Find Your Score**

## HOW DID YOU DO?

| Age | 20–29 | 30–39 | 40–49 | 50–59 | 60–69 | 70–79 |
|---|---|---|---|---|---|---|
| EXCELLENT | ≤11 | ≤14 | ≤16 | ≤18 | ≤18 | ≤19 |
| GOOD | 11–16 | 14–17 | 16–20 | 18–22 | 18–22 | 19–22 |
| AVERAGE | 16–19 | 17–21 | 20–23 | 22–24 | 22–26 | 22–27 |
| BELOW AVG. | 19+ | 21+ | 23+ | 24+ | 26+ | 27+ |

—DAN BENSIMHON

before and during a workout. If you're exercising for more than an hour, go for a sports drink, which replenishes both water and carbohydrates.

One last piece of advice: Don't buy complicated diet books.

—PETER JARET

# Transform Your Body

T HE WHOLE IDEA of this 12-week regimen is to shake the tree," says Bob Shaw. "Your body is adapted to its current program—especially if it's just sitting on the couch—so we've got to shock it, force it to make some changes."

---

### [WEEK 1] FOUNDATION STAGE

*Objective:* Incorporate postural balance into the strength program; acclimate weak joints and muscles; begin to build cardiovascular condition. All exercises should be done in 3 sets of 15 to 20 reps unless otherwise noted.

### Day 1: Abs, Chest, Back, Posture

*Cardio:* Walk or run at easy intensity for 30 minutes.

*Strength exercises:* Reverse crunch (20 to 30 reps), oblique abdominal crunch (20 to 30 reps), prone hyperextension, external shoulder rotation, internal shoulder rotation, seated row, bench press, reverse fly, dumbbell fly.

### Day 2: Abs, Lower Back, Legs

*Cardio:* Skip rope for 10 minutes; run at moderate intensity for 20 minutes.

*Strength exercises:* Bicycle (50 reps), crunch (20 to 30 reps), prone hyperextension, lunge, leg press, leg curl, calf raise.

### Day 3: Abs, Arms

*Cardio:* Skip rope for 20 minutes; walk or run at easy intensity for 20 minutes.

*Strength exercises:* Reverse crunch (20 to 30 reps), oblique abdominal crunch (20 to 30 reps), bicycle (50 reps), straight-bar curl, triceps extension, supinating dumbbell curl, bench dip.

### Day 4:
Rest.

### Day 5: Chest, Shoulders, Back, Posture

*Cardio:* Skip rope for 30 minutes.

*Strength exercises:* External shoulder rotation, internal shoulder rotation, incline bench press, seated row, lat pull-down, standing cable crossover, dumbbell shoulder press, reverse fly.

### Day 6: Abs, Legs, Arms

*Cardio:* Run at moderate intensity for 30 minutes.

*Strength exercises:* Reverse crunch (20 to 30 reps), oblique abdominal crunch (20 to 30 reps), bicycle (50 reps), straight-bar curl, triceps extension, supinating dumbbell curl, bench dip, lunge, leg press, leg curl, calf raise.

### Day 7
Rest.

### [WEEKS 2 to 4] BUILDING

**Objective:** Begin building muscular endurance and strength; slowly increase cardiovascular capacity. All exercises should be done with heavier weights in 3 sets of 12 to 15 reps unless otherwise noted.

### Day 1

**Cardio:** Run for 30 minutes at moderate intensity; skip rope for 20 minutes.
**Strength exercises:** Same as in week 1.

### Day 2

**Cardio:** Spend 10 minutes at a high level on a stairclimber; run for 20 minutes at moderate intensity; skip rope for 10 minutes.
**Strength exercises:** Add squats to exercises in week 1.

### Day 3

**Cardio:** Run at high intensity for 40 minutes.
**Strength exercises:** Add hammer curls and close-grip push-ups to exercises in week 1.

### Day 4

Rest

### Day 5

**Cardio:** Skip rope for 30 minutes; do the stairclimber at a high level for 20 minutes.
**Strength exercises:** Add shrugs and decline presses to exercises in week 1.

### Day 6

**Cardio:** Run at easy intensity for 30 minutes.
**Strength exercises:** Add squats to exercises in week 1.

### Day 7

Rest.

### [WEEKS 5 to 7] TRANSITION

**Objective:** You should be seeing real results at this point. Now you're shifting toward real strength. All exercises should be done with heavier weights in 3 sets of 10 to 12 reps unless otherwise noted.

## Day 1

**Cardio:** Run for 30 minutes at moderate intensity; skip rope for 20 minutes.

**Strength exercises:** Same as in weeks 1 to 4.

## Day 2

**Cardio:** Do the stairclimber at a high level for 20 minutes; skip rope for 20 minutes.

**Strength exercises:** Add hip abduction to exercises in weeks 2 to 4.

## Day 3

**Cardio:** Run at high intensity for 40 minutes.

**Strength exercises:** Same as in weeks 2 to 4.

## Day 4

Do at least 1 set each of the abdominal exercises.

## Day 5

**Cardio:** Skip rope for 30 minutes; do the stairclimber at a high level for 20 minutes.

**Strength exercises:** Add lateral shoulder raises to exercises in weeks 2 to 4.

## Day 6

**Cardio:** Skip rope for 15 minutes; do the stairclimber at a high level for 15 minutes; run at high intensity for 15 minutes.

**Strength exercises:** Same as in weeks 2 to 4.

## Day 7

Do at least 1 set each of the abdominal exercises; skip rope for 15 minutes.

---

### [WEEKS 8 to 10] MASS

**Objective:** Now is the time to really push. You should be in solid shape, with your joints capable of doing some serious lifting. This stage primarily works on strength and muscle mass, with each exercise done in 3 sets of 8 to 10 reps.

## Day 1

**Cardio:** Run for 30 minutes at moderate intensity; skip rope for 20 minutes.

**Strength exercises:** Same as in weeks 1 to 7.

## Day 2

**Cardio:** Do the stairclimber at a high level for 20 minutes; skip rope for 20 minutes.

**Strength exercises:** Same as in weeks 5 to 7.

## Day 3

**Cardio:** Run at high intensity for 40 minutes.

**Strength exercises:** Same as in weeks 2 to 7.

## Day 4

Do at least 1 set each of the abdominal exercises; skip rope for 15 minutes.

## Day 5

**Cardio:** Skip rope for 30 minutes; do the stairclimber at a high level for 20 minutes.

**Strength exercises:** Same as in weeks 5 to 7.

### THE TIME-CRUNCH REGIMEN

Obviously, this program involves no small amount of commitment. If you simply can't manage to find time for five hour-plus workouts in their weekly schedule, though, you'll still get solid results by performing either the exercises from the first three days as a thrice-weekly regimen or those of the last two days as a twice-weekly program. (This is also the best way, using weeks 11 and 12 as a template, to create a maintenance plan once the 12 weeks are up.) And Shaw will grudgingly permit doing just one or two sets of each exercise.

## Day 6

**Cardio:** Skip rope for 15 minutes; do the stair-climber for 15 minutes at a high level; run at high intensity for 15 minutes.

**Strength exercises:** Same as in weeks 2 to 7.

## Day 7

Do at least 1 set each of the various abdominal exercises; skip rope for 15 minutes.

---

### [WEEKS 11 to 12] DEFINITION

**Objective:** Put on the finishing touches. You've got the muscles, you've dropped the body fat, and you're reducing the weight and increasing the number of reps—back up to 3 sets of 10 to 12 each—to give those muscles real definition.

## Day 1

**Cardio:** Run at moderate intensity for 15 minutes; skip rope for 10 minutes.

**Strength exercises:** Same as in weeks 1 to 10.

## Day 2

**Cardio:** Do the stairclimber at a high level for 10 minutes; skip rope for 15 minutes.

**Strength exercises:** Same as in weeks 5 to 10.

## Day 3

**Cardio:** Run at high intensity for 25 minutes.

**Strength exercises:** Same as in weeks 2 to 10.

## Day 4

Do at least 1 set each of the various abdominal exercises; skip rope for 15 minutes.

## Day 5

**Cardio:** Skip rope for 15 minutes; do the stair-climber at a high level for 10 minutes.

**Strength exercises:** Same as in weeks 5 to 10.

## Day 6

**Cardio:** Skip rope for 5 minutes; do the stair-climber at a moderate level for 10 minutes; run at moderate intensity for 10 minutes.

**Strength exercises:** Same as in weeks 2 to 10.

## Day 7

Rest; complete, utter, total rest.

—DAN BENSIMHON

---

**FLEXIBILITY**

# Stretching With Soul

STRETCHING IS ONE of those rare, sensible things that can just as easily hurt you as help you. The admonition to stretch before and after exercise is one of the golden oldies of fitness tips—yet now sports-medicine types are advising us to warm up (a light jog or a spin on the stationary bike) before we do that first stretch. Thus, the obvious question: Why stretch at all?

The answer: Stretching can definitely improve athletic performance and, if intelligently done, probably reduce the risk of injury.

When we stretch, we elongate our muscle fibers up to one and a half times their original length. That affords the joints a greater, smoother range of motion—that is, flexibility. The tennis phenom with a flexible, snappy shoulder, elbow, and wrist uncorks the speedier first serve. But as we age, our muscle cells change—they lose water and valuable elastin fibers and gain worthless additional collagen fibers—and we have to work at maintaining the limberness we once took for granted.

The reason smart stretching tends to be an oxymoron is because of something called the "stretching reflex," or in fancier terms, the "myotatic response." Pretty much any stretch will elongate the muscle fibers for a second. But if a stretch is done too fast or too forcefully, receptors attached to those fibers will trigger nerve cells to vigorously contract the muscle, the body's protective reflex against overstretching.

Quadriceps: Stand on your left leg, knee slightly bent (hold on to something for balance, if necessary), and grasp your right foot with your right hand. Pull the foot in close to your butt. Do not arch your back or twist your hips, and make sure the inner thighs touch. Hold for 30 to 60 seconds. Switch sides and repeat.

ROBERT DISCALFANI

Aggressively working a joint when the muscles are in a tense, contracted state can result in microtears in the connective tissues, contributing to the soreness and susceptibility to injury that the stretching was supposed to counter. Ballistic stretches that use the body's own momentum to extend range of motion in the joints—touching your toes, jumping jacks—are the surest trigger of the stretching reflex. Though dear to the hearts of high school football coaches everywhere, these movements are, for the most part, worthless.

The best stretching philosophies try to make peace with the stretching reflex. The dominant school is static stretching, which is essentially the opposite of the herky-jerky ballistic approach. You enter the stretch slowly and hold it for a while. The runner who's stretching out his calves and hamstrings by leaning against a wall, rear foot flat on the floor, might hold the stretch anywhere from 10 seconds to a minute, depending on what exercise book he's read.

Static advocates think that the long duration of the stretch encourages the muscle to relax by allowing the stretching reflex to be overridden by an "inverse myotatic reflex," the body's mechanism to protect itself against overvigorous muscle contraction. It seems to be the case that, with time and effort, the static stretcher can hold deeper stretches, increasing the distance the muscle fibers can lengthen before the stretching reflex kicks in. (Research suggests that over time the stretcher's muscles can actually change shape.

## TEST YOURSELF: SIT AND REACH

You hated it in gym class and probably still do, but the sit-and-reach test is the best measure of trunk and hamstring flexibility. Sit on the floor with your legs extended in front of you, your feet 12 inches apart. Place a yardstick between your legs, with the zero mark closest to your crotch. Tape the yardstick to the floor at the 15-inch mark and reposition yourself so your heels are even with the tape.

   Place your right hand over your left so that the tips of your middle fingers are even. Without bouncing, slowly lean forward and slide your fingertips along the yardstick as far as possible. Record the number closest to your fingertips. Make three attempts and compare your highest reading to the table below.

| Age | 20–29 | 30–39 | 40–49 | 50–59 | 60+ |
|---|---|---|---|---|---|
| ELITE | 19+ | 18+ | 17+ | 16+ | 15+ |
| AVERAGE | 13–18 | 12–17 | 11–16 | 10–15 | 9–14 |
| BELOW AVERAGE | 10–12 | 9–11 | 8–10 | 7–9 | 6–8 |
| POOR | ≤ 9 | ≤ 8 | ≤ 7 | ≤ 6 | ≤ 5 |

—DAN BENSIMHON

New muscle cells get added, and the fascial sheaths that cover the muscle fibers take on an elongated shape.)

In the flexibility world, the new kid on the block is "active isolated" stretching. With its origins in the physical-therapy research of the '30s, A-I is now being developed and promoted by father-and-son therapist/trainers Jim and Phil Wharton, the authors of *The Whartons' Stretch Book*. The Whartons say, plausibly, that they have a better way around the stretching reflex, taking advantage of the fact that muscles work in pairs, with an agonist that powers movement and an antagonist that brakes or counters it. As an example, let's take that same runner who's doing the static wall stretches.

Instead, he lies on his back and slowly raises a locked leg. The quadriceps (thigh) muscle is doing all the lifting (that's the "active" part), which means that the hamstrings are, out of physiological necessity, in a relaxed state, or "isolated," and are ready to be stretched. The stretches themselves are held only for a second or two, so the stretching reflex doesn't have time to fully kick in.

There's no consensus here, no definitive program for Body by Gumby. For now, whether you choose the static or the active route, the most important lesson is: Stretch, yes, but be smart about it.

—JOSEPH HOOPER

# Master the So-Called Measure of Manhood

IN THIS AGE of John Tesh and Yanni, three measures of manhood have managed to survive. The first is obvious. Bringing up a distant second and third are the size of a guy's salary and the heft of his bench press. And because it is not good form to discuss the first two, we're left with just the third station of the male-ego triumvirate as a viable yardstick of masculinity.

Probably more than anything else, it is the lift's simplicity—a straight push skyward from the pectorals—that has made it such a benchmark. Nearly everyone who has laid hands on a barbell has tried it once. It is the forge in which arm-spreading pecs, bazooka-like triceps, and a strong self-regard are wrought.

But the bench press hasn't always been the gold standard. "Back in the '30s, the standing military press was the barometer," says Herb Glossbrenner, the historian for *Powerlifting USA* magazine. The bench press didn't begin to become the measure until the '50s and '60s, when lifters started making the switch from the Olympic lifts to powerlifting. In the early '50s, Canadian Doug Hepburn powered up a record 550.5-pound press. The 600-pound barrier was broken in 1966, and in 1985 Ted Arcidi hoisted 705.4 pounds. Arcidi's lift, however, sounded the death knell for the pure man-versus-metal battle. Before slithering under the weight, he had his cronies cram his upper body into a suffocatingly tight canvas shirt. As Arcidi low-ered the weight, the shirt stretched across his chest, then rebounded to catapult his shoulders—and the bar—into the air. Since a good shirt can add 20 to 100 pounds per press, the best guess on the final count stands: Arcidi, 655.4; shirt, 50.

The race to 800 pounds is now being led by Anthony Clark (780 pounds) and Jamie Harris (760). Both use bench-press shirts. Only James Henderson has benched more than 700 pounds (705.4) without help from a hunk of fabric.

Still, the bench press remains king, and athletes of all stripes genuflect before it—a fact that gives strength coaches and personal trainers the itchies. "Most tennis players go into the gym, max out on the bench, do some curls, and say, 'Wow, I got a helluva workout,'" says Pat Etcheberry, who has trained Pete Sampras and Jim Courier. "Truth is, they haven't done anything to help them on the court." Bottom line: Training is sport-specific and unless you're an offensive lineman, you're getting very little return from the bench.

That said, if your boss asks you how much you bench, you'd still better have a number handy. Here's a quick guide: Bench your weight once and you're respectable. Bench it 10 times and you'll either get promoted or fired. Double your weight once and you'll be asked to perform at the company picnic.

———————

The bench press is the quickest way to build the strength and size of your chest. Lie on a bench with your feet flat on the floor and grasp the barbell with your hands slightly wider than shoulder-width apart, thumbs wrapped around the bar. Official bench-press rules dictate that there be no more than 32 inches between your index fingers. Keeping your elbows out, slowly lower the weight to your sternum, pause briefly without letting the weight sink into your chest, and then press the bar back up until your elbows are locked. Your head, shoulders, buttocks, and hamstrings must stay in contact with the bench at all times to be regulation. To maximize your gains, bench twice a week, doing three sets of 5 to 8 reps (with two to three minutes of rest between sets) early in the week and three sets of 8 to 12 reps (with 60 to 90 seconds of rest) two or three days later.

**—DAN BENSIMHON**

## SIT·UPS

# Crunch for Life

THE SIT-UP is the Richard Nixon of exercises. Rock-ribbed conservatives—staff sergeants and gym teachers alike—adored it; it promised more than it delivered; and, ultimately, it shuffled off in disgrace.

The traditional sit-up—legs straight, hands behind the head, feet unanchored—owes its erstwhile preeminence to Walter Camp. As the coach of the powerhouse Yale football team in the 1880s, Camp whistled his charges through the "daily dozen"—12 of his favorite exercises, including push-ups, jumping jacks, toe touches, and sit-ups. "Because the team was so successful, the daily dozen seeped into almost every fitness program in America," says Charles Kuntzleman,

*All this flat-belly bullshit is killing the country.*

**—JACK NICHOLSON**

Ed.D., an associate professor of kinesiology at the University of Michigan.

The sit-up's popularity grew steadily until the mid-1960s, when several physicians publicly surmised that the exercise might be a reason for the increasing number of bad backs they saw stooped in front of them. Hard evidence for impeachment wasn't available, though, for another 15 years. In the late '70s and early '80s, exercise physiologists placed electrodes into the abdominal muscles of volunteers and ran them through a series of stomach exercises. The researchers found that in addition to stressing the abdominals, traditional sit-ups relied heavily on the hip flexors, the group of muscles that connect the thighs to the lower back. "Anytime you jackknife your upper body toward your lower body, whether your feet are held down or not, you're going to get a tug at both ends of your hip flexors, and that can spell trouble for your lower back," says Lawrence A. Golding, Ph.D., the director of exercise physiology at the University of Nevada at Las Vegas. "On the other hand, the crunch—where you curl your upper back just 30 degrees off the ground and lower it slowly—isolates the abdominals almost exclusively."

The overdue inauguration of the crunch as our country's official ab exercise occurred when the YMCA replaced the straight-leg sit-up with the crunch in its standard battery of fitness tests, which schools, health clubs, and corporations across the country use to assess levels of muscle strength, endurance, and flexibility. "Twenty years ago, we realized that crunches were the better exercise," says Golding, who directed the group that created the Y's original testing regimen. "But we had no way to standardize the test and make sure people weren't going up too far or not far enough." Recently, Golding and one of his students developed a reliable crunch, thus consigning the straight-leg version to history.

With the proper protocol in hand, we can all proceed to building metal-jacket midsections, right? "After two to three months of serious crunching—four or five days a week—you'll have all the muscle tone you need to start showing an ab six-pack," says Kuntzleman. But to look like Rambo—and not Rimbaud—you need to watch your diet and burn calories with additional aerobic exercise. Even a few pounds of circumferential padding can turn the most chiseled six-pack into a beer ball.

## The Classic Crunch

Lie with your back flat on the floor and your calves resting on an exercise bench (or a chair) so that your legs are bent at a 90-degree angle. With your arms

folded across your chest and your chin gently tucked, contract your stomach muscles and slowly curl your shoulders off the floor. Raise your upper body only 30 degrees (so the bottoms of your shoulder blades are just about to leave the floor). Hold this position for a second as you forcibly contract your upper abdominals. Slowly lower yourself back to the floor.

To get the most out of the routine, do two sets of 30 crunches four or five days a week. Every other workout, replace one set of regular crunches with a set of twisting crunches. If you want more of a gut-blasting workout, resist the urge to do more crunches—that will primarily boost your muscular endurance without doing much for your size and strength. Instead, increase the resistance by holding a 5- or 10-pound weight across your chest.

## The YMCA Crunch

To develop national standards for crunch-testing, the YMCA had two main challenges: to devise an exercise that was a true test of abdominal-muscle strength and endurance and to devise a method that ensured the exercise would be done uniformly. Here's the result: Lie on your back with your arms at your sides, palms resting on the floor. Have a friend stick two strips of tape to the floor on either side of you—one at the tip of each middle finger and another three and a half inches below that. Keeping your palms flat, curl your shoulders off the floor so that the tips of your middle fingers slide from the first set of tape to the second. Almost without exception, this will bring your upper body 30 degrees off the floor. Consider your abs superior if you can do 60 in one minute, good if you can do 45, and average if you perform 30. If you score below that, lie.

## The Oblique Crunch

While the classic crunch is the state-of-the-art in ab-building, you can do minor variations. For example, twisting as you curl up will put extra stress on your obliques—the three sets of muscles at the sides of your waist—without any added stress on your back. Start the exercise the same way you would a classic crunch: back on the floor, arms folded across your chest, feet resting on a bench. But instead of curling your upper body straight up, curl your right shoulder up toward your left knee. Do not attempt to actually touch your shoulder or elbow to your knee—curl up only 30 degrees off the floor. At the top of your curl, contract your abdominals forcibly for a second and then slowly lower your upper body to starting position. Repeat, curling your left shoulder toward your right knee. Alternate throughout the set.

**—DAN BENSIMHON**

# Lift Yourself

I AM NOT TERRIBLY ATHLETIC. When I run, I get side cramps. When I bike, my knees ache. In high school gym I was always the guy left after sides had been chosen. So when I announce that there actually is an exercise at which I excel, you'll pardon my boast. I am exceptional at performing parallel-bar dips. I can manage 50, no problem. I can dangle a 25-pound weight from my waist and rip 50 more. People stare, some in awe, some aghast. I never quit. Up, down, lift, lower, over and over again.

Tell people you're into dips and they think you're crazy. "We used to have to do those in high school," they say. "I think my record is three."

Dips are the lonely stepchild of almost everyone's gym routine. Still, attention must be paid. After all, bench presses are performed more or less out of sight of anyone not standing over you. Dips, on the other hand, are executed on parallel bars a good four feet off the ground. Everyone in the room can see you. Collapse after a measly three and they know. But grip those bars and hold yourself aloft as you accomplish a respectable 10 or more and even if your bod is nothing special, you've at least proved your utilitarian worth.

Dips are all about strength. "They really challenge the muscles," says Greg Isaacs, the author of *The Ultimate Lean Routine.* You work out using your own weight, so, says Isaacs, "when you fail, you really fail."

Assuming you're in decent shape already, risk the failure. You might be surprised. Once you've descended as far as you can, your muscles and your mind begin to work in concert. There's that split-second oh-God-I-can't-do-this feeling, immediately followed by the knowledge that you are doing it. Suddenly, you give a good push and you're back up again. Better yet, just as you get there, just as everyone turns to see, your muscles do you a slight favor: They swell. Your lower pecs bulge slightly, your triceps deepen a bit, your deltoids do a funny little dance across your shoulders. It feels great and looks even better. Sure, no one applauds. It is, in

## MODIFIED CHIN-UP

Stand with your chest against a horizontal bar. Grasp the bar with your hands at shoulder width and your palms facing toward you. Take a full step forward with each foot. Slowly lower yourself backward while keeping your body straight. Once your arms are fully extended, pull yourself up until your chin reaches the bar, and then lower yourself all the way back down. Once you can do 3 sets of 8 to 12, it's time to move on to the real thing.

## CHIN-UP

Grasp a horizontal bar with your hands at shoulder width, your palms facing toward you. Lower yourself until your arms are fully extended. Pull yourself up until your chin reaches the bar; then lower yourself all the way and repeat. When you can do 3 sets of 12, ask a partner to add resistance by tugging downward on your legs.

**—JIM THORNTON**

DAVID BARRY

the end, just a moment in time. But, hey, it's your moment. Relish it.

## The Classic Dip

Dips are at once minimalistic and maximalistic. Decidedly low-tech, they push your body into high gear by exercising most of the upper body at once—pecs, triceps, anterior deltoids, and even your upper back. Stay straight and you emphasize the triceps workout; angle your torso slightly forward and your lower pecs bear the brunt of muscle-building stress.

No matter which muscles you want to work, grab the bars with your palms facing in, elbows at your sides. Cross your ankles. Bend your knees slightly. Now, slowly lower yourself as far as you can go, but don't bounce once you get there. And don't pause. Just do a U-turn, slowly raising yourself back up. How many dips you should do is subjective, but Isaacs suggests three sets to exhaustion: the first, going about three-quarters of the way down; the second, as low as you can go; and the third, again only three-quarters down.

**—DAN SANTOW**

# Be Your Own Machine

REMEMBER *ROCKY*? While undefeated heavyweight champ Apollo Creed wind-bagged his way into the title match, regular-guy Balboa knocked out push-up after push-up.

Creed won a split decision, but we all know Rocky kicked his ass.

Granted, Rocky also slurped raw eggs and sparred with frozen sides of beef. But it's no secret that extremists are drawn to the push-up. In fact, the exercise's very simplicity encourages the push-up's use as everything from an elemental test of strength to an instrument of humiliation (or motivation, as the torturers might put it). "A lot of people avoid push-ups when they get older," says J.P. Slovak, the fitness director at the Cooper Fitness Center in Dallas, "because when they were younger, coaches made them do push-ups if they did something wrong."

Childhood flashbacks aside, the physical benefits of the push-up are rarely enough for the exercise's true disciples. Witness, for instance, the case of Anthony Mauro, who, upon graduating from Marine Officer Candidate School in 1983, dropped to the stage in full-dress uniform and pumped out 20 single-arm push-ups before a packed house. "Everybody went crazy," says Mauro, now a major and the recruit-training operations officer at Parris Island. "It was all about unit identity, honor, and motivation. When you get down to it, the push-up is a matter of personal pride."

Tell that to Apollo Creed.

## The Classic

Place your palms on the floor, slightly wider than shoulder-width apart; this position works the triceps, the deltoids, and the pectorals equally. (Keeping your palms closer together works the triceps more; wider apart, it's the delts and the pecs.) Raise yourself to an erect position, with your arms extended but not locked. (Locking your elbows places stress on the joints and rests the muscles you're trying to work.) On the way down, lower yourself *slowly*—taking twice as long as you did

---

### THE DUMBBELL CURL

### Exercises the Biceps

Stand with your feet hip-width apart, holding a dumbbell in each hand with your arms down, palms facing forward, and the insides of your elbows resting lightly against your sides. Slowly curl the weight in one hand toward your shoulder by bending your elbow, trying to keep it pressed to your side. Return to the starting position; repeat with your other arm. (You can curl with a barbell, though dumbbells place less strain on the wrists.)

—JEFFREY J. CSATARI

going up—until you're two to three inches from the ground. The marines do push-ups with their eyes forward to see the exercise leader, but to avoid neck strain, maintain your head's neutral, relaxed position and look at the floor. Inhale on the way down; exhale on the way up. Shoot for 2 to 3 sets of 20. Anything more builds endurance, not muscle.

## The Single-Arm

There's one limitation with push-ups: You can't increase the weight you're lifting. Enter the single-arm version, a far more challenging take on the old standby—if muscle is what you crave, this exercise will deliver it. Keeping your right arm and leg in line, kick out your left leg two to three feet to the side to balance yourself. Place your left hand on your butt. You probably can't go down as far as you can while doing a standard push-up and still be able to get back up, but mimic the movement as best you can. Shoot for 8 to 10 reps in a set; then switch sides and do another set.

## The Fingertip

Try this specialized variation to build finger, wrist, and hand strength. The form and technique are the same as those of the classic push-up except for the positioning of your fingers. Create a wide base with your hands, spreading your fingers as far as they'll go, and balance your body on your fingertips. (Your hands should be raised, resembling small tents.) Go slowly; your hand is filled with tiny muscles that aren't accustomed to supporting that much weight. "Your fingers will fatigue before your triceps, pecs, and delts do," Slovak says. "So do your fingertip reps first, until you tire. Then continue with regular push-ups."

—BRETT FORREST

# Be Like Rocky

OVER 20 YEARS AGO, a silent revolution swept through grade-school gyms, turning gender stereotypes on their heads and inaugurating a bold, new era of self-expression for the youth of America. No, we're not talking *Rocky Horror* here—we're talking jump-rope. The year was 1979, and the American Heart Association glommed onto this simple cord once used almost exclusively by boxers and little girls and made it the centerpiece of an effort to train kids in a fitness regimen—and, not incidentally, to pry them away from the tube. Ultimately, more than 25 million impressionable young minds received full indoctrination.

Now those first converts are executing phase two of the AHA's plan: They're bringing the revolution to the rest of us, teaching aerobics-style rope classes at health clubs and marketing bouncy workout videos.

Not that the sport hasn't always had fanatic followers. The accepted theory is that jumping originated in ancient Egypt. Your average clothesline being useless for mooring massive barges laden with Nubian goods, ropemakers wove two-foot-

## THE SQUAT

### Exercises the Thighs and the Buttocks

Stand with your feet slightly wider than shoulder-width apart and your toes pointed slightly outward. Lift a barbell over your head and rest it across your upper back, with your hands also placed slightly more than shoulder-width apart. (*Note:* If you don't have a spotter, you can do this exercise with heavy dumbbells, holding one in each hand at chest level, palms facing out.) Keeping your weight on your heels, slowly bend your knees, as if you are sitting down on a chair. Stop when your butt hits the imaginary chair and your thighs are almost parallel to the floor. Looking straight ahead, pause for a moment, and then slowly stand up. Be sure you don't bounce at the bottom of the movement or lock your knees at the top. Repeat.

—JEFFREY J. CSATARI

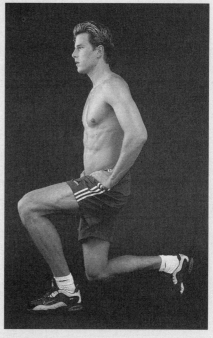

DAVID BARRY

diameter cables by laying three 10-inch-thick strands side by side and then swinging them, jumping over one strand and under the other. The process morphed into a game when children began to imitate this motion with smaller cords.

Most of us will never mix a back flip in with a double-under-front-cross, but with a bit of practice, we can spin a simple cord some two times per second and thus burn 118 calories in 10 minutes. The American Heart Association would be proud.

## The Classic Jump-Rope

Use a segmented-bead rope—the length is adjustable, and the weight of the beads allows for smooth turns and an arc that holds its shape. To find the right fit, put your foot on the center of the rope and lift the handles; they should just reach your armpits. Jump on a wooden or carpeted surface, and wear cross-trainers

### SQUAT JUMP

Stand with hands on hips, one foot a step ahead of the other. Squat (drop quickly) until your front thigh is at a 90-degree angle to the back leg; then immediately jump as high as possible, fully straightening the knees. Switching the position of your feet on the way down, land, squat, and jump again.

—JIM THORNTON

or aerobic shoes that offer support under the balls of your feet. Start with your hands in front of you, elbows by your sides and feet slightly apart. Turn the rope by making small circles with your wrists, not big ones with your arms and shoulders. When the rope approaches your feet, jump just high enough—no more than an inch or two—to allow it to pass underneath. Land softly on the balls of your feet and keep your feet barely apart throughout the exercise. Start with intervals of a couple of minutes and build slowly from there.

—DAVID DiBENEDETTO

# Get Out of the Gym

DURING HIS SIX years of study at the Latvian Academy of Sports, from 1985 to 1991, Vladimir Apanassov was trained in the great Soviet sports traditions, among them the all-important art of making do with meager resources. "There were sports centers where elite athletes trained," he says, "but even there machinery, like leg presses, was nonexistent." Out of necessity, Apanassov developed a healthy respect for the benefits of resistance training at its most fundamental level, using only the weight we carry on our own frames.

"You learn how to control your body," Apanassov says of his complex calisthenics. "When you are on a machine, you're just along for the ride." Apanassov's rigorous regimen of body-resistance exercises adds up to an intense workout that rivals any barbell-and-weight-stacks circuit (with no equipment required). And because the focus is so squarely on working muscles against one another, his routine also trains neuromuscular coordination.

He's found agreement even among trainers who weren't schooled in Soviet deprivation. "You really have to be in touch with your body to make these contractions," says Greg Isaacs, the author of *The Ultimate Lean Routine*. "What this will do is teach you to isolate the muscles." Which is an important skill for everyone from rock climbers to skiers to those who are simply trying to get the most out of a more traditional weight routine. "It's a great thing to do while you're traveling, when you don't have access to a gym," says Isaacs. "Then, when you go back to the weights, you'll have created a consciousness of your muscles, which is important in any kind of strength training."

So use these five exercises as a supplement to your regular routine, working them in one day a week or devoting yourself to them exclusively for a few weeks before returning to your regimen.

## Pectorals, Anterior Deltoids, Triceps

### Triple Push-up

Start with a set of standard push-ups: arms shoulder-width apart and perpendicular to the ground, hands pointing forward. Keep your entire body tight and breathe in as you slowly lower yourself to the floor, out as you push yourself up. Don't lock your elbows at the top. This primarily works your pecs, with support from your triceps. Then, without shifting your body position, move your arms back so they're at about a 75-degree angle to the floor. Point your hands behind you and slightly outward, as if your palms are on the bottom two sides of a hexagon. Perform push-ups as above. This works your delts, with support from your pecs. Finally, bring your arms forward to a reverse 75-degree angle, and point your hands slightly outward, as if they're on the top two sides of the hexagon. These push-ups work your triceps, with support from the front deltoids. Begin with 10 to 15 reps of each, and repeat the circuit once.

## Quadriceps Region

### Plyometric Squat

Stand in a modified "parade rest" stance: legs shoulder-width apart, toes pointing slightly to each side, hands clasped in front of your groin. Tilt your head back, contracting the muscles in your neck and back, and bring your shoulder blades together. Bend your knees and slowly crouch until your hands just touch the floor. Without pausing, exhale and jump as high as you can. Keep your knees slightly bent for a soft landing, and immediately begin the next squat. Do two sets of 25 repetitions.

## Abdominal Region

### Bridge

Start in a push-up position but with your elbows bent 90 degrees and your forearms resting on the floor in front of you, palms down. As you exhale, flex your abs and slowly push up even higher from your waist without shifting your weight forward or back. (Your arms shouldn't move, and your butt shouldn't stick into the air.) Your body should move no more than two or three inches. Return to the starting position and repeat without pausing at the top or bottom. Concentrate on maintaining perfect form for a minute and a half without worrying about how many repetitions you do.

## Hamstring/Gluteal Region

### Pelvic Push-up

Lie on your back with your hands resting lightly on your waist and both legs bent at a 90-degree angle. Lift your right toe and your left heel off the floor, thus shifting your weight toward your right side. Breathing out, push up from your right heel, slowly lifting your body until it's in a straight line from your knees to your shoulders. Keep your hamstrings, glutes, back, and abs tight. Slowly lower yourself to just above the floor before rising again—don't fully relax. Do two sets of 20 repetitions with each leg.

## Posterior Deltoids, Triceps, Abs

### Candle

Lie on your back with your legs extended straight up at the ceiling and your arms pressed against the ground at about a 45-degree angle to your body. While exhaling, push down with your arms and slowly lift your body straight up, leaving only your upper back and shoulders touching the floor. Slowly lower yourself almost to the floor before rising again. Concentrate on keeping your entire body tight throughout the exercise. Do two to three sets of 15 repetitions.

—MARK JANNOT

# Prevent Injury

IF YOU'RE LIKE ME, it has taken you years of swollen blisters, sprained ankles, and sore muscles to figure out that the best way to treat such common sports ailments is not to get them in the first place. Believe it or not, it's a feat more easily accomplished than a six-minute mile. In some cases it requires a little more strengthening, in others a bit more stretching, and in still others, more careful outfitting, but by knowing what the most common injuries are and why they occur, you can take steps to prevent everything from biker's shoulder down to athlete's foot.

In general you can prevent muscle soreness by warming up and cooling down with 10 to 15 minutes of light aerobic exercise before and after your workout. Taking an anti-inflammatory, aspirin or ibuprofen, 4 hours before you work out and up to 48 hours afterward can help as well. And while you've got the pill bottles out, take daily supplements of vitamins C and E, which are antioxidants that reduce the deteriorating effects of free radicals in your body.

That done, look at the following pages for a starting point to avoid certain specific kinds of pain. Remember, though, if you have any condition accompanied by intense pain or that doesn't diminish within a few days, consult a physician.

## Tennis Elbow

**DESCRIPTION.** A sharp pain on the outside of the elbow and forearm that affects both tennis players and golfers.

**PREVENTION.** Strengthen by doing three sets of wrist curls and tennis-ball squeezes a day. Stretch by extending your arm straight in front of you and pushing your hand toward the floor and then the ceiling.

## Sore Shoulder (Rotator-Cuff Tendinitis)

**DESCRIPTION.** A dull ache on the top or front of the shoulder, this very common injury can result from throwing, golf, tennis, swimming, or weight lifting.

**PREVENTION.** Do rowing exercises and rotator-cuff exercises three times per week. Also, stretch the back of your shoulder daily by pulling your arm across your body.

## Lower-Back Strains

**DESCRIPTION.** Pain or stiffness in the lower back that subsides when you're active but returns later. It affects many golfers and weight lifters.

**PREVENTION.** Do back extensions and crunches to strengthen your abdomen and lower back. While weight lifting, don't attempt weights you can't handle and wear a support belt. Bend at the knees and hips, not the waist.

## Runner's Knee

**DESCRIPTION.** Pain in the front or middle of the knee that hits not only runners but bicyclers and swimmers as well.

**PREVENTION.** Keep hamstrings and hips flexible. Wear good-quality shoes and padded socks. Avoid excessive running and don't increase your mileage by more than 10 percent per week. For biking, avoid excessive uphill riding and have a professional check your seat height and pedal position.

## Shin Splints

**DESCRIPTION.** Sharp pain in the front or back of the lower leg.

**PREVENTION.** Do heel raises, toe raises, and calf stretches at least three times per week. Run on soft surfaces, like grass or cinder tracks, and avoid running on crowned roads that cause one foot to be lower than the other.

## Biker's Wrist or Shoulder

**DESCRIPTION.** Ache or pain that results from absorbing the shock of riding over rough terrain. Usually intensifies when the body part is stressed and can cause numbness.

**PREVENTION.** Strengthen upper body using high reps and low weight. Stretch wrists, shoulders, and neck while riding. Check the position of seat and handlebars and change hand positions frequently. Wear padded cycling gloves.

## Ankle Sprain

**DESCRIPTION.** Ranges from sharp pain to mild tenderness and can include swelling and black-and-blue marks.

**PREVENTION.** Strengthen ankle by putting a five-pound weight on the top of your foot and raising your toes upward. If you're susceptible to sprains, tape the ankle before stressing it.

## Blisters

**DESCRIPTION.** A painful buildup of fluid between the inner and outer layers of skin.

**PREVENTION.** Make sure your shoes fit properly: When standing, the shanks (arch supports) should feel firm when you try to bend them, and the toe area, or toe box, should be at least as wide as your foot, with a quarter-inch to a half-inch of room above your toes.

## Blisters II

**DESCRIPTION.** A painful buildup of fluid between the inner and outer layers of skin.

**PREVENTION.** Wear two pairs of socks, preferably of different materials—silk or nylon covered by wool or cotton—which causes the friction to occur between the socks and not between your foot and the shoe.

## Athlete's Foot

**DESCRIPTION.** An itching, burning infection caused by a fungus that forms in hot, sweaty conditions.

**PREVENTION.** Wear flip-flops in public showers to avoid the fungus. Wash your feet well and dry them thoroughly, especially between the toes. Sprinkle your shoes and socks with an antifungal or even talcum powder.

## Jock Itch

**DESCRIPTION.** Symptoms and causes similar to athlete's foot.

**PREVENTION.** Slip on clean socks before you put your underwear on (so you won't transfer fungus from your feet to your groin). Wear cotton briefs under a jock strap to prevent abrasions that can be susceptible to fungus.

—JIM GORANT

## SPORTS AILMENTS

# Give It a Rest

D O BATTLE with your physiology and your physiology will always win," says David Pearson, Ph.D., an associate professor of exercise physiology at the Ball State University Human Performance Laboratory in Muncie, Indiana. Pearson's admonition reflects the dirty secret of working out: Pumping iron or running a 10K imposes just another form of stress not all that different from the kind induced by too little sleep or a blank 1040 on April 16. "A certain amount of stress is good," says Pearson, "but in excess the body defends itself by making you sick."

Overload your muscles in the weightroom for an hour, and you shock your body: Your temperature rises. Your heart beats faster. Your muscle fibers tear. You deplete amino acids, muscle-fiber proteins, and glycogen, your primary energy source. By the time your workout is over, your body is stressed. And that's okay, because it reacts to the stress positively, in what Canadian endocrinologist Hans Selye named the General Adaptation Syndrome. Freaked by the exertion and determined not to be caught unprepared again, your muscles "supercompensate" by packing on fresh proteins and additional water over the next 24 to 96 hours. Your muscle fibers grow and may even divide. As you eat, your body replenishes its energy stores.

But here's the rub: You don't get stronger during exercise; you get stronger while you're *healing* from it. The greater the intensity of your training—hefting heavy weights, running marathon distances or up and down steep hills—the more damage done to your body. And the more damage done, the longer you need to recover.

This is where things get tricky. Repeat your workout too soon, and you'll actually interfere with the rebuilding process; you'll get weaker. But wait too long, and your new strength or power gains will have already begun to decline. "You have to be careful to perform your next workout at the peak of your rebuilding process," says Wayne Westcott, Ph.D., the fitness research director of the South Shore YMCA in Quincy, Massachusetts.

But exactly when is that peak? Fast-twitch muscle fibers, such as those that predominate in the triceps, take longer to recover than do slow-twitch fibers. And the fitter you are, the faster your body

## SYMPTOMS OF BURNOUT

Overtraining can happen to anyone and can be particularly insidious because its most common symptom—a decline in strength or performance—only makes us want to train harder. Meanwhile, the best thing to do is rest: Start with two weeks off from exercise, then go from there. In addition, watch for:

- Persistent flulike symptoms, including a mild headache or a runny nose
- A marked decrease in your appetite
- Insomnia or other disruptions in your normal sleep pattern
- Excessive fatigue
- An elevated heart rate, even at rest

## Rebuilding Plan

Rest each muscle group at least 48 hours between workouts. If you are doing intense lifting with heavy weights, you may want to give yourself an extra day or two to recover. (Research conducted by Wayne Westcott at the South Shore YMCA in Quincy, Massachusetts, has shown that among nonathletes and recreational athletes the difference between the results of working out twice a week or three times a week is minimal.)

**VARY YOUR WORKOUTS.** You'll get better results and reduce the risk of overtraining by simply mixing things up once in a while. If you regularly do barbell bench presses, for instance, switch to dumbbells and a Swiss ball; if you run, try riding a bike.

**TAKE A BREAK.** If your workouts are primarily aerobic, don't go for more than three days in a row without a hiatus.

**EAT ENOUGH.** "Most people who run or bike or swim a lot are running on fumes, unless they eat plenty of carbohydrates," says David Pearson, Ph.D. That's especially true for anyone who's trying to lose weight. "You need to exercise and feed yourself, not exercise and starve yourself," says Pearson.

**GET PLENTY OF SLEEP.**

DAVID REGAN

recovers and the harder you have to push to keep squeezing out gains. "There's a really fine line," says Dan Wathen, the president of the National Strength and Conditioning Association and the strength coach at Youngstown State University in Youngstown, Ohio. "To get into peak condition you really need to overreach, to get to a certain edge, and that edge is different for every person."

Ride that edge by training smart, and you win. But push too far, and you fall fast and hard. That's because overtraining presents a vicious paradox: The more you train, the weaker you get. What's more, because the symptoms of overtraining sim-

ply constitute your body's reaction to stress, you don't have to be preparing for the Olympics to find yourself locked in its cycle.

"Any stress can be a fairly significant component to overtraining," says Jeffrey Potteiger, Ph.D., the director of the exercise-physiology lab at the University of Kansas. "If you're a Wall Street broker who works 18 hours a day and exercises a few times a week to relieve stress, well, that might work. But if you're a Wall Street broker working 18-hour days and you're trying to train for a marathon, then you're setting yourself up for a fall."

—CARL HOFFMAN

# Lean Machine

PERMIT ME a brief introduction. The words you are now reading have been written by a 177.54-pound chunk of animate matter, precisely 23.19 percent (or 41.18 pounds) of which is pure fat. In the course of writing these words, I have expended 2.6 calories per minute at my keyboard—exactly twice the 1.3 calories per minute you are now burning, assuming that you're reading this seated quietly (though not on a toilet, in which case you could be expending up to 2 calories per minute).

This morning, just after I awoke, my resting metabolic rate was such that if I'd followed my instincts and remained prone for the next 24 hours, I would have burned 1,823 calories simply by being alive. According to a Penn State labora-

tory analysis (see "Your Fuel Efficiency") of the amount of oxygen my body uses at rest and how much $CO_2$ it gives off, I burn roughly six times more fat than carbohydrates before breakfast, though that proportion surely changes after a couple of bagels replenish my muscle-glycogen stores. And in the course of digesting said bagels, I also begin to enjoy a "postprandial thermogenic burn"—an elevated caloric expenditure reflecting the metabolic work needed to process food.

My body mass index, or BMI, is 23.58—a tad under the 25 that a group of National Institutes of Health experts designated in June 1997 as the new statistical starting point for an "overweight" diagnosis. The old standard, provided by the National Center for Health Statistics, held that people weren't overweight until they hit a BMI of 28. With the downward shift, the United States became predominantly a nation of butterballs, with 97 million adults, nearly 55 percent of the adult population, officially declared to be overweight. (To torture yourself by calculating your own BMI, see "How Fat Are You Really?")

All that said, I'd like to indulge in a few qualifying remarks of the sort that rarely figures into weight-loss advice.

First, this BMI hoo-ha may make a modicum of sense in the aggregate, but it absolutely doesn't apply to quite a few men, especially those who are particularly muscular. "By these new standards, for instance, most professional athletes would be classified as overweight," says clinical nutritionist Dr. C. Wayne Callaway, a weight-control specialist at George Washington University School of Medicine. "It's silly."

Second, an influential study by Dr. Steven Blair and his colleagues at the Cooper Institute in Dallas found that fitness matters much more than fatness. Highly fit men with BMIs of 30-plus had substantially lower death rates than did couch potatoes with BMIs under 25. (Amazingly, these high-fit, high-weight guys even had lower death rates than did the high-fit, low-weight guys, though the difference wasn't statistically significant.)

Third, while many researchers agree that losing 5 percent to 10 percent of your body weight will improve your health if your heft has already triggered health problems—including high blood pressure, high cholesterol, or insulin resistance—the evidence for those with a BMI under 30 is much less compelling that losing weight will do the same in the absence of such so-called co-morbidities.

> *It pushes a man to the wall if he stands there in the buff and looks straight down and can't even see his own weenie.*
>
> **—JOHN WAYNE**

There's also another tricky distinction to make. Generally speaking, epidemiological studies suggest that men with BMIs between 21 and 25 live longer than those with BMIs over 25, though the disparity shrinks with age and disappears altogether by age 74. And the data on positive consequences of lowering a high BMI is surprisingly ambiguous. As an editorial in the *New England Journal of Medicine* put it, "We simply do not know whether a person who loses 20 pounds will thereby acquire the same reduced risk as a person who started out 20 pounds lighter. The few studies of mortality among people who voluntarily lost weight produced inconsistent results; some even suggested that weight loss increased mortality."

If you're the type of guy who's prone to denial, chances are that these points have just emancipated you from any further nettlesome thoughts on weight loss. After all, you're fairly muscular, right? And your health is pretty good—no major blood-pressure, cholesterol, or insulin-resistance problems. And what about this increased-mortality business? You'll damn well eat that chocolate bar! Any sacrifice to avoid dying young!

## Gut Check

Well, the guys in the denial crowd weren't going to try to lose weight, anyhow, so I now bid them Godspeed and adieu. For those of you still with me, most of whom I suspect aren't professional athletes, your excess pounds are probably contributing to at least some health concerns and—if nothing else—self-image problems. To get a gander at what is most likely imperiling your well-being, take a moment to look down at your waist.

Recovered yet? Unlike women, whose fat deposits tend to gather with the rapacity of barnacles around the hips and thighs, the typical male obesity pattern is the love-handled beer gut. Some experts believe that one of the best predictors of health problems from excess weight comes from the so-called waist-hip ratio. To calculate this, measure the circumference of your waist at its slenderest point, then that of your hips at their fattest, and divide the first number by the second. Depending on which expert you ask, this number should be below .95 or 1. If it isn't, odds are good that you have a surplus of intra-abdominal fat, also known as "visceral fat," which could lead, most dangerously, to heart trouble.

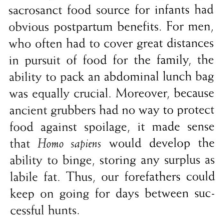

JOSEPH FIEDLER

Visceral fat is not the same as the relatively less harmful subcutaneous fat that lurks immediately beneath your abdominal skin. It resides instead under the abdominal muscles and the thick connective tissue, called the peritoneum, that lines the abdominal cavity.

The bad news is that visceral fat is highly labile, which means your body can readily mobilize it into the bloodstream for use as an energy source. And as endless public-health messages have reminded us for decades, a lot of artery-clogging fat in the blood is decidedly not a good thing.

The good news is that this same lability makes visceral fat relatively easy to lose, especially with exercise. In contrast, the hip- and thigh-fat stores so often suffered by females are notoriously resistant to elimination despite the helpful guidance supplied month after month by women's magazines. "This hip and thigh fat is a very deep energy store," says Dr. Louis Aronne, a clinical associate professor of medicine at Cornell University Medical College. "It's mobilized only during breast-feeding."

The discrepancy in how apple-shaped men and pear-shaped women put on—and take off—weight is likely the vestige of different gender-based evolutionary pressures applied in antiquity. For women, particularly in times of scarcity, saving a sacrosanct food source for infants had obvious postpartum benefits. For men, who often had to cover great distances in pursuit of food for the family, the ability to pack an abdominal lunch bag was equally crucial. Moreover, because ancient grubbers had no way to protect food against spoilage, it made sense that *Homo sapiens* would develop the ability to binge, storing any surplus as labile fat. Thus, our forefathers could keep on going for days between successful hunts.

The location of our internal larder also makes sense biomechanically: Weight is least likely to hamper locomotion when piled around the midriff. Moreover, abdominal fat has a short, expeditious route through the portal vein to the liver, where it can be converted into ketones during times of starvation, keeping the brain alive even in the absence of glucose.

It's difficult to imagine in this age of McNuggetized plenty how constant the threat of starvation has been for most of human history. But hunger-strikers and others given to fasting have clearly exhibited the body's biological adaptations to want: A man who starts out at a more or less normal weight can survive 55 to 60 days without food. If he's obese to begin with, he'll almost certainly last longer. The world record, held by a former 300-pounder, is more than a year without food.

The point is that we all have mighty, inherent safeguards against starvation, and some of us have extraordinarily effective fat-adding and fat-hoarding capabilities. When World War III is over, the hoarders will enjoy the last laugh. But until then, a full complement of antistarvation genes practically guarantees a protracted struggle against weight gain. And this struggle will continue as long as supermarket shelves stay stocked with cheap, palatable food and—even more importantly—as long as the siren song of sedentary living continues to seduce.

## The Settling Point

You've probably heard the old saw that says to lose a pound, you must create a deficit of 3,500 calories. Eat 500 calories per day less than your normal diet for one week; eat the same as always but burn 500 calories more per day through additional exercise; or do some kind of mix-and-match 500-calorie combination of lowering intake and increasing expenditure. Adhere religiously to any of these approaches, conventional thinking went, and in seven days there'd be precisely one pound less of you stomping about the earth.

Ah, if only weight loss truly worked this way in the real world!

In reality, the body's machinations are infinitely more complex and confounding. For most men, caloric restriction alone just doesn't cut it, especially over the long term. Eat less and the body doesn't get thinner—rather, it turns down the metabolic furnace a notch or two, hoarding stored fat as if it were life's most precious commodity (which, of course, it once was).

This metabolic bait-and-switch undergirds one of the more controversial theories about weight control—that each of us, depending on our genetic makeup, has a setpoint, or preferred weight, that the body strives to maintain regardless of how

much or how little we eat. Some researchers assert that thinking of this weight as a lone setpoint is too rigid; they agree that the body seeks to hold at a preferred weight but suggest that it's more of a range. "It's probably more accurate to think of this as a settling point," says Callaway.

Semantics notwithstanding, two early-1990s experiments conducted in Canada by weight researcher Dr. Claude Bouchard of Quebec's Laval University exemplify how powerful the body's adaptive response can be. In the first of these studies, Bouchard took 12 pairs of identical twins to a remote location where they could be closely monitored—and where no vending machines or other such temptations would induce dietary cheating. After determining the number of calories each per-

JOSEPH FIEDLER

## BLAME THE BEER

Alcohol is high in less-than-nutritious calories, but it's not calories alone that trigger the growth of the aptly named beer belly. A 1992 Swiss study found that, because of a quirk in how it is metabolized, alcohol interferes with the body's ability to use—and thus eliminate—the abdominal fat. The bottom line: You want to deflate your beach ball? Switching from a daily six-pack of Miller to a daily six-pack of Miller Lite isn't going to do it.

—J.T.

son needed to maintain his weight, Bouchard had everyone consume an additional 1,000 calories a day above this diet.

The experiment was conducted 6 days a week for 100 days. At its conclusion, two findings had emerged. First, there were large individual differences in weight gain: Some subjects put on nearly 30 pounds, while others, despite the chronic daily engorgement, gained less than 10. Second, the role of genetics was equally striking: The siblings in each pair of twins increased their weight by nearly identical amounts.

In Bouchard's follow-up study, different sets of twins ate a maintenance diet for 100 days while expending 1,000 calories daily more than they normally would through exercise (equivalent to jogging for 1 hour and 40 minutes). Bouchard expected that all subjects would lose weight, and they did. But once again there were wide variations. And once again, twins within each pair reacted nearly identically.

Other studies have tried to identify what happens metabolically when people are purposely overfed. "It turns out," says Dr. James Chenoweth, an exercise and weight-control specialist in Ann Arbor, Michigan, "that we have biochemical path-

ways known as 'futile cycles' that, when we overeat, allow us to basically turn excess energy into heat and thereby waste much of it rather than pack it all on." When we give our bodies too little food, on the other hand, the metabolic rate slows down to compensate. Researchers have identified a host of complex mechanisms that work together to preserve a steady status quo, mechanisms that make reductions in weight extremely difficult to maintain, especially if you rely on dieting alone.

## Liberating the Lean You

That's not to say that, given enough time and deprivation, stringent dieting alone won't shed some pounds, though if your genetic constitution has made you a superb fat miser, you probably won't enjoy the weight-loss rate of 1 pound per 3,500 calories. In fact, there's probably not much of anything you'll enjoy: Dieting practically guarantees gnawing hunger pangs orchestrated by brain chemicals, including neuropeptide Y. Such signals must be constantly countered with self-denial, something that is notoriously difficult to sustain long-term.

Even worse, the weight that you do lose by solely dieting will likely include a fair amount of lean muscle mass. Because muscle burns fuel and fat just sits there, your basal metabolism will further decrease, meaning you'll have to restrict your diet even more to keep up the new, hard-won status quo.

JOSEPH FIEDLER

## EATING OUT DOESN'T HAVE TO MEAN PORKIN' OUT

Sit down in almost any restaurant, and you might as well kiss your weight-loss plan goodbye. Portions have gotten so big that the average meal is off the calorie-counting charts. The average appetizer racks up a whopping 900 calories, according to the Center for Science in the Public Interest, which recently surveyed eateries around the country. Talk about supersized: CSPI found that portions in many restaurants are two to three times bigger than what nutritionists consider a standard serving. A single meal can easily pack more calories than most men should consume in an entire day.

"Luckily, you can enjoy a fine meal and keep the weight off," says nutrition expert Dr. John La Puma, who was once 35 pounds overweight, but he's lost those pounds and kept them off for 6 years. "What it takes," says La Puma, "is a little planning." Here's what he suggests:

Ask for it your way. "You're in charge of what you put in your mouth," says La Puma. "If you want a French meal without the heavy sauce, ask for it. If you like the fish but want it broiled instead of fried, tell the waiter. A good restaurant should be able to put anything together with anything else."

**ORDER ALL TOPPINGS ON THE SIDE.** A lot of calories lurk in fat-based sauces and oily salad dressings, so ask for these on the side and use them sparingly. Look for items that rely on subtle seasoning instead of heavy sauces for flavor.

**DIVIDE AND CONQUER.** Bigger is not better when it comes to good food. Even before the plate hits the table, ask your waiter to divide the entree in half; eat one portion and take the rest home. Or draw an imaginary line down your meal, finish half, and then push the plate away.

**FAVOR FRUITS AND VEGETABLES.** Fruits and veggies fill you up on fewer calories. Yet men average only about three servings a day—way under the five to nine nutrition experts recommend. You don't have to become a vegetarian to stay slim, but it's wise to look for dishes that offer plenty from the produce aisle, as well as rice, grains, or beans.

—PETER JARET

Surprisingly, statistics indicate that modern Americans are eating pretty much the same amount of food as Americans circa 1900 did. Now, however, many more of us are overweight. Obviously, this discrepancy hasn't been wrought by widespread genetic mutations. The big change has been the societal shift to desk jobs and away from the manual labor of agricultural and industrial employment. TV probably hasn't helped much either—where once we played sports, today we watch them.

The key to weight loss is to regain the extremely active life of our ancestors. Regular exercise is, in fact, virtually the only proven way to move your setpoint downward. If you don't exercise, you'll be constantly battling your own physiology, and it—unlike you—will never give up.

And not all forms of exercise are created equal. Aerobic workouts, it turns out, are significantly better than anaerobic training in promoting and maintaining weight loss. One reason is that such sports as running, swimming, hiking, and biking burn more calories per minute than weight lifting, says Ben Hurley, Ph.D., a resistance-training researcher.

Consider: An extremely vigorous circuit of 15 standard weight-lifting exercises, performed with almost no rest between sets, uses up only about 5 calories per minute. In contrast, jogging at a modest 12-minute-mile pace consumes twice as many. One reason for the difference is the energy source utilized. During moderate aerobic training, the body can burn sugar, but its preferred energy source is fat, which can be burned only in the presence of oxygen. Once you cross the anaerobic threshold, though, your body fails to supply oxygen fast enough to meet

YOUR FUEL EFFICIENCY

# HOW MUCH FOOD DO YOU ACTUALLY NEED?

An important first step in any weight-loss regimen is to get a handle on how many calories your body typically burns throughout the day. My own "resting metabolic rate" was calculated at the Noll Physiological Research Center at Penn State University, but to spare yourself the hassle and expense of a lab visit, you can use a formula called the Harris-Benedict Equation:

1. Multiply your weight in pounds by 6.3.
2. Multiply your height in inches by 12.7.
3. Add 66 to the sum of these two figures.
4. Multiply your age by 6.8 and subtract from the above number.

In most cases, this formula is remarkably accurate. When I used it, I came up with a resting metabolic rate of 1,802 calories per day. This deviates from the lab measurement by fewer calories than you'd consume by eating five large green olives.

Once you calculate your average resting metabolic rate, you know how much you can eat to maintain your weight without ever having to get out of bed. Obviously, most of us don't live like this, so an allowance must be made for our actual activity above and beyond rest.

A somewhat crude method of estimating this is to keep a log throughout the day; then multiply the minutes you spend at each activity by the calories per minute cited on standard tables. (See "The Burn Chart.")

Finally, if you just want a down-and-dirty estimate of the calories you burn in a day, take your resting metabolic rate and multiply it by 1.2 if you're modestly active, 1.4 if you're moderately active (for instance, you take a half-hour walk each day), and from 1.6 to 2 if you're very active (for the high end, you should have a physically demanding job and exercise the equivalent of an hour's run each day).

—J.T.

# EXERCISE IS THE ONLY WAY

If you're determined to lose weight and keep it off permanently, the highly rigorous program detailed here will help. Keep in mind a few general principles:

**THINK GRADUAL.** A week of starvation and hyper-exercise doesn't work; a long-term commitment does. A reasonable goal for weight loss is a pound or two per week, depending on how heavy you are to begin with. *Note:* Weight loss is not linear. Don't become discouraged if the pounds come off in fits and starts separated by plateaus. Persistence will pay off.

**ACTIVITY MATTERS.** Always take the stairs, never drive when you can walk or bike, and constantly look for ways to incorporate movement into your routine. The regimens described here are an adjunct to, not a substitute for, an active approach to daily life.

**MODERATELY RESTRICT CALORIES.** During the initial weeks, try to reduce your daily intake by about 500 calories a day. Whenever possible, look for easy ways to do this: Don't add sugar to your coffee and use skim milk instead of cream. Control between-meal snacks. Reduce portion size on everything but proteins. Scale back alcohol consumption—one less beer a day will save you 150 calories.

**BUILD UP WORKOUTS.** Whatever exercise your body is used to doing, it can do safely without too much risk of injury. If you commit to increasing your exercise load, however, do so over a period of weeks or months. A completely sedentary man should not try to run 20 miles in Week 1; in fact, it should take him 3 months to safely reach 10 miles a week. By the same token, a regular 30-mile-a-week runner shouldn't suddenly shift to 50 miles a week. Once again, think long-term. The following program is *not* a starting point but, rather, a goal to build toward over time.

**DROP THE DIET—BUT NOT THE EXERCISE.** Once you do reach your ideal weight, let your appetite guide how much you eat. Avoid too much fat, keep up your workouts, and chances are good that you can maintain your weight without further dietary self-deprivation.

—J.T.

the high demands. Your muscles thus have no choice but to start burning glycogen anaerobically (i.e., without oxygen), which produces lactic acid. As lactic-acid levels escalate, your muscles start to fatigue and cramp. Eventually you'll need to stop or greatly reduce the intensity of your workout. This is another reason why aerobic exercise is better for losing weight—you can keep going at it for a significantly longer period of time. The bottom line: Exercise at a moderate, sustainable pace for as long as you can, and you'll burn fat most effectively.

This said, however, it's important not to ignore strength training altogether. Though physiological studies are hardly unanimous, says Hurley, an increase of lean muscle mass from weight lifting can, in some cases, crank up your basal metabolic rate by as much as 7 percent. This means that the calories your body burns, even at rest, increase modestly. Unfortunately, this effect isn't as powerful as conventional wisdom would have it; even if a weakling transformed himself into Arnold Schwarzenegger, it would make a difference of no

# A SEVEN-DAY PRESCRIPTION. REFILLS: INFINITE

## Day One: Resistance and aerobic training

20 minutes weight lifting or calisthenics (about 100 calories burned)
  20 minutes easy-to-moderate aerobic training (200 to 300 calories burned)
  Example: Do one circuit on Nautilus equipment, followed by two miles of jogging.

## Day Two: Sustained aerobics

45 to 60 minutes moderate aerobic training (675 to 900 calories burned)
  Example: Jog three to five miles or swim 2,000 to 3,000 yards; or play competitive soccer, full-court basketball, or singles tennis for an hour.

## Day Three: Sustained aerobics

45 to 60 minutes moderate aerobic training (675 to 900 calories burned)
  Example: Repeat Day Two; or try cycling, skating, stairclimbing, or uphill hiking for an hour.

## Day Four: Resistance and aerobic training

20 minutes weight lifting or calisthenics (about 100 calories burned)
  20 minutes easy-to-moderate aerobic training (200 to 300 calories burned)
  Example: Repeat Day One; or do two sets of 8 to 12 chin-ups, crunches, push-ups, and squat jumps—with resistance if you're completing 12 reps without trouble. Follow this with a 20-minute power walk.

## Day Five: Sustained aerobics

45 to 60 minutes moderate aerobic training (675 to 900 calories burned)
   Example: Repeat Day Two or Three; or play competitive racquetball for an hour; or cross-country ski for 45 minutes; or row moderately to vigorously for 45 to 60 minutes.

## Day Six: Long-duration aerobics

90 to 120 minutes easy-to-moderate aerobic training (900 to 1,800 calories burned)
   Example: During this one "long day" of the week, the emphasis should be on duration, not intensity. Pick a pace that you can sustain for 90 to 120 minutes and then swim, bike, jog, hike, or engage in a similar activity that requires the use of your major muscle groups.

## Day Seven: Rest day

20 to 30 minutes light aerobic training (140 to 300 calories burned)
   Example: Take a half-hour walk but otherwise let your body recuperate.

# Weekly total: 3,665 to 5,600 calories burned

—J.T.

# A NO-EXERCISE DIET?
# OKAY, PAL.

Why are Americans getting fatter? What's the best way to lose weight? With dieting tomes perpetually clogging the bestseller lists, you'd think we might know something about the subject. But it's that very bookstore clutter that fuels the most resilient nutrition myths at large. Here are a few that can sidetrack even the best of weight-loss intentions.

**SUGAR IS FATTENING.** If only it were that simple. First starch was the enemy, then fat, and now sugar, according to diet superstars like *Sugar Busters!* and *Lick the Sugar Habit.* The books claim that sugary foods and refined carbs, such as white bread and pasta, increase insulin, which in turn encourages the body to store fat. But most nutritionists say that's just a small part of the explanation for our collective blubber. True, there are good reasons to reduce levels of refined sugar, which contains calories and not much else. And too much of a sweet thing *is* taking its toll. We've cut back on fatty foods in the past two decades (from 40 percent of calories from fat, on average, to 33 percent today), yet we're still getting rounder. Part of the reason: We're eating 30 pounds more sugar a year than we did in 1970. But no single type of food is the culprit. "The real problem is that Americans are consuming not just too much fat or too much sugar but too many calories," says John Foreyt, a professor of medicine and leading weight-loss expert at Baylor University in Houston.

**DIETING MEANS HAVING TO SAY NO.** Not always. Crash diets that ban people's favorite foods usually fail. They're simply too hard to stick with over time. A better bet, say experts, is to allow yourself occasional indulgences, but in small portions and only as a special treat. That means you don't have to give up Ben & Jerry's Cherry Garcia— just don't dip into the freezer every day.

**HIGH-PROTEIN DIETS MELT AWAY FAT.** Such hot sellers as *The Zone, Dr. Atkins' New Diet Revolution,* and *Protein Power* have led the craze for high-protein, low-carbohydrate diets. The approach is touted as a way to crank up fat burn-off without having to go hungry. A typical Atkins meal plan includes tuna for breakfast, chicken for lunch, and steak for dinner. But the secret isn't high protein, says Marion Nestle, who heads up New York University's food-science department. "The real reason these fad diets work is because behind all the fancy theories and biochemical jargon, they're low in calories." That's fine. But beware of diets that ban certain fruits and vegetables, says Nestle. Plant-based foods are turning out to be the source of many antioxidants. Eliminate too many and you could be putting yourself at risk.

**"LEAN" MEATS MEAN LOWER FAT.** True but misleading. Beef labeled "lean" can still be up to 22.5 percent fat. That means a "lean"-meat quarter-pound burger without cheese packs 21 grams of fat—about a third of the average man's daily limit; a serving of "lean" sausage has 9 grams of fat. It's not a bad idea to choose lean over fatty and to eat your chicken breasts skinless; but don't think that's a license to scarf as much as you want. You've still got to keep portions small. (Most experts say a piece of meat should be no bigger than a deck of cards.)

**ALL FAT IS BAD.** Not so. Gram for gram, fat is twice as high in calories as carbs or protein, so dieters are wise to look for low-fat alternatives. But not all fat is created equal. The worst is saturated fat, which is found in meat, dairy products, and tropical oils like coconut and palm and which gums up the arteries and increases the danger of heart disease. Also hazardous to the arteries, scientists have learned, are trans fats and hydrogenated fats, which show up in many kinds of margarine and processed foods. Monounsaturated fats (found primarily in plant-based oils like canola, peanut, and olive), on the other hand, are easy on the heart. In fact, diets with up to 40 percent of their calories from fat—as long as most of it is monounsaturated—may be even healthier for your heart than a low-fat, high-carbohydrate diet. "Unsaturated fats in the diet lower total cholesterol and improve the ratio of good to bad cholesterol," says Frank Sacks, a researcher at the Harvard School of Public Health. "They also keep blood levels of triglycerides, which have been linked to heart disease, from rising."

**SNACKING SPELLS TROUBLE.** Snacking is actually helpful if you're trying to lose weight, according to Evette Hackman, an associate professor of food and nutrition at Seattle Pacific University. Studies have found that volunteers who ate smaller, more frequent meals—five or six instead of the classic breakfast, lunch, and dinner—were less prone to overindulge at the big three. Steer clear of junk like candy bars and chips, of course, which have very little nutrition and lots of calories. Even many fruit juices are loaded with sugar and low in fiber. A better bet is a piece of fruit or carrot and celery sticks—even a handful of peanuts. Sure, they're high in fat, but it's mostly unsaturated fat. And nuts may not be fattening. Volunteers at the Health Research and Studies Center in Los Altos, California, each ate a whopping 590 calories' worth of almonds every day for nine weeks—and they didn't gain a single pound. Other research shows that nut eaters tend to be slimmer than people who never chew a cashew. "It may be that nuts are so dense in nutrients that they satisfy hunger on fewer calories," says nutritionist Gene Spiller, who conducted the Los Altos study.

JOSEPH FIEDLER

**SOME PEOPLE ARE DESTINED TO BE FAT.** Don't buy it. Certain genes may make it more likely for particular people to become fat, but that's only half the story. The rest is diet and exercise. "Here in the United States, the majority of Pima Indians are obese," says Eric Ravussin, a former researcher with the National Institutes of Health. "The Pimas in Mexico are physically active and eat diets very low in fat and high in complex carbohydrates, and they're generally very lean. Same genes. Different lifestyle. Very different outcome." With fewer work-related opportunities for physical activity and a glut of food, it may be hard for Americans to fight fat. But it is possible.

—PETER JARET

# THE BURN CHART

## WHY CLIMB A MOUNTAIN WHEN CLIMBING STAIRS IS JUST AS GOOD?

| ACTIVITY | CALORIES BURNED PER MINUTE |
|---|---|
| Sleeping | 1.2 |
| Standing | 1.5 |
| Driving a car | 2.8 |
| Golfing, foursome | 3.7 |
| Baseball (except pitching) | 4.7 |
| Calisthenics | 5.0 |
| Cycling, easy | 5.0 |
| Golfing, twosome | 5.0 |
| Gardening, weeding | 5.6 |
| Walking, 3.5 miles per hour (road/field/soft snow) | 5.6/7.0/20.0 |
| Basketball, half-court | 6.0 |
| Swimming, leisurely | 6.0 |
| Tennis, recreational | 7.0 |
| Descending stairs | 7.1 |
| Shoveling snow | 7.5 |
| Skiing, moderate hill | 8.0 |
| Basketball, full-court | 9.0 |
| Soccer | 9.0 |
| Handball, racquetball | 10.0 |
| Running, 12-minute-mile pace | 10.0 |
| Mountain climbing | 10.0–15.0 |
| Skipping rope | 10.0–15.0 |
| Ascending stairs | 10.0–18.0 |
| Tennis, competitive | 11.0 |
| Swimming, 50 yards per minute | 12.5 |
| Swimming, butterfly | 14.0 |
| Cycling, hard | 15.0 |
| Skiing, steep hill | 20.0 |
| Running, 5-minute-mile pace | 25.0 |

Add 10 percent for every 15 pounds over 150; subtract 10 percent for every 15 pounds below 150. / Source: *Fitness and Health*, 4th edition, by Brian J. Sharkey, Ph.D, more than 300 calories per day. Perhaps an even better reason to commit to some strength training is the "can do" factor. Simply put, a guy who gets stronger can be a lot more active in his day-to-day life. And if you can do it, you probably will do it.

Which brings us to the third "category" of exercise: daily activities that you probably don't even think of as exercise but that can add tremendously to your calorie burn. If, for instance, you walk or bike to work instead of drive. Swear off elevators and escalators and always take the stairs—you can expend up to 18 calories per minute in that stairwell. Such mini-bouts of exercise add up. In a study comparing the effectiveness of 40 minutes of continuous exercise with that of four 10-minute periods (each separated by as much as five hours), exercise physiologist John Jakicic, Ph.D., then at the University of Pittsburgh Medical Center, found that both worked about the same in fostering weight loss. "But the 10-minute approach gave people a lot more flexibility," he explains. "This helped with adherence."

Good as this sounds, the reality is that most people with a serious weight problem are going to have to do a lot more exercise to lose significant weight and keep it off. (One study showed that of those who were successful at maintaining weight loss long-term, at least 80 percent were exercising a minimum of five days a week.) Paul Williams, Ph.D., the director of the National Runners Health Study, says that his data reveals that when it comes to exercise, more is less. "Men running 50 miles a week are leaner than those who run 40 miles a week," says Williams. "We're seeing benefits accrue with every 10-mile increment."

A TEST OF STRENGTH
(MULTIPLE CHOICE)

MUELLER

P.S. MUELLER

For further inspiration, consider another twins study, this one conducted by Williams, who analyzed 35 pairs of identical twins, one of whom in each set was a committed runner, while the other lived the sweet, slothful life. The runners had consistently lean bodies and healthy BMIs. Yet the sedentary twins had BMIs all over the map. Some, no doubt thanks to their genes, had low BMIs despite not exercising; others had dangerously high BMIs. But it was impossible to predict from looking at the runners how fat or thin their twins would be.

What this means, says Williams, is that no matter how intractably fat-biased your genes may be, vigorous exercise can actually change your destiny. "Weight clearly does have genetic influences," concedes Williams. "But what we're finding is these influences significantly decrease, and may even be eliminated, as physical activity increases."

—JIM THORNTON

# Wise Up

"WHY YOU FEARING?" The deep bellow comes from above me, and even though my body is bent like a paper clip, there appears to be real sincerity to the question. The fact that I've been tortured for 90 minutes and am now being held upside down apparently makes little impression on my shirtless Brahman yoga teacher, whose understanding of things Western seems to end with the black Calvin Klein boxer-briefs he's wearing, which is to say well short of worry about American-style litigation. Not that I entirely comprehend yoga as it's taught in its motherland. For one thing, there's pain shooting from everywhere on my body save my earlobes. "Why you fearing?" comes the butchered syntax again. The 83-year-old, potbellied guru's strong hands are cinched on my waist. And I believe he's waiting for a response.

"Urgghhhh."

To Sri K. Pattabhi Jois (pronounced "joyce"), who is revered throughout the world as the keeper of the ancient ashtanga-yoga flame, this isn't the 64,000-rupee answer. Here in his dark sweatbox of a yoga studio in the small city of Mysore, in south India, I'm at Jois's mercy while he steadies me in bow pose, or what is essentially a Mary Lou Retton–esque backbend. Jois, who is called Guruji by his students (an affectionate form of "guru," which means "spiritual guide"), is sternly urging me to uncoil from my arch and then drop into a backbend again. "You stiff back!" Guruji lectures to my navel as my hands hit the floor. "You stiff shoulders!"

Such are the words of revelation I'm offered in exchange for traveling to the other side of the world on a 28-day intensive yoga odyssey. I've come to Mysore to experience the mind-body overhaul that my eastward-looking yoga classes at home in New Mexico suggested I might find. The discipline I'd practiced over the past couple of years had little in common with what I'd previously thought yoga was—a come-smell-the-incense gig, full of housewives reaching for their toes.

Instead, ashtanga is super-high-octane yoga, involving an unbroken chain of demanding poses, or asanas, that develop endurance, strength, and flexibility. Ashtanga had elasticized my limbs and fortified my body, making me a more agile and better-balanced runner, mountain biker, and skier. I also got a taste for the practice's more ethereal side, a deep, calming agenda that includes meditation via breath control and focused thought. Indeed, ashtanga yoga is a whole-body approach to fitness.

So it seemed like a prudent life-choice to order up a bigger hunk of such a fulfilling pie. After arranging for a long-term dog-sitter, my wife, Madeleine, and I sought out the master Jois. What I found was a teacher who was one sliver Gandhi and many parts drill sergeant. What I've learned, after now having spent a month with the guru in a nation so mercurial that it stirred V.S. Naipaul to call it the country of "a million mutinies," is that if I can bliss out here, I can bliss out anywhere. Not that it took beyond my first day to have an epiphany: You'll bend very far before you break. The word *yoga* may mean "to form union," as in that of man and God, but I swear the octogenarian looming above me sees it as the joining of my face with his studio's worn green carpet, soiled with the sweat of thousands of yogis. For my finale, Jois wants me to form a human wheel. Curl backward so that the hands grab the feet, the belief goes, and the body changes from a lightning rod dispersing electricity to a circle pulsing with energy. But my wheel looks more like a card table.

"Tomorrow, practice," grunts Guruji before turning around to stick someone's knee behind her head. "Hands and feet touching," says Sharath, his 28-year-old grandson and sidekick, sporting a wry smile.

Our first few days on the mat yielded nothing but Guruji-inflicted aches, and within a week Madeleine and I realized that in order to survive we need to get up at 5:30 A.M. at our $4-a-night cement-block hotel to prepare ourselves for another bout with Jois: first with bucket showers, followed by copious amounts of a salve called Moov, India's version of Ben-Gay. By 6:15 every morning, the odors of burning trash, dung, and menthol blending in our nostrils, we're on our one-speed bikes, riding through the city streets, our muscles loose and tingling. Given ashtanga's six increasingly difficult series of poses, watching the advanced students practice is almost like visiting a Coney Island sideshow: Sharath sticking his heels in his armpits, middle-aged women holding handstands while resting their toes on their foreheads. But then there came the sobering realization that Guruji expected contortionism from *me*.

By Day 10, he was looking for such feats as *I performed uthita hasta padangustasana*, which involves balancing on one straight leg while holding the other up as straight as you can—picture a cancan dancer frozen at maximum kick. Guruji spied me struggling: "Lift," he said.

I raised my left leg, and as testimony that my body was already becoming more supple, I proudly stood with my thighs forming a right angle, a per-

sonal best. Yet this didn't satisfy the guru as he shoved my hamstring-challenged gam skyward. The pain swirled, and my only recourse was to flex both knees and hop in place.

"Bad man!" exclaimed Guruji, who was still holding my left foot. "Why you dancing?"

There were muffled giggles from the yogis in the studio and the 20 or so others waiting in the stairwell, a Greek chorus of acolytes nervously awaiting their turn with a living legend. Pattabhi Jois has been a yogi since age 12. He spent two decades learning ashtanga from the esteemed T. Krishnamacharya, who lived to be 101 and made Guruji seem like Mister Rogers: A young Jois once had to remain in an extreme backbend—knees and elbows resting on the ground—for 30 minutes while Krishnamacharya stood on his prize student's chest.

What makes Krishnamacharya's venerable ashtanga style more demanding than other, more static forms of yoga is that each of its hundreds of asanas is connected by a strength-building, push-up-and-squat-thrust move that keeps your heart pumping and your body in a lather. And sweat equity is something Westerners readily understand. It's not surprising that in recent years ashtanga and its "power yoga" variants have become arguably the fastest-growing styles of yoga, embraced by athletes and Hollywood alike, making a spot on Guruji's studio floor all the more coveted.

After two weeks under Guruji's tutelage, I found that flexibility and strength were starting to blend with the ever-present soreness, and I even noticed new definition in my shoulders and abs. The problem is, even now—our last week in India—I'm having trouble finding the on-ramp to the nirvana highway.

The spiritual goal of yoga can be summed up tidily enough: Steady the mind. To that end, the breathing you do when performing ashtanga is deep and intentional, meant to springboard you from a meditative state in the studio to a peaceful

# FIVE YOGA POSES FOR FLEXIBILITY AND STRENGTH

Anyone can benefit from practicing ashtanga yoga. "It is physically, spiritually, and psychologically rigorous," says David Life, the codirector of the Jivamukti Yoga Center in New York City. "After you do it, the StairMaster will never be the same." The exercises, which take the form of asanas, or poses, will make you more limber and improve your muscle tone. If you are recovering from a sports injury, yoga is also an ideal rehabilitation program.

Before willing your foot to meet your forehead, however, try the following sampler from ashtanga's 35-move primary series. Use the regimen to complement other sports or do it as a stand-alone exercise routine. Lay a yoga mat over a hard floor for traction and practice in loose clothing with your feet bare.

One key to ashtanga is *ujjayi* breathing: With your mouth closed, slowly inhale and exhale deeply from the back of the throat, which produces a distinctive, meditative hiss and generates body heat, thanks to the large exchange of air. Hold one asana for five to eight breaths before moving immediately on to the next pose.

To perform ashtanga properly, you should do the following push-up leg thrust between poses. Warning: It's not easy.

Sit on a mat with your palms on either side of you. At the same time, lift your legs and push down with your palms so that only your hands touch the floor. In one motion, bend your legs into your torso and swing them underneath and then behind you, landing in a straight-legged, bent-armed, push-up position. Gently push forward with your toes while straightening your arms. Your shoulders should be directly over your wrists, and your spine should be arched. Now use your hips to help lift you into an upside-down V pose—the "Downward Dog." Bend your legs and hop them forward, between your arms, landing in a seated position with legs straight again.

Another caution: Be careful not to strain; yoga is a controlled stretch. Also, always see a doctor before starting any rigorous exercise routine.

1. **TRIANGLE** Spread your feet about a yard apart. Bend to the left so that your outstretched arms windmill until your right hand points toward the ceiling and your left to the floor. Keep legs and hips in line as you twist your torso and gaze upward. Repeat to the opposite side.

2. **SHOULDER STAND** Lie on your back. Keeping your legs together, lift your hips and bring your palms to the small of your back. Now extend your legs skyward with your toes pointed. Make sure your neck isn't strained.

3. **BENT-LEG TWIST** Sit with your left leg straight and your right leg bent. Rotate clockwise from

the waist and wedge your bent left arm against the outside of your right thigh; your right arm should extend behind you, palm on the floor. Repeat the pose to the opposite side.

4. **FORWARD BEND** Standing with your legs straight and your feet hip-width apart, bend at the waist and try to hook the index and middle fingers of each hand around each big toe while letting your head dangle. Take the sting out of your hamstrings by drawing your quadriceps toward your pelvis and relax your shoulder blades so that the stretch is focused in your legs and midsection.

5. **MODIFIED FISH POSE** Lie flat with your legs straight, your arms at your sides and your palms facing down; now arch your back, rolling your head so that your crown is resting on the floor. Increase the arch in your middle back by using your hands to press into the floor.

GREGORY HEISLER

existence out in the world. Ashtanga's meditative qualities can actually be *heard:* The asana room sounds like a giant scuba regulator, with each student producing a hollow hiss while he or she practices what's called *ujjayi*, or "triumphant breath." By narrowing the throat and slowly, rhythmically, forcing air in and out of the nostrils five times with each pose, you supply your body with oxygen and your brain with a metronome. That consistent beat is what helps settle the mind so that you become simultaneously calm and undistracted, yet remain highly aware, like an athlete in the Zone. But what's proving messy is trying to clear my thoughts of the everyday enemies of yogic equipoise— anger, doubt, and despair, among many others— particularly when I'm feeling a lot of them toward my instructor.

"You do *upavishta konasana*," Guruji says one morning. This has become my most dreaded pose. Unless you have a body like overdone vermicelli, the asana is a horrible concoction whereby, in a sitting position, you grab your feet while your legs are straight and widely splayed and then attempt to lean forward at the waist so that you can set your chest on the ground.

I calmly perform my half-baked version. Then Jois gives me that extra guru *oomph.*

"Touch your chin," he gruffly urges while pressing a waxy foot on one of my thighs and kneeing me in the back until I do an ashtanga face-plant.

"You breathe!" he demands.

I'm sure the pose looks as impressive as when Jois did it for Krishnamacharya. And yet there is

## 10 REASONS TO PRACTICE YOGA

1. Improves balance.
2. Calms the mind; reduces stress.
3. Reputedly lowers blood pressure.
4. Increases flexibility.
5. Improves posture.
6. Helps ward off sports injuries.
7. Boosts endurance and sports performance.
8. Reputedly relieves mild depression and helps alleviate asthma symptoms.
9. Ashtanga yoga burns roughly 440 calories per hour (based on a 175–pound man).
10. A lot of very flexible women take yoga classes.

no peace, no healthy indifference, as I pant while a terrifying agony runs up my back and down my legs. In the spasmodic aftermath I can't understand why an enlightened being is yanking me two angry steps back with every spiritual inch I move forward.

That afternoon I sulk poolside at the Southern Star, a popular yogi hangout. I wander over to John Scott, a yoga instructor from New Zealand, who has been to Mysore nine times. He has already consoled me on days when the Shakti power seems to be short-circuiting.

"Guruji doesn't want to hurt you. If he asks, 'Why you fearing?' then ask yourself, 'What really *is* there to fear?'" says Scott in a soft Kiwi accent. "When Guruji gives you a strong adjustment, he wants you to learn to surrender to the unknown." I realize that Scott is right; the guru has been pushing me to find in myself one of the great survival tools for the studio, no less life. Fear, it's true, has been making my body stiff and my mind rigid. How much agony am I experiencing in the studio, really, that I haven't endured through years of sports? The philosophy goes against what was instilled in me as a never-say-uncle punk in the schoolyard, but all these years I

was wrong: It's actually far braver to yield than to fight back; and besides, implies Scott, pain is only a passing sensation. "Physical issues are also emotional issues," he says. "You may have gotten into this for the fitness, but at a certain point spirituality takes over the journey."

Twenty-eight days is a long vacation for Americans but not a scratch on the timeline of a Hindu existence, once you account for reincarnations. So I'm not entirely surprised that by the last day of my trip I've been sucked into the disorienting vortex that grabs so many naive Westerners on an eastward quest: I feel as if I'm groping for the way to yoga's starting blocks instead of crossing a karmic finish line.

I am, however, planning to go out with a yogic bang.

Guruji is holding my hips as I bend backward into the hated bow pose. "Touch your feet," he commands. I claw at the mat, my fingertips in search of my heels. I'm thinking about the 12 long inches that still separates them.

But at least I'm thinking, and I'm breathing triumphantly, and there is no murky fear.

I go maybe another inch before Guruji pulls me up. "Gradually is coming," he says, his warm, odorless breath meeting my sweaty cheeks. "You take patience."

He tells me to sit down and, while keeping my legs straight, bend over and grab my feet. Then he climbs on my back like a frog onto a lily pad, teetering as his weight folds me in half.

As Jois stretches my spine, his belly presses against my lumbar with every deep, clear breath,

and I try my best to synchronize our breathing. When the guru grabs my feet, his electricity finds its conductor.

Then my mind drifts uncontrollably: I'm overcome with the fear that my hamstrings are about to snap.

—ANDREW TILIN

TAI CHI

# Slow Your Nerves

TOUGH GUYS don't get much softer-looking than William C.C. Chen. No matter. Receiving a blow from the easygoing 64-year-old tai chi chuan teacher feels like getting hit by a sledgehammer.

Ditto for Morihei Ueshiba. In his later years, the founder of the martial-arts form aikido was a fragile-looking bald fellow with a scraggly gray beard who regularly tossed around young studs as if they were Nerf balls.

The ability of small, benign-appearing people to level explosive power against their foes is the hallmark of the martial arts' apparent triumph of mind over body, and there's no more dramatic example than tai chi chuan (pronounced "tie-chee-chwann"). Literally "supreme ultimate fist," tai chi chuan, or tai chi for short, is a series of foot and hand

*If any thing is sacred the human body is sacred.*

**— WALT WHITMAN**

strikes and evasive maneuvers strung together in slow, flowing motions, or "forms."

The continuous, full-body movements of tai chi stimulate your muscles' sensitivity, raise your heart rate, and oxygenate your blood; they also boost flexibility, coordination, and strength. And ultimately, as the San Diego Cardiac Center Medical Group concluded in its studies of tai chi and yoga, "muscular activity with an internally directed focus . . . [has] significant mental and physical value." In other words, body and mind are one.

"The whole idea of tai chi chuan is to slow your nerves," says Chen. "When you keep your mind and body relaxed, your whole self loosens up, your circulation gets better, and you start to feel your energy flow." It's tai chi's deliberate, fluid maneuvers—almost as if you're swimming through the air—

that differentiate it from the so-called "hard" martial arts like karate (though Chen says hard and soft styles are simply "like PCs and Macs; the same things that just work a little differently") and that make it particularly appealing to athletes recovering from injuries, to people looking for a low-impact workout, and to anyone interested in learning a nonfighting art.

While talk of "energy flow" may be too New Agey for you engineers out there, there's a growing body of hard science backing up tai chi's benefits: Research shows that the exercise lowers blood pressure and improves cardiovascular fitness, balance, and coordination, all while diminishing stress, anxiety, and depression. "Tai chi surprised me," says Deborah Young, Ph.D., assistant professor of medicine at the Johns Hopkins University School of Medicine, who conducted a study on the effect of aerobic exercise on hypertension. Half of her subjects did aerobics, half practiced tai chi. She expected 12 weeks of moderate aerobic exercise to show a far greater effect on blood pressure than 12 weeks of slow-motion tai chi. It didn't. The aerobic group's systolic blood pressure fell by an average of 8.4 millimeters of mercury, compared with an average of 7 millimeters in the tai chi group. "The differences were not significant," says Young, "plus we never suspected that such light-intensity exercise would even be sufficient to drop blood pressure."

Young's research is hardly unsupported:

• In a similar English study, subjects doing aerobics and tai chi all saw their systolic blood pressure fall significantly, but only those practicing the latter experienced a decrease in diastolic pressure as well.
• Research conducted at La Trobe University in Australia found that tai chi reduced levels of stress hormones just as effectively as meditation and brisk walking did and was even more effective in doing so than reading.
• A study at the Center for Rehabilitation Medicine at Emory University in Georgia showed that elderly people in a tai chi program experienced significant boosts in balance and an elevated "sense of well-being."

Tai chi, however, isn't just mobile meditation; it's a martial art. No one knows exactly when and how it started, but one Chen Chang Shen is thought of as its modern father. In the mid-1700s he taught an art that was both hard and fast and slow and soft to a handful of family members and a particularly eager neighbor named Yang Lu Shann. From Chen, and then Yang, we get tai chi's three main styles: Chen, Wu, and Yang, all of which are characterized by measured, graceful attacking and defensive moves.

Stick with tai chi long enough and you'll progress from doing these movements with an imaginary opponent to working with a real one in an advanced series called "push-hands."

Even in combat, tai chi continues to cultivate the *chi* (inner energy) from a point in your abdomen two inches below your navel called the *dan tien*. (Western athletic trainers call this sacred spot "the core.") The power of tai chi takes years to develop, but William Chen says it has less to do with cultivating mystical strength than it does with simple body mechanics. By keeping your body loose and your mind clear and by using the strength of your *dan tien*, you can redirect your opponent's force at just the right moment and appear to have superhuman power.

"Just think about a bullet and a small amount of gunpowder," says Chen. "With the right amount of tension, suddenly that bullet explodes out of the gun with incredible force. A person has to control his muscles like that."

## Wave Hands Like Clouds and Other Tai Chi Basics

"Proper posture is one of the key goals of tai chi. Begin by imagining you're a marionette," says Brooklyn-based tai chi instructor Rubin Torres, "as if you're being held upright lightly with a string." Your back should be straight yet loose and relaxed. Evenly distribute your weight over both feet, slightly bend your knees, and keep your shoulders rounded, your arms loose at your sides, your eyes wide open but not focusing on anything, and your tongue resting lightly on the top of your mouth with your teeth slightly clenched. Breathe through your nose. Exercise in loose clothing and soft-soled shoes (or with feet bare). Practitioners normally exercise in the morning and again in the evening.

To get a taste of tai chi, try the following six moves, taken from its primary twenty-four movements. Because tai chi's forms flow gracefully from one to the next without interruption, you'll need personal instruction to learn transition maneuvers and get the full effect.

JOE MCNALLY

Descend and stand on single leg.

### 1. WHITE CRANE SPREADS WINGS.
Stand with your knees slightly bent, most of your weight on your right leg and your left leg forward. Raise your right arm, palm facing in, and extend your left arm to your side, with palm down and wrist turned in slightly.

### 2. WAVE HANDS LIKE CLOUDS.
Position your bent left arm in front of your chest, palm facing in; move your right arm, palm down, to your right side. Without moving your arms, rotate slowly at your waist to the left as you step with your left foot. Switch arm positions, turn right, and step with your right foot. Do this sequence three times.

### 3. SINGLE WHIP.
With your knees slightly bent, extend your right arm to the side, making a small circle with your hand, as if you were turning a door handle. As you turn, squeeze your fingers together and bend your wrist to form what resembles the beak of a pecking bird.

Now lift your left hand in front of you and push it forward.

### 4. STEP BACK AND ROLL ARMS.
With your legs bent and your weight supported by your right leg, extend your left hand, palm facing up, elbow bent. Meanwhile, roll your right arm forward as if you were about to strike someone with your fingertips.

### 5. WORK AT SHUTTLES.
Lift your left hand, your palm facing forward, in a blocking pose until it's just above your left temple. As you do this, push your right hand in front of your chest in a striking position. Alternate your hand positions three times.

### 6. DESCEND AND STAND ON SINGLE LEG.
Step out to the side with your right leg, keeping your left leg straight. Form a hook with your right hand, and sweep your left arm across your chest, ending along your left leg.

—CARL HOFFMAN

# Stretch for Power

PILATES HAS BEEN generating much media attention of late, from which a guy might deduce that the method is all about medieval-looking exercise machines equipped with leather straps and pulleys and of interest only to spandex-clad women who've accepted Madonna as their personal-fitness savior. But that would be a mistake.

"We're getting manly men involved," says Elyssa Rossenberg, the associate director of the Pilates Studio of New York, "and we're kicking their butts." The evidence: good reviews from some Cincinnati Reds and San Francisco '49ers players and an article in *Trucking '98* magazine about drivers using Pilates ("puh-LAH-teez") to counter the spine-squeezing effects of sitting for a living.

The exercise routine was developed almost 75 years ago by Joseph H. Pilates, a rickets-plagued German who transformed himself into Mr. Body Beautiful. By the '50s, he had become a guru to New York dance types. Today the stiff-limbed are filing into hundreds of certified Pilates studios across the country for sessions with such strength and flexibility machines as the Universal Reformer and the Cadillac, which Pilates designed during World War I so that the wounded could exercise in hospital beds. But the same principles of proper breathing and muscle control are at work in mat exercises you can do at home.

The idea is to concentrate on the midsection, what Pilates trainers call "the powerhouse," the area from the bottom of the rib cage to the top of the hipbones. If you increase the flexibility and strength of your abdominal muscles, the thinking goes, you'll also shore up your spine, which Pilates disciples believe is the key to a healthy body. In addition, your posture will improve, and your breathing will become deeper. The emphasis here is on a low number of repetitions done with precision, indeed with an almost Buddhist-like attention to process that has endeared the method to mind/body types of different persuasions.

This may sound like a lot of metaphysical freight to load on a humble sit-up. But give it a try with the following Pilates mat exercises. At the very least, you'll get a great ab workout.

**THE HUNDRED.** Lie back on a mat and bring your knees to your chest. Then push your legs toward the ceiling so your thighs are at a 45-degree angle to the mat; keep your heels together and your feet turned out, and try not to bend your knees. Tuck your chin to your chest and bring your head up, tightening your abdominals. Holding this position, pump your arms (held straight, palms down) as if you were doing a stiff-arm basketball dribble. Inhale for five pumps; exhale for five pumps. That's one rep—do 10 (hence, "the Hundred").

**ROLL-UP.** Lie on a mat with legs straight and arms extended behind your head. Bring up your arms and then your head (with chin to chest), rolling over from the waist until your hands reach your toes. Your body should make a C. Then slowly roll back down, "one vertebra at a time," in Pilates-speak. Exhale on the roll-up; inhale on the roll-down. Repeat three to five times.

**ROLL LIKE A BALL.** Sit on a mat and bend your knees, bringing your feet in until your heels touch your butt and you're in a "ball" position. Wedge your hands between your thighs and your lower legs, keeping your chin to your chest. Now tip back toward the mat; then roll forward into the seated position, breathing normally. Repeat up to six times.

**DOUBLE LEG STRETCH.** Lie back on the mat, bring your knees to your chest, and grasp your ankles. Then inhale, and raise your arms above your head, in line with your ears, as you extend your legs at a 45-degree angle to the mat. Exhale and bring your knees and hands back to the starting position. Repeat 5 to 10 times.

—JOSEPH HOOPER

## 100 QUICK FIXES

# A Cheat Sheet for the Healthy Male

IN 1964, when Robert DeBusk was a young-buck intern at Boston City Hospital, he experienced a small but significant revelation that he says has stayed with him. Climbing 60 to 90 flights of stairs a day, he lost 12 pounds in two weeks. "I lost that weight without breaking a sweat," he says.

Today, at age 56, DeBusk still weighs 185 pounds, from which he hasn't deviated by more than 5 pounds through the years. He bikes five miles round-trip to the Stanford University School of Medicine, where he's a professor of medicine and cardiology. If he has to do errands in nearby Palo Alto, he gets there by pushing pedals. It's faster than driving in traffic, but it is also an example of his attitude about exercise: Do a little; gain a lot. A philosophy that works, studies say, better than a dramatic self-improvement campaign with a strict deadline.

Although every man has a personal wish list—run a marathon, eat healthier, lose 10 pounds, last longer in bed—it is all too often beyond his grasp. "Most of us are creatures of habit," says psychologist Alan Elkin, director of the Stress Management & Counseling Center in New York and author of *Stress Management for Dummies.* "Major life transformations like losing weight and getting in shape demand lifestyle adjustments that are more ambitious than most people's tolerance for change."

The solution? Break goals into manageable pieces, biting off only what you can chew comfortably. "Don't set out to lose 10 pounds," advises Elkin. "That's too daunting. Instead, commit to losing one pound a month. In a year, you're 10 pounds lighter."

But how can you lose that one pound? More easily than you might think. We've compiled 100 small changes that can add to your fitness and well-being. Each by itself is no big deal, but that's the point. One small change often leads to another. (Many of these pointers are expanded in essays throughout the health section.)

## Exercise

1. Divide up your exercise. In one study of men who walked briskly five days a week for 12 weeks, those who split their daily jaunt into three 10-minute sessions experienced the same fitness gains and weight loss (an average of 4 pounds) as those who walked in straight 30-minute shots. So lack of time is no excuse.

2. Do three minutes of office calisthenics. Although they won't work muscles through their entire range of motion, these simple exertion exercises can tone and strengthen, says Bryant Stamford, Ph.D., of the University of Louisville. Hold each for six seconds and repeat 10 times. 1. Palm press, for the pecs (force hands together). 2. Desk curl, for biceps (place palms face-up on bottom of desk and press upward). 3. Wall squats, for quads.

3. Exercise after eating. Riding a bike or walking after a meal almost doubles your resting metabolic rate for several hours, according to Stamford. That means when you watch the late news afterward, you'll be burning twice the calories you would have if you had sat down right after dinner.

4. Run on sand or grass. According to researchers in Italy, running on softer, uneven surfaces can burn 40 percent more calories than running on hard, even surfaces like asphalt and cement.

5. Set your workout to music. One study's subjects were able to pedal 30 percent longer on stationary bikes while listening to tunes.

6. Meditate before working out. A University of Glasgow study found that meditating 8 to 15 minutes a day for two weeks lessened the physiological toll of running. Participants' heart rates, for example, dropped 2 to 15 beats per minute at training pace and 4 to 12 at race pace.

7. Pedal in low gear. Cyclists who pedaled at 90 rpm in a lower gear burned almost 10 percent more calories than

the group that cruised at 60 rpm in a higher gear in the same amount of time.

8. Swim or use a rowing or cross-country skiing machine. A 1994 University of Wisconsin at La Crosse study found that activities that involve arms *and* legs burn about 55 percent more calories.

9. Lay out your workout clothes before going to bed. Put them on first thing in the morning and don't take them off until you do some sort of exercise.

10. Boost your aerobic workout from one to two or more times a week. Among other benefits, it reduces the risk of diabetes by up to 39 percent.

11. Set the treadmill at a 10 percent incline. Studies by Kenneth Cooper, M.D., at the Cooper Clinic in Dallas show that if you do you'll burn 40 more calories.

12. Hit the stairs and live longer. Researchers at Johns Hopkins University School of Medicine say you can gain an extra two years of life with just six minutes of stairclimbing a day. So whenever you can, take the stairs instead of the elevator or escalator.

13. Work your heart rate down. Two months of working out on a cross-country machine every day can drop your resting pulse 10 beats per minute.

14. Do compound lifts in the weightroom. Exercises that work two or more muscle groups (such as squats, bench presses, lat pull-downs, and leg presses) can burn up to 50 percent more calories than ones that work only single groups (such as biceps curls and leg extensions).

15. Walk backward. Retro-walking burns 38 percent to 119 percent more calories (depending on your speed) than walking forward at the same pace.

16. Do 10 minutes of treadmill exercise to reduce blood pressure. In one study, the blood pressure of hypertensive subjects dropped significantly for 30 minutes after a 10-minute treadmill workout. After three weeks of these sessions, blood pressure stayed down. Studies show that regular exercise in general lowers diastolic blood pressure 3 to 15mm Hg, and systolic 5 to 25.

17. Exercise in the late afternoon, if you can. That's when most people's heart rate, manual dexterity, and reaction time are highest.

18. Limber up before breakfast. Here is a simple yoga posture you can do while waiting for your toast to pop up. Called the Dog Pose, it stretches the glutes and increases flexibility, especially in hamstrings. Kneel on all fours with your hands directly under your shoulders and knees under your hips. Raise your butt in the air so that your arms and legs are straight and your weight is on your palms and the balls of your feet. Push your heels to the floor and breathe deeply, holding the position for one minute.

19. Warm up to make exercise easier. Muscles work best at 100 to 104 degrees—so before you work out, warm up. Five to 10 minutes of light exercise—jogging in place or doing jumping jacks—followed by a few minutes of gentle stretching improves mechanical efficiency and also increases the flow of blood to muscles. Both of which make exercise easier and reduce the risk of injury.

20. Take a 20-minute swim to help prevent cancer. A quick crawl in the pool stimulates the muscles of the large intestine, shortening the transit time of food and reducing your risk of colon cancer. Regular exercise in general can reduce your risk of developing colon cancer by 30 percent to 75 percent.

21. Cool down to make the next day easier. Five to 10 minutes of cooling down after you work out—even just slowly marching in place is enough—make a difference in recovery. Lactic acid, which causes muscle fatigue, decreases 50 percent faster when you cool down before relaxing.

22. Be a role model. Here is a sure way to keep you *and* your spouse exercising: A survey found that a child with one physically active parent is twice as likely to exercise as a child with two sedentary parents. If both parents are exercisers, the child is six times more likely to follow suit.

—GARY LEGWOLD

## Diet

23. Substitute low-fat potato chips or baked tortilla chips for their full-calorie versions. You'll save about 20 calories per serving and cut fat by up to 80 percent.

24. Switch from whole to low-fat milk and from low-fat to no-fat yogurt. The difference in fat between whole (4 percent) and low-fat (1 percent) milk is more than 5 grams a cup, which means that every 2 cups substituted eliminates the equivalent of the fat found in a regular serving of fries.

25. Drink espresso instead of cappuccino. A half-cup of whole milk, about the amount in a standard cup of cappuccino, yields 75 calories and 4 grams of fat.

26. Remove the skin from chicken before cooking. White-meat chicken with skin has almost 150 percent more calories than the skinless version and six times as much fat.

27. Pick roast beef over chef salad. An extra-lean roast-beef sandwich with mustard instead of mayonnaise contains only about 160 calories and 3 grams of fat, while a small chef salad with ham and cheese contains roughly 320 calories and 28 grams of fat.

28. Choose the leanest cuts of beef. Select cuts are lower in fat than choice or prime. Select sirloin contains 15 percent fewer calories and almost 35 percent less fat than choice.

29. Make soups and stews a day in advance, chill, and skim the fat before reheating. Each tablespoon skimmed saves 120 calories, most of them from fat.

30. Use a nonstick skillet and cooking spray when sautéing meat. Rub chicken breasts with an herb-and-spice mixture; then "dry sauté" them for six to eight minutes, turning once, over medium-high heat. This cooking method amounts to a savings of about 30 grams of fat and 300 calories over cooking with three tablespoons of margarine.

31. Use only one yolk in your weekly three-egg omelet. You'll eliminate 3,500 calories during the course of a year and help keep your cholesterol level down as well.

32. Go to the bottom for the freshest produce. Supermarket clerks often put the items that have been sitting around on top of the pile. If you want fresher romaine, start digging.

33. Substitute whole-grain bread and breadsticks for their white-flour cousins. You'll triple the fiber in your diet.

34. Use jam instead of butter. You'll save up to four grams of fat with every teaspoon.

35. Eat more garlic. A half a clove a day cuts your heart-attack risk by about 18 percent by reducing your cholesterol. (Stephen Warshafsky, M.D., and colleagues at the New York Medical College in Valhalla reanalyzed five previous studies of the garlic-cholesterol connection and concluded that a half a clove a day cuts cholesterol by 9 percent. And, according to a study in the *Yale Heart Book*, for every 1 percent decrease in cholesterol, heart-attack risk drops about 2 percent.)

36. Dilute fruit juices and flavored drinks to cut calories in half. Also, watch out for flavored seltzers that are, in fact, soft drinks and for "natural" drinks, which may contain 100 calories or more a serving.

37. Choose the right candy. Chuckles, jelly beans, and spice drops all contain around 100 calories and no fat per serving. Just one Reese's Peanut Butter Cup has 120 calories and seven grams of fat. And when was the last time you ate just one?

38. Have a fajita instead of an enchilada. Three beef fajitas (with no cheese or sour cream) contain 10 grams of fat, while three beef enchiladas contain more than 20 grams.

39. Start your day with a hearty breakfast. People who don't eat breakfast are more likely to overeat later in the day. Furthermore, an adequate breakfast (one that equals about 25 percent of your daily caloric intake) raises your metabolism by 20 percent for four to five hours. So think of your eating day as a pyramid: Start big and eat progressively smaller meals as the day goes on.

40. Substitute turkey for salami and ham and cheese. Three ounces of turkey have about 100 calories and 3 grams of fat, whereas three ounces of salami have more than 350 calories and 30 grams of fat.

41. Forget pie a la mode. Have the pie *or* the ice cream. Most pies weigh in at a couple of hundred calories and 10 grams of fat per slice; most ice cream, at more than that.

42. Choose the right popcorn. Low-fat microwave varieties contain two-thirds the calories of regular microwave popcorn and less than half the fat.

43. Pick one food each month and substitute a low-fat version. Low- or no-fat salad dressing, for example, has about 75 percent less fat than the regular kind; part-skim-milk mozzarella has half the fat of whole-milk varieties.

TODD GRAVELINE

44. Eat hamburgers instead of cheeseburgers. There are typically 100 calories and 9 grams of fat in a single slice of American cheese.

45. Eat more tasty, low-calorie foods. The following contain less than 100 calories and no more than a gram of fat: six large shrimps, one half cup of cooked rice, one half pound of strawberries, a pickle, a bottle of certain light beers, a fig bar.

46. Make a leaner, more flavorful burger. Mix three quarters of a pound of lean ground meat with one-half cup of cooked rice, a tablespoon of parsley dill, a tablespoon of steak sauce, salt, and pepper (makes four). You've just cut the fat in your burger by 25 percent.

47. Substitute a glass of water for a soda once a week. You'll save 7,500 calories over a year, which is the equivalent of more than two pounds.

48. Bring an apple or a carrot to work. If you eat it as a snack instead of a serving of potato chips, for example, you'll save 10 grams of fat, cut calories by 50 percent or more, and boost your intake of nutrients and fiber.

49. Have a piece of fruit with each meal. The National Cancer Institute recommends five servings of fruits and vegetables a day: Have a piece of fruit with every meal and you'll need only a salad and one cooked vegetable to make your daily five.

50. Slim down the salad bar. Take two pita pockets (100 calories, 1 gram of fat each), cram them full of fresh vegetables, and drizzle on some low-fat dressing. You'll eat less fat, fewer calories, and more fiber than if you had chosen a mayonnaise-drenched salad or one loaded with bacon bits and croutons.

51. Eat cereal for lunch or dinner once a week. Many cereals fill you up with a minimum of calories and fat. But choose wisely: General Mills' Oatmeal Crisp with Almonds contains 230 calories and only 4 grams of fiber, while Kellogg's All-Bran with Extra Fiber has 180 calories and 30 grams of fiber per cup, with milk.

52. Have low-fat or fat-free frozen yogurt. For every half cup you indulge in, you'll save at least 60 calories and 10 grams of fat.

53. Choose frozen desserts that are individually wrapped. They build in portion control.

54. Whip up a fruit drink instead of a milkshake. When you're at home and craving something sweet, combine a cup of orange juice, a banana (peel and freeze them as they get too ripe and you'll always have one on hand), and some ice in a blender. It makes a frothy treat with about 200 calories and 1 gram of fat. Compare that to a milkshake made with a cup of whole milk, a half-cup of generic ice cream, and a tablespoon of chocolate syrup: 400 calories, 21 grams of fat.

55. Drink a glass of cold water before every meal. It stems your appetite without adding a calorie.

56. Switch to low- or no-fat mayo. Regular mayonnaise sports big numbers: Many tuna-salad sandwiches contain as much fat as a Big Mac (about 35 grams). Use low-fat mayo, which has up to 90 percent less fat and a quarter of the calories.

57. Don't go nuts. The package of peanuts served on airplanes contains up to 15 grams of fat, about a quarter of your daily allotment (67 grams). Don't ask for seconds.

58. Skip the French fries once a week. It will save you at least 520 grams of fat a year—more than a week's recommended intake.

59. Choose ham instead of bacon. Lean ham (or Canadian bacon) weighs in at 6 grams of fat per serving; three slices of bacon, at about 10.

60. Cut meat calories. If you're cooking for four, buy a piece of meat that weighs about a pound to keep each portion to a modest four ounces.

61. Use butter sense. Cut the amount of butter you use on vegetables gradually by mixing it in equal parts with lemon juice. Gradually increase the amount of lemon juice until you've eliminated the butter.

62. Stir it up. Prepare stir-fries, soups, and stews using meat as an ingredient rather than the main attraction.

63. Order thin-crust pizza. Thin-crust varieties have just two-thirds the calories of thick-crust.

64. And hold the meat. Pepperoni, for instance, can increase the fat content of pizza by a third.

65. Alternate alcoholic drinks with nonalcoholic ones. Not only does alcohol add between 100 and 180 calories; it is metabolized in such a way as to put weight around your middle.

66. Eat white-fleshed fish. A serving of cod contains less than 100 calories and less than one gram of fat, while the dark-fleshed salmon, for example, will sock you with 120 calories and five and a half grams of fat.

—MARK BITTMAN

## Lifestyle

67. Stand up. Standing an additional hour over the course of a day can burn an extra 10 to 20 calories—that's 3,650 to 7,300 (a pound or two of fat) a year.

68. Pace yourself. About one calorie is burned for every 15 steps paced, which can add up as you yak on the phone,

brush your teeth, or work on that speech you're giving next week.

69. Park a block or two away from your destination. It can burn an extra 30 calories a day, or three pounds of fat a year.

70. Spend 15 minutes cleaning up. Straightening up the kitchen, cellar, or garage for just 15 minutes burns about 40 calories—four pounds a year if you clean up ever day.

71. Walk before you talk. If you walk to another part of the house to talk to your wife or children—rather than sitting and bellowing, Archie Bunker style—you burn three calories or so. Big deal? Well, walking, not shouting, five times a day could mean a pound of fat loss in a year. And less stress for everyone.

72. Do two errands a week on foot. In one study of heart disease, researchers found that 20 minutes or more of walking was associated with a 33 percent lower incidence of heart problems.

73. Breathe deeply during sex. Sex therapist Bernie Zilbergeld, Ph.D., author of *The New Male Sexuality*, recommends deep breathing from the diaphragm as a quick, easy way to improve ejaculatory control.

74. Let her get on top. This position has advantages for both sexes: It eliminates the physical stress a man experiences while supporting himself in the missionary position—a stress that can trigger quick ejaculation—and allows the woman more freedom of movement.

75. Keep a bottle of water-based lubricant by your bed. "Many women do not produce enough natural lubricant to allow comfortable intercourse, and many who do find that a lubricant turns them on a lot more," explains Louanne Cole Weston, Ph.D., a clinical sexologist in Sacramento.

76. Short-circuit sudden stress. Stress expert Robert Cooper, Ph.D., has devised a five-step "instant calming sequence": 1. Keep breathing. Stress often makes people hold their breath, which increases anxiety. 2. Smile. It helps you to relax. 3. Maintain good posture. Stress often causes slumping, which increases tension. 4. Accentuate the positive. Imagine a wave of relaxation washing over you; picture yourself on vacation lying in a hammock. 5. Take some control. Even when things seem to be veering out of control, you still have power. Use it.

77. Call a good friend once a week. During the course of a nine-year study conducted by Leonard Syme, Ph.D., a professor of epidemiology, and Lisa Berkman, Ph.D., those adults with the most social connections had half the death rate as those with the fewest.

78. Take 100 to 400 international units of vitamin E each day. A recent Harvard study of 40,000 male health professionals showed that those who took at least 100 IU of vitamin E daily suffered 37 percent fewer heart attacks.

79. Speed pain relief with caffeine. A 65-milligram dose of caffeine boosts the pain-relieving power of aspirin by about 40 percent, according to a study in the *Journal of the American Medical Association*. Try Anacin, a commercial aspirin-caffeine combination, or take two aspirins with Coke, coffee, or tea.

TODD GRAVELINE

80. Check your vitamin label. Vitamins can't do any good unless they dissolve in the gut. Some don't. The better brands should dissolve within 45 minutes. Look for a statement saying the product passes the dissolution test.

81. Buy the cheapest vitamins you can find. Inexpensive store brands are just as pure and effective as expensive national brands. Quite often they're identical.

82. Make an appointment for a checkup on your birthday every year. Women live, on average, 7 years longer than men (79 versus 72), partly because they are better about having annual physical exams. Among the most important tests for men: blood pressure and cholesterol. If you're 50 or over, the PSA, the early-detection test for prostate cancer, is also a must.

83. Get a doctor you like. If you're unhappy with your physician, ask five friends or coworkers for recommendations; call the doctor who receives the best reviews and also accepts your insurance. Finding the right M.D. gives you one less excuse to put off that annual physical.

84. Know when to call the doctor. Anne Simons, M.D., coauthor of Before You Call the Doctor, says you should call if a fever doesn't subside after two days of taking aspirin or another painkiller; you suffer an injury that does not respond to RICE (Rest, Ice, Compression, and Elevation) within 72 hours; you have severe pain for 12 hours; you experience persistent low-level pain or achiness for six weeks or a single symptom becomes multiple—nausea yields to headache and diarrhea, for instance.

85. Cover your ears. Every loud noise damages the microscopic hairs in the ears that transmit sound impulses to the brain. Once injured, these hairs do not grow back. To hold on to the hearing you have left, buy ear plugs.

86. Ask your parents and siblings about their health. Heredity is not destiny, but many serious illnesses run in families. If your parents, grandparents, or siblings had a fatal disease, you're at a greater-than-average risk of death from the same cause.

87. Take a sip when you pass a water fountain. You need more water than your thirst indicates. Metabolized food provides about 4 cups a day, but breathing, urinating, and nonathletic perspiration cost you 10 cups a day. That's a six-cup deficit before you even lace up your running shoes.

88. Get a flu shot every November. It doesn't provide absolute protection, but it cuts risk by about 80 percent for healthy adults.

89. Don't go barefoot in a health-club shower or locker room. Keep a pair of thongs or sandals in your locker and wear them religiously. On any given day, some 4 percent of Americans have athlete's foot—chances are someone at your club is one of them.

90. Wash your hands several times a day. People touch their noses unconsciously several times an hour; cold sufferers deposit the virus on hard, nonporous surfaces—doorknobs, countertops, telephones, and so forth. You may become infected when you touch a contaminated surface and then touch your own nose.

91. Watch your testicle health. Once a week when you are in the shower, roll each testicle gently from side to side in your fingers. If you come across a hard lump, call your doctor. A tumor is hard and painless, so if it hurts, it probably isn't cancerous—but it's always better to be sure.

92. Drink to your health. Moderate drinking helps prevent heart disease, according to many studies.

93. Head off a hangover. The darker the alcohol, the greater the hangover risk. If you're prone to head bangers after a night of drinking, skip the bourbon, Scotch, and red wine. Go instead with vodka or white wine.

94. Sip teas for indigestion or anxiety. A cup of peppermint or spearmint tea can settle an upset stomach, and chamomile can ease anxiety.

95. Laugh at least three times a day. It's no joke. William Frey, M.D., a professor emeritus of psychiatry at Stanford University, estimates that 100 laughs provide a muscular workout equivalent to about 10 minutes on a rowing machine. Laughter also increases pain tolerance and bolsters the immune system.

96. Leave the plastic at home. "Money troubles are a major cause of men's stress," says Alan Elkin, Ph.D., director of the Stress Management Counseling Center. Men spend impulsively when they're tense, and plastic slides out of the wallet much too easily. Bring cash and spontaneous buying will diminish. Or, if there are only a few places where you lose control—say, record or sporting-goods stores—take the cards out of your wallet before you visit them.

97. Take low doses of aspirin regularly. A Harvard study shows that half an aspirin (165 milligrams) a day reduces the risk of heart attack by about 40 percent. And according

**98. Take vitamin C in two doses.** Because vitamin C is quickly excreted, taking one tablet in the morning and one before bed keeps a steady level of the vitamin in your body.

**99. Buy a plant to protect yourself from indoor air pollutants.** For effective air cleaning, all you need are two plants—Boston fern, English ivy, spider plants, and potted palms are best—per 100 square feet of floor space.

**100. Pick a tip a month.** Adopt the one tip that would make the most difference to you now. Next month, adopt one more and add another every month after that. In just one year, you will have made a dozen positive changes that add to your health, energy, and well-being.

—MICHAEL CASTLEMAN

to researchers at the American Cancer Society, the same dose also cuts risk of colorectal cancer, the most lethal among nonsmokers, by about 40 percent. (Don't take aspirin if you have a clotting disorder, ulcer, any chronic gastrointestinal condition, or asthma.)

CHECKUPS

# Full Body Check

W E LIKE TO THINK that disease is self-evident. We like to think that we don't need a doctor as long as we restrain our bad habits and develop our good ones. We like to think the patterns of illness are as predictable as the seasons. As generalities, all of the above are true, which is why today's physicals are less about finding problems and more about preventing them.

For many men, nothing is more humbling than the moment when a physician tells them to drop their shorts—which could be one reason males shun regular checkups. The National Center for Health Statistics' 1998 figures show that just 62 percent of men surveyed saw a doctor in the past year, compared with 83 percent of women.

Is that such a bad thing? Although having regular checkups seems like a smart thing to do, the rationale for full-scale, top-to-bottom examinations has come into question over the years. In fact, during the mid-1980s, a federally appointed panel of health researchers—the U.S. Preventive Services Task Force—determined that exhaustive health checks didn't do much to improve survival rates in the general population. Only blood pressure, weight, and cholesterol tests and flu shots for people over age sixty were shown to save lives.

## Turn Your Head and Cough

I underwent a three-day blizzard of medical tests at the behest of *Men's Journal*, which sent me to experience firsthand what is arguably the best physical exam that money can buy: the Mayo Clinic's Executive Health Program. Designed as an intensive, one-stop health screen for busy execs in high-stress jobs, the examination costs several thousand dollars, lasts two to three days, and is far more intensive than the run-of-the-mill physical you'd get from your family physician.

Ironically, the things people associate most with a physical—the poking and prodding—consumed 10 minutes at best. Dr. Donald Hensrud, the director of the Executive Health Program, inspected my eyes, nose, ears, teeth, hair, nails, skin, and posture. He listened to my heart and lungs and felt my lymph glands, abdomen, underarms, and groin. After asking me to drop my drawers, he checked for testicular cancer. He conducted the standard hernia test and then told me to turn around, bend forward, and take a deep breath. I took quite a few deep breaths, as it happens. Using a lubricated glove, he spent a seemingly interminable 10 to 15 seconds with his finger in my rear, feeling for signs of rectum or prostate cancer.

At 34, I was statistically too young for this. The American Cancer Society doesn't recommend men having a digital rectal exam until age 40, because controversy surrounds the test's usefulness. At age 50—or 40, if you are African-American or have a family history of prostate trouble—an additional cancer screening is recommended, the PSA (prostate-specific antigen) blood test. (The medical community is also split on the need for a PSA test mostly because of the high number of false-positive results. But at least one study indicates that PSA tests can reduce the overall death rate from the disease.)

Medical exploration of your nether regions only intensifies as you age. At age 50 you should also have your rectum examined for cancer with a short, flexible device called a sigmoidoscope. Fortunately, I was also too young for a colorectal-cancer screening, even by the Mayo's rigorous standards. So, off for my chest X-ray I went. This test checked for lung cancer and other hidden problems.

The medical community agrees that even a 34-year-old needs to have his cholesterol monitored. The most accurate and useful blood test breaks down your high-density lipoprotein (you want to have at least 35 milligrams per deciliter of HDL, the so-called good cholesterol), low-density lipoprotein, or LDL (you want less than 160 milligrams per deciliter of this "bad" cholesterol), and another type of blood fat called triglycerides. (Less than 200 milligrams per deciliter is best.) Total cholesterol should be under

| HOW OFTEN SHOULD YOU HAVE A COMPLETE PHYSICAL? | |
|---|---|
| **Age Range** | **Recommended Frequency of Health Evaluation*** |
| 30s | Once every four years |
| 40s | Once every three years |
| 50s | Once every two years |
| 60s or older | Annually |
| * More frequent if individual medical issues warrant. | |

## WHAT TESTS SHOULD BE DONE WHEN

# RECOMMENDED TESTS FOR MEN—BASED ON THE MAYO CLINIC'S EXECUTIVE HEALTH PROGRAM

### BEFORE AGE 40

Blood pressure • Height–weight index • Immunization update • Waist circumference • Visual inspection of skin • Thorough physical inspection of body, including a stethoscope check of heart and lungs • Urinalysis • Blood tests: total cholesterol level; HDL cholesterol; LDL cholesterol; blood triglycerides; glucose level (diabetes); white–blood–cell level (leukemia or anemia); iron saturation; calcium; electrolyte; renal; and liver function

### ADD THESE AT 40

Digital rectal exam • Chest X–ray • EKG • Stress test

### ADD THESE AT 50

PSA (prostate–specific antigen) blood test* • Barium enema and flexible sigmoidoscopy every five years† • TSH blood test (thyroid function)

### ADD THESE AT 65

Hearing tests • Eye exam • Influenza vaccination • Pneumonia vaccination‡

*Yearly starting at age 40 for those with a family history of prostate cancer or for African-Americans. †For those with a relative (or relatives) who had colorectal cancer, screening should begin 10 years prior to the age the relative was when his or her cancer was diagnosed.
‡Earlier for those with diabetes or heart or lung disease.

---

200. For the record, my cholesterol profile was pretty good: HDL 42, LDL 129, total 191.

Next, I met a rail-thin registered dietitian named Mark Glen. Glen spent an hour and a half reviewing my daily food intake and dispensing unsurprising advice: Obey the food pyramid; get 25 grams of fiber or more a day by eating a plant-based diet. I listened, collected an assortment of pamphlets, promised to nibble on reduced-fat Wheat Thins instead of cheese, and promptly repaired to the local steakhouse.

But the next day's exercise electrocardiogram, or treadmill stress test, confirmed that my heart was doing well under pressure despite 92 grams of saturated fat from that T-bone. I was beginning to feel rather proud that I'd aced my Mayo physical when a hearing test, of all things, sent up a red flag. It appears I've lost the ability to detect high tones in my left ear. Bilateral hearing loss is common, especially in men, but a unilateral drop, I learn, could signal the presence of something serious: an acoustic neuroma (or brain tumor). So I was hustled over to a specialist who asked me whether I've ever fired guns or driven farm machinery. No, I've never operated a combine, but I did play bass in a new-wave power trio back in 1983. (A good physical causes you to reflect upon all your detours in life.) No brain tumor. A 100-watt bass amp and bad Police covers did my hearing in.

## Epilogue

All told, my two and a half days of testing cost $2,000. A few weeks later, Hensrud sent me a lengthy report outlining my health status. A life-insurance agent seemed measurably impressed when I told her I just got the thumbs-up from the Mayo Clinic. Still, my inner cynic wondered, *Was all that necessary?*

"When somebody comes here, they want a clean bill of health," says Hensrud. "And unless we've done some of these things, I can't give it to them. We're in the business of being complete."

—PAUL SCOTT

## HEART HEALTH

# Is Heart Disease in Your Future?

DESPITE CHANGES in our collective habits, cardiovascular disease remains the country's number-one killer, and in some form it afflicts one of every five adults in the United States. Approximately 450,000 American men die from it each year. So cardiovascular experts have been emphasizing the importance of identifying risk factors early.

A heart-disease score sheet, published in *Circulation: the Journal of the American Heart Association*, may become an important clinical test for determining heart-disease risk. The score sheet is based

on a series of groundbreaking findings from the celebrated Framingham Heart Study, a rich data collection that for the past half-century has taught the world how people develop coronary artery disease.

The original study tracked 5,209 healthy men and women between the ages of 30 and 60 who agreed to undergo health evaluations every 2 years. Back in 1948, doctors accepted that atherosclerosis—or hardening of the arteries—was a normal result of aging. Popular belief held that a person's blood pressure rose naturally as he got older in order to keep blood flowing through arteries narrowed by years of high-fat foods and other unhealthy habits. "In those days," says Dr. Daniel Levy, the study's director since 1995, "it was unconventional to think of diet as a risk factor."

Or cholesterol levels, smoking, obesity, or lack of exercise, for that matter. Framingham brought all of these factors into the American health-care lexicon with stunning effects. In the years since the study's results began trickling in, death rates from heart attack and stroke have fallen by more than half.

"The Framingham score sheet helps to motivate people," says its lead author, Dr. Peter Wilson, the director of laboratories at the Framingham Heart Study. "We think of it more as an educational tool than pure science."

The following questionnaire allows men to calculate their general risk of developing coronary disease in the next 10 years. Score yourself for each step; then add up the total points and locate your total in Step 7. If you don't like your results, take heart: By changing your lifestyle, you can reverse the damage done. Start with the suggestions in "Slash Your Risk" (page 154).

**—REBECCA VOELKER**

## THE FRAMINGHAM HEART STUDY TEST

| Step 1 | | Step 2 | | Step 3 | |
|---|---|---|---|---|---|
| AGE | POINTS | TOTAL CHOLESTEROL | | HDL (GOOD) CHOLESTEROL | |
| 30-34 | -1 | Under 160 | -3 | Under 35 | 2 |
| 35-39 | 0 | 160-199 | 0 | 35-44 | 1 |
| 40-44 | 1 | 200-239 | 1 | 45-49 | 0 |
| 45-49 | 2 | 240-279 | 2 | 50-59 | 0 |
| 50-54 | 3 | 280+ | 3 | 60+ | -2 |
| 55-59 | 4 | | | | |
| 60-64 | 5 | | | | |
| 65-69 | 6 | | | | |
| 70-74 | 7 | | | | |

### Step 4
BLOOD PRESSURE

The systolic number (the top figure) measures how much force your heart puts behind the flow of your blood, while the diastolic (the bottom number) measures how relaxed your arteries become between heartbeats. On the chart below, read down and across for your point score. For example, a reading of 120 over 82 scores zero.

| | DIASTOLIC | | | | |
| | Under 80 | 80–84 | 85–89 | 90–99 | 100+ |
|---|---|---|---|---|---|
| SYSTOLIC | | | | | |
| Under 120 | 0 | 0 | 1 | 2 | 3 |
| 120–129 | 0 | 0 | 1 | 2 | 3 |
| 130–139 | 1 | 1 | 1 | 2 | 3 |
| 140–159 | 2 | 2 | 2 | 2 | 3 |
| 160+ | 3 | 3 | 3 | 3 | 3 |

**Step 5**

ARE YOU DIABETIC?

Yes       2

No       0

**Step 6**

DO YOU SMOKE?

Yes       2

No       0

**Step 7**

Find your score on the chart below to determine your percentage risk for developing heart disease.

| POINTS | RISK (%) |
|---|---|
| Under 0 | 2 |
| 0 | 3 |
| 1 | 3 |
| 2 | 4 |
| 3 | 5 |
| 4 | 7 |
| 5 | 8 |
| 6 | 10 |
| 7 | 13 |
| 8 | 16 |
| 9 | 20 |
| 10 | 25 |
| 11 | 31 |
| 12 | 37 |
| 13 | 45 |
| 14+ | 53+ |

**Step 8**

How do you measure up with other men? Find your age category below and read across to compare your score (from Step 7) with those of average- and low-risk men in your age group.

| AGE | AVERAGE RISK (%) | LOW RISK (%) |
|---|---|---|
| 30–34 | 3 | 2 |
| 35–39 | 5 | 3 |
| 40–44 | 7 | 4 |
| 45–49 | 11 | 4 |
| 50–54 | 14 | 6 |
| 55–59 | 16 | 7 |
| 60–64 | 21 | 9 |
| 65–69 | 25 | 11 |
| 70–74 | 30 | 14 |

## SEVEN SECRETS FOR A GOOD HEART

- Stop smoking. Smoking contributes to nearly one-fifth of all heart-disease deaths by narrowing blood vessels and making the blood more prone to clogging.
- Drop pounds. According to data from the Framingham Heart Study, men who tip the scales at 30 percent over their ideal weight double their chances of heart disease.
- Eat a low-fat diet. The American Heart Association (AHA) recommends you get less than 30 percent of your total calories from fat and no more than 10 percent of those from the saturated kind—fats like butter and lard that are solid at room temperature.
- Combine a healthy diet with exercise. A study at Stanford University found that people who ate a low-fat diet but never exercised didn't lower their cholesterol significantly. Those who ate properly and worked out regularly for a year, however, experienced significant decreases in their LDL (bad) cholesterol.
- Don't dog it. Exercising vigorously for at least 30 minutes three to four days a week at 50 percent to 60 percent of your maximum heart rate obtains the greatest heart-health benefits, according to the AHA.
- Switch to olive oil. Studies show that monounsaturated fat, the kind found in olive oil, tends to lower LDL cholesterol while leaving good HDL levels intact.
- Eat oats. They're rich in water-soluble fiber, which surrounds LDL cholesterol in your gut and escorts it out of the body. You can also find soluble fiber in beans.

—JEFFREY J. CSATARI

SEMINAL HEALTH

# Taking Care of Your Plumbing

WE TAKE HOME plumbing for granted—until the sink backs up, which is why all the repair manuals urge preventive maintenance. The same goes for a man's reproductive plumbing. A little attention to prevention can minimize risk of annoying—

even potentially fatal—health problems down the road.

## Erections Forever

There's a lot more to an erection than having your honey unzip your pants. Physiologically, an erection is a complicated process, one that can easily go awry. No wonder that some 10 percent of men report erection problems and that when Viagra, the erection pill, was approved, its sales took off like a rocket.

When a sexually arousing thought registers in the brain, nerves in the penis release nitric oxide, which triggers a substance called cyclic GMP (guanosine monophosphate) in the cells of the penis's spongy erectile tissues. GMP causes the penile arteries to dilate, allowing increased inflow of blood, which fills the erectile tissues, producing an erection. As an erection grows, it also compresses the veins that carry blood out of the penis, which helps maintain it. After orgasm, an enzyme, phosphodiesterase type 5 (PDE5), breaks down GMP, reversing this process, and erection subsides.

When erection impairment develops, it's usually

DAVID REGAN

caused by (1) blood vessel (vascular) problems—not enough blood getting into the penis, (2) nerve problems, for example, a spinal-cord injury, or (3) both—as in diabetes, which damages the vascular and nervous systems, or chronic stress, which can disrupt the coordination between the two.

The key to preventing impotence is to keep your vascular and nervous systems healthy and working well together. On the vascular side, that means taking the same steps that prevent heart disease, because the factors that keep blood gushing into the penis are the same ones that keep it flowing smoothly into the heart:

- **Don't smoke.**
- **Get regular exercise.**
- **Keep your weight, cholesterol, and blood pressure at recommended levels.**

On the neurological side:

- **Shun narcotics.**
- **Limit your alcohol consumption.**

---

### THE RISE OF SEX SCIENCE

★**INDIA, CA. 1000 B.C.** Ayurvedic medical texts recommend rock salt from a mine in Sind as an effective sexual stimulant. The *Kamasutra* suggests that potency can be restored by drinking a tonic of clarified butter, honey, sugar, milk, licorice, and bulb juice. Alternative suggestion: imbibing a ram testicle that's been boiled in milk.

★**GREECE, CA. 315 B.C.** Aristotle notes the presence of a *baculum*, or "littlestick," inside the penises of the fox and the wolf. These cartilaginous structures aid in penetration. Later observers find the same thing in whales, though at more than two yards long, these bacula can hardly be called littlesticks. Humans lack this structure.

★**EGYPT, CA. 30 B.C.** Cleopatra dissolves pearls in vinegar and drinks the concoction; she credits the potion with her seduction of Julius Caesar and Mark Antony.

★**EUROPE, CA. 1350.** Erections thought to be boosted by ingesting a mixture of dried black ants and olive oil. Other miracle cures: topical anointment of the penis and vulva with jackal bile; lubrication of the penis with melted fat from camel humps; the use of leeches that have been allowed to rot in a dunghill as a penile ointment.

★**ENGLAND, 1605.** In *Macbeth*, Shakespeare observes that alcohol "provokes the desire, but it takes away the performance." Miller

Time is still nearly 400 years away.

★**PARIS, 1659.** The first shipment of cocoa from the tropics reaches France; Parisian doctors initially endorse it as a tonic but later wonder if it has "malevolent" aphrodisiac powers. Chocolate becomes a popular Valentine's Day gift.

★**ITALY, 1754.** Italian Lothario Casanova boosts his legendary sexual prowess by eating 48 oysters each morning, using a comely female breast as his plate.

- Ask your doctor if any medications you take have sexual side effects. Antidepressants are notorious for wilting erections (and libido).
- Manage your stress by learning to relax. Ever wonder why you look better hung after a hot shower? It's because heat is relaxing and, even without sexual arousal, more blood finds its way into your penis.

If you think your erections are not the stand-up guys they used to be, start with a complete physical exam to check for possible vascular or neurological problems. Lose weight. And if necessary, take medication to lower high cholesterol or blood pressure. (Just make sure that your blood-pressure medication doesn't cause erection impairment as a side effect.)

If you still need a boost, try Viagra. It dilates the penile arteries, providing the extra blood necessary for erection. But don't take Viagra if you take any nitrate drug for heart disease, especially nitroglycerine for angina. The combination of Viagra and nitrate drugs can be fatal.

Viagra is not the only medication that produces an erection. Yohimbine also works for many men. Ask your doctor about it.

Drugs can help produce an erection, but they can't repair a damaged relationship. If your relationship is stressful and your little guy is suffering as a result, consider sex therapy.

## Preserve Your Fertility

In about half of cases, infertility has to do with the man. The reason is that sperm cells are remarkably delicate, and an enormous number of things—many seemingly innocuous—can harm them.

A big one is heat. The scrotum hangs outside the body because the optimal temperature for creating healthy sperm is lower than normal body temperature. Although quick, hot showers don't depress sperm count, frequent extended soaks in hot tubs might. Prolonged periods of sitting with your legs together, as you might if you have a desk job or drive for a living, can also result in a lower count. Keep your legs apart to keep your testicles cool. Finally, varicose veins in the testicles (varicoceles) are linked to infertility, presumably because the extra blood in them exposes developing sperm to excess heat. Urologists can detect varicoceles with a simple manual exam. If you have any, they can be surgically removed in a simple operation.

Another cause of infertility is genital infection. If you're concerned, have your doctor test you for prostatitis and all the sexually transmissible diseases, especially chlamydia.

Drugs can be hell on sperm. Smokers tend to have lower sperm counts than nonsmokers. Other recreational drugs can also depress sperm count: alcohol, marijuana, cocaine, and narcotics. An

★**1912.** Sigmund Freud writes: "We must reckon with the possibility that something in the nature of the sexual instinct itself is unfavorable to the realization of complete satisfaction." The father of penis envy suggests that impotence is a neurotic response resulting from repressed conflicts.

★**1936.** The first successful reconstruction of an amputated penis takes place; later, battlefield injuries during World War II provide surgeons with opportunities to refine the procedure.

★**1948.** Alfred C. Kinsey publishes *Sexual Behavior in the Human Male*, following it five years later with *Sexual Behavior in the Human Female*. His findings bust such widely held myths as the alleged inability of females to have orgasms and the pious notion that most couples engage in sex only for procreation.

★**1952.** Acrylic splints are used as a form of penile implant to help impotent men regain the ability to penetrate during sex.

★**1966.** Though early penile-implant procedures appear to have a high success rate, surgeons are cautioned not to perform this operation on "neurotics," who will likely be dissatisfied with any result. Myths about the causes of impotence continue to reign: excessive masturbation, prolonged abstinence, *coitus interruptus*, monogamy monotony, homosexuality, and male menopause.

★**1967.** Ads for penis enlargers with vacuum-pump technology appear in men's magazines.

Famed English secret agent Austin Powers authors self-help book entitled, *Swedish-Made Penis-Enlarger Pumps and Me: This Sort of Thing Is My Bag, Baby.*

★**1969.** Researchers discover that high levels of serotonin can inhibit sexual response in rats, while a chemical that blocks serotonin, PCPA, increases the rate at which male rats mount. Later, the scientists find this applies only to homosexual mountings—heterosexual-mounting rates appear unchanged.

occasional beer or joint probably won't kick you in the nuts, but long-term use has been linked to infertility. Prescription drugs can also cause damage, notably medications used to treat ulcers, colitis, fungal infections, high blood pressure, and cancer. If you take any medication, ask your pharmacist if it has been implicated in infertility. If so, you might be able to take another less sperm-toxic drug.

Because sperm are among the most delicate cells in a man's body, they are quite sensitive to the toxic effects of even low-level exposure to pollutants: pesticides, heavy metals, solvents, and estrogenic compounds that have been seeping into the environment. Occupational exposure is a big risk, and the federal Occupational Safety and Health Administration (OSHA) requires employers to notify employees of potentially toxic chemicals by posting a Material Safety Data Sheet (MSDS). If you have a fertility problem, jot down the MSDS list and ask your doctor if any of the chemicals might be responsible for your problem. If so, work to limit your exposure.

Diet and exercise also factor into healthy fertility. Don't go overboard with exercise: Ordinary workouts are fine, but ultrastrenuous exercise—for example, extended daily training for marathons or iron-man events—can lower your testosterone level and might interfere with sperm development.

Nourish your sperm. A good diet helps, of course, but in addition, two supplemental nutrients have been shown to improve sperm count and quality. Studies suggest benefits from daily doses of zinc (50 milligrams) and vitamin C (1,000 milligrams).

Finally, sperm take about 90 days to develop, so don't expect any lifestyle changes to improve sperm count for about three months.

## Prevent Prostate Cancer

Prostate cancer strikes almost 180,000 American men each year, killing 37,000. The vast majority of them are over 60, but some are younger (Frank Zappa died in his early 50s). Unfortunately, the prostate cancer rate has been rising steadily for 25 years, and you're getting older every day.

There's more bad news: Just about everything having to do with prostate-cancer detection and treatment is currently controversial. Consider the screening test that detects prostate-specific antigen (PSA). PSA rises in men with prostate cancer, but it also rises for many other reasons. As a result, you can wind up having surgery to remove a purportedly cancerous prostate—a procedure that risks impotence—and not have cancer at all. Many distinguished medical organizations now oppose routine PSA screening for prostate cancer, among

★**1970.** In their book *Human Sexual Inadequacy,* Masters and Johnson declare that 90 percent of all impotence is caused by some form of psychological or emotional conflict.

★**1973.** The first report on vascular surgery to restore erectile function is published in the *World Journal of Surgery.* The successful use of penile prostheses, including inflatable implants, is detailed in *Urology,* inaugurating a new era of impotence treatment.

★**LATE 1970s.** Evidence accumulates that impotence is most often caused by physical, not emotional, problems. Diabetes, atherosclerosis, high blood pressure, depression, cigarette smoking, and side effects of prescription drugs are seen as more likely culprits than psychodynamic conflicts.

★**1981.** The AIDS epidemic signals the end of the Sexual Revolution.

★**1983.** At the American Urological Association's annual

meeting, British neurophysiologist Giles Brindley pulls down his pants mid-lecture, announces that he has injected himself in the penis with a long-acting alpha-blocking drug, and parades around with an erection.

★**1984.** The use of erection-stimulating injections allows urologists to better identify the causes of a patient's impotence.

Medical-grade vacuum pumps, as opposed to novelty devices long advertised in men's magazines, are intro-

duced as a viable treatment for impotence.

★**1985.** A new generation of self-contained penile implants hits the market. They prove easier to insert and more reliable than older models.

New vasodilating drugs promise a pharmacological "cure" for many cases of impotence.

★**1989.** The FDA issues a statement that no over-the-counter impotence remedies or aphrodisiacs—from jackal bile to green M&M's—have any scientific basis.

them the National Cancer Institute, the American College of Preventive Medicine, and the U.S. Preventive Services Task Force. Even PSA testing's two biggest promoters, the American Cancer Society and the American Urological Association, have recently backed off a bit from recommending the test.

Then there's the controversy over treating early prostate cancer. Many prostate tumors are "indolent," meaning they grow so slowly that they never become life threatening. Urologists have a saying: More men die *with* prostate cancer than *from* it. Only a fraction of prostate cancers ever spread. Unfortunately, current medical technology cannot distinguish between metastatic and indolent tumors, so again, you might endure the trauma of treatment for a disease that poses no real threat.

Finally, the standard treatment, removal of the gland (prostatectomy), often leaves men impotent. Recently, a number of surgical refinements have reduced the risk of erection impairment, but still, one slip of the knife, and it's bye-bye Mr. Woody. A number of other treatments have been developed, notably implantation of radioactive pellets, but these are still somewhat experimental. The best way to steer clear of all the controversies surrounding prostate cancer is to try to prevent it. Fortunately, preventive approaches are simple and clear:

• **Eat less meat.** Good research shows that saturated fat in meat and whole-milk dairy foods increases risk.

• **Eat lots of tomatoes and tomato-based foods.** You can consume soups, pasta sauces, and even pizza as long as you limit the cheese and avoid meat toppings. Tomatoes contain lycopene, a form of vitamin A that reduces risk.

• **Take selenium.** As consumption of this essential trace mineral increases, prostate cancer risk decreases. The selenium content of foods varies with the mineral content of the soil in which it was grown. Supplements provide more consistency. Look for one that supplies around 200 micrograms. Some foods rich in selenium include rice, certain kinds of fish, and eggs.

• **Take vitamin E.** It, too, reduces prostate-cancer risk. Most experts recommend 400 international units a day. Nuts and green leafy vegetables are terrific sources of vitamin E.

## Avoid HIV Infection

Although HIV is widely known to be transmitted through same-sex intercourse and unsafe drug use, heterosex is the main route of transmission around the world and increasingly in the United States. The more sex partners you have, the greater your risk. Use condoms every time with all new lovers. Condoms do not offer perfect protection, but they largely eliminate

★**1992.** Nitric oxide (NO) emerges as a key to vasodilation and erectile response. Arginine, a naturally occurring amino acid that the body uses to manufacture NO, is touted by some as a natural remedy for impotence.

Doctors and researchers finally agree on a definition of impotence: the consistent inability to attain or maintain an erection for sexual activity.

Pharmaceutical giant Pfizer works on Sildenafil, a new oral drug for the treatment of angina. The drug fails to pro-

vide heart patients much relief, but some formerly impotent test subjects report getting erections after taking it.

★**1995.** The FDA approves the sale of Upjohn's Caverject, an injectable form of prostaglandin E1—the first prescription drug for treating impotence.

The failed angina drug Sildenafil, now also known as Viagra, shows promise as an oral treatment for impotence.

★**1996.** The company Vivus, Inc. gains FDA approval to

market prostaglandin E1 delivered via a transurethral "microsuppository" pellet instead of by injection.

★**1997.** Because the drug Viagra appears to have the potential to improve marital relations, the Vatican reportedly gives it a thumbs-up.

★**1998.** The FDA clears Viagra for sale as the first effective oral treatment for impotence. Shortly thereafter, the world goes bonkers.

★**1998**
President Clinton redefines the term "sexual relations." His misconduct with a White House intern and consequent dealings lead to the first impeachment of a sitting president in over 100 years. Altoids sell out everywhere.

★**1999**
Former senator and presidential candidate Bob Dole discusses his seminal health problems in controversial ads for Viagra.

—JIM THORNTON

risk. Condoms also prevent the spread of every other sexually transmitted disease. If you and your honey decide to be monogamous, get yourselves tested. Public-health departments, AIDS organizations, and private physicians offer HIV testing. You can even get a home test. Ask your pharmacist.

—MICHAEL CASTLEMAN

# Pharm Aid

IT STARTS WITH A TICKLE in the throat or a subtle sneeze, and before you know it, the floodgates of sinus hell open wide. You could tough it out and let your immune system spar with the cold virus. But nobody has patience with a runny nose these days. So you hoof it down to the local drug warehouse, where you find a dizzying array of remedies for every conceivable physical glitch that threatens your otherwise phlegm-free existence.

"Men are very much into pill popping to solve a problem," says pharmacist Michael Hughes, the spokesman for the American Pharmaceutical Association. "They tend to gravitate toward the multi-ingredient medicines, to overmedicate with chemicals they don't need, which increases the chances of suffering side effects. It's far better to treat the symptoms you have one medicine at a time."

But to do that you have to know what's in those boxes and bottles that crowd the drugstore shelves. So we talked with pharmacists and,

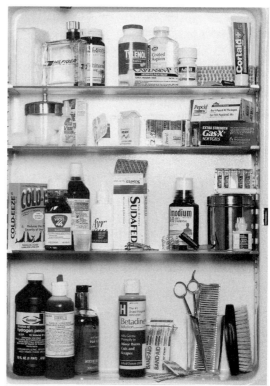

CHARLES MASTERS

Use these quick remedies and nothing save a compound fracture should send you home.

**BLISTERS.** Cut a small slit in the blister with a sterile knife and allow the fluid to seep out. Then squirt a drop of Krazy Glue through the opening to fill the cavity. It hurts for a few seconds, but it's fast and safe. To avoid blisters, rub an antiperspirant stick over your feet and ankles. This treatment prevents moisture from accumulating and contributing to the friction that leads to blisters.

**DIRT IN AN EYE.** Pull the upper lid of the affected eye down over the lower one; the lower lid's lashes will act as a broom, sweeping out the grit. If you have dirt under the lower lid, pull down on the skin under the lid and try gently flushing the speck away with water.

**FISHHOOK IN A FINGER.** The "string jerk" method has nothing to do with a noose or with the jackass who snagged you with a bad cast. Take a loop of fishing line (string or dental floss will work, too) and pass it around the bend of the hook. Have a buddy grasp the ends of the string; then, as you apply gentle downward pressure on the shank of the hook (disengaging the barb from your flesh), yank the string firmly and smoothly. The hook will pop right out.

**RASHES CAUSED BY POISONOUS PLANTS.** Poison ivy, oak, and sumac secrete urushiol, an oily resin that can penetrate your skin and cause a rash. If you know that you have just brushed against a poisonous plant, wash the skin with soap and water as soon as you can; you have about an hour before the toxin can penetrate deeply enough to cause a rash. Technu, an over-the-counter solvent, can dissolve the resin and halt a rash up to six hours after contact. In a pinch, gasoline or paint thinner will work just as well. Rub it on the skin with a clean rag; then wash it off. If you do develop a rash, apply a cream containing 100 percent–natural aloe-vera or real–peppermint oil. That maddening itch, meanwhile, is caused by your immune system's releasing chemicals called histamines. You can short-circuit this response by popping an antihistamine like Benadryl.

based on their recommendations, stocked a medicine cabinet with everything you need to make it through a year of colds, allergies, sports injuries, and more. Everything, perhaps, except this word of caution: Seemingly benign over-the-counter (OTC) drugs can cause dangerous interactions if taken with certain foods or prescription medications. "If you have high blood pressure, diabetes, heart disease, glaucoma, or prostate problems, you should consult a pharmacist or physician before taking any OTC remedy," says Hughes.

*Gesundheit.*

## 1. Your Pal Herb

Hundreds of herbal remedies line the pharmacy shelves. Are any of them worth taking? These five come highly recommended by William Keller, Ph.D., the chairman of pharmaceutical sciences at the

McWhorter School of Pharmacy at Samford University in Birmingham, Alabama. (For more in-depth information, see the following essay, "Vitamins and Supplements.")

- **ECHINACEA** Several international studies suggest that this immune-system stimulant can minimize cold symptoms or even prevent them altogether if taken at the first sign of sniffles or a cough.
- **GINKGO BILOBA** This remedy increases blood circulation, particularly in the brain, which may improve memory and clarity of thought.
- **GINSENG** It boosts energy and helps you manage stress, says Keller. Look for the more potent Korean variety, Panax ginseng. The body builds up resistance to the herb, so don't take it for more than two months at a time—and never if you have high blood pressure, which it tends to raise further.
- **MILK THISTLE** Keller says this herb "protects the liver from insult." In other words, it will block some of the damaging effects of a night out if you take it beforehand.
- **ST.-JOHN'S-WORT** Touted as a natural Prozac that eases mild depression, it also helps people cope with stress, and it's an excellent natural sleeping aid.

## 2. Rashes and Insect Bites

Choose an ointment with 1 percent hydrocortisone, which is the strongest concentration you can get without a prescription.

## 3. Pain Due to Injury and Overuse

Ibuprofen will help lessen the pain of an injury, but it won't easily reduce inflammation from, say, a

---

### KITCHEN AID: QUICK FIXES FROM MOTHER CUPBOARD

**BAG OF FROZEN PEAS.** A makeshift ice pack.

**CORNSTARCH.** Soothes chafing or body rash (except jock itch and athlete's foot).

**CUCUMBER.** Has anti-inflammatory properties. Place a slice over each of your puffy eyes during allergy season.

**EGG WHITE.** Dries up acne.

**GARLIC CLOVES.** Mash a fresh clove and rub it on a cut or scrape; then cover with a bandage. For a cold or sore throat, sip garlic soup.

**GINGER.** Chew on a piece of fresh ginger root to combat nausea caused by the flu or motion sickness.

**HONEY.** The antimicrobial properties of honey make it a great instant ointment to apply to all sorts of wounds, burns, and abrasions.

**ICE.** The next time you get the hiccups, rub an ice cube on your Adam's apple. This supposedly interrupts the nervous-system misfire that is triggering the involuntary contractions in your diaphragm.

**OATMEAL.** Combine with a little water and apply the mixture to rashes caused by poisonous plants.

**PARSLEY.** Chew a fresh sprig to sweeten bad breath.

**TEA.** Make a cup of black tea. Once the tea has steeped, remove the bag from the cup and let it cool for a couple of minutes, then squeeze a few drops of the liquid into your eyes. Tea contains soothing ingredients that are similar to those found in many over-the-counter eyedrops.

sprained ankle unless you take prescription-strength doses, says Irwin Reich, an instructor at the University of the Sciences in Philadelphia. You're better off with aspirin, which alleviates pain and inflammation. Plus, taken daily in 81-milligram doses, aspirin may reduce the risk of heart attack, stroke, and colon cancer.

## 4. Headache

Head pounding? Reach for acetaminophen, especially if aspirin upsets your stomach. It's also a good choice for reducing fever.

## 5. Backache and Arthritis

Back in the 1940s and 1950s, baseball pitchers used to rub homemade hot-pepper creams on their arms to warm them up and relieve muscle aches. You can now get the same results with creams containing capsaicin.

## 6. Gas

Look for anything with the antiflatulent chemical simethicone.

## 7. *Turista*

Loperamide is the most effective remedy for traveler's diarrhea.

## 8. Upset Stomach

Antacids in liquid form traditionally neutralize excess stomach acid faster than those in tablet form do, while the newer tablets, such as Pepcid AC, work best if you take them before eating an acid-producing meal. But now Pepcid also comes in a chewable form that can work almost as fast as the liquids and is a lot easier to carry in your pocket than a bottle of Maalox.

## 9. Stuffy Nose

If it's due to a cold or an allergy, take a decongestant containing pseudoephedrine. Use saline nasal spray to keep your nostrils moist; dry nasal passages are prime entry points for cold viruses. For a runny nose, try an antihistamine containing diphenhydramine.

## 10. Jock Itch and Athlete's Foot

Both infections are caused by the same family of fungi, says pharmacist Jonathan Marquess, the director of continuing education and professional affairs at Mercer University Southern School of Pharmacy in Atlanta. The most effective remedy, he says, is the active ingredient clotrimazole, found in Lotrimin AF.

## 11. Colds

At the first sign of a cold, suck on zinc-gluconate lozenges. Studies have shown that zinc can help lessen the severity and the duration of symptoms.

## 12. Coughs

To muzzle a hacking cough, get a cough suppressant with dextromethorphan. For a rattling, phlegmy cough, choose an expectorant with guaifenesin. Avoid remedies that have both ingredients; they can cancel each other out.

## 13. Cuts and Scrapes

Sterilize wounds the way hospitals do, with Betadine solution. Or select a double- or triple-antibiotic ointment. (If you're allergic to neomycin, which is the third antibiotic in the triple preparations, choose the double-antibiotic ointment.) If you need a bandage, opt for one of the new Band-Aids with antibiotic cream right on the pad.

—G.S. STEVENS

# Health in a Bottle?

A LL YOU HAVE TO DO is open a magazine or watch an infomercial to figure out that pills and potions are a big deal. Dozens of vitamins, herbal medicines, and dietary supplements promise to make you healthier, smarter, even happier. Some have proved effective, but if you're hoping for a magic pill, keep dreaming. None of these take the place of healthy living and a balanced diet. (That's why they're called *supplements.*)

## Vitamin Therapy à la Carte

**ANTIOXIDANTS.** Beta carotene. Vitamins C and E. Folic acid. The ever-growing alphabet soup of "essential" supplements can make your head spin. Lost in the confusing evidence and conflicting reports, though, is one simple truth: In the words of Jeffrey Blumberg, Ph.D., a professor of nutrition at Tufts University, "Certain nutrient supplements are closely connected

ROSS MCDONALD

with the prevention of specific diseases." Thus, it's a good idea to take vitamin and mineral pills—in specific combinations and dosages—if you're concerned about a particular problem.

"For a long time the medical community has been saying a good diet is all you need to meet the government's recommended daily allowance for the essential vitamins and minerals," says Iris Bell, M.D., Ph.D., a prominent vitamin and mineral researcher and an associate professor of psychiatry and family and community medicine at the University of Arizona. "That may be true if all you want to do is prevent deficiency diseases, but if you want to optimize your health, you probably need more. Besides, very few people even come close to meeting all their RDAs from diet alone."

While researchers can't guarantee every supplement will work for everyone, those here, taken in the specified amounts, have certainly proved to be safe, and they represent the best regimen to date for keeping your disease-fighting powers in peak condition.

### Heart Disease

**SUPPLEMENT.** *Folic acid, 400 micrograms*

Folic acid, one of the B vitamins, has been proven to lower blood levels of homocysteine, a chemical in the blood that some researchers believe may be even more important than cholesterol for predicting heart-disease risk.

### Muscle Strength

**SUPPLEMENT.** *Vitamin E, 100 to 400 international units*

Preliminary evidence suggests that vitamin E may help build muscle. Studies have shown that E may help men over fifty who lift weights recover more quickly after exercise, enabling them to increase their muscle size in a shorter period of time. Whether younger athletes, who typically recover faster, can benefit the same way has yet to be determined, but because

there's no harm in taking this much E, it's worth a shot.

### Cancer

**SUPPLEMENTS.** *Vitamin C, 250 to 500 milligrams; vitamin E, 100 to 400 international units; mixed carotenoids (including beta carotene and lycopene), 5 to 50 milligrams*

Even staunch supporters of supplements say this one's a tough call and more research needs to be done. While more than 50 epidemiological studies correlate a high intake of antioxidant-containing foods to a lower risk of developing a number of cancers (colon, prostate, lung, skin, and oral, among others), several studies in which researchers added one or two supplements to subjects' diets failed to show any decrease in cancer rates. For now, researchers say, evidence leans toward moderate supplementation with antioxidants. One promising area is prostate cancer; a 1996 study suggests that lycopene may provide some protection.

### Immunity

**SUPPLEMENTS.** *Multivitamin/multimineral containing 50 percent to 100 percent of the RDA for most vitamins and minerals; vitamin C, 250 to 500 milligrams; vitamin E, 200 to 400 international units; beta carotene, 5 to 10 milligrams*

A clinical study has shown that people over age 59 who took a daily multivitamin/multimineral supplement had significantly stronger immune-system reactions to seven different bacterial particles than did subjects who took placebos. Studies have also demonstrated the immune-system benefits of supplements. But the immunity-boosting benefits of supplementation may take six months to a year to accrue, and younger people whose immune systems are already strong probably have less to gain.

### Vision

**SUPPLEMENTS.** *Vitamin C, 250 to 500 milligrams; vitamin E, 400 international units*

Several studies suggest that an increased intake of vitamins E and C may decrease your risk of developing cataracts. Preliminary research also suggests that E and C may help guard against macular degeneration, an age-related change in the retina that can lead to blurred vision or blindness.

## Fertility

**SUPPLEMENTS.** *Vitamin C, 500 milligrams; vitamin E, 100 to 400 international units; mixed carotenoids (including lycopene), 5 to 50 milligrams*

Research suggests that without adequate levels of vitamin C in seminal fluid, sperm viability and motility can drop dramatically. Preliminary research also suggests that vitamin E and the carotenoids (a wide mix of related compounds, including beta carotene, alpha carotene, and lycopene) may also provide your sperm with protection from oxidative damage by free radicals.

## Brain Function

**SUPPLEMENTS.** *Multivitamin/multimineral with 50 percent to 100 percent of the RDA for most vitamins and minerals; vitamin C, 500 milligrams; vitamin E, 200 international units; B-complex vitamins, including 25 milligrams each of $B_1$, $B_2$, $B_3$, $B_5$, and $B_6$, 250 micrograms of $B_{12}$, and 400 micrograms of folic acid*

Studies show that even people with normal blood levels of the B vitamins (especially $B_{12}$ and folic acid) may be able to improve their memory and learning ability by taking supplements. Because brain function begins to decline when we reach our late forties, these compounds may be especially important to us as we age. Researchers also theorize that the high intake of vitamins C and E may protect brain cells from oxidative damage and preserve mental clarity through the years. Decreased levels of B vitamins, particularly folic acid, may also be linked to a higher risk of depression.

## Colds

**SUPPLEMENT.** *Vitamin C, 500 milligrams twice a day at the first sign of symptoms*

Clinical studies have shown that vitamin C supplements can modestly reduce the severity and duration of cold symptoms. However, they won't prevent you from catching a cold, and the benefits are typically less than what you'd get from an over-the-counter decongestant or antihistamine.

## Overall Health

**SUPPLEMENTS.** *Multivitamin/multimineral containing 50 percent to 100 percent of the RDA for most vitamins and minerals; vitamin C, 250 to 500 milligrams; vitamin E, 200 to 400 international units; beta carotene, 5 to 10 milligrams, or mixed carotenoids (including lycopene), 5 to 50 milligrams; B-complex vitamins, including 25 milligrams each of $B_1$, $B_2$, $B_3$, $B_5$, and $B_6$, 250 micrograms of $B_{12}$, and 400 micrograms of folic acid*

This program should provide you with a basic insurance policy against many major diseases and keep your mind and body performing at their best.

—DAN BENSIMHON

# Back to Nature

The dietary-supplement industry, its milquetoast moniker to the contrary, is a hopping little sector of the economy that has of late been stirring deep passion. In 1994 the industry and its chief political champion, Utah Republican senator Orrin Hatch, persuaded Congress to pass the Dietary Supplement Health and Education Act, which gave the industry the power to define what it wanted as a dietary supplement and, as such, remove it from meaningful Food and Drug Administration scrutiny. As long as the companies stop short of making drug claims for their herbs and hormones—no mention of disease prevention or risk reduction—the FDA was essentially defanged. So let the experimenter beware. Because the marketplace is so wide open, you need to arm yourself with as much solid information as possible before taking that fateful trip down the General Nutrition Center aisle.

## Herbals

Herbal remedies, increasingly fashionable, are a classic good news, bad news proposition. The good news is, they work. In 1978 the German government created an herbal division of its equivalent to the FDA, Commission E, that has reviewed and approved some 200 medicinal herbs and herb combinations for use with or without prescription. "For the top dozen or so herbs," says Purdue University's Varro Tyler, Ph.D., the world's preeminent medicinal-herb researcher, "we now have substantial research and a clinical base."

The bad news is, if you purchase an herbal product at the local health-food store, God knows what you're likely to get. A 1979 study of ginseng products on the American market found that 60 percent had so little ginseng in them as to be of questionable value, and around 15 percent had no ginseng at all. In general, herbalists recommend sticking with established national brands. Check the label to ensure that the herbal remedy is made from a standardized extract, which is designed to provide a strong, consistent therapeutic dose. That label should also contain information about any known contraindications.

**ECHINACEA.** What is it? If you're familiar with any traditional remedy, it's probably echinacea, the top-selling herb on the U.S. health-food market. Also known as purple coneflower, it was the favorite healing herb of the prairie Indians, and it remained one of the most frequently prescribed medicinal plants in this country into the 1920s.

What does it do? According to two German double-blind studies, echinacea is an effective flu fighter, shortening its duration and severity. No drug can claim that. Echinacea is also used (and has been vetted by the Germans) to treat lower-urinary-tract infections and, in salve form, hard-to-heal wounds.

How should I take it? Capsules of the ground root and leaf as well as a liquid extract are popular here, but the German studies were done with extract. Take 900 milliliters or between four and eight 500-milligram capsules a day. Echinacea is not recommended as a treatment for diseases of the immune system.

**GINKGO BILOBA.** What is it? The small, bushy ginkgo biloba is the world's oldest living variety of tree (200 million years old); an extract made from the green ginkgo leaf has been a best-selling herbal medicine in Europe for nearly 20 years and is newly popular here.

What does it do? Years of clinical tests in Europe have confirmed ginkgo's ability to improve impaired peripheral circulation, particularly to the brain. Ginkgo's flavonoid and ginkgolide compounds (the latter found nowhere else in nature) are thought to be doing the work. In two studies in the mid-'90s, ginkgo showed promise as a therapy for the various forms of mental impairment that often accompany old age. The Germans use it to treat certain forms of tinnitus (ringing in the ears), as well as short-term memory loss and senile dementia, and as a blood thinner, to prevent stroke.

How should I take it? Take 120 to 240 milligrams a day as therapy, 40 to 120 milligrams as a prophylactic brain tonic.

**HAWTHORN.** What is it? The red berries, flowers, and leaf extracts from this plant (*Crataegus*, a member of the rose family) are used to make jam in England and medicine in Europe, China, and America.

What does it do? Hawthorn was a standard

treatment for heart disease in the United States in the early part of the century. A number of more recent studies have confirmed that it dilates the coronary arteries, increasing blood flow to the heart, and thereby strengthens heart contractions. Research conducted in China also suggests that it can lower blood pressure and blood cholesterol levels.

How should I take it? Even though hawthorn has no known adverse side effects, you should never self-medicate a heart condition. Find a physician who would be willing to work with hawthorn. A healthy person might take 80 to 95 milligrams of the standard extract twice a day as a prophylaxis.

**KAVA-KAVA.** What is it? For centuries, Polynesians have been brewing up a dark, bitter drink from the massive, gnarly rootstock of the kava-kava shrub.

What does it do? Supplement companies have been introducing products that tout kava's antianxiety properties, and one even rolled out an elixir called Erotikava. Taken in sufficient quantities, kava can produce a mild natural "high" that in the right context might be described as sensual, though the established supplement companies are nervous about marketing anything purely for recreational enjoyment. The German Commission E approves kava for treating conditions of nervous anxiety, stress, and restlessness. Compounds called kavalactones and pyrones are primarily what give kava its kick, resulting in a numbing of the mouth, mild pain relief, and muscular relaxation.

How should I take it? Either in liquid or powdered extract form—and in moderation, increasing your dosage in small increments. With the help of a reliable label, translate the kava product into units of kava pyrones. A daily total might be in the range of 60 to 100 milligrams. Taking kava with alcohol, barbiturates, or psychoactive drugs will

result in a multiplier effect; no driving cars or operating heavy machinery.

**ST.-JOHN'S-WORT.** What is it? A preparation of the dried top of this modest wildflower (*Hypericum perforatum*) outsells Prozac in Germany, 7-to-1. But people have been fascinated by St.-John's-wort's medicinal properties since the ancient Greeks. Britons in the Middle Ages ascribed mystical properties to it.

What does it do? In August 1996 the *British Medical Journal* reviewed some 23 clinical trials and concluded that St.-John's-wort is effective in the treatment of mild to moderate depression. The theory is that the active ingredient in the plant— hypericin—boosts the brain's serotonin levels. The side effects (including possible photosensitivity) are negligible, especially compared with prescription antidepressants. St.-John's-wort has antiviral properties as well.

How should I take it? Take 2 to 4 grams of the powdered herb or the equivalent of .2 to 1 milligram of hypericin in the standardized extract. Please check with your doctor before taking this, however; recent studies have shown taking St. John's-wort may decrease the effectiveness of other medications.

**SAW PALMETTO.** What is it? This greenish, berry-sized fruit comes from a palm-family shrub found in the American Southeast. The Seminoles ate the greasy-tasting berry.

What does it do? Saw palmetto is one of the most effective treatments available for benign prostatic hyperplasia (BPH), the enlarged-prostate condition that bedevils most older men. German studies found that saw palmetto does not actually reduce the size of an inflammation; it just alleviates its symptoms, increasing urine flow and reducing retained urine (and the number of nocturnal trips to the bathroom).

How should I take it? Saw palmetto is available

in various forms. Make sure you're getting 320 milligrams a day of the standardized extract.

## Hormones

Pioneers in "antiaging medicine" contend that aging itself is a treatable disease. At least in part, they say, it's defined by a decline, beginning in middle age, in levels of certain crucial hormones, chemical messengers that help regulate virtually every activity in the body. According to this boosterish way of thinking, keep a guy's hormones supplemented at a twenty-year-old's levels and he'll stay hale and hormonally buff until he reaches, say, 120, whereupon he'll hit a genetic limit to longevity and contentedly expire.

Take any hormone under the supervision of a physician and have blood or saliva tested regularly to make sure you don't supplement yourself beyond physiological levels.

**MELATONIN.** What is it? The pineal gland, a pea-sized structure in the brain, secretes melatonin in response to light. Less light, more melatonin, we go to sleep. Melatonin supplements in very small doses, .1 to 1 milligram, are said by some researchers to be an effective natural sleeping pill and at a larger dose, like 3 milligrams, a remedy for jet lag. But what triggered the melatonin craze was Dr. William Regelson's 1995 bestseller, *The Melatonin Miracle*, which stopped just short of declaring the hormone the Fountain of Youth. Regelson's hypothesis is that the hormone somehow sets not just our daily sleep-wake cycle but the aging clock itself. In experiments conducted by Regelson, his coauthor, immunologist Walter Pierpaoli, and others, mice who were fed melatonin or who received a transplanted pineal gland from a young mouse looked younger and lived markedly longer. Not surprisingly, the hype suggests that melatonin supplementation protects against everything from stress to cancer to heart disease.

Does it work? Most likely, for everything sleep-related. Touting the hormone as a life extender seems premature at best.

Should I take it? Take too much of any hormone and its effects can be counterproductive; the cell receptors in the brain become overloaded, interfering with the body's ability to make its own hormone supply. Melatonin seems particularly finicky. Doses of over 1 milligram can cause insomnia, morning grogginess, and vivid dreaming. Most researchers recommend using it like a sleeping pill: only occasionally, not as a nightly tonic.

**PREGNENOLONE.** What is it? Pregnenolone is the "parent hormone." Cholesterol, ingested in food and produced by the liver, is first converted into preg and then morphs, as needed, into other steroid hormones: DHEA, testosterone, estrogen, progesterone, and cortisol. In the '40s, industrial psychologists at the University of Massachusetts recorded that subjects dosed with preg scored measurably better on an airplane flight simulator—a good test of learning, hand-eye coordination, and memory—and, in a separate study conducted by the same group, factory workers, particularly those in stressful situations, handled their jobs more ably and enthusiastically. The hormone also showed promise as a treatment for rheumatoid arthritis.

Does it work? Alas, being a natural product, preg isn't patentable, so drug companies invented side-effect–laden synthetic cortisone in the late '40s instead. Now preg's back and showing some strong preliminary results in enhancing the memories of mice in one study and older men and women in another. Regelson hopes that preg will establish itself as a natural Prozac.

Should I take it? So little is known about preg at this point that you probably ought to hold off unless you're an ardent experimentalist. Consult a doctor, particularly if you're planning on being a guinea pig for more than a month.

—JOSEPH HOOPER

**Magic Potions?**

Americans spend an estimated $4.2 billion annually on pills and potions loosely categorized as "dietary supplements"—such as androstenedione, creatine monohydrate, DHEA: dehydroepiandrosterone, ephedrine, and HMB (beta-hydroxy-beta-methylbutyrate)—are used in over-the-counter products, such as protein powders, "carbo" fuels, muscle builders, and weight elixirs (for loss or gain). Fret all you want about whether professional athletes ought to be allowed to use such products. The more fundamental questions are: *Do they work?* and *Are they safe?*

Answers, unfortunately, aren't easy to come by.

Credible studies, where they exist, don't yield simple conclusions. In many cases, manufacturers rely on questionable theories and on reports from scientists and laboratories in foreign countries to bolster their claims. As for U.S. government regulations, they are minimal. Under the Dietary Supplement and Health Education Act, this class of products is beyond the FDA's reach. Until these products have been tested more thoroughly, buyer beware. And always remember, consult your doctor before embarking on any exercise program.

—TED G. RAND

ALCOHOL

# Drink to Your Health

WHEN THE WORD got out that one or two drinks a day could reduce your chances of developing heart disease by 30 percent, it seemed reason enough to celebrate. It's intoxicating to think that the same martini or merlot that takes the edge off the day also increases the level of beneficial high-density lipoprotein (HDL) cholesterol—which helps reduce artery-clogging LDL cholesterol.

But just as everyone was getting comfortable with the millennial notion of drinking to your health, there's the constant reminder that the same spirits that protect the heart might also increase the chance of a heart attack. How, you say? Alcohol—three ounces of pure alcohol a day, equivalent to a whopping six beers—can downshift the body's fat-burning engine by about one-third, eventually causing upper-abdominal obesity. In other words, the classic beer belly. And this is bad for your heart. Abdominal fat, according to cardiologists, enters the bloodstream more easily than fat on your hips or thighs. But there is a happy medium with drinking and health, so read on.

# NO, I'M FINE — REALLY

People have come up with ingenious reasons to justify the drinking life. Here are some of the more common ones and the truth, if any, behind them.

*Sure, I drink, but I sweat it out.* Dream on. The primary enzyme system that breaks down alcohol is called dehydrogenase, and exercise and diet won't persuade your liver to make more of the enzyme. Nor can you sweat alcohol out through exercise. "Breathing and sweating aren't a significant route of excretion for alcohol," says Mark Messin, Ph.D., R.D., professor of nutrition at the University of Southern California Medical School.

*Alcohol doesn't make me fat; it goes right through me.* The reason you urinate more is that alcohol causes production of an enzyme that stimulates urination. In other words, it's a diuretic. You lose water but keep the calories.

*Beer is a great way to carbo load.* A beer may be 150 calories, but about 100 of those come from alcohol and only about 50 from carbohydrates. So if you are looking for carbohydrates to boost your performance in endurance sports, think pasta and potatoes, not brew.

*A nightcap helps me sleep.* Alcohol is a central-nervous-system depressant, so a nightcap can indeed help you fall asleep—but it may not be a good sleep. Alcohol disrupts slumber patterns, so your shut-eye may be "fragmented and unsettled," according to the University of California at Berkeley Wellness Letter. "After a nightcap, many people wake up suddenly in the middle of the night and can't get back to sleep."

*It takes a lot to get me drunk.* If you find that you are drinking more without getting drunk, it means you're drinking too much. Heavy drinkers are forced to tap into a secondary enzyme system, and the body can produce more of these enzymes in response to alcohol.

## Toasting Your Heart and Waistline

Okay, here's the bottom line: One or two drinks a day, 10 to 14 a week, according to the experts, provides heart protection without inflating your waistline. Alcohol not only raises your HDL levels but prevents the formation of dangerous heart-threatening blood clots. Yet more is not better. Saving up those one or two drinks a day for the weekend is a perilous strategy. First, "six or seven drinks [a day] does some damage to the liver and the heart," says Eric Rimm, Ph.D., a Harvard epidemiologist. Second, you don't derive any extra coronary advantage because alcohol's salutary effects last only a day or two. Third, half a dozen drinks add up to an inflationary number of calories.

This doesn't mean you can't *occasionally* have three or four drinks but doing so daily may yield few heart-protective benefits, thicken your waistline, *and* increase your overall mortality rate to boot. (This is a statistical average, not a hard-and-fast number; for bigger individuals, these levels do. To make matters worse, consider what you're eating while under the influence. "Among men, those who drink more tend to have diets that are fattier, heavier in calories, with more cholesterol, fewer fruits and vegetables, less fiber and less carbohydrates, than those who drink less or not at all," says Barbara Posner, Ph.D., who directs the nutrition component of the Framingham Heart Study, a definitive ongoing report on diet and disease.

## Eat, Drink, and Be Lean

Furthermore, alcohol causes the liver to burn fat more *slowly*; most of the calories from, say, your accompanying (and fatty) Beer Nuts or slices of pizza will head straight for your gut, butt, and hips. Studies indicate that moderate drinkers who are consumers of high-fat foods put on weight *much* more quickly than their drinking companions with low-fat diets.

Alcohol can also trash your best dietary intentions. "Al-cohol stimulates the release of insulin, so your blood sugar drops, and you get hungry," says Mary Donkersloot, R.D., a nutritionist in private practice in Beverly Hills, California. "Alcohol also lowers inhibitions, so you're more likely to eat not only the wrong kind of food but more of it." One solution is eating—preferably in a low-fat mode—before you drink to blunt the desire to munch that alcohol engenders. And while you're eating, make sure to hydrate yourself as well. Alcohol is a diuretic, which initiates a drink-pee-drink cycle that, depending on your tolerance and capacity to hold alcohol, can be a major source of weight gain. How? To make up for fluid loss, you wind up drinking more alcohol and absorbing the calories that come along with it. So pace your drinking and make it a practice of ordering a pitcher of water along with your beer and alternate the two.

may have lessened effects.) In general, research indicates that this quantity of alcohol can raise blood pressure, damage brain cells, weaken the heart muscle, cause abnormal cardiac rhythms, and increase the risk of cirrhosis (abnormal growth and scarring) of the liver. Liver damage is irreversible, and it can be fatal. Continuous heavy drinking can also cause cancer of the esophagus, rectum, and colon.

In terms of weight gain, it's simple addition: Have three or four drinks a day and you're adding 450 to 600 calories that you'll have to run, cycle, or somehow burn off to break even—something, nutritionists note, most men never

## What to Drink: Wine, Beer, or the Hard Stuff?

First, science told us that red wine beats other alcoholic beverages cold when it comes to protecting the heart. Then researchers at Cornell University found that the skin of red grapes (from which red wine and red grape juice get their color) contains a chemical called resveratrol, which raises HDL levels in laboratory studies. Recent evidence suggests red wine's reputation as a coronary savior is accurate but not for the reasons researchers originally thought. According to Arthur Klatsky, M.D., who conducted a study at the Kaiser Permanente Medical Center in Oakland, California, drinkers who preferred wine were indeed less likely to die from coronary disease than those who preferred beer or liquor. But it isn't because red wine possesses any inherent biochemical advantage. (In fact, in the study, white wine offered slightly more protection.) Rather, wine drinkers simply tend to be healthier, less likely to smoke, and possibly better informed about good health habits than those who indulge in booze and beer. To further muddle the picture, in a Harvard study of 50,000 men, liquor was shown to reduce heart-disease risk more than either wine or beer. If anything, the conflicting research suggests you should stick with your preference—whether wine, beer, or the hard stuff—and follow the two-drinks-a-day advice.

—ROBERT BARNETT

# Lighten Up

CALL IT AN EXPERIMENT in worse-living-through-chemistry. In 1997, Yale University psychiatrist J. Douglas Bremner gathered a group of former depression patients and had each one down a cocktail spiked with an amino acid that blocks, for up to six hours, the brain's ability to absorb serotonin, the sanguinity-inducing neurotransmitter without which the depression-prone slip into a dismal funk. He then took pictures of each person's brain with a special camera that captures brain activity as a series of glowing multicolored blobs.

This wasn't some cruel Dr. Feelbad ruse to force

people to relive their misery. The good doctor instead sought to pinpoint the parts of the brain responsible for triggering depression—in hopes of finding better, more targeted ways of fighting the disease.

But what was most fascinating about the experiment wasn't that the pictures revealed depression-related changes in three brain regions. What surprised Bremner, rather, was the starkly gender specific ways in which men and women reacted to the potion. Typical of the males was "John," a middle-aged business-man who had fully recovered from a bout of depression. Within minutes of drinking the brew, however, "he wanted to escape to a bar across the street," recalls Bremner. "He didn't express sadness . . . he didn't really express any-thing. He just wanted to leave and go to Larry's Lounge."

Contrast John's response with that of female subjects like "Sue." After taking the cocktail, "she began to cry and express her sadness over the loss of her father two years ago," recalls Bremner. "She was overwhelmed by her emotions."

Venus and Mars, indeed. Although depression appears to have the same biological triggers in both men and women, we often experience it as if we were, literally, from different planets. Which begs the question of whether depression treat-ments could be improved by tailoring them specif-ically for each sex.

## Gender Blues

Until recently, depression research and treatment have been aimed mostly at women. Conventional psychotherapy generally focuses on plumbing the sorts of heart-wrenching emotional issues that are routinely addressed by women but often give men the heebie-jeebies. And while such modern anti-depressants as Prozac and Zoloft (which are both selective serotonin reuptake inhibitors, or SSRIs,

drugs that keep the brain awash in serotonin) aid both genders, their sexual side effects tend to afflict men more severely, causing impotence and libido loss so unbearable that many end up blow-ing off treatment altogether (though more sex friendly pills do exist). Combine that with a genetic and cultural predisposition to "hanging tough" and feigning emotional in-vulnerability and it's little wonder men are about two-and-a-half times less likely than women to seek help in the first place.

## Flirting with Divorce

At least Bob knew *something* was wrong and had the gumption to seek help. Too many men simply "hold on to depressive pain until it becomes unbearable," says Dr. Frederick Goodwin, the former director of the National Institute of Mental Health and a leading expert on depression. "And the result is failed health and failed relationships."

Indeed, each year roughly 23,000 American men commit suicide (four times more than women), while countless others suffer depres-sion-related heart disease. Moreover, there's increasing evidence that untreated or undertreat-ed depression—particularly that experienced early in life or during highly stressful periods, such as combat duty—may damage the brain's hippocampi, two sea horse–shaped parts of the limbic system believed to regulate emotions, as well as memory, appetite, and sleep. The likely result: a predisposition to depression later in life. "Severe stress and mental trauma are predictors of depression," says Bremner, who points to research that demonstrates half of all people who suffer major depression will experience a recur-rence of the condition.

Such waves of misery can push even the most committed relationship to the breaking point. And when we complain that we've "fallen out of love" with our partners or spouses, the truth may be that

## Prozac

The first of the SSRIs, Prozac was introduced in 1988 and soon became the most prescribed antidepressant in the world. Its active ingredient, fluoxetine, blocks nerve cells from recapturing serotonin and removing it from the brain.

**UPSIDES:** One pill a day brings relief not only from depression but also from panic attacks, obsessive-compulsive disorder, and bulimia.

**DOWNSIDES:** In addition to the sexual dysfunctions reported by up to 50 percent of users, SSRIs can disrupt sleep and cause "micro-awaking," which can contribute to fatigue. Other side effects can include nausea, nervousness, insomnia, drowsiness, diarrhea, and tremors.

## Zoloft

Introduced in 1991, this SSRI is highly similar to Prozac.

**UPSIDES:** See Prozac.

**DOWNSIDES:** In addition to sexual side effects and sleep disruption, Zoloft has been blamed for nausea, diarrhea, dry mouth, insomnia, drowsiness, dizziness, tremors, excessive sweating, and indigestion.

## Paxil

An SSRI introduced in 1992, Paxil is also highly similar to Prozac.

**UPSIDES:** See Prozac.

**DOWNSIDES:** In addition to sexual side effects and sleep disruption, Paxil can cause nausea, drowsiness, dry mouth, weakness, constipation, dizziness, insomnia, diarrhea, excessive sweating, and tremors.

## Serzone

Approved in 1995, this is one of the newest antidepressants available. Its active ingredient, nefazadone, interferes with the removal of serotonin and norepinephrine from the brain.

**UPSIDES:** Unlike SSRIs, Serzone causes few sexual side effects and doesn't induce sleep problems; in fact, it increases REM sleep. In addition to treating depression, it also helps counteract anxiety. And because it affects both serotonin and norepinephrine, some people find it more effective than SSRIs.

**DOWNSIDES:** Serzone needs to be taken twice daily. Its side effects can include dry mouth, drowsiness, nausea, dizziness, constipation, weakness, lightheadedness, blurred vision, and confusion.

## Wellbutrin

Brought to market in 1985, Wellbutrin, whose active ingredient is buproprione, inhibits serotonin and norepinephrine uptake and also affects another neurotransmitter, dopamine.

**UPSIDES:** Few sexual side effects have been reported. It's also an effective aid to quitting cigarette smoking.

**DOWNSIDES:** It needs to be taken either twice or three times a day and can cause substantial drowsiness—enough to impair motor skills. Other side effects can include loss of appetite (which can lead to weight loss), agitation, dry mouth, constipation, excessive sweating, dizziness, tremors, and blurred vision.

## Effexor

Approved in 1993, this drug—whose active ingredient is venlafaxine—inhibits uptake of serotonin and norepinephrine and, to a lesser extent, dopamine.

**UPSIDES:** Although Effexor can cause sexual side effects, ejaculation problems are reported by only 12 percent of male users and impotence by a mere 6 percent. And because the drug affects both serotonin and norepinephrine, it can be more powerful—and act faster—than SSRIs.

**DOWNSIDES:** Must be taken with food and requires two to three dosages daily. In addition to sexual side effects, it can induce nausea, drowsiness, dry mouth, dizziness, constipation, weakness, nervousness, excessive sweating, and loss of appetite.

## Nardil and Parnate

Older antidepressants that have become less popular because of their side effects, these drugs interfere with the enzyme monoamine oxidase (MAO), which helps clear serotonin, epinephrine, and norepinephrine from nerve-cell synapses.

**UPSIDES:** In some cases, it is the only drug that works.

**DOWNSIDES:** A dangerous spike in blood pressure can result from taking MAO inhibitors with such foods as cheese, salami, red wine, avocados, bananas, chocolate, and beer. Other side effects can include dizziness, headaches, tremors, muscle twitching, confusion, memory impairment, anxiety, insomnia, weakness, drowsiness, chills, blurred vision, and heart palpitations.

## St.-John's-Wort

This flowering plant has been used in traditional European medicine for centuries, primarily for wound healing. German scientists have proved that it's a natural MAO inhibitor.

**UPSIDES:** It costs only about $10 a month and can be obtained over the counter. Furthermore, it doesn't appear to cause the large number of side effects that other MAO inhibitors do.

**DOWNSIDES:** MAO inhibitors have largely been replaced by new drugs that are more powerful, and St.-John's-wort is considered effective only for mild to moderate depression. Side effects reportedly include photosensitivity, dry mouth, fatigue, dizziness, rashes, and itching.

## Tricyclics (Elavil, Aventyl, Acsendin, and Others)

These decades-old antidepressants effectively inhibit reuptake of serotonin and norepinephrine, but their significant side effects have led to a sharp decline in their usage.

**UPSIDES:** Few; as with MAO inhibitors, these are prescribed nowadays only as a last resort.

**DOWNSIDES:** In addition to the side effects exhibited by more modern antidepressants, tricyclics have been associated with vomiting, coughing, laryngitis, rashes, hives, acne, numbness, anemia, bad breath, excessive sweating, elevated blood pressure, nasal congestion, and ringing in the ears.

our gloomy outlook is responsible for our change of heart.

Depression's judgment-clouding effects are reason enough to get evaluated mentally before making any final decisions about ending a long-term relationship. "Unrecognized depression is one of the greatest risk factors for divorce," says Dr. Peter D. Kramer, the author of *Listening to Prozac* and *Should You Leave?* "And I'd hate for a marriage to end because of an unrecognized treatable illness."

### Don't Be a Man

So why do men continue to resist diagnosis and treatment? The answer probably lies in some tangled combination of nature and nurture, a genetic and cultural makeup passed down through generations and perpetuated by every John Wayne or Clint Eastwood movie ever made. "It's how we're raised," says Terrence Real, the codirector of the Family Institute of Cambridge Gender Research Project. "To learn to be a man means to pretend to be invulnerable . . . to play through the pain . . . to tough it out. The very phrase 'Be a man!' means 'Stop being vulnerable!'"

"Natural selection chose men who could redi-rect or contain most of their emotional responses," says Dr. Helen Fisher, an evolutionary anthropologist at Rutgers University and the author of *Anatomy of Love: A Natural History of Mating, Marriage and Why We Stray.* "If you're looking into the yellow eyes of a leopard coming your way, it's not adaptive to experience your emotions like fear. You have to concentrate on killing the beast. Reveal your heart and you perish."

Yet in a modern world in which day-to-day survival is largely a given, our predisposition to turn melancholy and anguish into anger and aggression is only slightly more useful than our vestigial appendixes. "The very mechanisms that evolved to help contain men's emotions can also short-circuit their ability to cope," says Fisher, who believes men are susceptible to "emotional flooding," an explosion of pent-up feelings that often takes the form of violence. "Your heart pounds, your face gets red, and you do dumb things, like drive too fast, drink too much, and put your fist through walls."

Which isn't exactly the kind of behavior that fosters healthy relationships, let alone self-actualized men. And whether or not we're willing to admit it, we need emotionally intimate connections in order to do more than just survive.

## The Prozac Droop

Ironically, while all those serotonin-enhancing drugs can help break down male inhibitions about exploring emotional intimacy, their side effects have also created major hurdles to our favorite way of expressing it: Approximately 60 percent of men who take SSRIs report impotence, reduced sexual pleasure, or decreased libido. Such reactions can worsen the deadening effect the depression itself can have on the sex drive, sabotaging any chance for successful treatment.

That's exacerbated by our reticence to discuss sexual dysfunction with doctors, as well as the failure of some internists to thoroughly explain the potential for sexual side effects. Although Dr. Wise, a psychiatrist and depression expert at Inova Fairfax Hospital in Virginia, recommends that those who suffer acute sexual dysfunction due to SSRIs consider switching medications, there are other options as well. Many men need only reduce their dosage of SSRIs to restore their sex drive, while others find relief by taking "drug holidays," two-day breaks from medications during which virility is restored, though the depression-alleviating effects of SSRIs aren't dampened. (Either option should be discussed first with a doctor.)

## The Talking Cure

Men who are averse to spending time on the psychiatric couch may look forward with relish to the day when pharmacologists develop the real-world equivalent of Aldous Huxley's soma—a miracle cure for all symptoms of depression. But for the time being, pills alone typically aren't enough. Studies show that the likelihood of depression's recurring increases substantially when psychotherapy isn't in the treatment mix. "While antidepressants alleviate depression's symptoms," says Dr. William S. Pollack, the director of the Center for Men at Harvard Medical School's McLean Hospital, "they can't take away the trigger for the stress."

Pollack cites studies indicating that psychotherapy may have the same biological effects as antidepressants, increasing the brain's uptake of serotonin and inducing a sense of well-being—without any side effects. Yet research also indicates that talk therapy without medication often prolongs treatment, risking the possibility that men might succumb to their suicidal tendencies. "[Antidepressants] give men back the capacity to do something about their depression," Pollack says.

"Doing something" doesn't necessarily mean undergoing the intense emotional introspection that terrifies some men so thoroughly that they flee from treatment. "Men have this false notion that therapy is only talking about feelings," says Pollack. "It's really about talking about whatever things are essential in their lives—their sense of struggle at work, the sense of failure or success at achieving the goals in their lives."

In fact, he believes the key to improving depression treatment for men may lie in changing the "feminized" mode most psychotherapists now employ. Instead of forcing men to explore their inner selves right off the bat, he favors an approach that doesn't threaten their fierce sense of emotional invulnerability but instead offers the kind of advice and consultation that physicians treating physical ailments might give. For example, an initial discussion of depression's biological basis can mollify much of the angst about submitting to therapy.

Another effective tactic is to focus first on altering depression-linked behaviors, such as substance abuse, which is twice as common among depressed men as women. Most depressed men can admit—at least to themselves—the debilitating effect drug and alcohol abuse have. And it's often easier—and more productive—to plot a step-by-step strategy for overcoming such habits than to explore the deeper issues that initially drove us to them.

All this assumes, however, that we're even willing to seek treatment and that our therapists take an approach that doesn't push us away. "Depression is bad enough without having to deal with a doctor who treats you like some sick, helpless patient," says Pollack. "You should interview multiple people. And if they're arrogant or huffy, you shouldn't hesitate to leave and find someone else."

Just as long as you don't leave and head straight to Larry's Lounge.

**—ALEX MARKELS**

MEN-O-PAUSE.

P.S. MUELLER

W
o
m
e
n

RICHARD PHIBBS

WE'RE NOT EVEN going to pretend that we can give you a lot of help with this one. When it comes to women, every man is on his own. F. Scott Fitzgerald probably said it best: "He knew that when he kissed this girl, when he wed his unutterable visions to her perishable breath, his mind would never romp again like the mind of God." In other words, we're all done for. You only have to spend one afternoon walking through midtown Manhattan in the summertime to realize the astounding power of the slit skirt, the long brown hair, the playful laugh. Fitzgerald was no slouch when it came to women, but he knew better than most that we don't stand a chance. If a man defines his life by the challenges he faces, then understanding women is surely the most dangerous—and definitely the most fun.

Since *Men's Journal* was founded, we've tried to give readers a little harmless ammunition. We've talked to dozens of women over the years, always trying to find the elusive answer to that impossible question: What do they want? We've also asked sex therapists and doctors to explore the chemical and psychological mysteries of the libido. Of course, this part is not just about sex, though there is enough sophisticated sex advice in here to make any man a better lover, a better husband, and a better friend. It's about knowing how to cook for a woman, how to give her a good massage, how to buy her presents, and how to do the little things—the thousands upon thousands of little things—that on occasion will put you in her good graces.

# What Women Want

"HOTTIE LIST," my 10-year-old son Ben announces as we walk home together from the school bus. He shakes his head in wide-eyed bewilderment. "Brooke calls it her Hottie list, and I found out I'm second on it." It turns out that Hottie (root word: "hot") is girl-speak for an attractive boy. Brooke is Osborne Elementary's head cheerleader and thus vested with the job of keeping such a list properly culled and up to date. You may have never actually met Brooke, but if you're a guy, you know her. She is, in short, an early incarnation of that lifelong evolving prototype of female pulchritude that, for most of us, is doomed to forever recede just out of reach, like Xeno's Paradox.

A few decades earlier, when I was in fifth grade, I once made it up to No. 5 on our own class beauty's list. I was beside myself with rapture, determined to crawl and scratch my way one more impossible rung up the hierarchy. But how to do this? What do feminine supermagnets like Jennifer Moony actually find attractive in the grown-up versions of those hopeless Fourth Place Hottie wannabes?

Sari Locker, the twenty-something author of *The Complete Idiot's Guide to Amazing Sex*, a striking brunette who's been lionized by *Playboy* magazine as "our favorite tantalizing sex writer," tells me, "Guys *think* women want them to be rich and pow-

erful. If the stereotype for women is 'sex object,' then the stereotype for men is 'success object.' This may be true for some women, but many others just want a nice guy who knows how to express love, be sensual, and be a good boyfriend or husband.

*The great question that has never been answered and which I have not yet been able to answer, despite my 30 years of research into the feminine soul, is "What does a woman want?"*

— SIGMUND FREUD

Real love, for most women, is based on how much a guy *cares*, not how much he *has*."

What about looks? I ask. "Men," she continued reassuringly, "really don't need to feel insecure about their looks because you can almost always find some woman somewhere who will like them. Even if a man is not very physically good looking or doesn't have much money, he can still find love

# HOW A GUY CAN MAKE THE MOST OF WHAT HE'S GOT

So you want to optimize your attractiveness to women, but you don't have $5,000 for pectoral implants or even $1,600 for a chin augmentation? It's probably just as well, suggest scientists and sexperts alike, who argue there are a lot less draconian (and much more effective) routes to the feminine heart.

A smattering of their suggestions:

• **STRIVE TO EMBODY BEHAVIORAL QUALITIES THAT WOMEN WANT,** says psychologist Donald Buss, author of *The Evolution of Desire.* These include ambition and industriousness, emotional stability, and commitment. "Women don't want losers," he says. "They do look for a guy who is in love with *them,* one who will stay around for the long term."

• **CULTIVATE A SENSE OF INNER CONFIDENCE.** "Even if a man thinks he's not good-looking," says sex educator and author Sari Locker, "he can always find aspects of himself that are attractive. Confidence comes from the inside."

• **DRESS FOR SUCCESS.** You don't have to spend a fortune on Armani, but cleanliness and a modicum of fashion sense do score points. Studies have shown that the exact same guy, dressed first in a nice suit and later in a burger-flipping uniform, provokes wildly different reactions in women. The bad news for fast-food workers: It's not that your outfits make you look ugly to women—they make you *invisible.* Tip: Stop at home and change first before going out on dates.

• **BE NICE FROM THE GET-GO.** "Plan the date, pick a nice restaurant, and offer to pay," suggests Locker. "Don't do this out of some stereotypical notion of gender roles; do it to be nice. Bring her some flowers or a Hershey's kiss on the first or second date."

• **JUST DON'T BE *DESPERATELY* NICE.** Declaring your undying love on, say, the second date signals low mate value—like damaged goods being auctioned off at a fire sale. It's been suggested that the trick in winning a woman's affections is to first show her you *don't* need her, then show her you *do.* But when is it safe to make this shift and declare genuine affection? "I don't know for sure," concedes Buss, "but I would wait at least a month."

• **ACT LIKE A GOOD POTENTIAL FATHER.** Photos showing guys interacting positively with babies win great acclaim from typical female viewers. Men ignoring the same little tykes, especially when they appear to be in distress, prove to be a consistently powerful turnoff.

• **BE YOURSELF.** "As trite as this sounds, it's true," says Locker. "If you portray yourself one way on a date, then in a month she sees who you really are, you've lost her."

• **LOOK FOR COMPATIBILITY.** A woman who likes your friends and lifestyle is much more likely to keep liking you even after the initial infatuation begins to wane.

with a wonderful woman with whom he's compatible. Almost everyone gets into a lasting relationship." As much as I want to believe this infinitely more humane view of romance and attraction, can it possibly be more than greeting-card pabulum?

So I asked real women, in the real world, what they think. I start with the often strikingly attractive wives and girlfriends of my buddies, females who have already demonstrated by their own mate selection an encouraging lack of Zarathustrian standards. These women, in turn, not only generously answer my questions but also pass the inquiries along to their female friends, who soon begin bombarding my e-mail address with their own thoughtful replies. Truth be known: Women do seem *at least* as preoccupied by us as we are by them. And their range of tastes is exhilarating.

One, for instance, told me she is most turned on by "noticeably bobbing Adam's apples." Another confessed she looked for guys with "strong noses, nice mothers, some degree of motor-headedness, and no guns." And still another likes "guys who know a lot of trivia about world history, literature, and pop culture—like Burgess Meredith's birthday, for instance, or the date of the signing of the Magna Carta, or how many slices of pizza Americans consume in a year."

Not that the absence of such specifies is always a deal breaker. "While I am partial to blue eyes," a twenty-something brunette New Yorker told me, "the last two guys whom I dated had muddy eyes. I have noticed that many people have supposed types, but they rarely end up with that type. One friend of mine once claimed that the most important thing in a prospective mate was that he be active, yet her husband is a coach potato. She's afraid that their daughter, a baby who loves to play on the floor, will think her father is simply a voice from behind the coffee table. Love seems to have no rhyme or reason." Somewhere between the "by-the-numbers" approach of science and the indecipherable vagaries of actual desire, love does manage to find its eccentric way.

If there exists any unifying principle whatsoever in this business of attraction, perhaps it's the insight contained in a joke by a woman named Emma: "I'm attracted," she sums up, "by a man who understands it's all about me. Me! Me! Me! Focus on me!"

In such a sentiment, both genders appear to have at last found common ground.

**—JIM THORNTON**

# Woo Her With Words

WHAT DO YOU DO when it's 1833 and you've fallen for an older woman named George? "My dear George," writes 23-year-old Alfred de Musset to novelist and gadfly George Sand, "I have something stupid and ridiculous to tell you. I am foolishly writing you instead of having told you this, I do not know why. . . . You will laugh in my face, will take me for a maker of phrases in all my relations with you hitherto. You will show me the door and you will think I am lying. I am in love with you."

Cute. As de Musset knows, love makes idiots of men; sometimes, it even turns them into letter writers. Short of the balloon-gram, perhaps no form of expression is more un-hip than the love letter. Here's a secret, though: Love letters work. They radiate personal touch; their old-fashioned charm lends them the aura of the genuine. Only the truly hardhearted letter recipient can fail to be swayed by the spectacle of a man trying—and inevitably failing—to find words for his love jones. Love letters will make your inarticulateness seem endearing, if you are willing to follow a few simple rules.

Consider the example of de Musset. Young pup though he is in 1833, he displays an uncanny knack for the basics. He pretends to struggle to hold himself back. He adopts the tone of a confession. He strikes a posture of humiliation. Like de Musset, if you claim to be overwhelmed by love ("It's not me speaking, it's the love"), you have a shot at eliciting a useful blend of pity and erotic curiosity; at the same time, if your pleas are rejected, you are left with the timeless excuse of not having been in your right mind.

Practicalities: Go low-tech, and avoid anything that smacks of the generic. No e-mail, and no fancy fonts (e-mail is for sex, not for love). Your handwriting can be sloppy, even illegible at times—that's part of the personal touch. Use plain paper (simplicity), note-size (intimacy).

Keep the letter down to a few paragraphs, and at all costs avoid the kinds of exaggeration that are the stock in trade of traditional love letters. We live in a suspicious age, and exaggerated promises and claims ("always," "forever") may backfire.

Try to appear motiveless in the letter, especially in regard to sex. Don't thank the addressee for sex, don't apologize for sex, and don't appear to want sex too badly, even though you will be lying.

Don't send the letter on obvious milestone dates—anniversaries, holidays, payday. If your emotional patterns are transparent, you become uninteresting and may deserve not to be loved. Avoid clichés. Clichés are for men who don't need love badly enough to be writing letters. The language should have the texture of you in it—your personality, your humor, even your vulnerabilities. It should reflect a deep knowledge of your partner as well. Some years ago I wrote what I thought was a rather convincing letter to a woman I'd recently met. She was less persuaded. I had spelled her name wrong, eight times. She took it as a sign. She was right.

—MARK LEVINE

# He Said, She Said

I'LL NEVER UNDERSTAND why, but when it comes to communicating in relationships, men and women insist on playing dodge ball. Whenever I played the game in grade school, I got hit in the head. You'd think such adverse conditioning would have left an indelible impression. Unfortunately, it hasn't for many people. Relationship analyses like *Men Are From Mars, Women Are From Venus* have made things even

more difficult for men and women. Both sexes seem to be happier carrying on the traditions of Men Are Walking Dicks and Women Are Hormonal C-words because those lanes of communication are still easier to navigate than the New Age psychobabble of "getting in touch with your partner's feelings."

The "men and women are different creatures from different planets" theory just doesn't work in real life when the chemistry between a man and a woman sets off fireworks in each other. It's like saying, "Let the games begin." They can no longer be honest with one other, and communication gets confusing, if not outright ulcer-inducing.

For ages there has been a seemingly undisputable belief that men are incapable of talking about their feelings, almost as though they lack a gland that would permit it. Yet I constantly hear about guys going to bars with their buddies and pouring their hearts out over a load of longnecks. I support male support groups, but common sense would dictate that talking to the babe you're talking about (and not while hammered) might get better results. The bottom line is, in order to get a good level of communication going, you have to actually *communicate*. Why is it such a terrifying thought to bare your mind to the person with whom you routinely bare your butt? It doesn't matter why it's terrifying. Think of it as an extreme sport—rock climbing, sky surfing, talking to your girlfriend. There's no expensive equipment to go with this death-defying act, just a piece of advice: Be nice. Women tend to take "we need to talk" moments as rejection. If you just stick to the thing you need to fix and reassure her, you'll get results. If you're going to be away on a business trip during her birthday, give it to her straight, but back it up with something sweet, like promising to do something special when you get back and sending flowers on her birthday. That way, she won't take it personally, and you won't get your head ripped off. If you want to try something new in bed, compliment her bod, tell her how much she excites you, and then make your suggestion. See how easy it is?

If a fight is unavoidable, keep it fair. Don't bring up past stuff that's been resolved, don't lob any physical insults, and don't veer off into "I don't like how you fight" tangents. Stick to the problem at hand, come to as much of a compromise as you can, and have great makeup sex afterward. Lastly, if you're having the kind of communication problem where the only thing you talk about is whether to go for burritos before or after the movie, it's time to reassess. It might be that this is the kind of relationship where the sex is so good that you never noticed you don't have anything to say to each other when you're both dressed. But if she's someone you used to talk to like a best friend, you know what you should at least *try* to do. *And no, I don't mean you should hit her upside the head with a ball.*

— SUZAN COLÓN

# The PMS Playbook

JENNIFER MADE IT EASY. "Dad, I've got PMS," my daughter would say. "Please stop at the store and get me Advil and chocolate. Oh, and for the next few days, *stay out of my face.*"

So I brought home the supplies and gladly deferred

parental nagging—at least until Jennifer entered a more congenial state. Aware that the chances for conflict rose exponentially during her premenstrual phase, we forged a well-defined strategy to avoid it.

With other women, the rules may be less clear. In fact, few men have any idea about how to handle the emotional component of premenstrual syndrome. Whether it's affecting a daughter, wife, girlfriend, or coworker, PMS is a facet of female behavior that can sting and exasperate the most imperturbable among us.

Without a cautionary shadow crossing her countenance, the mood of an otherwise tender and levelheaded woman can go south. Devolving into a hybrid of Thelma and Louise, she may yell over imagined slights, give you the withering deep freeze, even toss a casserole dish at your cranium. While PMS is transitory, its emotional fallout can turn a relationship into Chernobyl.

"I've heard more than a few women say their divorces were caused by PMS," says Diana Taylor, R.N., Ph.D., director of the Premenstrual Symptom Management Program at the University of California at San Francisco's School of Nursing. "A woman may have other underlying problems, or the relationship may not have been great to begin with—and PMS magnifies these flaws. The condition causes the woman to have an abnormal response to a normal event."

Most men find these responses baffling. Thus, they make jokes about PMS or ascribe *any* assertive female behavior to its influence. Yet as many as 95 percent of women experience some physical or emotional symptoms of PMS at some point during their childbearing years. Next time you're at the receiving end of monthly unreasonableness, remind yourself that women don't like PMS or its results any better than you do—and that it ain't going away.

## In Harm's Way

It is, therefore, a management problem. And the skillful use of various strategies can help a woman manage her symptoms. Call it an act of kindness or enlightened self-interest. But be warned: Compared to handling PMS, negotiating an end to the baseball strike is cake.

Indeed, PMS stems from a complex interplay of physiology and psychological reactions to stress. But alas, scientists know more about DNA sequencing than about how hormones drive PMS behavior. Linked to roughly 150 symptoms, PMS is an enigmatic affliction that defies easy definition.

"There are theories associating PMS with estrogen excess, an estrogen-to-progesterone imbalance, vitamin deficiencies, and low blood sugar," says Taylor, who has evaluated the cycles of more than 5,000 women and conducts nationwide clinical studies of menstruation and women's health. "You can make arguments for all the causes. But none has been substantiated. And no single treatment has been proven effective."

But none of this is terribly helpful to the average man trying to understand a woman who suddenly feels physically cruddy, snaps at his every suggestion, or becomes uncharacteristically daft. "It's silly. But PMS heightens feelings about everything," says Janet R. Laubgross, Ph.D., a Fairfax, Virginia, clinical psychologist who treats many women who have PMS.

Many guys are flummoxed by a PMSing woman's heightened hostility. There's usually a reason at the root of her ire, but the virulence of the attack may be way out of proportion to the importance of the issue. "Women aren't always good at expressing minor anger," says Leslie Hartley Gise an associate clinical professor at the Mount Sinai School of Medicine in New York and director of the school's Premenstrual Syndromes Program. "With PMS they kind of have a chemical and social license to let go, and it doesn't always turn out well."

Unfortunately, relatively few women warn us when we're in harm's way. Part of the reluctance is cultural. Since men have used PMS to discount female behavior, a woman may fear that her partner will ignore legitimate concerns. Admitting to

PMS at work suggests that a woman has lost command of her professional self.

Despite the cyclical nature of menstruation, PMS can sneak up on and overtake a woman when she least expects it. "The onset of symptoms can change throughout a woman's life, varying from month to month," says Gary Galante, vice-president of research and development for Chattem Inc., which manufactures an over-the-counter PMS medicine. For most women, symptoms arise 1 to 10 days before menstruation and disappear once the period starts. But as new research indicates, some suffer through PMS-like symptoms at other times. My wife, for example, gets a little cranky about a week after her period. Go figure.

"Perhaps the most difficult thing to understand is that just when women are most unbearable is often also the time when some of them most enjoy sex," says PMS researcher Katharina Dalton, author of *Once a Month*. Indeed, many women report an increased libido during the PMS phase. But sex, too, can fall victim to interpersonal conflagrations.

## Confronting Your Fate

Recognizing the onset of PMS is the first step in dealing with the condition; once you've known a woman for a while, this may become easier. One clue might be when, as Taylor says, "a woman reacts with a level of anger that's out of proportion to the event or issue that caused it."

The second step, and the foundation of PMS management for men, is to provide tea and sympathy—served with the steely nerves of an explosives technician. In that vein, don't tip your hand. "Never, never tell a woman she has PMS," says Galante. "I've sat in on focus groups, and women agree that nothing makes them more angry." Let her diagnose herself.

Tone of voice is helpful: Speak with empathy but avoid a patronizing edge. Use "I" and "feeling" statements. "Body language also becomes very

important," notes Taylor. "Crossing your arms indicates you're defensive." Granted, this Machiavellian appeasement may seem ridiculous, but remember that you're trying to deflect Big Trouble.

"In a close relationship," adds Laubgross, "a man might be able to ask the woman where she is in her cycle. This is an indirect way of allowing her to acknowledge the PMS." Just make sure not to ask in the middle of an argument.

Once the women I know confess to the obvious, the she-devil is half-whipped. And it stays whipped as long as you reassure her that whatever was bothering her has at least some roots in reality and—since she may feel guilty after launching a verbal barrage—that you haven't taken the barbs personally.

## The Five Circles of Hell

Researchers have tried to define PMS using every explanatory model short of chaos theory—which, to be frank, probably best applies. During the past decade, PMS experts grouped the symptoms into common "clusters." It made sense, since for some women PMS results in muscle stiffness, headaches, cramps, and backaches. For others, it produces water retention and bloating, tender breasts and sensitive skin. Still others experience anger, tension, irritability, anxiety, depression, and mood swings. And in a small minority of women, PMS induces obsessive thinking, concentration problems, and a loss of interest in just about everything.

According to Leslie Hartley Gise, such groupings produced little in the way of effective treatments. So new categories have recently emerged that focus on gradations of the syndrome's severity while accounting for conditions that aren't caused by PMS but are magnified during the premenstruum.

**Level 1: One or two mild symptoms that don't track with the menstrual cycle and can manifest themselves even right**

after the period. Treatment: dietary changes, exercise, over-the-counter medications, pain reliever.

Level 2: One relatively mild symptom, whether a headache, bloating, or a minor case of the blues. Treatment: dietary changes, exercise, over-the-counter medications, pain reliever.

Level 3: Two or more mild-to-moderate symptoms (fatigue, irritability, pain) that don't greatly interfere with a woman's daily life. Thirty percent to 50 percent of all women fall into this category. Treatment: same as for Levels 1 and 2.

Level 4: Five or more serious symptoms—from depression to anger, lethargy, anxiety, and physical pain—interfere with a woman's ability to deal with relationships at work or home. Only 3 percent to 5 percent of women are saddled with this condition. Treatment: See a doctor.

Level 5: Multiple symptoms exacerbate an underlying health condition—psychiatric problems or organic illnesses. In other words, PMS makes clinical depression worse or magnifies the problems of diabetes, chronic fatigue syndrome, or other conditions. Treatment: See a doctor fast.

—JAY STULLER

# Man the Kitchen

I WAS LUCKY ENOUGH to grow up in a household with a father who cooked—and cooked well. Considering the times—the '50s, '60s, and '70s—this was pretty unusual, particularly in our small southern town. Just recently, I asked him what motivated him to learn the culinary arts. "I had to or I would have starved to death!" he said, laughing. It turns out that when my mother was pregnant with me, she had severe and enduring morning sickness and couldn't go anywhere near the kitchen. Dad decided to take matters into his own hands and taught himself to cook, using an Italian recipe book as a training manual. Before long, he found that he enjoyed the process; it became a relaxing pastime for him—and our family and friends benefited from his hobby.

*Give me a woman who loves beer and I will conquer the world.*

—KAISER WILHELM

You don't have to wait for a situation like my dad's to impress the love of your life, however. Even if you're just dating, you can really earn points by making dinner for your gal. When you choose your menu, don't forget to consider any food restrictions she may have due to allergies or a vegetarian diet.

So whether you'd like to whip something up to romance the new woman in your life or turn the tables on the one who's been doing all the cooking since you started living together, or should you find yourself in a situation where you *have* to cook for the two of you, the following tips can help you put together some tasty repasts.

Go with what you know. When you start out, don't try complicated recipes filled with exotic ingredients. Next time you order pasta in a restaurant, take note of the ingredients you enjoy; then experiment on your own. Buy fresh vegetables in season, such as zucchini or tomatoes, and simply sauté them in olive oil with garlic, oregano, and salt. Serve, if possible, with fresh pasta; follow the cooking directions on the package and top with your vegetable sauce. Toss lightly so that the liquid is dispersed throughout the pasta; then grate fresh Parmesan cheese on top. Serve with crusty bread and a green salad.

Lasagna was my dad's intro to cooking; he used a recipe in a 1952 cookbook called *The Art of Italian Cooking;* it's long out of print, but there are plenty of others on the market—and even the recipes on the side of a pasta box, believe it or not, offer simple directions for making this hearty dish. (For a healthier version, you can substitute spinach—either freshly chopped or frozen that's been thawed—for the meat.)

If you're good with a grill, let her sit back and sip a beer while you barbecue steaks, shishkebabs, salmon, or chicken; wrap fresh corn (left in the husks) or Idaho potatoes in foil and place them in the coals. Test with a fork for softness to see when they're ready.

## COOK WITH PASSION

Every guy needs to know how to cook, and to cook well, if for no other reason than that cooking is the best path to seduction. I'm not talking here about developing a signature dish. That inevitably becomes a caricature dish ("You're having dinner at Bob's? I hope you like calamari"). The thing to master is real cooking.

I could rant about the need for the right tools, especially a gas range, a food processor, and some excellent knives, and about how simplicity tends to yield the finest results (Paul Prudhomme roasts garlic by holding a complete head with tongs in a gas flame set on high). But I've come to believe that what separates a real cook from a signature cook is the use of fresh herbs and spices.

I've got four favorites: garlic, ginger, jalapeño peppers, and basil. No aphrodisiac can match the power of a leaf of basil crushed between the fingertips, or the scent of freshly peeled and sliced ginger under a would-be lover's nose, or the sensory explosion that occurs when a tablespoon of minced garlic encounters a cast-iron skillet containing hot olive oil. (Never use spray-on oil. It's the culinary equivalent of combing hair over a bald spot.)

As a test of these ingredients, try this: Dice garlic, jalapeños, and ginger to produce a tablespoon of each. Toss these with great flourish into an iron skillet containing two tablespoons of hot oil. Add two gutted but otherwise whole trout (or fresh scallops, shrimp, or calamari). Drizzle with fresh lime juice. Garnish with four large leaves of basil sliced into thin strips. Pour the wine—I recommend a Cale chardonnay. Put on some Keith Jarrett. Serve the trout when the flesh is opaque. This could easily become a signature dish. But it could also open the door to a new realm of culinary and sensual experimentation. And that's cooking.

—ERIK LARSON

Fresh ingredients need the least amount of "work." Just as nothing beats fresh-picked vegetables, the same can be said for seafood—particularly fish you've caught yourself! After cleaning and filleting, lightly dust the bass or trout in flour, then briefly sauté in olive oil and butter. Be careful not to overcook fish; to know when it's done, try pressing on it, and if it springs back, it's ready.

An old-fashioned shrimp boil is easy and fun. Put an onion or a celery stalk, along with crab or shrimp boil seasoning, in a big pot of water; when it comes to a boil, throw in the shrimp, cover, then turn off the heat and let the shrimp cook for three to five minutes; when the shrimp turn a darker color, they're done (again, be careful not to overcook). You can make your own cocktail sauce by mixing ketchup with some horseradish and a little Tabasco and Worcestershire sauce and a squeeze of fresh lemon. (Speaking of lemon, always place a few slices on the plate with any seafood dish—for taste and visual appeal.)

Another easy dish is a pot of fresh steamed mussels. Sauté garlic in olive oil, and add that plus two more tablespoons of olive oil and a half cup of white wine to a pot full of carefully washed mussels. Cover, turn on medium heat, and remove when the mussel shells open up. Serve with hot bread.

It's amazing what a tablecloth, cloth napkins, candlelight, and a good bottle of wine can do for a meal. Also, have those Frank Sinatra CDs handy—especially if you're cooking pasta.

**—HOLLY GEORGE-WARREN**

# Risk-Free Lingerie Buying

AN IMMODEST SCENARIO: It's an occasion—a holiday, a birthday, *an anniversary*—and you've risen to it. You present your wife or girlfriend with an elaborately wrapped trifle: silver box, black taffeta ribbon. She frowns at first, fearing the worst kind of lingerie gift. But what's this? Nestled in the folds of the tissue paper rests something silky and wispy and absolutely fabulous. She looks at you with a new level of respect and interest. A man who actually knows how to buy lingerie—now *this* is a rare gift. She retreats; she replaces her white cotton with this incredible item; she holds her breath and looks in the mirror. Not only is she your most exciting fantasy; she's her own.

An hour later, the gift that you selected in sweat and agony and presented in hope and terror lies in tatters around the bed. A hundred dollars, and it lasted five minutes.

WILLIAM WALDRON

That was the best hundred dollars you ever spent.

And here is how to get there, to that scene of ultimate satiation: a return-proof guide to buying your lover the kind of lingerie she'd choose for herself.

## Start Simple

The very first piece of lingerie you give a woman can set the tone for how finery will play into your relationship, so it's vital to choose wisely. You don't want to scare her off by making her feel as if you're setting the stage for black leather corsets and handcuffs down the road, yet you also don't want to give her something that looks as if your grandmother picked it out. Try a white eyelet demi-cup bra with matching panties

or an ethereal peach silk nightgown. Both are innocently sexy without being the least bit sleazy.

## Know Your Stuff

But once you move beyond bras, panties, and nightgowns, you enter a jungle of foreign and mysterious garments that might make the perfect purchase—if only you knew what they were. A lexicon:

**FULL SLIP.** A slightly old-fashioned but highly elegant item that resembles a knee-length dress with a low-cut neckline and thin shoulder straps. Think Catherine Deneuve in *Belle du Jour.* Getting a woman a full slip is more like buying her clothes than lingerie, except with higher voltage.

**CHEMISE.** A chemise (French for *shirt*) is essentially a truncated version of a full slip: simple and relatively demure on top; short—barely butt-length. It's stylish, hides a multitude of figure flaws, and can be extremely sexy, especially when worn without panties.

**TEDDY.** A teddy is a bathing suit on aphrodisiacs—one-piece, fitted to the body, unmistakably erotic. Men generally love them, but women are more ambivalent. On the plus side, teddies can be flattering and, if oh-so-slightly snug, can act as a turn-on for both of you. (Skintight bodysuits—updated versions of teddies in such fabrics as stretch velvet that can be worn as shirts—are most likely to make a woman happy.) But most teddies are impractical for anything but posing in—and that includes any kind of sex.

**TAP PANTS.** Tap pants are distaff boxer shorts, sexiest when full and sheer. They make great foreplay gear, but they don't really work any other way, under clothes or in bed.

**CAMISOLE.** A camisole is a waist-length chemise—a feminine undershirt—pretty and classy but, again, not too practical or erotic.

## Size It Up

"Men always estimate that the woman they're buying for is about the saleswoman's size," says Rebecca

Apsan, the owner of La Petite Coquette, a downtown Manhattan lingerie shop. "I ask men if their girlfriend's breasts are the size of a lemon, an orange, or a grapefruit—that's A, B, and C. Better yet, men can go through her lingerie drawer and write down sizes from the labels."

When choosing a garment, be sure it's geared to your partner's body type. If she loves her breasts, you might investigate top-of-the-line bras that look like a scrap of lace but are engineered like the Verrazano Bridge. A woman who is in great shape but who is small on top might prefer a bodysuit that shows off her muscles without emphasizing her lack of curves. If she's sensitive about her weight, go for maximum coverage and a loose fit and invest in a supremely sexy fabric (a creamy satin or rich lace).

## Don't Be Cheap

Money is key to buying the kind of lingerie a woman will adore. Not that you have to spend hundreds, but if you've got only 20 bucks, squander it all on a tiny pair of panties. In real silk. And think with your fin-

gers: slippery satin, sheer chiffon, elaborate lace. And ultrafeminine pale pink or cool leopard skin are on most women's A-list.

## Listen to Your Relationship

The ultimate success of a lingerie offering will depend on your relationship. If you have an untried or a testy lingerie history, the best gift may be something distinctly nonsexy (like a terry-cloth bathrobe), along with an erotic sidelight (a G-string, say) that you can laugh off as a joke if she freaks.

Like love, lingerie buying is a cumulative experience, building over time. Tasseled pasties and crotchless panties, presented prematurely, can be disastrous. But after the terry robe and the silk chemise and the teeny bikinis and the leopard skin Wonderbra have been offered, accepted, and enjoyed, you might find success with lingerie that's more adventurous. Way more adventurous.

—PAMELA REDMOND SATRAN

SEX

# Curse of the Bedroom Blahs

S EX, WHEN TRULY transcendent, defies time and space. It's as close to nirvana as mere mortals are allowed to wander. It frees the mind, relaxes the body, and nourishes the soul. It's the salve to life's petty aggravations.

The first decade of our sexual awareness unleashes a ravenous beast within us whose endless hunger is never sated. The libido is on overdrive, searching, stalking, sexualizing, and devouring each new experience with a fevered gluttony akin to frenzy.

Then, just as the body giveth, the body can taketh away. With a mind of its own, boredom sets in, and the libido simply goes on strike. Shut down. Atrophy. Feels stale. Wrung out. The result of slim pickens on a playing field littered with sexual burnouts? Overexposure to the American fetish of using gorgeous females as mere marketing ploys to sell you everything from toothpaste to sport utility vehicles? Or is monogamy to blame for your bedroom blahs? Before wolfing down a fistful of black-market Viagra, here are a few suggestions.

1. **Relax.** Although a good romp may relieve stress, stress is not an aphrodisiac. It's a turnoff for both you and your partner. Work out, swim, bike, get your mind off the job, the boss, the rent, the bills, and let the mind wander. And if that's a broken record of worry and insecurities, it will greatly decrease your sexual performance. (Unless you've got an Oedipus complex and your partner is someone who enjoys hearing a grown man whine, this is not good.) The enduring sex appeal of Bogie and James Bond is that they were never mama's boys.

2. **Treat yourself.** Redo the boudoir. Paint it burnished gold, put up heavy velvet curtains, buy new sheets and pillows. Dim the lights. Program sexy music. Buy yourself a satin smoking jacket. Think opium den. Keep it immaculate even if the rest of the house is a bachelor-pad pig farm. Take the TV away from the foot of the bed, or at least hide it in an armoire and use only for European soft- or hard-core skin flicks. Dedicate your "sex palace" as a special retreat, eliminate utilitarian drab, and crown yourself the king of sex.

3. **Practice on yourself.** Masturbation is the next best thing to being there. Sometimes it's actually preferable. Use your imagination, break out the lube, and practice the tantric art of withholding ejaculation. Do this a few nights in a row and I guarantee your partner will thank you.

4. **Be spontaneous and take it out of the bedroom.** The most exciting part of those horny teenage years was the risk of getting caught. Take chances. The car, the roof, the roof of the car, stairwells, basements, public parks at sundown, the bathroom at the library, the golf course, the tennis court at the crack of dawn. *Note:* These should be done with a partner—in case you get busted, the courts are far more lenient to couples than to an odd man out. Remember, it helped Hugh Grant gain respect.

5. **Experiment.** If you have a high-pressured job or are a control freak, relinquish every now and then. It helps to blow off steam. Takes the onus off performance. Beg to service her.

6. **If there are consistent problems, seek professional help.** A temporary flagging of sexual interest is normal. Sure, there are more important things than a satisfying sex life, but good sex is a gift we owe ourselves. You deserve it, don't you?

—LYDIA LUNCH

# The Sensual Rubdown

I N THE FINE ART of giving pleasure to the body's largest organ, the skin, everlasting gratitude can be yours if you take the time to master a few basic strokes. (I can attest to this, as can my well-oiled wife-slash-research assistant.) The art of sensual massage is steeped in history, mostly

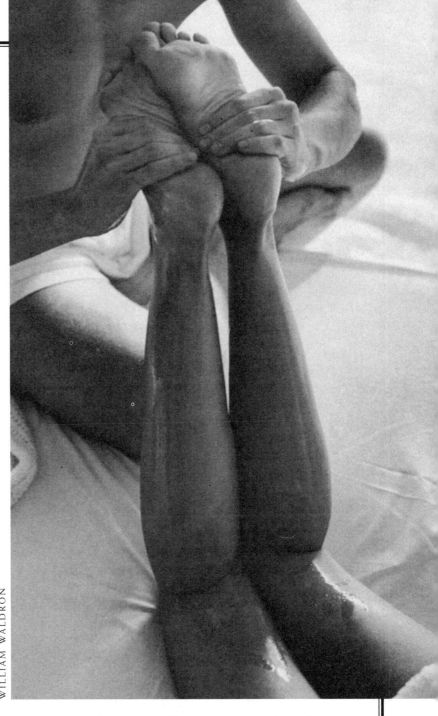

Eastern. It's lauded in a 5,000-year-old Chinese treatise called the *Nei Ching*. The *Kamasutra's* take: "If lovers spend time playing with and caressing each other, then their ecstasy and confidence increase. Love-play enhances pleasure."

With all respect to ancient Eastern sages: *no kidding*. And yet, simple though it sounds, my wife and I recently found ourselves in need of a little rudimentary love play. She'd just given birth, and between kid, sleep deprivation, and busy schedules (we both work), we'd been going through an extended *coitus hiatus*. And when we did get horizontal, it was somewhat mechanical. We had stopped communicating and experimenting.

We were, in short, poster children for sensual massage. According to experts on matters sexual, massage is the perfect Rx for couples who have hit a plateau. For starters, it provides a forum to work on those crucial coital communication skills. "It helps people learn to talk about what they want—in a less threatening situation," says Dr. Geoffrey White, a Los Angeles psychologist who specializes in sex therapy. During a massage, he explains, "it's easier for people to say 'try it this way' or 'do it harder' than if they're having genital contact."

White, in fact, prescribes massage as part of his couples counseling, using it to combat specific performance problems, such as rapid ejaculation for men and difficulty achieving orgasm for women. He instructs patients to rub, caress, massage—just

WILLIAM WALDRON

so long as they steer clear of the genitals. Knowing that intercourse is off-limits relieves them of potential performance anxiety. "You want to get back to the process, the moment," he says, "and not be thinking about the performance or the goal."

For my part, I'm sometimes selfish in the sack, looking out for No. 1 while leaving my wife in orgasmic limbo. Men of the wham-bam-thank-you-ma'am school are the most resistant to massage, says White, yet they have the most to learn. "For people who are only in it for themselves," he says, "massage is a way to learn how to develop empathy or sensitivity for their partner."

One thing I've never been averse to is a little learning.

## Rules of Thumb

**LESSON ONE.** Slather up. A dollop of massage oil will lubricate the body, allowing your hands to glide easily over the skin. Meanwhile, the friction heats the oil, turning those hands into burning mitts of passion. "Your hands are hot," my wife purred during our first road test. "That feels really, really good."

Don't use hand cream or body lotion, which are too easily absorbed into the skin. Any vegetable oil will work, but I prefer an oil designed specifically for massage. A subtle scent—lavender and ber-gamot are nice; rosemary is reputed to be an aphrodisiac—enhances the erotic effects. Always warm the oil before starting (a small dish for 10 seconds in the microwave works well and also infuses the air with the scent), and pour it into your hand before placing it on your partner's body. Don't use too much; you're not marinating a chicken.

**LESSON TWO.** Review the available literature. Books are helpful for learning the strokes. (See, for example, *The Complete Guide to Massage* by Susan Mumford.) Look for copious photos and illustrations: Some of these moves are easier seen than

described. Better still, rent one of the many videotapes on the subject. (*Massage . . . the Touch of Love*, from MCA Home Video, is my favorite; I found it for $30 at my local Borders superstore.)

Be warned, however, that many authorities on the subject tend toward New Age goop that can be hard to stomach. In *Exotic Massage for Lovers* by Timothy Freke and *The Tao of Sexual Massage* by Stephen Russell and Jürgen Kolb, there's much talk about "cleansing auras" and "removing negative energy" in chapters titled "Pleasuring the Jade Stalk," "Pounding the Rear Door of the Crimson Palace," and "Playing Siva's Flute."

And don't let the books and videos make you neurotic. The best way to start is to just dig in and get your hands oily. Sensual massage is like golf: It's hard to do well, but any moron can tee it up, mess around, and have a good time.

## Different Strokes

So your hands are oiled; your partner is splayed across the bed. Now what?

Commence rubbing. Start with broad, easy strokes to apply the oil. "It's better to begin with very, very gentle strokes and then work up," says Roger Hicks, the coauthor, with Victoria Day, of *A Lover's Guide to Massage*. "You'll feel through your fingers where you need to push harder." Use the whole of your palm together with your fingers, which you should keep relaxed. Tense fingers are the mortal enemies of sensual massage.

Keep the strokes reliable, rhythmic—no herky-jerky motions that will rouse your partner from her reverie. Although you'll be working on one body part at a time, the massage should feel like a continuous sequence.

Day, a British masseuse, recommends a sequence that begins with a simple neck massage, calling it "one of the most immediately relaxing and effective techniques you can possibly learn." With your partner lying facedown, use your thumbs to relax the muscles on either side of the spine. Using small rotational movements, work across the upper part of the shoulders. Then place your hands on either side of your partner's neck and stroke outward across the shoulders, using firm pressure on the outward stroke and lighter pressure as you return.

Next, kneel astride your partner's butt (a highly erotic position for both parties) and work your hands up her back, on either side of the spine, returning with light pressure along the sensitive border where back and stomach converge. Progress to deeper, kneading strokes, feeling with your fingers for stiff muscles. Now run your forearm up the middle of her back for a spine-stretching tingle.

To complete the back, massage the arms and legs, again applying added pressure on the upward stroke. Pay particular attention to the inner thighs, up to but not yet including the genitals. Most women find this extremely relaxing. But keep your ears open for indications that *your* partner might not. "Don't assume that what you like, the other person likes," explains Day. "Check as you go along that you've got it right for both people." In our case, my wife told me she didn't appreciate the more percussive strokes, the pounding and chopping. I, on the other hand, enjoy a bit of the rough stuff. As they say, different folks, different strokes.

## The Naughty Bits

As you wend your way up, down, and around your partner's body, exploring her landscape like an eager tourist, you'll begin to discover certain parts that— shall we say—respond particularly effusively to sensual massage. I once had a girlfriend who could be transported to the portals of passion with a simple (albeit lengthy) foot massage. My wife also likes foot play, but she's more partial to leg massages. She also feels a sweet release of tension whenever I massage my thumbs along the top of her buttocks, at the base

of the spine. The stomach is, for many women, another hot spot. "There are areas that are highly sensitive," Day says, citing "the navel, just above the thighs, and just inside the hipbone."

A sensual massage is one that stops just shy of touching the naughty bits, though inevitably you'll get to the point where you'll want to cross the line. When caressing the breasts and genitals, keep in mind the cardinal massage rules: Begin gently, to maintain the relaxing atmosphere, and make certain your partner is comfortable communicating her wishes and desires.

Another erotic treat is going skin to skin—massaging her body with yours and vice versa. By the time you're done rubbing and you're ready to rumble, your bodies are oiled up and wondrously slippery. If you're feeling particularly amorous—and ambitious—try a body slide. Smear the front of your body with still more oil and, starting at her feet, slide your greasy body up her legs, buttocks, and back. Make sure she reciprocates.

Don't be afraid to get creative. Use your fingernails, alternating between rubbing and light scratching so that your partner is never sure which to expect. Or try massaging each other with something other than your hands. Use soft fabrics like silk or velvet. If your partner has long hair, have her trail it slowly down your back. Ask her to rub your body with her breasts. Arousal is the mother of invention.

## Hands-on Approach

Did sensual massage totally transform my love life? Wrong question. As Hicks points out, that's exactly the type of goal-oriented approach you're looking to avoid.

For the record, though, it definitely got us through our fallow period. Before starting, we decided that intercourse would be off the menu. Thus, I concentrated solely on the task at hand. This did not go unnoticed by my wife. "When you're not fixated on the goal of penetration and ejaculation," she said (sounding strangely like Dr. Ruth), "then your mind is more focused on what you're doing at the moment rather than what's coming—if you'll pardon the expression."

Not surprisingly, on the occasions when we did opt for the wild thing, I was eager to earn the same positive feedback. We talked about pleasure, about what turned us on, what felt good and what did not. For the first time in years we found ourselves looking at the clock and saying, "Wow, is it midnight already?"

—STEVEN EDWARDS

SEX

# Eight Big Myths

WHEN IT COMES to sex, there's an odd sort of erosion that afflicts sexual certitude. No matter how enlightened we are—no matter how fearlessly we explore and explode our misconceptions—discredited but perversely persuasive notions keep sneaking back, fueled by the dynamic duo of insecurity and defensiveness. Of course, we're too savvy to still believe, for instance, that size begets her satisfaction. Right? But somehow the anxiety still lurks in a corner of your subconscious, ready to pounce at inopportune moments. So it is with the eight topics arrayed below. You've heard that they're not true, but you've never really been convinced. And so they keep creeping back into your consciousness, like a drug-resistant virus.

Consider this your booster shot.

1. Men reach their sexual peak between the ages of 18 and 25. Yes, men between the ages of 18 and 25 are in their physical prime: Bodies work faster, athletics are easier, and we have a harder time keeping it down than coax-

ing it up. "But that's a far cry from a sexual peak," says Dr. Judy Seifer, the host of the *Videos for Lovers* videotape series. "The truth is, the majority of men haven't had nearly enough sex by their mid-twenties to beget mastery. I've found many men over 50 who were convinced that they'd had lousy sex all through their twenties, thirties, and forties, and it wasn't until their later years that the experience was of the earth-shattering variety." Far from being petered out after 25, most of us are just getting up to speed.

2. Women have less energy for sex than men do. "During the Victorian era," says Bernie Zilbergeld, Ph.D., the author of *The New Male Sexuality*, "women's sexuality was officially repressed. That legacy is still with us." This idea seems to rely on the distortion of a number of tenets of our cultural common wisdom, among them the recognized truth that men obsess about sex much more than women do. But there's a difference between how often you think about it and how deeply that urge runs. According to Dr. William Masters (of Masters and Johnson fame), "Women are usually physically capable of having more sex than men are. One of the most common com-

plaints issued by couples seeking sexual counseling is that they're not having enough sex. Who's doing most of the complaining? The women. Furthermore, women can have multiple orgasms, and when they do, often their third or fourth orgasm is more intense than their first." Now *that's* sexual energy.

3. Women always take longer to build toward orgasm than men do. This one falls into the sad category of defensive mythology. The idea that women don't come as quickly as men do reassures us that we're not bad lovers; it gives us an excuse. But the truth is far more complicated. "Biologically, women can orgasm as quickly as men," says Sherry Lehman, the author of *Seven Days to Better Sex and a More Loving Relationship.* "But, often, psychologically they can't. How fast you can orgasm is dictated by, among other things, how comfortable you are with your partner."

To help speed up the process, Lehman says, you have to understand that most really good foreplay takes place outside the bedroom. To ease psychological barriers in the evening, start in the afternoon—call her from work, ask how her day is going, tell her you're going to make it better, let her imagine the possibilities. "If you want to turn a woman on," says Lehman, "the organ to focus on is her brain."

4. Bigger is better. Despite the ego salve of the male mantra "It's not the meat, it's the motion," this phrase still lingers somewhere in the back of every guy's closet of insecurities. It's time for an anatomy lesson. The average vagina is three and a half inches long. Masters and Johnson called it an "organ of accommodation." Not only does the vagina expand with arousal to make room for that beef; it then contracts, shrinking and locking around it. "Unless you have an exceptionally small or exceptionally large penis," says Dr. Robert Birch, the author of *Oral Caress,* "once you're inside the vagina, women can't really tell how big you are."

5. Rapid ejaculation is caused by too much arousal. How many times have you counted sheep, gone over stock quotes—done anything you possibly could to ward off the big E? "All those 'think of something else' thoughts might just be your problem," says Judy Seifer. "Sexually,

it's impossible to be in two places at the same time—it screws up the machinery. The usual scenario is, anxiety of some sort caus-es the first few rapid-ejaculatory experiences, but after that the mind takes over. Every time you climb into bed you think, *Is it gonna happen again? Shit, I'd better count sheep.* So all of a sudden you're in two places at once, and you're not really feeling what sex feels like, and if you're not 'feeling the feelings,' there's no way to control them."

Instead, try to focus all your thoughts on the physical sensations of intercourse. You'll leave no room for anxiety, no room for what's causing rapid ejaculation in the first place. And slow down. Try simply pausing inside your partner for a while, get used to those feelings, then build back up to that mad-dog sex you'd like to be having.

6. Men can't have "bad" orgasms. "Most men want to believe that the only bad orgasm is no orgasm," says Seifer. "Actually, men and women experience orgasms in varying degrees, and some of those orgasms are deeply satisfying, while some just fizzle. Often young men will tell you that there is no such thing as a bad orgasm, but the fact is, they've never had a really good orgasm, so they don't have a basis for comparison."

To up the intensity of your orgasm, try not to fixate on the end result. Focusing on the O from the moment you kiss to the moment you come is kind of like worrying about whether or not you're going to pass the bar exam the day you start law school. Forget about it and you'll soon discover just how bad some of those old orgasms have been.

7. A vibrator in the sack is a sure sign of an unsatisfied lover. Since the beginning of the beginning we've been told that we should be able to please our women strictly through the old in-out. Our egos hang in the balance, but we're setting them up to take a pretty big hit. Only about 35 percent of all women can have an orgasm through vaginal stimulation alone, and of those, most can't do it every time. This isn't a question of sexual prowess; this is biology. If you want to please your partner, you're going to have to use more than just your tool. Which is where that other one comes in.

"There are very few guarantees in life," says Lonnie

Barbach, Ph.D., the author of *50 Ways to Please Your Lover (While You Please Yourself)*, "but if you want to bring a woman to orgasm, vibrators are as close to a sure bet as you can get."

Sherry Lehman suggests that you overcome your inhibitions by getting in on the action yourself. "Let her use it on you," she says. "Get into the feeling of it. And when you use it on her, let her guide your hand. Remember that many women just use a vibrator externally, so don't go in there and try to drill for oil. Try it with her on top and both of you can use the vibrator on her clitoris."

8. Women know when men orgasm. "This idea," says Birch, "is one that came from literature: 'She felt his powerful manhood exploding within.'" Sorry, but the vagina doesn't have a receptacle that's waiting to be filled. And its back wall is almost devoid of nerves, so even if you can come mightily, there's very little chance she's going to realize it. "In fact," says Birch, "very few women are sensitive enough to feel even the spasms of orgasm." Women know that men come the same way men know that women come: by listening to us grunt and watching us make funny faces.

—STEVEN KOTLER

SEX

# Her Orgasm

PRETEND I'M YOUR new girlfriend and this is my user's manual—everything you need to know to give me reliable, earth-shattering orgasms. No, I don't work exactly the same as every other woman, but if you can master my operation, you should be well on your way to proficiency with other makes and models.

All you need is a few pieces of equipment you probably already have lying around the house: a pair of opposable thumbs, a working tongue, a willing member, and a keen interest in your lover's pleasure.

Let's start with the good news: Most women are reasonably easy to please. Researchers estimate that just 10 percent to 25 percent either never have orgasms or have difficulty having them. (If you've met more than a couple of women who fit this description, this probably says more about you than it does about them.) Dr. Derek Polonsky, a Boston-based psychiatrist and the author of *Talking About Sex*, says some women are nonorgasmic because of a repressive or religiously strict upbringing or because they're on Prozac or another antidepressant. But most women who have difficulty getting off, says Polonsky, suffer from nothing more serious than a lack of knowledge—their own or their partner's—about what makes them feel good.

Not to worry, boys. It's never too late to learn.

## The ABCs of the O

Surprisingly, a woman's orgasm feels essentially the same to her as yours does to you. Not only are the major physiological responses identical—the changes in blood pressure, heart rate, muscle tension, pain threshold, and pupil diameter—but the emotional experience is remarkably similar as well. In the 1970s researchers at the University of Washington in Seattle asked 24 men and 24 women to describe their orgasms. When the names were removed and the responses were shuffled together, no one could tell which were the men's and which were the women's.

According to Dr. Beverly Whipple, a Rutgers University sex researcher and the coauthor of *The G-Spot*, the activities that most frequently bring a woman to orgasm are, in order, masturbation, masturbation by a partner, oral sex, intercourse, and fantasy. (Whipple has conducted experiments in which she observed women reach orgasm simply by imagining a sensual experience—anything they considered pleasurable—with no physical stimulation whatsoever.)

The reason for this hierarchy is anatomical. Activities that directly stimulate the clitoris, such as masturbation and oral sex, are the most likely to make women light up. That tiny bundle of soft tissue and nerves tucked between the top of the outer labia is the one and only organ in the human body—bless its little soul!—whose exclusive function is to transmit sexual sensation.

Techniques that stimulate the G-spot are the second most likely to trip a woman's trigger. This acorn-shaped mass of spongy tissue surrounding the urethra is located behind the front, inside wall of the vagina, usually about halfway up. If your partner doesn't get turned on by G-spot sex, though, there's no reason to worry. While early research tended to portray the G-spot as a kind of instant-ecstasy button, sex experts now know that women's reactions to such stimulation run from "Oh, my god, don't stop!" to "What the *hell* are you doing?"

Don't despair that "helping ourselves" is the No. 1 way most women get off. Just because it's the most reliable method doesn't mean it's the most desirable. It's certainly not what we opt for when we have a choice. What it does mean is that you should encourage a woman's self-discovery because the more she knows about what makes her feel good, the easier it will be for you to give her pleasure. This has certainly been true in my case: After spending half of my childhood afraid I was addicted to masturbation, my hours of practice paid off. I entered the world of grown-up sex with my clitoris in Olympic shape, ready to produce orgasm after orgasm in response to a wide variety of sexual escapades. If women were video games, I'd be Level 1 difficulty.

## Hand It to Her

The easiest way to get a woman off is with your fingers. The basic concept is to rub the clitoris rhythmically either up and down or in a circle. Don't go straight for the head itself—for most women, it's too sensitive. Instead, caress the area immediately surrounding it, starting slowly and gently and increasing the speed and frequency based on her cues. Watch how she moves her hips; notice when she tenses her arms, legs, and hands; listen to the rhythm of her breathing and don't be afraid to ask for help—if you need it, most of us will be happy to oblige.

Once a woman is warmed up, try sliding your fingers into her. In addition to giving her a psychological tingle from having a part of you inside of her, you can use your fingers to caress her G-spot. A gentle in-out action works well. If you're aiming for maximum G-force, curve your fingers, push softly on the spot, and waggle them in a "come hither" motion.

Consider using your mouth and tongue as well. The basic principles are the same as for digital stimulation: Go slowly, work in rhythmic strokes, and pay attention to your partner's responses. Yes, there are women who feel inhibited about the sights and smells that men encounter between their thighs, and you, too, may be less than enthusiastic. Well, get with it. If you master the art of oral sex, I guarantee your partner will thank you. Think of it this way: Would you rather get a great hand job or a great blow job? I thought so.

The long and the short of it is, you cannot pay too much attention to a vagina. Don't be afraid to venture to underexplored areas like the mons veneris (the mound where her pubic hair grows) and the inner and outer labia. Or give dildos and vibrators a whirl. Personally, I enjoy having my nipples caressed or licked while my partner's fingers or tongue are inside of me—I like to think of it as a sexual combo pack.

Consider this: A popular sexual legend has it that lesbians tend to have multiple orgasms far more often than straight women. If that myth is true, I think I know the reason: Lesbians devote the lion's share of their sexual explorations to each other's vaginas.

## The Electric Slide

Getting a woman off through intercourse is a bit trickier; even the 30 percent to 40 percent of women who report having orgasms during coitus don't have them every time or with every lover. Anatomy and position are the keys. The width and length of your penis come into play, but it's not just size that matters: Curvature, angle, your relative heights and widths, and a variety of other factors are equally important. (By the way, most women prefer a medium-sized member to one hat's too big; too big makes you feel like you're having a baby or something.)

Unfortunately, there's not much you can do about anatomy—you and your partner either fit together or you don't. But what you lack in fit, you can make up for with technique.

I'm most likely to climax, for instance, in the missionary position with my legs spread not too far apart—I get just enough direct clitoral stimulation that way.

Another way to coddle the clitoris during sex is to try the coital alignment technique (C.A.T.). Essentially, C.A.T. involves "riding high" with your pelvis slightly above hers, so that the base of your penis rubs against her clitoris constantly as the two of you press your hips together and rock slowly into each other with a minimum of thrust-

ing. (This method is even more effective if she tips her pelvis slightly upward to increase the friction.) Another tip: Try stimulating your partner's clitoris with your hands during penetration. This tends to work best if she's on top or if you enter her from behind.

Women who are G-spot-sensitive usually come quickest in the missionary position (with you kneeling rather than lying down), from rear entry (try it with her hunched up on her knees instead of flat on her stomach), or when they are on top. (Experiment with both squatting and kneeling.) Using a device that monitors brain activity, Whipple uncovered evidence of a new source of sexual pleasure—a nerve pathway that runs directly from the cervix to the brain that may trigger some orgasms. The best positions for stimulating this nerve, Whipple says, are those that involve deep penetration.

## Ready and Willing

More than anything else, sex experts say, whether a woman comes during intercourse may depend simply on how horny she is. A state of ready-made arousal can develop because she hasn't had sex for a few days, because she's madly in love with you, or because she just had an incredible martini. Or she may be in the hormone-induced state of lust a woman typically experiences right before her period.

Long, slow foreplay is always a good way to get your partner primed. Another is fantasy. In the same way many men get turned on by erotic films, sexy thoughts make many women hot. While I've personally never gotten off just from thinking about sex, I discovered the value of fantasy during a weekend I spent in the country with my boyfriend. There was nothing to do at night, so we decided to play Scrabble with the following stakes: The point spread between winner and loser would be translated into minutes of sexual slavery.

I won by 35 points. What I asked my slave to do was this: Tell me an erotic story with him and me as characters while touching only my breasts. The last thing I expected out of this was an orgasm; I just thought it would be fun. But as the story progressed, I felt a tidal wave rising inside of me. Before ten minutes had passed, I came like a woman possessed. It may seem unfathomable to you that listening to a few sexy sentences could elicit such ecstasy. Well, women are equally baffled by the notion of watching big tits on a videotape. Repeat after me: "We're at a party. I see you across the room in a tight, red dress. I find myself irresistibly drawn to you. . . ."

Although there is no hard data on the percentage of women who experience multiple orgasms, researchers estimate the number lies somewhere between 30 percent and 40 percent. Usually the first few climaxes are the biggest, and then they get smaller. Sometimes women need a short break in between (stop rubbing or just go slower) so they can rest a minute and recharge. At other times, there's just one explosion of pleasure after another until your partner finally maxes out. There's no special secret to inducing multiples; just do the same thing you'd do for singles—and keep at it.

---

### Relax . . .

Finally, don't obsess about your partner coming every time you have sex. If you get hung up on giving a woman the ultimate O, you'll lose sight of the real goal, which is to relax and enjoy each other's bodies. If you put enough pressure on a woman to perform, in fact, you're practically begging her to fake one (and no, there is *no* way you can tell).

Difficult though it may be to imagine, there are actually times when a woman doesn't even want to come. Take me, for example. Sometimes I prefer simply to concentrate on the feeling of a lover inside me, the way he touches my hips or breasts, the psychological thrill of sex. I want to relax and experience all of these sensations without getting too focused on being rubbed the certain way that will reduce my whole world to that tiny, escalating, imploding pinpoint of mind-blowing fireworks known as an orgasm. Then again, don't get me wrong. More often than not, fireworks are good.

**—MARISSA SPRING**

<br>

SEX

# The Sapphic Report

WHAT IS IT about grown men and lesbians? Even the most phallocentric male quivers like a prairie dog when the talk turns to girl-girl sex. Part of it, of course, is the kid-in-the-candy-shop fantasy—what would it be like to be in bed with two women doing succulent things to each other and (this being the fantasy) get taken along for the ride? But it could also be a tongue-tied curiosity about whether lesbians know ways to please a woman that men don't.

"Most men perceive sex in one way—penis and vagina," says Kurt Brungardt, coauthor of *Lesbian Sex Secrets for Men: What Every Man Wants to Know About Making Love to a Woman and Never Asks.* "Knowing that lesbians don't do it that way makes what they actually do kind of mysterious. It opens up men to listening to what sex is for a woman."

With their captive audience secured, Brungardt and his coauthor, lesbian activist Jamie Goddard, surveyed gay (and straight) females about the art of pleasing women and conducted focus groups in which straight men could talk to lesbians about the mysteries of the terra incognita known as "down there." So what do lesbian women know? Some of the secrets are not so secret: First of all, they know how to talk to their partners about what feels good and what doesn't, and how to ask questions to get a sense of a lover's predilections. The authors emphasize the importance of communication between partners and even note the old chestnut that "your most important sex organ isn't between your legs. It's between your ears." Apparently, this sort of thing still comes as a news flash for many men. "It's a sad state of affairs that men and women can't talk about this, and that it still needs to be said," says Goddard.

From their surveys, Brungardt and Goddard came to the unsurprising conclusion that cunnilingus was by far the most intimidating aspect of sex for most guys. Thus, they provide a breezy, informative breakdown of the intimate geography, as well as sound advice on how to proceed once you've got your bearings. "For a great cunnilingus session, you've got to be prepared to go the distance," the authors advise. "Be ready for fifteen rounds if necessary. Don't think you're going to be down there for a few minutes and she'll explode in a mind-blowing orgasm, then beg you to bang her afterward . . . A good work ethic is an important part of giving great head." Even if male readers go no further, the authors will have earned the grateful thanks of millions of women everywhere.

But the best thing about lesbian sex from the straight woman's point of view is that it's not confined to the usual practices that still define most heterosexual encounters. With no penis to please, lesbians feel free to lavish their attention on every part of the body. The authors report that hardly a crevice or ridge is overlooked, from the roof of the mouth ("curling your tongue slowly or briskly along the top is often a crowd pleaser") to the spine ("a soft tongue doing little circles around each vertebra sends pleasure sensors directly to the brain") to more familiar terrain ("don't forget those little bumps around the perimeter of the areola—it's like caressing a dozen miniature nipples all at once"). You half expect to receive instructions for fondling the pancreas. Still, in this department, there's probably no such thing as overkill.

Not having a penis in the picture also means that the alternatives are not so threatening. Many lesbians like to play with gender roles, taking turns with who is the doer and who is the done to, experimenting with what it is like to surrender and what it is like to wield power. They play with toys too— vibrators, harnesses, dildos, anal plugs, strap-ons. As can you. Toys are one way of making sure your partner's pleasure isn't entirely dependent on what you're up for at any particular moment, and they can help the two of you turn the tables in an interesting way—you'll be surprised at how many women love to know what it's like to use an ersatz penis on someone else. Not going there? Brungardt and Goddard will at least have you thinking about your limits and finding hers. (There's one exercise that actually lets you feel what it's like inside her womb though we'll spare you the details here.)

The point is, sex isn't all about your penis. You knew that, right? So. Slow. Down. Appreciate the machinery. Learn how to tease and how to play. Nothing a straight girl couldn't tell you, but then again, many a straight girl won't.

—LYNN DARLING

# Build a Better Orgasm

*I've never had the wrong kind.*

*My worst one was right on the money.*

**—WOODY ALLEN, IN *MANHATTAN***

WOODY ALLEN'S observation notwithstanding, one orgasm isn't necessarily as good as another. Some can feel as powerful as a rocket engine igniting, while others can be as weak as taking a leak. You know this. Urologists know this. In fact, research shows that many men complain that the force, so to speak, ain't with them. Fortunately, there are ways to make sex feel the way it did when you were nineteen.

## Master the Mechanics

A quick review of Sex Ed 101 will remind you that as orgasm nears, two important things happen: Muscle tension increases throughout the genital region, and fluid collects in the seminal vesicles. When you finally reach the point of no return, the tension gets released in a series of rhythmic spasms that also pump out semen. In layman's terms, the intensity of an ejaculation depends on both the volume of your ejaculate and the power of your pubococcygeal muscle, says Dr. Larry Lipshultz, a professor of urology at Baylor College of Medicine in Houston, Texas.

The latter—your PC muscle, for short—is the one you use to stop the flow of urine. It can be strengthened simply by clenching and unclenching it. (Do 3 sets of 10 repetitions twice a day.)

As for increasing the amount of your ejaculate, the first step (believe it or not) is to have sex a little less frequently. Your body needs a day or two to replenish its supply of semen, says Dr. E. Douglas Whitehead, a urologist in New York City. And then take it slowly when you do have sex. "Ultimately, the more foreplay you have, the more seminal fluid builds up," says Lipshultz. Allow a certain amount of sexual tension to build—then ease up. Withdraw if you must. Each time you restart, things will get a bit more intense. "It's like climbing a mountain," says Jennifer Duffy, Ph.D., a Long Island–based clinical psychologist. "You take one step back, then two steps forward toward a higher peak."

Practice this start-stop technique while masturbating, suggests Dr. Richard Kogan, a New York City psychiatrist and sex therapist. "Take your time," he says. "See how much you can boost your arousal before letting go."

## Master the Mental Game

If you want orgasms that are more satisfying, you need to be more emotionally attuned to your partner, says Marty Klein, Ph.D., a sex therapist in Palo Alto, California, and director of the website SexEd.com. In other words, in the context of sex, your mind is just as important as your penis.

*Look* at your partner. Notice how she feels, smells. Notice her hair. Peer into her eyes. Think of how you're feeling all over, not just between your legs. If that all sounds a little too Kenny G for you, just keep thinking: *Better orgasms to come.*

And, finally, relax. If you're worried about how well you're doing in bed, you're hurting your chances of achieving a superorgasm. Anxiety sends norepinephrine, the "fight or flight" hormone, surging through your body, directing blood away from your groin and into your arms and legs to prepare you either for running like hell or for putting up your dukes. To ensure body-wide relaxation, focus on breathing deeply from your abdomen rather than shallowly from your chest. On the local level, concentrate on unclenching the PC muscle just as you're about to come. This reduces the pressure on the seminal vesicles.

## Random Tactics

Here are more ways to optimize your orgasm.

**BLOW HARD.** A loud, forceful expulsion of breath just before you reach your climax helps release the tension in your PC muscle, generating more staying power.

**GET MORE CONTROL.** Give the rear-entry position a try. This method can give you greater control over the rhythm of the strokes and the depth of penetration, says Duffy.

**TRY IT IN THE LAUNDRY ROOM.** Having sex out of your bedroom can stoke your passion and make your orgasms more explosive, says Bernie Zilbergeld, Ph.D., the author of *The New Male Sexuality.*

**EAT LIGHTLY.** Don't have sex on a full stomach. Blood will rush to your stomach to help with digestion, leading to reduced sensitivity in the genital area. A general principle: Safe-swimming rules apply. Allow an hour to an hour and a half after a big meal.

**DRINK LIGHTLY.** Booze dulls sensation, which can make it difficult to get an erection, let alone have a turbocharged orgasm. But you knew that already.

—STEVEN SLON

# Tantric Moves

TANTRA, THE SO-CALLED yoga of sex, has always stirred Occidental passions. Indeed, the tantric sex manual, *The Kamasutra of Vatysayana,* with its garish depictions of well-hung maharajahs blissfully diddling their contortionist consorts, still inflames Western imaginations—and flies off bookstore shelves—more than a century after it first shocked Victorian England.

Lately, however, tantra has moved beyond mere titillation. Over the past few years, through a spate of new books, magazines, newsletters, X-rated educational videos, and West Coast weekend workshops, the idea of using yoga to enhance sex has gone more or less mainstream. (It even has its own celebrity poster boy—rock star Sting, who can reportedly go at it for five hours running.) And why not? In an era in which fear and familiarity conspire to take the sizzle out of sex, it's hard to turn down the kind of love life that's promised by Alan Verdegraal, publisher of *Tantra: The Magazine*, a bimonthly New Mexico–based quarterly with a circulation of 12,000. "Most men's orgasms are genitally oriented," Verdegraal says. "But when we get beyond that, we can have these *super*orgasms where the entire body becomes sensitized. We are talking about a major leap in experience."

You don't necessarily have to buy into tantric beliefs about mystical internal energy centers, or chakras, in order to pick up some secrets about prolonging and/or enhancing your own coital encounters. Unlike other forms of yoga in which spiritual enlightenment is achieved through assuming difficult postures, undertaking fasts, and practicing celibacy, the central mystery of tantra—a metaphysical system whose roots date back some 2,000 years—is the union of *lingam* and *yoni*: sexual intercourse.

Still, reaching sexual nirvana requires a distinctly non-Western journey. Thanks to Masters and Johnson, most of us view the human sexual response as a four-stage process: excitement (get-

JOSE ORTEGA

ting an erection), plateau (doing something about it), orgasm, and resolution (rolling over and falling asleep). Tantra, by contrast, is about going to the edge of orgasm—and then stopping and starting over and getting even closer. Again and again. So that when you finally do climax, it's transcendent. Tantra instructor Charles Muir, coauthor of *Tantra: The Art of Conscious Loving*, describes it as "climbing the peaks of the Himalayas."

Still, you don't have to be a slave to that prolonged rhythm to enjoy tantra. "If you like to [go at it hammer and tongs]," says Muir, "you still get to [go at it hammer and tongs]."

## Sexual Inspiration

One of tantra's key means of achieving heightened sexual awareness is through breath control. In other words, certain breathing patterns help you and your lover get in sync for sex. Others—so-called heating, or yang, breaths—are used to induce and intensify orgasm. Still others—cooling, or yin, breaths—help you to delay or extend it.

**INTIMATE BREATHING.** These simple breathing exercises are designed to help you and your lover reach a level of intimacy and nonverbal communication that practitioners of tantra, or tantrikas, say is sorely missing from Western-style sex. Instead of jumping into heavy foreplay, take a few minutes with your lover. Just lie there and relax. After a while, you should become aware of her breathing. Get yours in sync with hers. Inhale deeply, hold it, then exhale fully. Together. Feel the rise and fall of your lover's chest; feel her heartbeat against your body. Do this for a few minutes. (Concentrate on your chakras, if you can manage it.) In Muir's book—written with his wife, Caroline—this is known as "the harmonizing breath." After you feel harmonized, vary your breathing so that you're inhaling when she's exhaling and vice versa. The Muirs call this "the reciprocal charging breath."

**YANG BREATHING.** Once you get into your lovemaking, there are several techniques to make it more vibrant and enjoyable. In their book *Sexual Energy Ecstasy: A Practical Guide to Lovemaking Secrets of the East and West,* tantra gurus David and Ellen Ramsdale suggest that you pant in order to intensify the experience of both coitus and orgasm. To pant properly, breathe rapidly from deep down in your belly with your mouth open. (Added bonus: The Ramsdales say panting helps relieve the postorgasmic hypersensitivity of a woman's clitoris, allowing her to achieve multiple orgasms quicker and easier.)

Beyond panting, there's pelvic breathing. Coordinate your breathing with your thrusting.

Exhale as you and your lover push toward each other, inhale as you pull away, breathing deeply and exhaling completely.

**YIN BREATHING.** Sometimes, of course, getting heated up isn't the problem; rather, the danger is blowing a gasket too soon. This is when you need to practice a yin breath. The simple way is to breathe slowly and rhythmically through your nose. If that doesn't get the job done, try opening your mouth slightly. Place your tongue either against the back of your teeth or between them—if you're capable of doing it, roll your tongue into a tube—and inhale slowly and deeply through your mouth. Exhale gently through your nose. Close your eyes. Think serene thoughts.

## Hold Everything

For men, the unique precept of tantra is that orgasm and ejaculation are not synonymous. "The pleasure that is experienced in a typical orgasm-ejaculation response is nothing compared to the feeling a man can experience in a true full-body orgasm without ejaculation," insists Alan Verdegraal.

Tantra adepts use a number of techniques to stave off the Big Moment, ranging from breath control to mind control. And who's going to argue with getting a better handle on that penultimate moment of male sexual responsiveness Masters and Johnson called "ejaculatory inevitability"? Here are a few simple mechanical tricks. (If they sound familiar, they are. Though tantrikas have known about them for millennia, they've also been "discovered" over the past couple of decades by Western sexologists.)

**PC MUSCLE MANIPULATION.** Despite its name, the PC muscle, or Kegel muscle, is the least politically correct piece of connective tissue in the body. PC in this case stands for pubococcygeal, and it's the muscular hammock that hangs beneath your pelvis, supporting your rectum, urinary tract, and genitals. Adept women tantrikas are said to be able to play a man's lingam like a sitar simply by fluttering and flexing their PC muscle. Men have PC muscles, too. To test yours, the next time you urinate, try stopping the flow by abruptly tightening your groin. Do this twice every time you pee to gain strength and control. (You can also work out the PC muscle by twitching your penis whenever you get an erection—although this is a routine you should practice with some discretion.) To postpone ejaculation during sex, stop moving, hold your breath and clench your PC muscle—hard.

**THE SCROTAL PULL.** When a man is about to ejaculate, his testicles draw up close to his body. Thus, tantrikas reason, you can delay orgasm by pulling them down. When you feel that you're about to pop, have your partner encircle the top of your scrotum with her thumb and middle finger . . . and tug. Have her apply some traction and hold it for a few seconds. A word of caution: Make sure she yanks on the top of the scrotum and not on your testicles. This is supposed to be a *pleasant* exercise.

**THE SQUEEZE.** When you're about to ejaculate, pull out and gently squeeze the tip of your penis to force the blood back down. (Your partner can do it if that turns you on.) Crude, perhaps, but effective.

**THE PRESS.** Anatomists give the name perineum to the space between your scrotum and your anus. Some sexologists call it the external prostate spot. Because of its erogenous sensitivity, tantrikas call it "the missing three inches of lingam." To stave off imminent ejaculation, either you or your partner should press firmly on the perineum until the skin indents about half an inch; keep the pressure on from 10 to 30 seconds or until the potential for spillage subsides.

## The Positional Game

Tantric tradition comprises more than 100 tantras, or holy texts. These texts, in turn, comprise hundreds, if not thousands, of individual sexual techniques. And although many of them may simply be variations on tricks you already know, there are a few lovemaking positions tantrikas claim as uniquely theirs. Here are two that deserve a spin.

**MAITHUNA.** Tantrikas refer to ritual sexual union as maithuna. In his 1964 book *Tantra: The Yoga of Sex*—one of the first tantra books to become popular in the United States—writer Omar Garrison describes the initial maithuna position. It's worth trying as an experiment if you're interested in seeing just how long tantric lovemaking can last. Once you've gotten past the initial breathing exercises and are thoroughly harmonized, lie on your left side. Your lover should be on her back, perpendicular to you; her right leg should drape over your right hip, her left leg between yours. Now insert yourself. Stop. Relax. Concentrate on your sensitizing breaths. *Don't move.* For half an hour.

Garrison promises that after 28 or 29 minutes, you and your partner will be swept up in an overwhelming wave of pleasure. If it doesn't happen, follow the Ramsdales' advice: Don't change positions . . . but *get busy. Don't* ejaculate, however. After another 30 minutes, stop everything and remain motionless for an equal length of time. Eventually, you should have yourself one of those full-body orgasms that tantrikas talk about. And if not, you might wind up outlasting Sting.

**YABYUM.** To the Westerner, it might seem like merely a variation on the sitting position, but tantrikas insist Yabyum is different. To get it right, you should sit cross-legged on the bed. Your lover then sits on your thighs and touches her heels behind your back. According to the rules of tantra, this position is a favorite because your chakras (again, your energy centers) are aligned with your lover's, which supposedly facilitates the transfer of sexual energy. On a practical level, Yabyum makes bouncing and rocking easier than it would be in a regular seated position.

One final note for newcomers to the tantric practice: Don't forget that tantra is ultimately about the long haul—"superorgasms," like spiritual enlightenment, don't necessarily (and probably won't) happen overnight, but rather over *many* nights. You should remember that climbing the Himalayas, even the sexual ones, takes time.

**—LAMAR GRAHAM**

# Skills

THERE ARE certain things in life that a man should know how to do. First, and not necessarily most important, he should know how to open a bottle of beer under any circumstance. He should know how to read a topographical map. He should know how to win a fight, especially against a guy who is bigger (and hopefully drunker) than he is. He should know how to order a good Scotch or a good red wine without referring to the price and then be able to describe it after the first sip. He should know how to give a good toast at his best friend's wedding or to a girl he just met. He should be able to pack a bag so small that his friends will be astonished when he throws it into the car. ("That's all you're taking?") He should know how to cook a perfect steak, a perfect salmon fillet, and a perfect hamburger. He should know better than to wear a collarless shirt on a golf course, khakis after Labor Day, or suspenders with a belt. He should know how to build a log cabin and where to build it. And, most important of all, he should know how to relax. Someone once said that specialization is for insects, which is exactly why we came up with this chapter. In a world of adventure travel "packages," propane grills, and cybersex, there are a lot of skills that men have forgotten or never had time to learn. We're barely scratching the surface in this chapter, of course, and even then, it all depends on your priorities. The point is, you have to know it all, so you might as well get started.

# Build Your Dream House

PROSPEROUS MEN buy them, industrious men build them, and *all* red-blooded American men dream of owning a log cabin. No "kit home" of milled logs for us, but an authentic Northwoods-style cabin of felled fir and honest sweat. And for that, there is no finer example than the "Scandinavian full-scribe" structures built by Ron Brodigan, presiding druid of the Great Lakes School of Log Building.

Since 1975, Brodigan has been building cabins in northern Minnesota the purist's way: no nails, no chinking—just lots of elbow grease. In the time-honored method he practices, logs are not just notched at the ends to fit together and then stacked on top of one another (the heretical "half-scribe method," which requires chinking). A shallow trough is also carved lengthwise on the underside of each log so that it sits on the one below it like a hand gripping on a rail. No fancy tools are employed, just a chain saw, an ax, an adze, and a scribe, the compasslike device used to mark the logs for precise cutting. Tightness of notches and grooves is the standard by which one's cabin-building skills—as well as one's character, I fear—are judged. Properly prepared, full-scribe logs fit together so tightly that it's impossible for a piece of paper or a breath of air to slip between them, yielding the most energy efficient and durable handcrafted log cabin there is.

How do *you* get one? Well, you could buy it from Brodigan. He'll cut the trees from his 320-acre forest, build you a full-scribe frame himself, and transport it to you by truck, charging by the square foot, plus the cost of the timber and delivery. The peeled, scribed, and marked logs will arrive in three to six months; raising them and building the floor and roof are your problem. Or you can become, like me, one of the nearly 3,000 people who have learned firsthand from Brodigan at North America's only full-time, year-round log cabin–building school. After his 10-day course, for the price of a few tools and some gasoline, you and some willing friends could raise the whole thing yourselves, and every knot on the walls, every nick and perfect groove, will carry something of your sweat and blisters and skill. But don't kid yourself about how long it might take. Expect to put in six man-hours per log—and about 70 go into a 300-square-foot

*Above all, try something.*

**— FRANKLIN DELANO ROOSEVELT**

cabin. In our 10-day seminar, my class put up only 6 logs.

"Log building is damn hard work," acknowledges Brodigan, who retains a sense of humor about the process, bunking students in monastic cabins outfitted with privies, wood stoves, and kerosene lamps—but no running water. Brodigan, with his grave eyes and scraggly beard, is a patient teacher who nonetheless demands an intensely focused effort. For one thing, a miscut the size of a half-dollar can hang up an entire log and leave a gaping crack in a wall. More importantly, a wailing chain saw can recoil dangerously if used improperly, as I discovered at one point. "Someone almost lost his face to kickback," Brodigan told my class without pointing at me. He then demonstrated, for the fifth time, how to make cuts without using the tip of the saw.

All this for a *cabin*? If you need to ask, you'd better order yours. I'll be in the woods.

—BILL OLSEN

# Bring What You Need

AFTER NEARLY 15 years of writing about the outdoors, I've come to the conclusion that the two guiding principles of camping are protection and comfort.

Protection not only relates to the clothes and equipment best suited for a particular season or terrains but to understanding and, sometimes, predicting the weather. For instance, if you're headed to the 10,000 feet in the mountains above Taos in mid-August, you might expect hot days and cool, clear nights. A little research, however, would reveal that August in New Mexico is monsoon season and you stand a good chance of getting rained on. Once you've determined the probable weather conditions, it becomes a simpler matter to choose the right equipment. If you expect hot and dry conditions, you'll want the option to ventilate as much as possible. You should have a three-season tent with wide mesh openings, an external frame pack, and a lightweight, synthetic bag with side zips. Spring and fall conditions dictate a bit more bulk, such as a 0- to 10-degree bag (a synthetic bag will dry faster in wet conditions but is heavier and takes more pack room); a tent and canopy with a vestibule large enough to store wet gear and cook in; a couple of layers of fleece clothing; a poncho; and an interior frame pack with a large sack. Winter camping, of course, requires the most layers and therefore the most bulk and weight. A four-season tent (either single-wall or with canopy) should have vents and openings that can shut down tight and hold in the most body heat. A –25-degree down bag is necessary, as is an inflatable pad. If your interior frame bag is large enough, it's a good idea to take two primary layers: socks, thermal underwear, and lightweight fleece zip T-shirt, as these items can get soaked quickly if you're cross-country skiing or snowshoeing.

Setting up a good camp is mostly common sense with a few tricks. Obviously, pitching your tent on a hillock on an exposed plain or on top of even the smallest ravine is unwise. Wind might buffet you on the former, and even a 15-minute cloudburst can turn a little cut into a river. An ideal spot in a forest is in a clearing with the trees close enough to provide protection (and a place to hang your food out of the grasp of animals) but far enough away so you're not getting bombarded with pine cones or deadfall. In a more denuded environment, you want a tent clearing with a few feet of rise to your back. Generally, all winds precede a change in weather. In the summer or fall, a north or northeaster portends heavy, cold weather, as does an east wind. A south wind also can precede rain. Winds from the west are generally the most favorable. Therefore, it's important to determine direction and then set up camp accordingly.

The first step is to lay down a tarp, usually a thick piece of plastic slightly larger than the tent floor. After setting up the tent on top of the tarp and stretching your guy wires, you should dig a small channel a few inches from the edge of the tarp if you have any expectation of rain. This is

## BUILD A BLAZING CAMPFIRE

Over the past 30 years, Jim Blair has taught some 5,000 people how to construct a toasty campfire. So we called the Denver-area Boy Scouts of America council commissioner and got his cheat sheet. Cold? Here goes:

• **DECIDE IF A FIRE IS APPROPRIATE.** This is not as obvious as it appears. Many wilderness areas forbid open fires; low-impact camping holds that you limit them; and if fire danger is high, you ought not to light up.

• **PICK A SPOT.** Going to spark? Find an area with no overhanging branches, then clear it for six feet around. Try to find dirt, sand, or rock to build upon (assemble a rock ring if you like, but it isn't necessary), then remove any brush or tinder. "If you're in a pine forest," says Blair, "line the ground with rocks to keep the duff from burning."

• **COLLECT TINDER.** Dry pine needles, toilet paper, and steel wool work best. Form a fist-size pile of tinder, then assemble a tepee of pencil-size twigs around it. "The tepee funnels heat, creating an oxygen vortex, which fuels the fire."

• **LIGHT THE TINDER.** "After that, just continue adding larger and larger pieces of wood in the same tepee form," Blair says. The structure will eventually collapse, creating a bed of coals on which to cook your Dinty Moore or some tasty woodland critter. And remember, don't move on to your next campsite without being certain the fire bed is completely out (it should be cool to the touch). You burn down the forest, Blair will sic five thousand Scouts on your ass.

—JOHN TAYMAN

especially important in winter camping, as you don't want moisture to accumulate between the tarp and the tent floor.

Staying warm through the night is the next priority. A common mistake in winter camping is to put on all your clothes and then climb into your down bag. In fact, down works more effectively when you're wearing just a primary layer. The best thing to do with your parka and fleece sweater is to lay them flat under your sleeping pad. This extra layer of insulation between you and the snow can make all the difference.

Keeping yourself well fed falls in both the protection and comfort categories. Especially in winter, you can use up an extraordinary number of calories in a day, and while this sounds like a great weight-loss program, it's also dangerous as hell and can lead to hypothermia. Always clean and test-light your camp stove before leaving home. A couple of hot meals a day, accompanied by energy or candy bars, are going to make you a happy camper. It will not only increase your energy level during the day, but having extra calories to burn (especially at high altitude) will help you sleep a lot better.

–KENT BLACK

# Gear Up for an Expedition

PACKING FOR a wilderness trip requires a dollop of ingenuity if you don't want to feel like a pastured pack mule by the time you reach your first campsite. As a rule, you can load up to 30 percent of your body weight in your pack (normally about 55 pounds) for relatively easy hiking trips, but if you're scaling high peaks, you should tote no more than 22 pounds. The first items to jettison are clothes (just pack one of everything, except socks, underwear, and T-shirts) and your hardback copy of *Infinite Jest*, but stick with things that can serve dual purposes, such as a poncho that can double as a tarp and a tent groundsheet. For a pillow, just stuff clothes into a fleece jacket.

But don't forget the niceties of camp life when lightening your load—simple, yet indulgent, items, like a small flask filled with your favorite sipping whiskey or a pair of river sandals for crossing streams and walking around camp, are worth their extra weight. Incidentally, the safest place for vital equipment is not your pack, since it can be lost in an accident. Instead, carry your compass, whistle, and even your penknife on a string around your neck. If you're still questioning the load you've packed before the trip starts, it may help to remember an old woodsman's adage: Dump it out and lighten by half.

Here's a breakdown of what you'll need in your pack, starting from the bottom up. For added protection, line the entire pack with a garbage bag to keep your things dry during downpours.

**Sleeping bag**
**Clothes**
**Tent**
**Food**
**Stove and fuel**
**Rain pants, poncho, and sweater**
**Plates and utensils**
**Toiletries**
**First-aid kit**
**Maps**
**Paperback book/journal**
**Water bottles**
**Wool hat**

—DAVID DiBENEDETTO

# Get Your Bearings

THERE'S NOT a man alive who *likes* asking directions. It might even be a particularly American malady, given our ancestors' propensity to strike out for new, unknown territories. Unfortunately, most modern-day explorers don't stand much of a chance in a real wilderness without learning the simplest and most useful survival tool: a map and compass.

Quite simply, a compass is a piece of magnetized metal floating in liquid that always points to the magnetic north pole. The most common compass used to follow topographic maps (most often U.S. Geological Survey [USGS] survey maps, drawn to scale, with longitude, latitude, contours, and elevations) is an orienteering compass. The base is clear plastic, so it can be lined up on top of a map. The major components are the direction-of-travel arrow, the orienting arrow, the compass housing, the graduated dial (marked in 20-degree increments, with north, east, south, and west markers), and the red magnetic needle.

The first step in compass work is learning to take a bearing: the degree reading from one position to another. First, face the desired destination and, holding the compass level, point the direction arrow toward it. Next, rotate the dial until the needle and the orienting arrow line up. Now, even if your destination, say, a hilltop, drops out of sight, you need only raise up your compass (being careful not to rotate the housing), line up the orienting arrow and the needle, and then follow the direction arrow.

In laying out your course on a USGS map, the first step is to look at the bottom of the map and note the degree of declination. This is the degree difference between the magnetic north pole to which your compass is oriented and the geographical north pole to which the map is oriented. Say you're in the Wind River Range in Wyoming. You might have an eastern declination of 16 degrees. Therefore, the housing must be rotated 16 degrees so that your compass and the map will agree.

The next step is to align the edge of the compass on your map so that a straight line exists between your present location and your destination. Your bearing is set by rotating the dial so that north on the map and north on your compass are lined up. Your bearing now appears at the direction-of-travel arrow.

To determine your course, you then take the compass off the map and hold it level in front of you so that the magnetic needle swings free. Pivot yourself until the orienting arrow is aligned with the needle. Your directional arrow now points you the way you need to travel.

The last step is to orient the map to your direction of travel. To do this, simply lay your map on the ground and align your compass to the true north of the map. Turn the map so that the orienting line and the needle line up. To make sure the map is lined up with your perspective, look for a nearby contour or landmark on the map and check to see if it's where it should be in front of you.

—KENT BLACK

# Land a Plane (But Only If You Really Have To)

S AY THE PILOT of the small jet or passenger plane you're riding in has fallen ill, and no one else is available. Bummer. According to David Borgenicht, your proxy pilot and the coauthor of *The Worst-Case Scenario Survival Handbook*, here's what to do:

•**HAIL THE TOWER.** Assuming the plane is on autopilot, get the incapacitated pilot out of his seat, put on the radio headset, and immediately summon help. If no one answers on the current channel, try the emergency channel at frequency 121.5.

• **IDENTIFY YOUR EQUIPMENT.** The yoke for steering (pull it to ascend, push it to descend, turn it left or right to bank); the altimeter, usually a red dial at mid-panel; the heading indicator, a compass with an image of the plane on it; the airspeed indicator, at the panel's top left; the throttle, a black lever between the two seats; the fuel gauge, in most aircraft just above the throttle; and the landing-gear level, just to the right of the throttle.

• **SLOW DOWN.** Once your radio helper clears you to reduce altitude, throttle back while watching your airspeed indicator. Drop your speed by about a quarter. As you slow, the plane's nose will drop. On descent, the nose should be about four inches below the horizon. "If it goes much deeper than that," says Borgenicht, "you're descending too fast."

• **DEPLOY THE LANDING GEAR.** "Now's as good a time as any."

• **FIND AN OPEN SPACE.** If no airport is visible, look for a mile-long field, but any clear, flat area will do. It's an emergency!

• **LINE 'ER UP.** Reduce your altitude to 900 feet. Steering with the yoke, fly past your landing strip, keeping it two football fields or so to the right of you. When you're at a 45-degree angle to the far edge of the strip, make a right-hand U-turn.

• **SET 'ER DOWN.** Ready for showtime? Gradually align the plane with the landing path. At the same time, reduce power by pulling back on the throttle, making sure that the nose of the plane doesn't drop more than six inches below the horizon. You want the craft to be 100 feet off the ground when you're just above the beginning of the strip. The plane will stall at around 55 to 65 miles per hour; you should be within that range when you touch down. Try to get the rear wheels to touch first by gently pulling back on the yoke. When you hit terra firma, pull the throttle all the way back and continue pulling on the yoke to level the plane.

• **HALT!** Once on land, steer clear of obstacles with the floor pedals, not the yoke, and brake to a stop: The lower pedals control the steering, the upper pedals activate the brakes. Buy yourself a six-pack. Await your call from the president.

—JOHN TAYMAN

# Locked Up in a Foreign Country

I T WAS like being dropped into hell," says photographer Michael "Nick" Nichols, who once found himself hurled into jail in West Africa. After three months of working in the Congo, Nichols, his assistant, Neeld Messler, and filmmaker Bryan Harvey had taken a day-long canoe ride to the city of Ouesso to catch the weekly flight to the capital, Brazzaville, the first stop on their way back to the States for vacation.

The trouble started as the three Americans prepared to board the plane and were asked for their passports. Nichols and Messler didn't have theirs; they had sent the documents ahead to Brazzaville for visa extensions. The two men explained to airport personnel that they were planning to pick up their papers in the capital and get official approval before leaving the country—wrong approach. One guard, it became apparent, was drunk. He had a gun. Harvey reluctantly got on the plane alone, and the aircraft left without two of its scheduled passengers.

"For a few hours," Nichols says, "we sat outside of the police station. Then somebody decided we needed the full treatment."

Within minutes, Nichols and Messler were stripped to their underwear. Their clothes, money, and gear—including expensive photo equipment—were disseminated across the country within the day. The men were tossed into a small dirt-floored cell; light seeped in only when their jailers cracked open the door to peer inside.

---

## On Your Own

Landing in the clink in a foreign country is easier than you might imagine. On any given day, there are about three thousand Americans imprisoned outside the United States, half in detention for major offenses, the other half doing time for just hours or days as punishment for minor infrac- ❧ tions. "These might include rowdy behavior, domestic disputes, disagreements with hotel managers, that kind of thing," says Maria Rudensky, a former spokesperson for the U.S. Department of State. Other violations can be far less obvious— in the Central African Republic, for instance, it's a jailable offense to photograph a government

building (and many are unmarked). "It's up to you to know the laws of a country before you go. Once inside, you're subject to those rules," says Rudensky.

Many incidents can be avoided by using common sense. Among the more obvious advice the State Department offers about overseas travel: Don't leave luggage unattended and deal only with authorized agents and merchants. Yet, as in Nichols and Messler's case, sometimes events simply stack up against a traveler's favor. "There was nothing we could do to prevent what was happening to us," says Nichols.

What should you do if you are arrested abroad? "The best strategy is to try to contact the consul at the nearest embassy or consulate," Rudensky says. In more than 160 international capitals, the U.S. maintains embassies charged with assisting its citizens abroad. In addition, there are almost 100 American consulates worldwide. But while staffers at these bureaus are perfectly useful for helping with things like passport replacement and contacting home in an emergency, they are often as walled out as anyone when it comes to springing fellow Yanks from prison.

"The consuls do what they can to ease things, but there are no guarantees they can be of assistance in getting you out of jail," says Rudensky.

What then? A canvass of international defense lawyers, global businessmen, veteran television producers, and traveling journalists turned up these tips:

- **Don't try to bribe or bully your way out of the situation—that only angers the police. Not that bribes are a bad idea; in many places, they're a time-honored mode of doing business. But let the enforcement or military make the approach. Never do it yourself.**
- **Remain calm. Request politely but immediately to get a message to friends in the area or to the nearest American embassy or consulate. (Though staffers**

may not be able to free you, it's important that they know about your plight.) And always be respectful: In foreign countries, clashing with authority figures is unwise. A no from them closes off every avenue of negotiation. Recognize the circumstances and try to work within them.

As for Nichols and Messler, their imprisonment lasted 24 hours. Upon landing in Brazzaville, Bryan Harvey collected consuls from the American embassy and hired a plane back to Ouesso the following day. By midafternoon, the two men were free, and the police were instructed to round up every bit of their belongings. Their little side tour cost Nichols and Messler an extra $5,000 in plane-charter fees, but, says Nichols, "I promise you I would have paid more. To get out of there, I would have paid almost anything."

—DONOVAN WEBSTER

# Survive a Bullet

WHEN I was first in Sarajevo during the war, the big question among journalists was whether or not to wear a bullet-proof vest. The United Nations required passengers to don one on its C-130 transport flights into the besieged city, but after that you were on your own. There was a considerable risk of having them taken at gunpoint by gangs; yet there was also a considerable risk of getting shot, and we agonized over what to do. Personally, I rarely wore my vest—it was a loaner and far too expensive to replace. But while I was in Sarajevo, another American journalist caught a machine-gun round in the chest. He was wearing his vest, fortunately, and he staggered backward and then made it to safety before the sniper figured out the situation. As soon as a Serb gunman realized you had on body armor, his second shot was to the head.

It was a sobering story, and when I returned to the States I bought my own vest, knowing I'd be going back to Bosnia. I was in good company, as it turned out: Three quarters of all law-enforcement officers wear them while on duty, and an association of jewelry-store owners in Georgia recently began recommending body armor to its members. Perhaps half a million vests have been sold in this country.

The vest I chose—the Hardcorps, manufactured by a Michigan company called Second Chance—was made of Kevlar; a nylon fabric with five times the tensile strength of steel, it has roughly the heft and thickness of those lead aprons you wear during X-rays. (Cops normally use this sort of concealable vest; the president of Second Chance made his company's reputation by pulling one on at a police convention and shooting himself in the stomach.) Because I'd be facing machine-gun fire, however, my vest also has steel plates enclosed in its front and back. The plates are heavy—imagine hanging two eight-pound Olympic-class discuses around your neck—and have stickers on them detailing the kind of ammunition they stop: 7.62 × 39 Soviet armor-piercing incendiary rounds, as well as all other known AK-47 rounds, plus those from M-16, M-14, M-60, and M-1 rifles.

The physics of thwarting a pointed piece of steel traveling 1,500 miles per hour are formidable and underline the damage a machine-gun bullet can do to the human body. The vest's plates are made of a steel alloy three sixteenths of an inch thick that has been hardened on the outside by a special carbonizing process and then bonded to a ballistic-nylon composite one quarter of an inch thick. The bullet blunts itself against the superhardened exterior, punches through, and then continues to flatten out as it plows through the rest of the steel. The more it flattens, the more resistance there is, and by the time it reaches the composite, it's shaped like a mushroom and moving relatively slowly. It then gets tangled up in layers of nylon and finally comes to a halt. The whole process takes about two thousandths of a second.

Although the vest checks the bullet, it does not completely dissipate the accompanying force, and shock waves radiate out from the point of impact in a phenomenon known as "back-face deformation." The sensation is a stinging blow that has been compared to getting whipped. The waves travel through the largely liquid medium of your body and can cause damage to internal organs and tissue—blunt trauma. In the overwhelming majority of cases, though, blunt trauma simply results in a bad bruise.

Away from war zones, however, the biggest threat is from small-caliber handguns, and so most cops get by with a concealable Kevlar vest that weighs less than four pounds. According to DuPont, which manufactures Kevlar, about 2,100 people have been saved by such vests in the past 10 years—including one Florida state trooper who was hit in the chest by a bolt of lightning and literally had the pants blown off of him. Vests are made of 10 to 20 layers of the material, which has been used as protection from chain saws and to lash oil rigs to the ocean bottom. The woven nylon stops small-caliber rounds in basically the same manner the plates stop steel bullets; the only way for a bullet to penetrate Kevlar is to resist the initial blunting and blast through the minute holes in the weave. But ammunition capable of doing this is rare on the streets.

At the moment, manufacturers are scrambling to develop new fabrics and designs—to keep pace with both the evolution of high-tech ammo and an increasingly competitive market—and research is going full-bore to make the vests lighter, more comfortable, and more discreet. Recent innovations include a molded Spectra Shield panel that fits entirely around the torso, as well as a vest for armor-piercing rounds, made of overlapping titanium plates.

However tough the vests get, though, scientists will never be able to predict the differing human reactions to taking a bullet. According to Ed Bachner, the vice-president of Second Chance, one cop fell down hollering even though his vest had stopped a .22 slug. On the other end of the spectrum was a Texas policeman who burst into a house and was greeted by two 12-gauge-shotgun blasts to the chest. The vest he was wearing saved his life, but he was so keyed up that he didn't even realize he'd been shot. He returned fire, killing his assailant, and then walked back out onto the porch.

"Hey, look," another cop said to him, "your chest is smoking."

—SEBASTIAN JUNGER

# Be Cool in a Stickup

AT 6 P.M. on a Wednesday, a six-foot man dressed in a bright yellow dress, a wig, and high heels walked into a crowded grocery store in Des Moines, Iowa, pulled out a gun, and headed for the customer-service desk, where he demanded money from the register. Holding a bagful of cash, the robber motioned to a customer to come to him, but she fled out the front door in a panic. The man grabbed the customer-service clerk, held his gun to her head, and barreled out the door with her. Then the bullets started flying.

Handgun violence, as anyone who reads a newspaper knows, has become frighteningly common in the United States: There are 575 robberies committed with a handgun every 24 hours. According to statistics from the Department of Justice, Americans stand a greater chance of being victims of violent crime than they do of being injured in a car accident. It's not something that bank tellers alone need to worry about. Anytime you go into a credit union, a gas station, or a convenience store— or just down the wrong street at the wrong time— you run the risk of being caught in a holdup.

## Stay Cool

"There are two things to keep in mind during an armed robbery: compliance and nonresistance," says John D. Moore, a retired police officer and an armed-robbery expert based in Spokane, Washington. "Too many times, people don't think; they just react. They try to be heroes, and they end up making a bad situation even worse."

Robert Quigley, formerly an officer on the police force of Cobb County, near Atlanta, and now a crime-prevention specialist, agrees. "Your best bet for survival in a holdup is just to blend in with everybody else," he advises. "And do your best to control your panic."

Moore notes that there are several myths about armed robbery. "Most people think they will increase their level of risk if they look at the perpetrator, which is completely untrue. The reality is that if you can establish some type of a relationship in a short period of time, even if it's only eye contact, your risk diminishes." You will also be able to describe the offender to the police if you get a good look at his face. "People tend to believe they can't talk to the robber," says Moore. "But communication is crucial." Always indicate to the thief—with gestures, if need be—what you're going to do before you do it.

If an armed robber accosts you on the street, these rules still apply. Resist any temptation to struggle or fight. To prevent any misinterpretation of your actions, keep your hands in full view and turn very slightly to either the right or the left so that you are not directly facing your attacker. This will lessen the likelihood of your being viewed as a threat.

## Busted

The bullets flying at the grocery store came from an off-duty policeman who had burst from the deli and opened up on the crook. The two exchanged gunfire; then the robber pushed his hostage aside and plunged into a getaway car. Thanks to eyewitness accounts, the dolled-up robber was quickly arrested and sent to prison.

—COY BAREFOOT

TROUBLE

# Throw a Good Punch

DAVE JACOFSKY was minding his own business at a watering hole in Whitehall, Pennsylvania, several years ago, when he noticed three men at the end of the bar harassing an unaccompanied woman who was in one of his college classes. Jacofsky walked up to the woman and proceeded to talk to her. The threesome got the message, finished their drinks, and left. Two hours later, Jacofsky headed out, only to find Larry, Moe, and Curly waiting for him in the parking lot.

Before he could get inside his car, the three were whaling on him. Jacofsky doesn't go into detail about what happened next, but having studied martial arts since the age of four tends to make you modest about your fighting abilities. He guesses the whole thing ended in less than a minute.

Jacofsky, now a black belt in tae kwon do, aikido, and kenpo and a surgery resident at the Mayo Clinic in Rochester, Minnesota, has spent the last decade since the incident teaching street-fighting and self-defense courses. And though we don't advise anyone to go looking for a fight, should one come looking for you, here's his advice on how to open up your own can of whup-ass.

## Be Cool

"Your first goal should be to talk your way out of it," said Jacofsky. "As humbling as it is to apologize (even if you didn't do anything in the first place), it's a lot less humbling than picking up your teeth in front of everybody."

If talking doesn't work, says Jacofsky, there's no shame in walking away, or even in running. Your third and final escape route is to look for an ally. But don't just call out into a crowd for assistance. "Grab somebody," says Jacofsky. "Make eye contact and say 'Can you help get this guy off me?'"

If all else fails, of course, chances are you're going to have to rock and roll. "In that case," says Jacofsky, "you need to imply that there's a degree of psychosis within you. If you can cause your opponent to hesitate a bit, it will make a huge difference in the fight."

Then, in the midst of your head-case impersonation, assess the gravity of your predicament.

"If your antagonist is just some fraternity brother who's upset that you talked to his girlfriend, you don't need to punch him in the throat (which can crush the windpipe and be fatal). But if some guy has you cornered and you think you're in danger of being injured or killed, that's different." There's only one thing to do then: Throw the first punch, and make damn sure it's definitive.

The best way to do this is to create a distraction before striking. "Toss your hat, coins, or drink in his face," says Jacofsky. "Once he raises his hands, there's your opportunity." Consider kicking him in the groin or throwing a punch below the sternum to knock the wind out of him. Punch with a tight fist, keeping your wrist locked in a straight line and your thumb sitting above, not inside, your fingers. Strike with the knuckles at the base of the second and third fingers: "If you hit with the knuckles of your ring and pinkie fingers," says Jacofsky, "you increase the chances of fracturing your wrist." Also, try to stand at a slight angle to your opponent, so you will offer a reduced profile for him to retaliate against.

Jacofsky notes that it's vital to finish what you start. "If it's a true self-defense situation, you can't fight him halfway. You need to keep hitting him, because now he's pissed and, unfortunately, now-adays you have to assume everybody's carrying a weapon." But be aware that defending yourself involves certain responsibilities. "You may be mad as hell," says Jacofsky, "but if he isn't coming back at you, you have to lay off, because at that point it's no longer self-defense."

*Serious sport has nothing to do with fair play. It is bound up with hatred, jealousy, boastfulness, and disregard of all the rules.*

**— GEORGE ORWELL**

–PAUL SCOTT

# The Appetite for Thrill

IT'S DIFFICULT to argue that anyone—man, woman, or child—actually *needs* to know how to ride an 800-pound, mostly steel motorcycle capable of hazardously great speeds, susceptible to all sorts of maiming mishaps, requiring a lot of money to purchase and maintain, and affording only the most fanciful service as transportation. No, a motorcycle is definitely a luxury—although you could argue that everybody, even a Jainist monk, needs at least one luxury.

My bike is a Harley-Davidson FXSTS Softail that I bought showroom-new in 1988. I'd ridden various sorts all my life—Cushman scooters, baby Harley 125s, a 400cc Triumph that fell on me and scarred my leg, my friend Barry Hannah's old Sportster, and a big red '79 "Fat Bob" from the dark days when Harley was owned by the AMF bowling ball company. I've always *wanted* a motorcycle, even in the years when I couldn't have one because of money or because of my wife's reluctance to see me risk my neck, or because we lived in Vermont or Montana and the weather was wrong.

Why I've wanted one (and I've always liked really big ones—sleek, heavy, shining, throbbing, intimidating, powerful things) is probably not very difficult to understand. It has everything to do with the Springsteen lyric from "Born to Run," in which the Boss, in a younger, less contemplative epoch in his charmed life, invites his girlfriend, Wendy, to wrap her legs around his velvet rims and strap her hands 'cross his engines. I really just wanted an engine.

But I also wanted what went along with such a power source, namely the basic know-how for keeping such a great machine erect, balanced, and headed straight. This involved familiarity with the bike's rudimentary protocols: gears, brakes, clutch, horn, lights, blinkers, dipstick, battery, tires—all of which, when mastered, delivered a consoling if minimal feeling of competency. I had, as well, my usual novelist's wish to impersonate someone—in this case, all those other riders I'd seen—and to know what their experience might be.

And last, because a motorcycle is so continuously and indifferently dangerous to whoever rides it, I must've wanted one because I wished to keep something in my life that could kill me—something besides the slow tedium of my work, or my thankless uphill efforts to become a better person. You could say, in other words, that an appetite for thrill lurks within me. (What other use would I have for death?) And the art of this thrill involves finding the evanescing line where focusing my mind on those tasks of competency and feeling the natural fear of disastrously "putting the bike down" can be said to communicate, with the result being not just a cheap buzz, but a fragile and clarified skill—the skill involved in not whacking myself.

This, of course, is not a pleasure unknown to the ages. Call it grace under pressure. Call it riding the balance of one's fear. Call it idiot's delight. As I said, no one *needs* to experience it, and it's not for everybody. It's merely one of the available markers to remind you that you're alive—lest you veer off the road into the limbo (and you know the limbo I mean) and forget.

—RICHARD FORD

# Ride a Hog

ALL RIGHT. So you've watched *Easy Rider* over 300 times—do you think *that* makes you ready for the chrome-laced machine? Sure, it's fun and carefree, but it is also much more dangerous than driving a car that safely pads you with several inches of reinforced steel. So, with that in mind, here are five pointers about getting started, but please don't substitute this mini-lesson for some intensive classes.

1. Obviously, the first step is sitting on the bike and figuring it out. If the bike's not in gear, hold down the front brake (the lever on the right handle grip) to keep the bike from rolling forward. You should position yourself on your bike so that your center of gravity is directly behind the bike's center of gravity—the latter usually dead center between the wheels. This provides the greatest stability. In certain situations, however, you may want to shift your position. For instance, moving your weight back on a bike increases the traction of the rear wheel; lowering yourself toward the gas tank and extending your arms toward the handlebars will decrease wind resistance. No matter where you sit on a bike, your knees should always press into the gas tank, and your arms should only be flexed out slightly at the elbows. Knees and elbows splayed out from the bike not only increases wind resistance but lessens control.

2. Play with your controls. Endlessly. Though you'll never know how the controls integrate without actually taking the bike out, you should make yourself as familiar as possible with all the controls' positions.

You drive a car, but you *ride* a motorcycle. This truism is especially important when learning to corner. You don't steer through a corner; you lean through it. As you do this, your center of gravity shifts to the inside. Your downward weight, combined with the centrifugal force caused by the change in direction, creates a traction point—that is, where your tire meets the road. It takes experience to gain confidence in this small traction point's ability to hold you up. Unfortunately, a good percentage of accidents among neophyte riders happens in cornering, either because they panic and brake, downshift too rapidly, or try to remain upright.

3. There's an old race-car adage about cornering: Go in wide; come out close. In cornering a motorcycle, you want to give yourself the widest and most graceful possible arc coming into a corner so that you can maintain the greatest

degree of control coming out of it. Obviously, most tight corners are going to necessitate a decrease in speed. This adjustment should become second nature: Brake evenly front and rear; downshift, lean into the corner, accelerate, and realign your center of gravity. The most helpful lesson I've ever learned in cornering is to see your line clearly and prepare for it before you take it.

4. Though you've probably seen motorcycle racers drop their inside foot to the ground on a tight corner, this should never be attempted in street riding. You should always keep your feet firmly on the footrests so you can access your gears and rear brake. You should always try to brake as evenly as possible: Too much back brake will send you into a skid.

5. Even big old hogs are fairly delicate pieces of machinery. There are dozens of things to learn about their workings and operation. For instance, any motorcycle should be driven slowly when the engine is cold; taking a bike to high speed when the oil's not flowing is a sure way to burn a piston. Unless you're on a cross-country trip and can't stop frequently for gas, you should never fill up a tank. One gallon of gas equals eight pounds. When you top off a tank, you're adding 30 to 40 pounds. This will destabilize any bike and, unless you're used to it, cause you problems on the first corner you take out of the gas station. Also be aware that a passenger on the back of the bike is going to change the bike's center of gravity. A lot of weight is going to be shifted to the rear wheel, and it's usually necessary for the driver and passenger to move forward as much as possible to maintain good balance.

Lastly, it's highly advisable to invest in a good helmet and a set of leathers even if you think they make you look like some Hell's Angels wannabe. After all, there's a lot of nothing between you and the hard, unforgiving highway.

—KENT BLACK

# Stake Your Claim

THE THREE fundamental rules of real estate apply to buying a country cabin as much as they do to purchasing a house or an apartment: location, location, location. As Gene GeRue, the author of *How to Find Your Ideal Country Home*, says, "The biggest mistake you make is buying into the wrong community." So how do you conduct your hunt?

First, ask yourself some tough questions, says GeRue. Be honest with yourself about how much you want to spend and how much land you need. Do you want something in the mountains, by the ocean, or in a valley? Should the locals mainly be urban refugees or lifetime rural residents? Do you want to use your home seasonally or year-round? How far from a decent-sized town do you want to be? Once you've made your checklist, stick to it. Next, take a detailed map of the region and draw a circle to represent the distance you're willing to travel from home; then look for towns within that area that meet your criteria. Local chambers of commerce and regional guidebooks are helpful. Outdoor and sporting-goods stores in your hometown are also a good resource.

Once you've narrowed your search to two or three potential communities, reconnoiter them. While it's ideal to check out a place once in each season, that's often not practical. Try to visit at least twice, though. Stay for several days, preferably through a weekend and into the week, so you can see how the area changes. Read the local paper; speak to the people at the grocery store and at the bank. Eat where locals eat. Talk to neighbors, and listen. How do they feel about newcomers? Has there been a high turnover in the region? What's the future likelihood of development?

Next, decide if you want to buy a site and build a cabin or buy an existing structure. If you think you'll want to build, be sure to research local codes and contractors. When you feel sure about the location and the type of property you want to own, your last visit should be to a realtor. By then you'll have a clear idea of what you want, you'll know the turf, and you won't be vulnerable to a snow job. Get a recommendation for a full-time local real-estate broker from a bank mortgage officer or escrow agent in the area.

Don't bother hiring a lawyer to draw up your contract, says GeRue. For country land, a standard realty contract usually suffices; in most cases, an attorney will only bog down the process and drive up your fees. Buying purchase-of-title insurance should provide adequate protection; such a policy will protect you from any problems uncovered during the course of a title search, conducted by the insurance company, just as a lawyer's custom-written contract would. Title insurance also safeguards your property's easements in terms of access from a public road, secure water and mineral rights, and available power. And it will determine if anybody else has through access or water rights on your land.

Generally, the best time to buy is when the weather is at its worst. Extreme conditions slow down the real-estate market and can make both agents and sellers eager. And if you love your land when it's at its least desirable, you'll only love it more the rest of the year. If you live in the heat belt, midsummer is the time to purchase; if you live in the North, buy your dream escape in the winter. But wherever you are, now is the time to start looking.

—ALEX BHATTACHARJI

# Build a Doghouse

YOU DON'T SEE them much anymore, but when I was a kid growing up in the Midwest, most dog owners kept their canine companions in the literal doghouse. Some of these abodes were quite elegant. I remember Victorian pooch palaces adorned with

A doghouse's length should be one and a half times the animal's length (excluding the tail); its width two-thirds of the dog's length; and its height one-fifth higher than the distance from the top of the dog's head to the ground. Three-quarter–inch plywood is a good building material. A peaked roof requires a strip of aluminum flashing at its apex to prevent leaks. Use synthetic or cedar shingles to avoid rot; caulk all seams. Persian rug optional.

bedazzling gingerbread, others in a more rustic mock–Tudor style, and one solid, no-nonsense dwelling built of brick, a miniature of the home it abutted, complete with a peaked roof of split cedar shakes topped off with a cute but nonfunctioning brick chimney. The poorer quarters of town were where you found the more typical American doghouse of that period. The average man's approach to canine housing in those days was to throw a packing crate into the backyard, slap on a few boards to keep out the wind, and then toss in a tin pail to serve as both food dish and water bowl.

Many dog owners today prefer a portable plastic kennel. If you start your puppy in one of these compact, lightweight shelters—or so the theory has it—he'll quickly learn to prefer his kennel to anyplace else on the *estancia*—such as the recently upholstered sofa. Some dog owners keep the portable kennel in the kitchen, calling the dog out of it only when he has a job to do. The drawback to this scheme is predictable: The kids start bringing Fido out to play, first in the family room, then to sleep on their beds at night. Pretty soon Ol' Pard is just another member of the household, but a whole lot messier.

Or you could do what I did some years ago: build your dog a proper home away from home— a fenced run and a snug, weatherproof shelter. I'm not sure how the pup felt about it, but I certainly found the construction of Chez Max to be a soul-satisfying summer project.

---

## Homesite

I began by scoping out a decent locale in the backyard. I wanted the dog to have both shelter from the prevailing northwesterly winds, especially in the winter, and exposure to direct sunlight during part of the day, but ample shade as well, for when the summer sun blazed hot.

Once I'd found my spot, I broke out pick and shovel. A dog run should be at least 20 feet long by 4 feet wide, with the doghouse at one end, and bedded in a foot or more of pea gravel (for drainage) or a layer of cambered concrete. In retrospect, I can see that concrete would have been the better choice for Chez Max. Plucking a bucketful of dewy dog shit from a bed of stones is not an inspiring way to begin a workday.

Next, I had to erect a fence. I quickly learned that the best way to develop bulging pecs, strong lats, a neck like a rutting bull, and chronic lower-

back pain is to grub a dozen deep holes in rocky soil with a dull posthole digger.

Beforehand, I'd bucked up an equal number of 10-foot-long four-by-fours, soaked the lower 3 feet of each in creosote for a few days, and allowed them to cure. Fairing the fence posts so they stood plumb upright was another day's work in itself. To these sturdy stanchions I stapled an enveloping eight-foot-high web of thick sheep wire.

Then came the fun part: actually building the doghouse. Bricks were too fancy for what I envisioned. No gingerbread, either. For the basic material, I settled on three-quarter-inch plywood—tough and rot-resistant. After all, the navy had built PT boats from the stuff during World War II.

The design I came up with would have pleased Frank Lloyd Wright: a low, clean, simple box, three feet on a side, with a roof that pitched back from the door so that rain and snowmelt would spill from the rear of the structure rather than into its front yard. The walls of Chez Max were secured with stainless-steel screws, the roof was weatherproofed with shingles, and all seams were caulked. I painted it a rich barn red, and over its square-cut open doorway inscribed in Gothic lettering and white enamel the single word "MAX."

I finished the project on a hot, humid Sunday afternoon in late August. When I stepped back and squinted, it looked just as I'd always imagined my dream doghouse would. Tough, austere, no frills: the abode of a sensible, hard-working field dog. What it lacked, though, was a touch of something elegant, something traditional, yet offbeat. I had just the item. Years earlier, my mother had given us an expensive Persian rug. By this point it was threadbare, and my wife planned to exile it to the attic. It was just the right size for Max's parlor, so in it went: the one thing about the doghouse the pup really loved.

—ROBERT F. JONES

# What Should Be in Everyman's Tool Set

TOOLS ARE not the dull gray bludgeons you remember as a youth. They have evolved with the higher technology of the machines they service. These days they are stronger, smaller, and more efficient than their predecessors, thanks to the demands put on toolmakers by the aerospace industry. And all of us, even mechanical primitivists, are the beneficiaries. Screwdriver handles, for instance, are ergonomically enhanced for a firm but comfortable grip. They are also brightly colored so you won't leave them in the tight, dark confines of your car engine. Sockets and wrench heads have been reduced in size and thickness so they can be maneuvered in, say, hard-to-reach spark-plug chambers. One company, Snap-on—the acknowledged leader in toolmaking—even improved the standard box wrench so that it delivers up to 50 percent more torque to loosen stubborn bolts. (By the way, it's called a flank-drive wrench.)

And tools are stronger than ever, sometimes outliving their owners. Snap-on adds chrome, nickel, and molybdenum to toughen its hand-polished steel tools. But you pay for that durability. Sears, a more affordable alternative, cold-forms many of its sturdy Craftsman sockets; cold-forming makes tougher sockets than hot-forging because heating steel can weaken its molecular structure.

## Home Improvement: The 45 Essential Tools

So, what to buy? First, decide on how you will be spending your tool time. If you are the typical home handyman, selecting a set of tools can be a complex procedure. Prepackaged house tools rarely include all the essentials simply because there are so many. Unlike boats and cars, a house is comprised of wood, glass, metal, tile, and a host of other materials. Without the right tool, simple jobs like installing a door lock, cutting a piece of pipe for under the kitchen sink, or splicing a wire become impossible or, worse, dangerous to your health.

So we asked John Houshmand, a self-confessed toolaholic and a partner and general manager at Clark Construction—a high-end residential and commercial contractor in Manhattan—to assemble the perfect bag of tools for home repairs. Most items can be bought in any good hardware store. The 45 items listed below cost around $500 and will allow you to handle just about any job. In fact, given ambition and talent, you could do quite a bit more. "If you gave me a power saw along with this stuff, I could build a house," says Houshmand, who has worked on everything from Park Avenue penthouses to New York's trendy Paramount Hotel. "And add plumbing and wire it, too."

At the top of everyone's toolbox is usually a hammer, and Houshmand recommends one with a wooden or fiberglass handle. "Never get a steel handle," he cautions, "because the vibrations will make your elbow fall off very quickly."

When it comes to cutting, a Sandvik saw is invaluable because it has teeth that run around the end of the blade. If you had to cut a hole in the middle of a floor, you could actually do it with this saw. Also, be sure you have a hacksaw for cutting metals and a coping saw for cutting fine, rounded edges. Houshmand's favorite is a flush-cutting saw called a *dozuki.* Flexible as a ballerina and capable of bending a full 90 degrees so you can cut on a variety of angles, a dozuki cuts while pulling *toward* you, resulting in much greater control.

"The next tool of choice is a little modular screwdriver with 28 interchangeable heads for just about every weird screw in the universe, including the Torx head (a six-pointed star) and the Roberts head, which is known as the square drive."

Measurement is integral to just about any woodworking job. The Stanley 30-foot Powerlock with a 1-inch-wide blade can be extended 20 feet straight up before the blade collapses, a plus if you're working alone. Thinner-blade models can't come close to that kind of rigidity. A Lufkin folding extension rule with a graduated brass slide allows you to get a precise inside measurement of, say, a doorjamb because you don't have to bend it like a tape measure.

Got a screw that won't turn? Rub the threads with a bar of soap and the screw will go into wood as if it were butter.

Other items in Houshmand's bag of tricks include:

- Wiss brand tin snips for cutting rain gutters and washing-machine vent pipes
- a good caulking gun for applying roofing adhesive and silicone caulk
- a glass cutter
- a torpedo level ("good for leveling the stove so your eggs don't run to one side of the pan")
- try-miter square for right angles
- an awl for marking points on metal and punching holes in anything
- a selection of pencils
- two planes
- a set of drill bits ("use brad points for fine wood-work")
- chisels
- a file
- a putty knife
- a wire-stripping tool for electrical work
- a cat's-paw for leverage
- a three-to-two-prong adapter
- a set of screwdrivers
- offset screwdrivers for tight spots
- a nail set for finish work
- a utility knife with a bright handle so you can find it on the lawn
- a 100-foot chalk line
- electrical tape
- a pencil compass
- pliers (adjustable, needle nose)
- vise grips
- a small set of Allen wrenches
- razor-blade holder
- a bevel gauge
- two clamps—a screw type and a steel-bar model

—EVAN McGLINN

# Find a Good (and Honest) Mechanic

A LITTLE HOMESPUN advice from Tom and Ray Magliozzi (a.k.a. Click and Clack), the founding owners of the Good News Garage in Cambridge, Massachusetts, and the hosts of National Public Radio's weekly call-in show *Car Talk*:

**TOM:** "The best way to find a good mechanic is by word of mouth."

**RAY:** "The second-best way is by cloak and dagger. Park your car across the street from a prospective shop and slink down in your seat. Then watch for the two telltale signs that you don't want to use this guy as your mechanic."

**TOM:** "Number one: Tow trucks keep taking cars out of his shop. That's a bad sign."

**RAY:** "Number two: He drives out on Saturday morning towing a 36-foot cabin cruiser behind him. That tells you on the day his boat payment is due you might come in for brake pads and drive out with a rebuilt engine and new carpets."

**TOM:** "Actually, if you move to a new area or don't know anybody with a good mechanic, we recommend you check the 'Mechan-X-Files.' That's a nondenominational, online database of great mechanics, recommended by people who use our website, the *Car Talk* section of *www.cars.com*."

**RAY:** "Every mechanic listed here has been personally recommended by one or more customers. Mechanics are listed by city, state, and the type of cars they specialize in. Then they're rated on honesty, the bacterial infestation of their waiting room, how they respond to screw-ups, their prices, et cetera."

**TOM:** "And if you have a great mechanic, recommend him to the rest of us."

—MIKE GRUDOWSKI

# Grill to Perfection

ACCORDING TO my father, the three things a man needed to learn to make his place in the world were carpentry, basic accounting, and grilling. He conceded the first two could be dodged a bit, but he could not understand any man who doesn't have the facility to stand around a barbecue with a third martini in hand, cracking jokes with his pals, and still perfectly barbecue a steak.

His philosophy was: Keep it simple. Even later in life, when I had a chance to observe the artists at Flint's BBQ in Oakland, California, or my friend Charlie, a master pig roaster, I noticed that these gentlemen observed a few basic rules and kept it as pure and simple as possible.

No single type or make of grill is really better than another, whether it's a hibachi, a Weber kettle, or a rebar in a grid across cinder blocks. The main thing is adequate surface area; your coals should always spread out a few inches beyond your intended grilling surface. The last thing you want is to bunch up the meat. It doesn't cook as well, and it's hell to turn.

I have a lot of friends who spend a small fortune on hardwood briquettes, dried grapevines, and exotic woods for the supposed flavor they impart to the meat. I've never tasted it. The fact is, most grilling takes less than 15 minutes, so there's not really much time for the meat to absorb a lot of smoke. The exception is grilling a whole pig or leg of lamb for several hours. In that case, briquettes made from applewood, for instance, may infuse the meat with a slight flavor. For the most part, stick to regular commercial briquettes and sometimes (if the price is reasonable) hardwood lump charcoal. The charcoal is preferred if cooking for a large party and grilling a succession of meat and veggies, since they hold their heat longer.

For a meal for four, use a cylindrical piece of sheet metal with a wood handle and a screen welded in the bottom to light the charcoal. Drop in a wad of newspaper and then the charcoal and light. As heat rises, the charcoal lights. This method takes about half an hour for the coals to be ready. For larger batches of charcoal, use regular lighter fluid. Charcoal is ready when the outside turns to a film of whitish ash. Plan on about 45 minutes.

Generally, you'll want hotter coals for red meat if your intention is to char the outside and leave the interior rare. If you want to make sure meat such as chicken is cooked all the way through, then it's best to wait until the coals are on their way down. You can test this by holding your hand a few inches from the surface. If you can only hold your hand above the coals for a second or two, then they have reached the peak temperature. If you can last six seconds, then they're on their way down.

With the exception of marinated meats, sauce should not be applied before or during grilling. Sauces heavy in oil or traditional tomato-based BBQ sauces cause the coals to flare, and you'll usually end up with blackened chicken a la carcinogen. Try a dry rub instead. This is almost any combination of dried spices, herbs, salt, pepper, and garlic cloves that you rub into the meat. Charlie says dry rubs won't flavor the meat more than an inch, so a finishing sauce, one that is slopped on toward the end of the grilling, doesn't necessarily need to be eliminated.

There is no way to estimate grill time. Since meats, grill types, and coal heat are all variables, there is no standard cooking time. It simply takes a lot of practice.

That's the good news.

—KENT BLACK

## BAR TRICKS

# Open a Beer Bottle

ALTHOUGH YOU MAY have impressed your college friends once by opening a beer bottle with your viselike chompers, using your teeth to open a bottle every time you forget your opener will only land you the opportunity to play in the remake of *Deliverance*. But rest easy, throngs of ingenious men have been confronted with the same problem and arrived at various solutions. In most cases all you need is a stout edge and a little force. (Use too much, however, and you'll be sifting your brew for glass chips.) Here are five of the best techniques.

**STRAIGHT EDGE.** One of the most successful ways to pop the top is to rest one side of the cap on a hard edge, like a wooden table or hand railing (steer clear of finished hardwood like your grandmother's antique dining-room table or it will look as if it were attacked by a rabid beaver), and with a forceful downward stroke of the palm, smack the cap. If you've done it correctly, you won't spill a drop.

**GIVE ME A LIGHT.** Use the butt end of a lighter to wedge beneath the cap; then pull down on the bottle while pushing up with the lighter. Don't try this method in front of people you want to impress until you've practiced it.

**BOTTLE TO BOTTLE.** For a showy but sloppy method, lock two bottles together cap to cap (parallel to the floor) and pull on both simultaneously. As the tops fly off, make sure to straighten the bottles quickly to prevent massive spills.

**KEY ME.** Take the key to your house or apartment (don't use your car's ignition key, since it's made with soft metal and can bend) and place one finger on each end; then slide it flat end first under the cap. Holding the bottle steady, pull hard with the key until you hear the sweet hiss of escaping carbonation and you'll know you're almost home free. If you're having problems, rotate the bottle and repeat.

**HUBCAP HEAVEN.** An automobile has an array of spots to open a beer bottle (like door handles), but rigid caps can wreak hell on a car's finish. Look for tougher, nonpainted parts like a hubcap. Using the same geometric principles as a mounted bottle opener, search for holes that the bottle top can be inserted in and then pried downward to pop off the top.

And if you can master none of these, just buy cans.

—DAVID DiBENEDETTO

## DINING

# Always Get a Great Table

ALL RIGHT, so you aren't dating a supermodel, and *Forbes* magazine isn't tracking your personal wealth. No matter. Any maître d' will tell you that a little confidence and old-fashioned manners are the fastest route to prime seating in any dining hot spot.

The first rule of the seating game is not to call a restaurant and say, "Give me your best table." They won't know what you mean. Instead, be personable and let them know the occasion. Getting engaged? That highly sought-after romantic corner table will be yours. Just got your big promotion? You'll be celebrating in the center of the room, where you can soak up the attention.

Of course, whether or not you're actually getting married—or even have a job for that matter—is strictly your own business. With or without a reservation, always introduce yourself to the maître d' when you arrive and shake hands. When you show that you want to get to know him, he will want to get to know you. Repeat customers are his lifeblood. Never be shy about handing over your business card and always ask for his.

If you haven't called ahead and are asked to wait at the bar, never be arrogant or pushy. Instead, request the wine list and ask if the sommelier is available. When they know they will be getting a decent check average from you, it can speed up your wait and give you preference for the table you want.

As for the old greasing of the palm? It won't work everywhere, but more often than not, a $20 bill has a way of making a table suddenly become available—though a few places are used to as much as $50 to $100 for that same magic trick to work.

If there's a hot new restaurant that's booked for months and all you can get is the 1 a.m. seating somewhere in their closet, take it and ask for the name of your reservationist. Send a thank-you note expressing your appreciation and mention that should a better table or time become available, you would love to have it. When something opens up, you'll be the one they remember.

If you follow these tips next time you make a reservation, not only will you have the best food in town, but, with a little charm, you'll have the best view as well.

—ADAM MORGANSTERN

# Say It With Class

IT IS SAFE to say that toasts offered at weddings tend to be the more painful of the species, both to the deliverers and to the listeners. The reasons are obvious: The principals in weddings tend to be young; the toasts they are expected to give will most likely be the first of their lives; and the terror of speaking in public has them by the throat and knees.

Perhaps the most important thing to remember about a toast, especially for those on the edge of panic as they tap a glass for silence, is that there is no length requirement, no need to embellish, or tell a story. "I'd like to toast So-and-So, the father of the bride," is sufficient for the best man to say, his only problem to get the toastee's name pronounced correctly. One toast I can remember was from a best man, nervous, who tapped for silence so concussively that the stem of the glass snapped; wine lapped over the edge of the table; he stumbled over his host's name; but he had the presence of mind to haltingly explain all this by saying he was so overcome by the occasion he couldn't think properly. He won everyone's heart.

Those who are responsible for toasts should be aware of what they're supposed to do, of course, and others who are good on their feet should be alerted. As with almost anything, preparation and practice are always in order. It is a mistake at a wedding to get carried away by the wine and what has been said by others and on impulse rise to speak. One recalls George Eliot's comment on this: "Blessed is the man who, having nothing to say, abstains from giving us wordy evidence of the fact."

Incidentally, a toast is called a toast because in medieval times a piece of toasted bread placed in an inferior wine was supposed to improve its flavor—thus, one raised a "toast" to salute the honoree. One quaint custom from the past (it's described by Martial, the first-century Latin poet) would have as many cups of wine consumed in succession as there are letters in the toastee's name . . . fine if it's Io or Jan being toasted but rather trying on the wedding party if it's Clytemnestra. When my daughter Medora was getting married, six letters in her name, I toyed with offering that particular kind of toast to her. But I resisted on the grounds of expense. Besides, I came up with something more appropriate. Thank goodness!

—GEORGE PLIMPTON

## BE RIGHT ABOUT EVERYTHING

"My core philosophy for winning an argument," says Harvard law professor and famed defense attorney Alan Dershowitz, "is to make certain the argument is conducted at the level of abstraction that will guarantee victory. If the strength of your position lies in the details, argue the details. If it lies in a broad philosophy, argue that philosophy." Take censorship, for example. "You'll lose if you try to defend a particular piece of pornography or racist nonsense or Nazi claptrap. Those things are easy to impugn. But you'll win if you stick to the high principle of free speech." And think of an argument as a chess match. "The winner is usually the person who can think three to five moves ahead and lead his opponent toward his own strength." Let's see. As in, *Detective Fuhrman, did you ever make certain statements about . . . ?* Uh-huh. We get it.

—JON GLUCK

# A Guy Walks
# Into a Bar . . .

**W**HEN STAND-UP comedian Jeffrey Ross was asked how to tell a joke, he deferred to advice given him by his mentor, Buddy Hackett. "It's like a painting. You have to put some time into it. You start with a frame, then paint the background. Then you start painting in the foreground until you've painted in a complete story. The last brush stroke is the punch line."

A Friars Club regular who's also produced a few televised roasts, Ross suggests that "timing is one of the most important aspects to telling a joke. I remember I used to play with my neighbors, the Antonelli boys. We were maybe eight or nine . . . and they were great athletes. I was terrible. The last picked. Every time they'd pass me the basketball, they'd scream at me, 'Shoot! Shoot.' So this one time, the score's tied eight to eight, they pass me the ball and immediately start screaming, 'Shoot, shoot!' So I just dropped the ball, cocked my fingers, and said, 'Bang, bang.' Timing's something you have or you don't. I don't think it can be taught. But if you watch enough and practice, you can learn.

"First, you got to know your audience. Among comedians, this is known as 'never tell a midget a midget joke.' When I do benefits or a country club, I test the waters by maybe saying 'fuck' once during the course of the first joke. If it gets a good laugh, then I know I can say almost anything without the crowd turning on me.

"It's always best when you can make the jokes conversational. Never, never start a joke by announcing, 'Hey, I got a great joke; you're going to love this.' That's death, man. You want to keep the people close around you; never try to tell a joke to someone at a party who's across the room. I was doing a benefit a few nights ago, and afterward I went upstairs with some guys to this private bar. It was so easy to tell these guys one joke after another . . . because they were no longer under the pressure of being entertained. Just having a few drinks, telling jokes. You want your audience as relaxed as possible."

Ross thinks this is most critical when it comes to joke telling on dates. "My experience is that you should never try to be too funny too fast. Get a couple drinks in her first. And yourself. If you start out too quick, it'll seemed forced. After a couple drinks, it'll be more natural. Along these same lines, I think the jokes that work best are personal. To be a successful comedian, all you need is a bad childhood and a sport coat."

One of the most common mistakes Ross sees among amateur comedians is not having your material down pat. "People who haven't practiced their jokes are sort of like five-year-olds when they tell a story. . . . "There was this guy . . . no wait . . . there were these two guys . . . no, three . . . and. . . ."

And that the number-one rule among all come-dians, according to Ross, "is never tell a joke to another comedian: They've heard it. And they're never going to admit it's funny."

—KENT BLACK

# Get the Shot

IT WAS a vacation to remember. You took in some great sights: breathtaking mountains, endlessly blue lakes, those incredible horses. But you also took some stunningly mediocre snapshots. Before you give up and decide photography is best left to professional artists, take some simple advice from Andy Anderson, *Men's Journal's* chief photographer since early 1998.

"The most important thing is that you have to be inspired by something," says Anderson. "Then you'll shoot it well. If [your subject] is something you like, think about how you want to portray that. Then think about what's going to make the shot better—the best light and things like that."

The choice of film is vital, probably more so than your camera. The lower the film speed, the tighter the grain and the sharper the image will appear when the film is processed. Anderson explains, "If I want to show a real gritty attitude, I'll shoot with a [fast] film that has big grain in it. If I want to make something that's beautiful and more detailed, then I use a smaller grain [slower] film."

But be careful of going too slow unless you have a tripod, and if you're shooting a moving object, too-slow film will yield a blurry image.

Obviously, light is crucial, too. The best photographs are generally taken early in the morning or late in the afternoon, when the sunlight illuminates your subject at an angle and creates interesting shadows. Direct midday sun can lead to washed-out, overexposed prints. If you're using low-speed film, however, you'll need the brighter light because your shutter speed will decrease even further in low light.

Once you've found your inspiration, chosen the correct film, *and* gotten up early to catch the dawn, think about framing your subject. Anderson suggests following the rule of thirds. Mentally divide what you see through the lens into thirds and place your subject—whether a cowboy or a tree—along one of those lines. True, you'll sometimes see professional photographs with the subjects in the center, but placing it slightly to the side is a fail-safe way to make a snapshot more interesting.

But the most important part of taking good

photographs is practicing. Anderson, who never took a photography class, didn't start taking pictures until 1986. After only a few years of trial and error, he was shooting professionally. "I just shot as much as I could," he says. "I made a lot of mistakes—exposure, quality of light, things like that—and learned from all of my mistakes. If I can learn it, anyone can. That's the truth." (You can check Anderson's work throughout this book. See the title page and pages 1, 5, 8, 25, 47, 211, and 296.)

—ANN ABEL

# Just Breathe

YOU DON'T NEED to go to Nepal or even to a yoga class to reap the stress-relieving rewards of meditation practice. Instead, you can become your own guru. By following five basic steps for about 15 minutes a day, you can train yourself to become what meditators refer to as "mindful," which is the ability to focus on the pres-ent moment and not be distracted by the myriad thoughts that clutter your mind.

1. Be comfortable. This is probably the only hard-and-fast rule with meditation. If you aren't comfortable, you're not going to focus effectively. You'll want to find a quiet place, wear loose clothing, and sit on a pillow on the floor or on a straight-backed chair. You can keep your eyes open or closed—again, whatever feels most relaxing.

2. Breathe consciously. Block out everything but your breath. While slowly inhaling and exhaling, say to yourself, "I breathe in, I breathe out. I breathe in, I breathe out." This is harder than it sounds. If you're lucky, you'll be able to go all of three breaths before being distracted by your ever-wandering mind. But that's the point. "Many novice meditators think there's something wrong with them once they experience just how hard it is to keep from being distracted," says Mark Epstein, M.D., a psychiatrist and author of the meditation book *Thoughts Without a Thinker.* "But everyone is in the same boat—very much out of touch with themselves, their minds going a mile a minute."

3. Label all thoughts. When meditating, any thought that takes your mind off your breath is a bad one. So when the enraged face of your boss at this morning's staff meeting suddenly appears in your mind's eye, interrupt your "I breathe in, I breathe out" litany and label the intrusion by saying the word *thinking* to yourself. Then return your consciousness to your breath.

4. At the end of 15 minutes, don't just jump up and rush back into the zaniness of your life. Keep sitting and gradually let your thoughts return.

5. Don't expect an epiphany. This 15-minute experience is an attempt to *practice* mindfulness so that your attention to the moment begins to imperceptibly carry over into your busy day. Without even realizing it, you'll be concentrating better at work and feeling less stress by nightfall.

—LARRY PLATT

# This Job Stinks

FATHERHOOD—it's an opportunity to pass down your name. Your values. Your pet theory about Larry, the unsung Stooge. On the other hand, over the next three years or so, something like 6,000 dirty diapers stand between you and the phrase "potty trained." Here's how to succeed in a dirty business.

**PLAN AHEAD.** Think of a diaper change as a teeny, tiny toxic-waste-removal project. Would you start excavating PCB-tainted soil from a Superfund site without knowing how you were going to dispose of it? Same with a stinky diaper. So before you even touch that Huggie, gather your gear. Changing pad clean? Check. Wipes open? Check. Diaper pail handy? Check. Finally, make sure you've got *two* new diapers unfolded and ready for action. Because Murphy's Law dictates that if you don't have a spare handy, you'll mess up the closure on diaper number one and end up having to explain that duct-taped disposable to the child welfare authorities.

**OPEN UP.** Think safety first. If the diaper pad has a strap, use it, but don't depend on it. Even the smallest infants can roll off a changing table, so keep one hand on the youngster at all times.

*Years ago, manhood was an opportunity for achievement, and now it is a problem to be overcome.*

**— GARRISON KEILLOR**

Now you're ready for the unveiling. As you undo the tapes on the old diaper, be aware of the fact that you're in the line of fire in case little Jason decides that it's time for target practice. Ray-Bans help.

**DO THE CHANGE UP.** The change itself should be done with all the high-speed choreography of a NASCAR pit crew. Pick the baby up by the legs with your left hand and slide the dirty diaper out. Without putting the baby down, grab a wipe with your right. Remember to wipe from front to back, being sure to clean all the, um, mess from the nooks and crannies of the youngster's privates—an especially important consideration for girls, since inadequate cleaning can lead to a serious infection. Finally, give the baby's bottom a quick once-over. If it's red, then the baby has diaper rash. Your options are (a) to apply some Desitin or A&D Ointment or (b) to yell, "Honey, the baby's butt is all red." If you choose (b) don't expect to win any Father of the Year contests. Then slide the new diaper home, attach the tapes securely, and you're home free.

**BE FUNNY.** That's the theory. In the real world, the key to successful diapering is being entertaining. Once that tape comes unfastened, suddenly the most interesting thing in the world becomes playing with a dirty diaper or running over to that suede sofa with a presanitized bottom. So dust off your Richard Nixon impression. Sing as much of "Louie Louie" as you can remember. Anything to keep your little one entertained while you gather up the dirties, fasten the clean one, sanitize yourself, and remember, there's only 5,999 to go.

—ALLEN ST. JOHN

# Look Sharp

FOR A SET of fashion dicta that you can't live—or at least look good—without, we consulted the sharpest character we know, *Men's Journal* fashion director John Mather.

• **MAKE IT FIT.** No matter what you're wearing, it won't look good sloppy. Your collar should be comfortable but not loose. Pants should be worn around your waist ("Too low is the most common mistake I see"), and they should break at the shoe ("Too short is the worst pants sin"). Have the jacket altered so that you can button it without it pulling across the stomach, back, or shoulders. How much shirt sleeve you show at the cuff is a matter of personal taste. "The quarter-inch rule doesn't apply anymore. Showing a little more or less can help you express personal style."

• **KEEP ACCESSORIES SIMPLE.** Many men try to add style by the piece—a watch, a ring, a pocket square, braces, a strong belt. "There's nothing wrong with those, but don't wear them all at once. The essence of style is restraint. Less is more."

• **PAY ATTENTION TO FOOTWEAR.** Always have a fresh shine and a perfect heel. ("Ever hear the term *well-heeled*?") Even if you're wearing jeans, wear good shoes that are well kept. "Especially if you're wearing a suit. Nothing ruins a champagne suit faster than Old Milwaukee shoes."

• **INVEST IN A GOOD UMBRELLA.** "Seriously. Why wear a cashmere topcoat and a fine suit and then carry a giveaway Totes knockoff? It drags down your whole act."

• **NEVER, EVER DO CREATIVE BLACK TIE.** The absolute best thing a man can wear is a classic tuxedo. "Formal wear tends to end up in photo albums a lot, and I promise you: You will regret that band collar and patterned vest."

—JON GLUCK

# Suiting Up

AT $300 TO $1,200 a pop, suits are an investment. To make the purchase worthwhile, Jarlath Mellett, Brooks Brothers vice-president of design, suggests the best way to go about buying a suit. "There are basically two ways to get the right fit," he says. "First, you could buy the entire suit, say a 44 regular. But with so many guys working out, getting bigger shoulders and smaller waists, it's really smarter to buy them as separates. Get the jacket first. Make sure it's not too baggy or tight across the shoulders. The sleeve length should just cover the wrists. A good coat should get you a desirable shape and hide the negative and accentuate the positive.

"Also buy two pair of pants for the jacket—one pair that makes the ensemble into a suit and the other in a complementary color. You want the waist to fit. The pants shouldn't be too tight or so loose that you have to cinch them up with a belt."

Mellett believes most suits in one's wardrobe should be tropical wool with a plain weave. Heavier-weight wools are pointless, since most suits are worn indoors, where there's some kind of temperature control. "One of the things to look for these days is mechanical stretch," he advises. "Mechanical stretch is created in the wool during weaving and spinning. It gives the fabric more elasticity and a much more comfortable fit. One reason people used to always hang their jackets on chairs was that they were stiff as boards. You want a suit to make you feel comfortable and at ease."

One aspect that really hasn't changed much over the years is the choice of colors. Mellett says that one's first and primary suit should always be gray but a second suit can have a little more color, like a charcoal or navy. "These colors are much easier to accessorize. You might only have a couple suits, but with a dozen different shirts and ties, you can wear them in a variety of combinations. You can start playing around a little with your third suit; try an off-brown or green."

Though Brooks Brothers still has a good-size rack of poplin suits, Mellett prefers cotton suits for summer. "They're not expensive, and a navy cotton suit will get you through the hottest days of summer."

Though Mellett believes that most workplaces have become more relaxed toward diverse styles, his final bit of advice is to "keep your eyes open at work to define what is appropriate."

—KENT BLACK

# Nice Shoes

COMING HOME and "kicking off your shoes" isn't enough for most men. After subjecting them to miles of repeated pounding, we show our gratitude by chucking them across the room, throwing them under the bed, or tossing them through the closet door. Anything to get them out of sight.

This abuse takes its toll. Your feet can perspire two to four ounces during the day, and for leather shoes this is enemy number one. When the wetness dries, the leather starts to crackle. Continue this vicious cycle and they'll eventually look like some topographic road map. Shame on you.

If you do only one thing for your shoes—and think of how much they do for you—buy some cedar shoe trees. These inserts not only help keep the shape intact; they also absorb all the moisture inside. This process takes one day, so never wear the same shoes twice in a row.

The outside of shoes need attention, too. Not everyone likes the look, but putting taps on the bottom of your heels will save them from much wear and tear. They come in plastic and metal—you can guess which ones make more noise. Purchase a water-stain protector with each new pair and reapply it every few months. Should your shoes ever get soaked in the rain, leave them to dry on their own. Do not use shoe trees or stuff them with paper; the shoes will dry and shrink to the shape of whatever is inside.

To keep that brand-new look, apply polish or cream whenever needed. Polish gives a brighter shine, but each coat builds up over the previous; you will eventually need a shoe wash or the leather will be unable to breathe. Shoe cream is preferable. It's less shiny but softens and moisturizes the leather. Of course, the best choice may be just to drop them off at a shoemaker. Give your shoes, and yourself, a rest while they make these weighty decisions for you.

**—ADAM MORGANSTERN**

# 65 Things Every Man Should Own

WHAT SHOULD every man own? Think about this for a minute and you'll discover that it's a matter of setting priorities. If you insist on being literal-minded about it, the list would start with, oh, a refrigerator, a television, toilet paper—and we would still be deciding between toenail clippers and Saran Wrap by the time we got to 50. If it's really essential, we'll assume you've already got it.

Our list consists of things that make an emotional connection. You know the kind of thing we're talking about. It may not be as indispensable as your laptop, but it's so beautiful or useful or just plain fun that it makes you smile every time you pick it up. Or it makes you feel smarter for owning it. Or it makes you want to meet the guy who designed it.

So here you go: 65 things that will make your life better.

*One good, sharp knifeis worth two of almost anything else, except women and horses, of course.*

—CHARLES JIMBY,
XIT RANCH, TEXAS,
C.1885

1. A Seattle Pilots Baseball Cap. Or one from some other baseball team that doesn't exist anymore. We choose the Pilots to honor Jim Bouton and the rest of the one-year wonder of a team that gave us *Ball Four.* You can choose the Birmingham Black Barons to honor their 17-year-old outfielder Willie Mays. Or the Homestead Grays to honor perhaps the greatest of them all, Josh Gibson. Whatever you choose, it sure beats a Tampa Bay Devil Rays cap.

2. A Pair of L.L. Bean Blucher Mocs. The four-eyelet leather uppers support your foot better than a pair of Tevas. The soles grip a slippery sailboat deck better than a pair of Top-Siders. They look as good in á canoe as they do on a yacht. And if you're willing to drive to Freeport, Maine, you can buy a pair at 3 A.M.

3. The Marantz RC2000 Mark II Remote Control. They do not call it the remote of the gods for nothing. It will replace every remote in your house. And your friends' houses. And the rest of the neighborhood's, too.

There is something very comforting about owning something that Bill Gates won't make a dime on but which is still so complicated that you'll never tap its full potential. Read the fine print in the directions and you can launch a cruise missile with three keystrokes. Lose them and you could be watching C-SPAN until the next millennium.

4. A Bottle of Old Spice. The bad news: You'll smell like your father. The good news: You'll smell like *her* father.

5. An Iomega Ditto Max Tape Backup. Every computer geek knows something that you should, too: Saving data to a hard drive is the information-age equivalent of writing in the sand. The only question is when the tide will come in. Maybe not today, maybe not tomorrow, but sooner or later you will get an error message that says something like "Drive C does not exist." If you have taken the half-hour or so a week that it takes to store up to 10 gigs of information on a single tape, this will be a minor inconvenience.

6. A Bic Pen. No, it doesn't cost $450. No, it doesn't have a rhodium nib. No, its tip won't conform to the distinctive pressure of your signature as would a very expensive fountain pen. It won't write on the moon. It does, however, have a cap as sleek as anything Brancusi ever sculpted. It has a little end-plug thingy that you can chew off and reinsert with your tongue. It has a tiny pinhole in the side for no apparent reason whatsoever. It has a transparent body that lets you know exactly how much ink is left—or if that remaining ink is about to explode in the inside pocket of your best blazer. And if you lose it, there are nine more just like it in the pack that you bought for $2.19.

7. A Nokona AMG400 Softball Glove. Of course, you can take your childhood baseball mitt off your trophy shelf and use it for the company softball game. But softball isn't baseball, and admit it, you need all the help you can get. So get the proper tool. Nokona's big glove is so huge—14 inches from tip to heel—that you couldn't use it in the majors, and it's reinforced in all the right places to withstand the abuse dealt out by the upsized orb. Best of all, the walnut-tanned cowhide makes it feel like an heirloom even before you apply that first dab of Vaseline.

8. A Silva Compass. No, it won't tell you how to get home. You need a map for that. But at least it will settle any arguments about the general direction of Canada.

9. An OXO Good Grips Peeler. Noble tasks do not require great tools. But is there anything less ennobling than stripping the skin off a potato? After all, KP duty is what passes for punishment during wartime. Well, with its chunky rubber handle and sleek, swiveling blade, the OXO can transform even this most menial of tasks. That it beat out nine other vegetable peelers in a comparison test by Cook's *Illustrated* magazine is proof of its greatness.

10. A Blue Blazer. You need a blazer if only for its versatility. You can wear it to a business meeting or a good restaurant or even pair it with blue jeans and never feel under- or overdressed.

11. A Terraillon Bathroom Scale. The first face you see in the morning—well, hopefully, the second, as well as the first—should be a beautiful one. Especially if it's going to be this brutally honest.

12. An Everlast Leather Jump Rope. Forget the gloves. It's the feet that connote real genius in the ring. But Sugar Ray Leonard was born with only half the twinkle in his toes. The rest came from his addiction to the incomparable sound of rope slicing through air. And the hard slap of leather against calf after every misstep. Positive reinforcement. Negative reinforcement. Guess you'd have to call it Skinner boxing.

13. A Black Gap Layering T-shirt. This is the ultimate sartorial chameleon, the Simon Templar of the fashion world. In a recent 24-hour period, one of mine went from a TV appearance (tucked in, paired with a gray blazer), to a barbecue (untucked, over a pair of chino shorts), to an impromptu game of hoops (sleeves rolled up, with a pair of Nike jams), to a long 3-point attempt at the laundry basket (rolled up into a ball, banked off the armoire). Try that with something Armani.

14. A Sears Craftsman Shovel. You never know when you'll have something to dig up or something to bury.

15. A Down Comforter. Did you ever stop to think how much your bed says about you? A well-made bed says you're neat. A large bed says you're sociable. A water bed says you're not prone to motion sickness. And a down comforter? It brands you as a sensualist. After all, a Hudson's Bay blanket will keep you warm, but you wouldn't want to sleep under it without your pjs.

16. The *Godfather* Trilogy. You need *The Godfather* to see how a cheesy potboiler can be turned into a work of art (and to get Clemenza's spaghetti-sauce recipe). You need *Godfather II* to understand how sheer ambition can sometimes drive a man to surpass that which he thought was possible (and to hear Lee Strasberg say, "Michael, we're bigger than U.S. Steel"). You need *Godfather III* to remind you why you should usually quit while you're ahead.

17. An Official WNBA Basketball. Let your friends think it's a symbol of solidarity, a way of saying, "You got net, sisters." But forget about being politically correct. This is the ball of choice for one reason only: Size matters. That crucial 1.2 inches is the difference between kinda sorta palming a regulation NBA ball and taking hold of this smaller two-toned rock as if it's a volleyball. Now you, too, can play hoops at its one-handed best, juking and jiving, channeling Allen Iverson's quasi-legal crossover, and even loading up for a tomahawk jam, Kobe style. Now if the sisters could just do something about the height of the rim.

18. Ace Pilot 404 Stapler. It all begins with that big, round button. This chrome-plated bad boy asks you—no, it *dares* you—to take aim and try to drive a staple through 23 sheets of 25-pound cotton rag bond. Pound a Swingline with its wimpy plastic case and you feel like a thug. But take a mighty whack at the all-metal Pilot and it just bounces right back, the office-supply equivalent of a *Romper Room* punching clown. And at $23, it's way cheaper than therapy.

19. A Cheater Plug. There will come a day when you'll be called upon by a beautiful damsel to install an air conditioner on the hottest night of the year. She'll be perched on the bed in a sports bra, watching you soak through your T-shirt as you wrestle the beast into the window. And as you bend down to plug it in, disaster: a three-pronged plug and a two-pronged outlet. Now comes your moment of truth. Do you reach into your pocket and whip out your trusty cheater plug, known in the trade as a grounded outlet adapter, and triumphantly flip the big unit to high cool, thus ensuring an NC-17 ending to the evening? Or will you be cast out into the dark to search in vain for an all-night hardware store?

20. A Metal Slinky. Understand this: A metal Slinky is to a plastic Slinky as real life is to a *Family Matters* marathon.

Feel its cold, clean heft, watch its lifelike gait, listen to its rhythmic oscillation, and deny if you can that for fun it's a wonderful toy. Yes, there will come a day when that Slinky, unlike its poseur polyethylene cousins, will uncoil once too often and develop the kink that will ultimately consign it to that Great Toy Box in the Sky. But isn't this realization—that every slink could be our last—what separates us from the animals? Perhaps John Donne said it best: Ask not for whom the Slinky chings. It chings for thee.

21. A Marmot Alpinist Jacket. Okay, so you're plotting strategy for the most technical section of the rainy two-block walk between the subway and your office. But there's something reassuring about knowing you could take this seam-sealed Gore-Tex shell to Everest base camp and not only stay warm and dry but also look as if you know what you're doing. At least until you try to put on your crampons.

22. A Master Combination Lock. Some absent-minded morning you'll go to the health club and find yourself turning the black dial to 6 right, 8 left, then back past 0 to 14. But when you yank on the lock, nothing happens. It's only then that you realize you've dialed the combination from your high school locker. Don't worry. With a little luck you'll stop having flashbacks to that Farrah Fawcett poster by lunchtime.

23. A Bottle of Ibuprofen. It's not just a little bottle full of relief. It's filled with third sets, eighth miles, back nines, fourth quarters, and extra innings. Not to mention tenth microbrews and fifth José Cuervos. Just think of it as Everyman's morning-after pill.

24. A Vaughan Super Bar. Entropy notwithstanding, there is almost as much craft involved in taking something apart properly as in putting it together in the first place. Used as a precision instrument, this multipurpose wrecking bar will let you extract the tiniest finishing nail, pry loose the most delicate molding. Wielded with more gusto, it will demolish a room quicker than Johnny Depp.

25. A Duncan Super Top Tournament Yo-Yo. Perhaps that plastic one that looks like an in-line skate wheel will spin faster, sleep longer. And maybe the one that lights up will do a better job of impressing a six-year-old. But with its hard gloss of enamel on maple, this vintage Duncan reminds you of the one you sent sailing through your mother's living-

room window when the Pima cotton string broke while you were trying to do 'round the world. And how surprised you were when she didn't yell at you.

26. A Maglite Flashlight. Survivalists love it more than canned food for its rugged reliability. Cops love it more than Dunkin' Donuts for its substantial heft. You'll love it because, well, sitting in the dark sucks.

27. Glide Dental Floss. This shred-free thread was not the official dental floss of the Marx Brothers. Right, Gummo?

28. A Vivitar 283 Flash. Pro photographers are a practical lot—you miss the shot and you don't get paid. Which is why Nikon users, Leica fans, and Hasselblad devotees alike have one of these 25-year-old flashes stashed in their Domke bags. It works. It's versatile, rugged (except for a flimsy plastic hot shoe mount), and cheap. And equipped with a diffuser, it provides illumination so natural, only you will know it's room light.

29. A Dog. A disclaimer: You don't own a dog. A dog owns you. My dog, Alison, considers me merely a hairless, lead-footed, flea-free member of her pack. Sure, she's content to let me play alpha male once in a while—usually when a walk or food is involved. But when a true threat to her and hers surfaces—the FedEx guy, a pizza delivery, another dog walking down the street—she pushes me aside and does her best Cujo imitation. A bodyguard that plays fetch? What more can you want?

30. A Hewlett-Packard HP 12C Calculator. Go to any brokerage house, where the Masters of the Universe buy and sell the world, and rifle through the top desk drawers. Depending on how long it takes for security to show up, you should find an HP 12C in almost every one. Sure, it does depreciation, amortization, and rate of return. But it's the reverse Polish notation that the big dogs love. To multiply 4,761 by 52, you have to punch its chunky square buttons in this counterintuitive sequence: *4, 7, 6, 1, enter, 5, 2, x.* Punch in *4, 7, 6, 1, x, 5, 2,* as you would on a regular calculator, and it won't compute correctly. No one figures it out without an explanation. Which is why it's Wall Street's secret handshake.

31. A Pair of Levi's 501 Jeans. Why a button fly? Because it's not only metal-mouth teenage dorks who have zipper accidents.

32. A Fender Telecaster. Basically a chunk of wood with a neck and a couple of pickups, the Tele was endowed by Leo Fender with a twang that's as American as the *ching* of a cash register. But you don't play, you say? That's why you don't want a Stratocaster—thinking about Jimi Hendrix can't help but give you an inferiority complex. On a Tele, the rhythm guitarist's standby, you can learn to play "Louie Louie" in about an hour. And that includes time for a beer run.

33. A Case XX Trapper Pocket Knife. There are more useful knives, but there are none that feel better slipped into the front pocket of your jeans. Dwight Eisenhower loved the Case XX spear-and-penknife so much, he gave it to special White House visitors. But if you plan to use a knife for more than touching up your manicure, you'll want the Case XX Trapper, with its beefier surgical steel, clip, and spey blades. The handle is still made from traditional cattle shinbone, polished smooth. And it will look just as handsome on the day you pass it down to your grandson.

34. The Orvis English Field Bag. Fiddle with the saddle-leather strap and the brass buckle, reach inside the cotton-duck main compartment, and you can almost feel the morning fog rising over the moors. At least until you remember that you're carrying a Walkman and a newspaper and not a box of shells and a dead duck. But it's nice to know that you could.

35. A Linn LP12 Turntable. At a time when the compact-disc player has all but run its natural life cycle, about to be replaced by the digital videodisc player, what's the best music-making machine on the planet? The Linn LP12 turntable, a 25-year-old spring-suspension, single-speed, belt-drive unit from Scotland. Believe it or not, when it comes to high fidelity, vinyl is kind. And while there are other turntables that dwarf the Linn in both size and price, they can't beat Linn at the old toe-tap test. Trying to sit still while listening to Al Green's "I'm So in Love With You" or the Contours' "First I Look at the Purse" on a Linn is like trying to concentrate on lingerie at a Victoria's Secret photo shoot.

36. Jumper cables.

37. A wooden tennis racket.

38. A scar and the story behind it.

39. Something your great-grandfather owned.

40. A video game you can beat any nine-year-old at.

41. A set of dumbbells.

42. A 175-gram tournament pro Frisbee.

43. A borrowed book that you know you'll never give back.

44. Cleats.

45. A real little black book.

46. Mirrored sunglasses that make you look like a cop.

47. A drawing made by a five-year-old.

48. A receipt from a dinner that cost more than your first car.

49. A real dart board and a picture to hang on it.

50. A souvenir from Graceland.

51. A bicycle you don't have to lock up.

52. The Bible.

53. The Talmud.

54. The Koran.

55. A 1-to-43 scale model of a car you'll never own.

56. Something made of cashmere that's not a sweater.

57. A picture of your first girlfriend.

58. Timberland boots.

59. A tuxedo.

60. A phone with a bell.

61. A T-shirt from a race you ran in.

62. A print of Manet's *Le Bar aux Folies-Bergère*.

63. A set of towels stolen from a really good hotel.

64. A garlic press.

65. An undergarment you'd be too embarrassed to describe to your mother.

—ALLEN ST. JOHN

CULTURE

# The 50 Best Books, Music, and Movies of the Century

BEST-OF-THE-CENTURY lists are arbitrary, contrived, and woefully overdone. And we love them. Argue all you want about this choice or that one. If you read these books, listen to these albums, and watch these movies, you'll be a richer man.

## Books

Where, you will ask, is *The Grapes of Wrath?* Why is there no poetry? Why isn't there more Hemingway? Why only one baseball book? Because this is a short list and there's not enough room. Because *The Grapes of*

*Wrath* is sentimental. Because great sports books are rare. And because in making my selections, I tried to choose books that are timeless.

As a result, works that may have had an enormous impact once but now feel dated (such as John Reed's *Ten Days That Shook the World*) are not to be found here. Such books have their place in history, but we're not historians. We're readers. And that's my point. Nothing made this list that isn't still a great read. The choices are split between fiction and nonfiction and arranged chronologically.

## Fiction

1. Joseph Conrad, *Heart of Darkness* (1902). Published in book form in 1902 after running as a magazine serial in 1899, the story is prophetic, thoroughly modern, and incontrovertibly ours. Having lived through this bloody century, we know now that brutality has no borders; we take it with us wherever we go. This novella fully justifies its persistently disquieting title.

2. Henry James, *The Ambassadors* (1903). The master's masterpiece. No one understood better than James the difference between America and Europe, and no one has ever written a better novel about that subject. This book is a love story, but it's also as good an explanation as any of why we are in, say, Kosovo.

3. Ford Madox Ford, *The Good Soldier* (1915). In his twentieth novel, Ford offered a definitive demonstration of what he had learned about the craft of writing while working on the previous 19, penning what some people consider the finest work of fiction of the century, bar none.

4. James Joyce, *Portrait of the Artist as a Young Man* (1916). If you read Joyce—and to be an educated man, you must—this is the book you'll finish: It's brilliant and accessible.

5. Franz Kafka, *The Metamorphosis* (1916). After all the comfy nineteenth-century certainties had vanished, along came Kafka to help us understand the only one that remained: No matter what we do, we lose. He gave the word Kafkaesque to the language, and we all know what it means: We may be turned into a giant cockroach at any moment.

6. F. Scott Fitzgerald, *The Great Gatsby* (1925). As close as you can get to a perfect novel and the one that most effectively goes to the hollow heart of the American Dream.

7. Ernest Hemingway, *In Our Time* (1925). The remaking of American prose style is Hemingway's greatest achievement, and these short stories are where he did it; they're his purest (he would have said "cleanest") work.

8. William Faulkner, *Light in August* (1932). *Light in August* may or may not be Faulkner's best, but it is the one that cuts closest to the bone of race relations in the South and the still-disastrous legacy of 250 years of slavery. And that style—call it the American rhetorical sublime.

9. Henry Miller, *Tropic of Cancer* (1934). You read Henry Miller for the raw, unapologetic pleasure he took from life and put into his books. This is Miller at his raunchiest and most outrageous, trying to survive in Paris on almost nothing while having the kind of time we all wish we had the courage to have.

10. John Dos Passos, *U.S.A.* (1936). Dos Passos's innovative trilogy, a vast collage of characters and "newsreels," snatches of song, interior monologues, newspaper clippings, and whatever else it took to portray the Depression, still stands as the singular angry literary achievement of the '30s.

11. Raymond Chandler, *The Big Sleep* (1939). "'Tall, aren't you?' she said.

"'I didn't mean to be.'"

Welcome to hard-boiled country, rendered to its full effect by Chandler. We have been living with his tough, cynical, and flawed-but-honorable heroes ever since.

12. Nathanael West, *The Day of the Locust* (1939). Misfits, lowlifes, and a rioting mob: It's the only Hollywood novel you'll ever need, the culture of celebrity as seen from the bottom up.

13. Jorge Luis Borges, *Ficciones* (1944). Who can forget Pierre Menard, the author of *Quixote,* writing his paradox, a word-for-word reproduction of Cervantes's great book? Or the infinite Library of Babel, where the certainty that "everything has been written" renders us as insubstantial as smoke?

14. Ralph Ellison, *Invisible Man* (1952). "What did I do/To be so black/And blue," sang Louis Armstrong, and

Ralph Ellison's answer is this long, astonishing discourse, by common acclaim the central novel of the African-American experience, grand both in scope and in execution. You finish it the way you finish Dostoevsky: staggered.

15. Saul Bellow, *The Adventures of Augie March* (1953). "'I am an American, Chicago born,'" says Augie, and his adventures are Bellow's attempt at an American epic. This is one hell of an exuberant book, Bellow's most uncharacteristic production, and the last gorgeous flower to bloom on the vine of American innocence before Vietnam.

16. Jack Kerouac, *On the Road* (1957). "'The only people for me,'" said Sal Paradise, "'are the mad ones, the ones who are mad to live, mad to talk, mad to be saved,'" and, of course, mad to drive. Kerouac was the Pied Piper who led us kiddies out of town. After this, our lives seemed hopelessly dull.

17. Joseph Heller, *Catch-22* (1961). We had to wait 16 years after the end of World War II for the storm of self-congratulation to die down; only then, it seemed, could Joe Heller find the perfect ironic tone to catch the particular insanity of that war. But he did, and Yossarian, albeit mad, lives, and now we are the world's policeman.

18. Vladimir Nabokov, *Pale Fire* (1962). This is a novel so clever, so strange, and so overpowering that it gives new meaning to the term tour de force. Reading *Pale Fire* is like wandering into some incredible maze, at the center of which, we know, stands the answer to the mystery of life. If only we could reach it.

19. Gabriel García Márquez, *One Hundred Years of Solitude* (1967). Márquez writes, and giant emeralds emerge from the mud. Life becomes baroque and vivid and unexpected, like a palace appearing around a bend in the Amazon. This is the book that reawakened the collective capacity for wonder.

20. Kurt Vonnegut, *Slaughterhouse-Five* (1969). Vonnegut himself, with his disarming charm, called it a "lousy little book," and it certainly has no pretensions to greatness. But nothing has diminished its power. In the face of the savage absurdity of the bombing of Dresden, Billy Pilgrim finds a loopy peace on Tralfamador, where "there is no why." Fantastic, direct, and whimsical, *Slaughterhouse-Five* tells it like it is.

21. Thomas Pynchon, *Gravity's Rainbow* (1973). You are in London late in World War II, the Germans have built the first rocket-powered missiles, "a screaming comes across the sky," and so begins this blockbuster of a book, one that discerns the (inevitably black) humor in history. It was only fitting that Pynchon sent a stand-up comic to accept his National Book Award. *Rainbow* is the twentieth century's *Moby-Dick*.

22. Jim Harrison, *Legends of the Fall* (1979). The story goes that Harrison wrote this in a whorehouse near Bozeman, Montana. No other author can compress so much action into a page, so large a story into so small a space. Harrison writes with the force of a fire hose, and this book is romantic and tragic and outsize and will make you cry with pleasure.

23. William Gibson, *Neuromancer* (1984). His prose on speed, his imagination on coke, Gibson wrote the cult sci-fi classic of our time, a book that, well before there was an Internet, saw reality collapse into cyberspace (the word is Gibson's invention) and knew from the start that it could come to no good end.

24. Thomas Harris, *The Silence of the Lambs* (1988). *Silence* made literature out of the thriller genre. Everything that followed is worthless imitation.

25. Robert Stone, *Outerbridge Reach* (1992). A man goes to sea alone and discovers in solitude and abandon the hallucinatory authority of his own ghosts and the logic of his own death, and he can go no further. This is the ultimate castaway book, and Stone is our maestro of metaphor, daring and profound.

## Nonfiction

26. Sigmund Freud, *The Interpretation of Dreams* (1900). Freud gave us the id, the ego, the superego, the unconscious, and the central insight that little boys have ambiguous feelings toward their mothers. He changed forever the way we think about ourselves, and he wrote like a novelist.

27. Jean-Henri Fabre, *The Life of the Caterpillar* (1916). Fabre spent his life studying insects with enormous patience and astonishing attention to detail in the fields of his native France. He was the first to see that some wasps

lay their eggs in paralyzed caterpillars, which the wasp larvae then eat from the inside. He wrote beautiful, tender, and fascinating books about such things. This is his best.

28. T.E. Lawrence, *The Seven Pillars of Wisdom* (1926). Lawrence hated his fame and spent years in the Royal Air Force under an assumed name. He translated Homer under a pseudonym. And he spoke Arabic like a native, led Bedouin tribesmen against the Turks in World War I, and years later, from memory, having left the first manuscript on a train, composed this magnificent account of his exploits.

29. F.A. Worsley, *Endurance: An Epic of Polar Adventure* (1931). There have been several retellings of Sir Ernest Shackleton's incredible (and successful) attempt to save his 28-man expedition team when they were trapped by pack ice in Antarctica in January 1915. But this is the original, a first-person narrative by the commander of Shackleton's ship, the *Endurance.* It is quite possibly the greatest modern adventure book.

30. *The Oxford English Dictionary* (1933). One of the supreme monuments of scholarship of any century. And if you love language, it is a delight to read.

31. Antoine de Saint-Exupéry, *Wind, Sand and Stars* (1940). Few pilots write well (which is why Charles Lindbergh didn't make this list), but Saint-Exupéry wrote like an angel. "Do you realize that there are lands on the globe where, when men meet you, they bring up their rifles to their cheeks?" This is *the* classic of flying.

32. John Hersey, *Hiroshima* (1946). You can read it in half a morning. You will remember it always.

33. Aldo Leopold, *A Sand County Almanac* (1949). Leopold watched the fierce green fire go out in the eyes of a wolf he had just shot and knew for the first time what the mountain knew—that the wolf is necessary to its health. Fifty years later, we are still learning to think like a mountain.

34. Maurice Herzog, *Annapurna* (1952). Before Everest, Annapurna. It is 26,493 feet high, and no mountain of that altitude had ever been climbed, but Herzog and his team, without good maps, oxygen, or the advantage of known routes, scaled it. Herzog dictated the book from his hospital bed, where he spent months recovering from the ordeal. It may well be the most compelling mountaineering book of all.

35. Eugen Herrigel, *Zen in the Art of Archery* (1953). The Zen master shoots at a target he can barely see and hits it dead center. With his second shot, he splits the first arrow, butt to head. This simple little book will send shivers down your spine with its understated eloquence. It remains the ultimate account of Zen training.

36. Albert Camus, *The Rebel: An Essay on Man in Revolt* (1954). Philosophy noir. Camus, who fought in the Resistance, understood clearly, after World War II, after the Holocaust, that "murder is the problem today," and he here asks, That being the way the world is, how do we live in it? He was perhaps the West's most courageous thinker, and he will be relevant as long as men go on killing each other.

37. Barbara W. Tuchman, *The Guns of August* (1962). History done the old-fashioned way, as a grand narrative account of World War I—replete with fascinating characters and remarkable events and told with verve and a deep awareness both of the tragedy that history always is and of how it could have turned out otherwise had men and women been wiser and their luck better.

38. Malcolm X, *The Autobiography of Malcolm X* (1965). Pimp, thief, bootlegger, and the best chronicler we have of racist America, Malcolm X did not so much write this book as dictate it to Alex Haley, but no matter—this is Malcolm, in our face, telling it like it was and mostly still is.

39. Edward Abbey, *Desert Solitaire* (1968). Much of his book, Abbey warns, will seem "coarse, rude, bad-tempered, violently prejudiced, unconstructive," which is just how we like him, all elbows and rough edges, a kind of cactus standing guard. *Don't touch me, above all don't touch my desert.*

40. Frederick Exley, *A Fan's Notes* (1968). Alcoholism and the worship of Frank Gifford do not seem like a likely subject for a great book, but against all odds Exley pulled the big bunny from his hat to produce the best book we have about what it means to be insane about sports, to have, in fact, no other reason to live.

41. Tom Wolfe, *The Electric Kool-Aid Acid Test* (1968). You were on the bus or off the bus—it was that simple—and Tom Wolfe, southern gentleman–journalist with

impeccable manners, got on the bus with Ken Kesey and the crazy, drug-laced Merry Pranksters and brought back this wonderful, electrifying report, in his signature mock-exclamatory style, of the century's zaniest cross-country trip.

42. Studs Terkel, *Hard Times: An Oral History of the Great Depression* (1970). Studs Terkel stood at the intersection of history and the lives of the individuals who lived through it, and he chronicled the collisions. No better record of the Depression exists.

43. Hunter S. Thompson, *Fear and Loathing in Las Vegas* (1971). Only Hunter Thompson would cover a prosecutors' convention in Las Vegas devoted to the drug problem with "two bags of grass, seventy-five pellets of mescaline, [and] five sheets of high-powered blotter acid" (and that's just for starters) in the trunk of his car. And only he, sacred monster that he is, could have written this wild, gonzo account of the whole inspired fiasco.

44. Roger Kahn, *The Boys of Summer* (1972). Kahn had the great luck to travel as a sportswriter with the Brooklyn Dodgers in the early 1950s, when Jackie Robinson was playing for them and they were specializing in breaking the hearts of their fans, usually in the final inning of the final game of the season. Years later, he wrote this loving memoir of growing up with the Dodgers and getting to know them. This is baseball's eminent book.

45. Carl Bernstein and Bob Woodward, *All the President's Men* (1974). What would the nation have done without these two brash young men? This was the summit of American journalism, two reporters using nothing but their own dogged persistence to wiggle the truth out of the most highly placed criminal class the nation had ever seen. They made history; they documented it.

46. Bruce Chatwin, *In Patagonia* (1977). As restless as a tribe of gypsies, Chatwin left a brilliant career at Sotheby's to wander the world, wound up at its bitter end, in Patagonia, and wrote one of the most concise, yet richest, travel books of our time. His page and a half on Buenos Aires tells you more about that city than most whole volumes do.

47. Michael Herr, *Dispatches* (1977). The news footage was raw and shocking, but it lacked depth. Herr gave us all the depth we needed, and then some. He was by far the best journalist in Vietnam, living with grunts and getting their life right, which was the same as getting the war right, and he wrote with an intensity that matched that of the war itself: "The moon came up nasty and full, a fat moist piece of decadent fruit." Vintage Herr, and an unforgettable book.

48. Norman Mailer, *The Executioner's Song* (1979). Mailer is a top-notch reporter, and this is his finest work, a hypnotic account of the life and times of Gary Gilmore, who caused a sensation when he was sentenced to die and asked the state of Utah to kill him forthwith. What is so vividly recorded here is the life as it was lived, the day-to-day experience of his hard-luck family, built up detail by detail to make a mountain from whose peak we get a long and all-embracing view of the contemporary West.

49. Tracy Kidder, *The Soul of a New Machine* (1981). Like a diver, Kidder vanishes into his subjects and returns from the deep with extraordinary tales. This one stars a computer nerd named Tom West, has all the drama of a novel filled with colorful, fully realized characters, and renders high technology understandable. Godlike, Kidder himself never appears.

50. Ryszard Kapuscinski, *The Soccer War* (1990). This astonishing Polish newsman—"Red" to his friends—made the armpits of the world his area of specialty and sent back dispatches from every conceivable war zone and hellhole on the planet. These are the stories behind those stories, featuring places and people you won't find in the suburbs or meet around the office water cooler. This is life as it happens beyond the edges of the known world, described with timeless, wry clarity.

—ANTHONY BRANDT

## Music

You want to bitch about all the great music I left out? Let me beat you to it! How about *Red Headed Stranger* by Willie Nelson or *Chocolate City* by Parliament? What happened to the Kinks, Paul Simon, Chuck Berry? How about Smashing Pumpkins, the Verve, and Pearl Jam? Where are *Making Movies* and *Every*

*Picture Tells a Story?* Given the endless hours I have spent listening to Steve Earle's *Train a Comin'*, how dare I leave that out? Hey, where's Hank Williams? Or would you prefer to fight over some of the things I put in? Wilco? Beth Orton? See, these lists are tough. Above all, this is a rock fan's list, with all the limitations and prejudices that implies. To keep it from being totally predictable, I have confined myself to a single album by each artist. Otherwise, I might never have gotten past the Johnson administration. Having said that, here are, indisputably, the best recordings of the century for men. (Listings are chronological based on the original recordings' release.)

1. Robert Johnson, *King of the Delta Blues Singers* (1961). In 1936 and 1937, a young bluesman recorded about thirty songs for producer Don Law in San Antonio and Dallas. Six decades later, we're still walking through the fallout. Earthy and spooky, otherworldly and familiar, this is the shape and the mythology of what would become rock and roll.

2. *Atlantic Rhythm & Blues 1947–1974* (1991). The mother of all boxed sets—the living history of the R&B titan from its founding to the end of the soul era. How could music have changed so much in 27 years? Because those 27 years saw a revolution in America. This is the soundtrack.

3. Frank Sinatra, *In the Wee Small Hours* (1955). Take Bogart's "Play it again, Sam" existentialism and set it to music. That's the flavor of this suite of late-night, stiff-upper-lip laments. If Sinatra was not the author of our fathers' notions of manhood, he at least held up a mirror to them.

4. Elvis Presley, *The Sun Sessions* (1976). If that boy from Tupelo had never walked into Sam Phillips's studio and mixed up country and R&B, well, someone else might have done it, but the result probably would not have changed the world. This is the turning point of twentieth-century popular music.

5. Sonny Rollins, *Saxophone Colossus* (1956). Rollins's legend is rooted in the image of a lonely genius playing to the darkness on the Williamsburg Bridge, yet this CD reminds us of his good humor and of the exuberant way he could embrace rhythms evocative of community.

6. Miles Davis, *Kind of Blue* (1959). This is the sound that most of the world thinks of when it thinks of jazz. Davis was a painter as well as a musician; each careful brush stroke here conspires to form a work of unbreakable integrity.

7. Sam Cooke, *The Man and His Music* (1986). For all the speculation about what might have happened had Hendrix or Coltrane or Kurt Cobain lived, the biggest what-if is surely Sam Cooke. At the time of his death, he was already a much-acclaimed singer, hit maker, songwriter, and producer. When he heard Dylan's "Blowin' in the Wind," he said it should not be left to white boys to write such songs and sat down and came up with "A Change Is Gonna Come," his greatest triumph. By the time it was on the radio, Cooke had been murdered. His music remains contemporary. His talent remains astonishing.

8. *Hitsville USA: The Motown Singles Collection 1959–1971* (1992). What are the odds against so much talent showing up in one small company in one mid-size city at the same time? It's as if the Beatles, the Stones, the Who, the Kinks, and the Faces had all come out of the same shop. The high point of American pop and a strong case for American capitalism.

9. Curtis Mayfield, *People Get Ready: The Curtis Mayfield Story* (1996). First, he was the voice of the civil-rights movement with *People Get Ready;* then he became the conscience of funk with *Freddie's Dead* and *Superfly.* Along the way, he wrote hits from "It's Alright" to "Givin' Him Something He Can Feel." His guitar playing influenced Hendrix and Clapton, and he produced Aretha Franklin. Mayfield did everything first—and usually best.

10. John Coltrane, *A Love Supreme* (1965). What the Beatles were then doing to rock, Coltrane did to jazz with an epic that was both devotional and revolutionary. He reached inside American music and pulled out India, Europe, and Africa—and redemption.

11. The Beatles, *Revolver* (1966). The pivot between the mop-top era and the creative explosion of the Beatles' long second act, this album was the Fab Four's greatest leap forward. George came into his own as a songwriter,

Ringo introduced "Yellow Submarine," Paul reached a new peak with "Eleanor Rigby" and "For No One," and John blew the world's mind with "She Said She Said" and the monumental "Tomorrow Never Knows."

12. Bob Dylan, *Blonde on Blonde* (1966). In 1965, Dylan made the greatest rock album ever—*Highway 61 Revisited*. Six months later, he topped it. This is moody, mysterious music, utterly compelling to this day.

13. Aretha Franklin, *Queen of Soul: The Atlantic Recordings* (1992). There is no longer a single CD that covers her finest period (1967 to 1976), so you have to spring for a boxed set to get "Respect" and "Chain of Fools" in the same collection as "Spanish Harlem" and "Bridge Over Troubled Water." How bad is that?

14. James Brown, *Live at the Apollo* (1968). Holy smoke! At the height of the Motown era, along came this sweat-soaked shot of unrelenting soul. There was nothing sweet about it, and it was catchy only in the sense that it got its hands around your neck and didn't let go. After you got over the shock, you didn't want it to.

15. Jimi Hendrix Experience, *Electric Ladyland* (1968). Writing and recording in stolen moments during an insane tour schedule, Hendrix was flinging out ideas faster than he could capture them on tape. Beauty, anger, lust, spirituality, and glimpses of eternity from a musician who created one of rock's most remarkable catalogs in just four years.

16. Johnny Cash, *At Folsom Prison* (1989). Every word Cash sings sounds true. That is the source of his authority. In a room full of prisoners, he articulated their rage, regret, homesickness, hardness, and yearning for redemption with a power that was almost telepathic. A year later he made *Live at San Quentin* which ran along the edge of a white riot, but *Folsom Prison* covered the whole human range, from love of jesus to love of murder.

17. Van Morrison, *Astral Weeks* (1968). A poetic, personal, jazz-inspired Irish song cycle about childhood, first love, wanderlust, and leaving home. Put this on as you go to sleep and let it carry you into Morrison's vision. One day, you'll wake up inside it.

18. The Band, *The Band* (1969). Some of the most perfect songs of the era sung by its most haunting voices,

*The Band* presented a new, grown-up version of rock and roll, based on country, R&B, and roadhouse rock. Everyone from Clapton to the Beatles to Elton John came away changed.

19. Neil Young and Crazy Horse, *Everybody Knows This Is Nowhere* (1969). Young had earned his place in history with Buffalo Springfield, and his first solo album was an intricate sonic montage, but he had not yet found his voice. The first time he teamed up with Crazy Horse and recorded live in the studio, he let go of his inhibitions and created a sound that would remain vibrant for decades.

20. Sly and the Family Stone, *Anthology* (1981). Where did he come from, where did he go? How could anyone make such a huge impact so quickly and then vanish? Every couple of years, it's rumored that Sly is about to reappear. He never does, but as P-Funk, Prince, and the Red Hot Chili Peppers will attest, his trail is warm.

21. Marvin Gaye, *What's Going On* (1971). In 1971, Gaye, already a major soul star, declared his independence from the Motown sound with an introspective evaluation of what was wrong inside and outside of people's heads in a time of war, urban strife, and environmental meltdown. Most protest records merely preach, but Gaye's struggled with questions. It was also the sexiest music he ever made. Which is saying a lot.

22. Joni Mitchell, *Blue* (1971). *Blue* is the crest of the confessional singer/songwriter wave, but its appeal comes from the precision with which Mitchell combined specific, novelistic details with universal emotional experiences. When Kris Kristofferson heard this music, he said, "Joan, save something for yourself."

23. Jesse Winchester, *Jesse Winchester* (1971). In 1969 the Band's Robbie Robertson returned to Canada to produce an album for a young man who had fled his native Tennessee and a military family to avoid the draft. The songs Jesse James Winchester sang were haunted by a sense of beauty and serenity lost forever, and his voice was up to the duty.

24. Jimmy Cliff, *The Harder They Come* (1972). Here is where the U.S.A. learned about reggae. The soundtrack to the film that was the *Hard Day's Night* of Jamaican music remains a wonderful entry point, and Cliff (perhaps

because he was a Muslim in a world of Rastafarians) remains a prophet without the proper honors.

25. The Rolling Stones, *Exile on Main Street* (1972). Ten years into their mission, the Rolling Stones were no longer British kids doing impressions of bluesmen—they were tough, burned, and experienced. *Exile* is a drug-fueled drive through the literal and metaphoric American South, a battered European take on blues, country, honky-tonk, gospel, and thick wads of rock and roll, set against images of voodoo, dance halls, deserts, and horse stalls.

26. Stevie Wonder, *Talking Book* (1972). You could pretty much jump in at any point on the odyssey from Wonder's breakthrough *Music of My Mind* to the climax of *Songs in the Key of Life* and find more ideas per square inch than most musicians express in their entire careers. *Talking Book* is the recording in which he seems most at ease with his own genius. It does not overwhelm; it seduces.

27. Bruce Springsteen, *The Wild, the Innocent, & the E Street Shuffle* (1973). Springsteen took inspiration from Dylan and Morrison but grounded his lyrical flights in a vivid, postadolescent American world of pinball joints, boardwalk romances, and urban fire escapes. Yes, he would further hone all his gifts, which pour out through every crack here—but this is where he first made the audience that just missed the '60s see the possibilities in their own lives.

28. Gil Scott-Heron & Brian Jackson, *Winter in America* (1974). As raw as a wound but as strong as a bone, this long-lost masterpiece has finally been reissued on CD. Scott-Heron was a street preacher, a radical, and a man whose anger could not hide his generous spirit. When asked why some of his jazzy proto-rap had echoes of country and western, he said, "I live in a western country."

29. Bob Marley & the Wailers, *Legend: The Best of Bob Marley and the Wailers* (1984). Music that created a new world order. Marley made something very personal and place-specific, and people all over the planet heard themselves in it. From Brazil to Africa to Thailand, people who thought they had nothing in common were united by Bob Marley.

30. Patti Smith, *Horses* (1975). Looking like Keith Richards, snarling like Bob Dylan, and free-associating like Allen Ginsberg, Patti Smith stepped up in 1975 and stopped the progress of '70s rock and roll in its tracks. It was as if one true believer, dismayed at seeing the music corrupted, seized the microphone and remade rock into what Dylan and the Stones had promised it would be.

31. The Sex Pistols, *Never Mind the Bollocks, Here's the Sex Pistols* (1977). If Patti Smith was the fierce poetess, standing on her chair to declaim, the Sex Pistols were the Marx Brothers, stealing the silverware while everyone else at the banquet was listening to the speech. The buzz-saw guitars and Johnny Rotten's astonishing voice helped disguise the Chuck Berry in their rhythm and the Beatles in their tunes—but, hell, they sure made the old formula sound fresh.

32. Elvis Costello, *This Year's Model* (1978). Ten Elvis Costello albums could claim to be his best, but one thing is for sure: This is the classic sound of Elvis and the Attractions. With so much anger and energy that you expect the wallpaper to peel off when you play it, this record let the world know that the music revolution of 1977 was not going to blow over.

33. The Clash, *London Calling* (1979). The moment when punk made good on its promise and, in doing so, stopped being punk. This is a CD full of warnings and alarm bells, but nothing can drown out the joy of listening to a band learning that it has no limits.

34. Richard & Linda Thompson, *Shoot Out the Lights* (1982). That their marriage was breaking up at the time has perhaps been given too much weight. This album was, and remains, peerless for her guileless singing, his reckless guitar playing, and their impeccable songs.

35. Pete Townshend, *All the Best Cowboys Have Chinese Eyes* (1982). For the Who at their peak as the best hard-rock band, buy *Who's Next*. But if you are one of the true believers who were most fascinated by Pete Townshend's journey as his generation's canary in the coal mine, this is the apex—a man stands on the brink of middle age, surveys his life, shares what he has learned about marriage, sex, and friendship, and explains why he didn't die before he got old.

36. Paul Kelly, *Post* (1985). It's worth spending the time to search the import bins for this Australian masterpiece; you'll play it forever. Rock songwriter Kelly stripped down

to bare bones for a series of intimate songs about missed chances and beautiful regrets.

37. The Replacements, *Tim* (1985). The last album with the band's original lineup and the moment when the Replacements' magic shone with the greatest clarity. "Little Mascara" and "Here Comes a Regular" were as truthful about the big disappointments in small lives as anything in Raymond Carver or George Jones. And these Minnesotans blew out their amps while they said it.

38. Prince, *Sign O' the Times* (1987). Great player, great producer, great showman—but Prince's real secret was, as fellow Minnesotan Paul Westerberg of the Replacements said, "The guy shits songs!" Terrific records came faster than anyone could keep up. Although everyone has a different favorite, no one denies that *Sign O' the Times* is brilliant.

39. R.E.M., *Document* (1987). Here R.E.M. achieved musical muscle combined with lyrical acuity—and it made their earlier work, plenty impressive in its own right, sound as though they had merely been beating around the bush.

40. Lucinda Williams, *Lucinda Williams* (1988). Williams's acclaimed *Car Wheels on a Gravel Road* was just as good, but this one achieved a once-in-a-lifetime impact by virtue of appearing out of nowhere. Written off by major labels as marginal, unfashionable, or difficult, Williams assembled a group of sympathetic pals, booked some studio time, and made a record of tremendous originality and power.

41. Lou Reed, *New York* (1989). New York City was always to Lou Reed what the South was to William Faulkner. After 25 years of circling the issue, he hurled a Molotov cocktail right onto the doorstep in a rigorous, savage, and bitterly funny song cycle about the greatest city in the world and the horrible people who live in it.

42. Nirvana, *Nevermind* (1991). When everyone thought rock had become too sanitized and diversified to be turned upside down by a single album, Nirvana changed the course of the music both creatively and commercially. This threesome set a new standard for honesty and struck terror into the hearts of the merchants in the temple.

43. U2, *Achtung Baby* (1991). The biggest band in the world tore down and then rebuilt its sound and image—and in doing so made its most vital music.

44. Freedy Johnston, *Can You Fly?* (1992). A clear, almost nondescript midwestern voice. Straightforward guitar strumming and rock instrumentation. Surprisingly agile melodies. Emotionally complex lyrics about misfits, a fallen angel, and a lonely man. A haunting CD that starts out strong and gets stronger.

45. James, *Laid* (1993) Just before Oasis made British rock okay again for Americans, this long-standing band teamed up with Brian Eno to make a haunted yet unexpectedly uplifting album. As soon as people hear it, they have to have it.

46. Townes Van Zandt, *No Deeper Blue* (1994). Van Zandt was a gifted songwriter and a fearless chronicler of his own darkness—and he just got better as he drew closer to the early death he often seemed to beckon. Still, his songs to his young children were as beautiful as Christmas morning, and his sense of humor was as rich as his sense of humanity.

47. Wilco, *Being There* (1996). A thirtyish guy with no real prospects sits down with his record collection and wonders if he's a fool or a failure because it's only in rock-and-roll albums that he still finds the closest thing he knows to transcendence. Does it make him an arrested adolescent? A bad lover, friend, or father? These two CDs answer the questions.

48. Lauryn Hill, *The Miseducation of Lauryn Hill* (1998). Hill reconfirmed the power of hip-hop to unite a vast audience without forfeiting inspiration. This CD raised the bar by suggesting that hip-hop has the power to lead and remake the mainstream at a moment when everyone else has abdicated.

49. Beth Orton, *Trailer Park* (1997). A human voice emanating from a net of electronica to prove that all styles are means to the same end: making connections between people. Orton's is the sort of talent you'll want to sign on with for the long haul. She's a lock for the Rock and Roll Hall of Fame as soon as she becomes eligible in 2021.

50. Tom Waits, *Mule Variations* (1999). Could Waits's thirteenth album really be his best? Fightin' words for sure, but look at it this way—his caustic wit is front and center, his musical inventiveness is on full parade, and the heart beneath the armor has never been more eloquently displayed.

—BILL FLANAGAN

# Movies

I would be happier if this list numbered 150 movies. My apologies to *Bonnie and Clyde, Citizen Kane,* and *McCabe and Mrs. Miller,* etc., etc. . . . And some of the greatest directors in the world are not represented here. (I decided no director would get more than one film on the list—then broke my promise.) I was appalled to realize how many essential male icons fail to make an appearance: Chaplin, Eastwood, Nicholson . . . Not to mention the women—from Garbo through Michelle Pfeiffer, who were just as important in forming men's tastes and identities. What can I say? It's a dirty job, but someone had to do it. My criteria for selection change shamelessly from movie to movie. Some I've included because they are movies guys love, others because they illuminate an aspect of the male experience. Some are here because they provided a role model or shaped the way we see ourselves. All are simply terrific films no man should go through life without seeing. Again, the movies are arranged chronologically. There's not one I wouldn't happily see tonight.

1. *Sherlock, Jr.* (Buster Keaton, 1924). In this silent classic, Keaton plays a movie projectionist who steps into the film he's showing. An athlete, a daredevil, and an artist rolled into one—and probably a genius—Keaton just wanted to make people laugh, but in the process he created a movie that can be appreciated as slapstick, as homegrown surrealism, or as a beautiful meditation on illusion and reality.

2. *Trouble in Paradise* (Ernst Lubitsch, 1932). Miriam Hopkins and Herbert Marshall are jewel thieves who steal each other's money and hearts in the best romantic comedy of the '30s. Set in art-deco back-lot Venice and Paris, it offers a window into a now-vanished style of male courtship. Marshall delivers the sparkling dialogue with velvety urbanity.

3. *Duck Soup* (Leo McCarey, 1933). Patriotism. Religion. War. Respectability. Name your sacred cow, the Marx Brothers were sure to lead it to slaughter. Their anarchic spirits were never so brilliant as in this hilarious martial satire, in which Groucho, as Rufus T. Firefly, the president of Freedonia, declares war on neighboring Sylvania—for no good reason.

4. *It Happened One Night* (Frank Capra, 1934). Compare Clark Gable's rugged masculinity in this Capra classic with Herbert Marshall's Europeanized suavity in *Trouble in Paradise,* and you can see a sea change that happened in just two years. Gable, appearing bare-chested, did famous damage to the undershirt industry. More significantly, this on-the-road romantic comedy made his gruff, Everyman style the paradigm of American manhood.

5. *The Thin Man* (W.S. Van Dyke, 1934). To this day, there hasn't been a more seductive husband-and-wife team onscreen than William Powell and Myrna Loy as Nick and Nora Charles. These martini-drinking, crime-solving, big-city sophisticates make us believe in matrimony as an ongoing party. Just add gin and stir.

6. *Swing Time* (George Stevens, 1936). Countless men have emerged from a Fred Astaire/Ginger Rogers movie fantasizing about crossing a dance floor with Fred's breezy style and class. Here he is in the springtime of his talent—the aristocrat of tap, the definition of debonair.

7. *La Grande Illusion* (Jean Renoir, 1937). A war movie that hoped—and, of course, failed—to end all wars, this humanistic masterpiece about French prisoners of war in Germany during World War I speaks volumes about class, loyalty, male bonding, and the vanishing world of the European aristocracy. Watching it now is sobering: With each passing decade, we seem to grow less civilized.

8. *Only Angels Have Wings* (Howard Hawks, 1939). Hawks may have been the ultimate "guy's director," and this great entertainment—set mainly in a bar in a South American banana republic where Cary Grant and his fellow mail fliers gather between hazardous hops over the Andes—is a perfect illustration of his elegantly hard-bitten code of heroism.

9. *The Best Years of Our Lives* (William Wyler, 1946). A moving, meticulous, and honest depiction of the problems that faced soldiers returning to civilian life after World War II. This was my father's favorite film and a touchstone for

a whole generation of men trying to come to terms with the outbreak of peace.

10. *The Big Sleep* (Howard Hawks, 1946). Bogart, Bacall, and Raymond Chandler rewritten by William Faulkner: hard-boiled heaven. Scene for scene, the private-eye movie doesn't get any better than this.

11. *My Darling Clementine* (John Ford, 1946). The Western in its purest, most mythical form. Henry Fonda's boyish, laconic Wyatt Earp was an American icon before the age of self-promotion, a diffident but fearless hero for a democracy that had just won the war. Ford enshrines him in grand, riveting black-and-white images.

12. *The Third Man* (Carol Reed, 1949). No matter how many times you see this dark, atmospheric thriller, it never wears out its welcome. The rubble-strewn streets of post-war Vienna glisten with corruption in Graham Greene's script, which gave Orson Welles his most spellbinding role, as Harry Lime. Joseph Cotten is the naive American hack writer who discovers that his best friend is evil. The great score and that haunting final shot in the cemetery are unforgettable.

13. *The Seven Samurai* (Akira Kurosawa, 1954). In this savage and lyrical epic set in the sixteenth century, villagers hire seven professional warriors to defend their town against an army of bandits. Kurosawa's choreographed violence set a standard against which filmmakers have been measuring themselves ever since.

14. *Men in War* (Anthony Mann, 1957). This gripping, bleak Korean War movie about a lost patrol, starring Robert Ryan and Aldo Ray, ponders what it takes to be good at the art of combat—and what it costs a man's soul.

15. *Sweet Smell of Success* (Alexander Mackendrick, 1957). This rancid stroll down the back alleys of the New York media world introduced us to a new breed of monster, personified by Burt Lancaster's nasty, power-mad Broadway gossip columnist and Tony Curtis's hustling, blackmailing press agent. Too dark for the times, the movie was a flop, but it has proved to be one of the more prophetic visions of America on the brink of the culture of celebrity.

16. *Vertigo* (Alfred Hitchcock, 1958). Hitchcock's most hypnotic and kinky film is still the definitive study of a man's obsessive objectification of a woman. Lush and very creepy.

17. *Breathless* (Jean-Luc Godard, 1959). Jean-Paul Belmondo's petty thief modeled himself on Humphrey Bogart, just as Godard's rule-breaking new-wave movie paid homage to Hollywood B-movies. Americans returned the favor by adopting Belmondo as the icon of existential cool.

18. *Room at the Top* (Jack Clayton, 1959). A British slum boy on the make (Laurence Harvey) sacrifices the woman he loves (Simone Signoret) to marry a rich man's daughter. What remains indelible is Signoret's worldly sensuality: For most men who saw this movie when it first appeared, she will always be the most alluring embodiment of the older woman, a concept that has sadly fallen out of movie fashion.

19. *Some Like It Hot* (Billy Wilder, 1959). Why do we so love comedies about men dressed as women? When they are this funny, we don't bother to ask. Jack Lemmon succumbs hilariously to the turn-on of cross-dressing, while Marilyn Monroe is so lusciously overripe as a real woman, she became a model for drag-queen parodies. Gender confusion at its most fun.

20. *The Hustler* (Robert Rossen, 1961). Fast Eddie, the two-bit pool shark who must find the inner mettle to conquer Jackie Gleason's Minnesota Fats, may be the quintessential Paul Newman tainted hero: a man who can't love and who, for all his flaws, we can't help but root for.

21. *Jules et Jim* (François Truffaut, 1961). It may be hard, almost 40 years later, to understand the exhilaration that this poetic, troubling movie produced at the time. Jeanne Moreau's complex femme fatale is at the center of a bohemian ménage à trois in the early decades of the century. Though the story ends tragically, the prewar world Truffaut evokes lingers in your mind like a paradise lost.

22. *Lawrence of Arabia* (David Lean, 1962) .It's the greatest of Lean's epics and, lurking behind the ravishing pictorialism, the most perverse. Lawrence is a warrior at war with himself, horrified and driven by his own demons. Truncated versions, unfortunately, cut out the crucial

scene in which he is tortured by a homosexual Turkish officer, and a whiff of sadomasochism seeps into this Oscar-garlanded classic.

23. *The Manchurian Candidate* (John Frankenheimer, 1962). A thriller about Cold War paranoia and an eerie harbinger of political assassinations to come, *Candidate* skewered both the right and the left, anticommunism and anti-anticommunism. Frank Sinatra was never better, and his flirtation with Janet Leigh on a train is one of the most peculiar seductions ever written.

24. *8 1/2* (Federico Fellini, 1963). A man's fantasy life brought to the screen as a sexual three-ring circus. Marcello Mastroianni is the glamorous film director Guido (Fellini's alter ego) in this gorgeously self-indulgent fantasia. A reminder of the days when any guy who didn't take movies seriously couldn't be taken seriously himself.

25. *Dr. Strangelove* (Stanley Kubrick, 1964). "Gentlemen! You can't fight in here; this is the War Room!" You can't overestimate how original this apocalyptic satire seemed in the mid-'60s. The visionary director boiled down the madness of the nuclear age to its primal slapstick core, and a generation facing Vietnam would never be able to look at the military with a straight face again.

26. *Goldfinger* (Guy Hamilton, 1964). No list of movies for men can be complete without one James Bond flick. (It goes without saying that it must star Sean Connery.) The third Bond outing, featuring such delights as Odd Job, Pussy Galore, and a Fort Knox finale, is male escapism at its most gilded and guiltless.

27. *A Shot in the Dark* (Blake Edwards, 1964). Peter Sellers's disaster-prone Inspector Clouseau, who can't enter a *rhuuem* without stumbling over his feet and his tongue, achieved instant immortality in *The Pink Panther*. But the second in the series is the true gem, a brilliant reinvention of silent-movie sight gags for the '60s.

28. *Chimes at Midnight* a.k.a. *Falstaff* (Orson Welles, 1966). There are more famous Welles movies and more polished ones, but this grand, heartbreaking Shakespearean adaptation—in which the playboy Prince Hal throws off his disreputable mentor, Falstaff, in order to assume the crown—strikes the deepest emotional chords. And when people talk about cinematic battle scenes, the muddy fight to the death at Shrewsbury should rank near the top.

29. *Faces* (John Cassavetes, 1968). The godfather of independent cinema, Cassavetes stripped the artifice from Hollywood movies, his improvisatory style blurring the line between documentary and fiction. Here he and his remarkable actors get down into the funk of marital infidelity and bad faith. Cassavetes gets so far inside the wormy male ego, it can make you squirm.

30. *The Wild Bunch* (Sam Peckinpah, 1969). Machismo at the end of its tether. "Bloody Sam," the poet of the slaughterhouse, showed us how far we'd come from the mythical West of John Ford in this unsettlingly beautiful orgy of self-destruction. Does it glorify or excoriate violence? People will argue that one forever.

31. *Murmur of the Heart* (Louis Malle, 1971). There have been dozens of coming-of-age dramas about adolescents plotting to lose their virginity—but nothing quite like this sensuous, sophisticated French comedy, which ends in the most unexpected of beds.

32. *The Godfather/The Godfather: Part II* (Francis Ford Coppola, 1972/1974). Don Vito Corleone and his clan have become our depraved, all-male royal family. We love them, we hate them, we imitate them, we can't get enough of them.

33. *Aguirre: The Wrath of God* (Werner Herzog, 1972). A unique epic about man's lust for glory. The images in this sixteenth-century tale, set in the Amazon jungles of Peru, achieve hallucinatory intensity. Klaus Kinski is the mad Aguirre, who vows to conquer a continent. Inevitably, this German masterpiece evokes a more recent *Führer* with conquest on his brain.

34. *La Grande Bouffe* (Marco Ferreri, 1973). A wild sendup of the male appetite, an over-the-top ode to excess. One woman and four men repair to a mansion, where they eat and screw themselves into oblivion. A cautionary tale made in a drug-addled era, it's not likely to lose its relevance anytime soon.

35. *Mean Streets* (Martin Scorsese, 1973). Catholicism, crime, guilt, and male bonding in Little Italy: All the great Scorsese themes are here, in his most urgent and personal film. A hundred inferior independent movies have

worked from this blueprint, but this is the real McCoy. De Niro's live-wire performance as the flaky, dangerously impulsive Johnny Boy made him a star.

36. *California Split* (Robert Altman, 1974). Loose and funky and strangely exhilarating, this crowded Altman fresco plunges us into the giddy world of compulsive gambling, from seedy L.A. poker halls to the back rooms of Reno. Altman's improvisational style captures the roller-coaster emotions of guys living on the edge of their wits and their luck.

37. *The Man Who Would Be King* (John Huston, 1975). A rousingly ironic Kipling adventure tale about two con men, Michael Caine and Sean Connery, who temporarily become the rulers of remote Kafiristan. The director of *The Treasure of the Sierra Madre* returned in old age to his great theme—the vanity of human wishes—and the edge of mortality gives this tale a surprising undercurrent of melancholy.

38. *The Black Stallion* (Carroll Ballard, 1979). The flinty perfectionist Ballard first proved himself a cinematic Scheherazade when he turned Walter Farley's classic adventure book into this mesmerizing cinematic poem. A children's film for everyone and for all time.

39. *North Dallas Forty* (Ted Kotcheff, 1979). Nick Nolte, the most physical of actors, plays a man who's paid to absorb pain: a pro-football receiver. It's a bitter comedy of Sunbelt manners and a locker-room satire with soul.

40. *Mad Max 2: The Road Warrior* (George Miller, 1981). A spectacular, original demonstration of action filmmaking. Australian director Miller animates charging trucks and flying bikes like an industrial Busby Berkeley, conjuring up a vision of a rusty, dusty, postapocalyptic world that is still being copied in Hollywood.

41. *The Right Stuff* (Philip Kaufman, 1983). In an age of media-concocted idolatry, what's real heroism and what's just manufactured hype? Kaufman's ambitious astronaut epic—part Western-in-space, part spoof—asks us to ponder what the right stuff is really made of. Few films have caught the texture of the early '60s so successfully.

42. *This Is Spinal Tap* (Rob Reiner, 1984). The funny thing about this "rockumentary" about a hapless heavy-

metal band is not just that it's the most hilarious movie about the music world, it's also one of the most accurate.

43. *The Times of Harvey Milk* (Robert Epstein and Richard Schmeichen, 1984). This moving, wildly dramatic documentary tells the extraordinary story of the election of the first openly gay politician in the United States, his assassination (along with San Francisco mayor George Moscone), and the outrageous trial of the killer, Dan White. You'll understand why it won an Oscar.

44. *Bull Durham* (Ron Shelton, 1988). The smartest and sexiest of sports movies, this literate comedy about minor-league baseball was Kevin Costner's personal best and gave Susan Sarandon her most beguiling role and Tim Robbins his big break.

45. *Drugstore Cowboy* (Gus Van Sant, 1989). Most movies about junkies are so determined to preach their antidrug message that they fail to acknowledge the fact that smack gives pleasure. Van Sant's honest and weirdly funny movie about an ad hoc junkie family doesn't make that mistake. It's vital and alive, even when its protagonists seem barely to be breathing.

46. *The Killer* (John Woo, 1989). No action movies have more action than those made in Hong Kong. The mad poet of the genre is Woo, whose operatic gangster melodramas merge religiosity and camp in indefinable ways. *The Killer* is Woo at his pre-Hollywood best.

47. *Hoop Dreams* (Steve James, 1994). Following two black high school basketball players for four years, the filmmakers hit documentary gold: not just a great movie about NBA dreams but a complex cinematic portrait of contemporary life in the inner city.

48. *Before Sunrise* (Richard Linklater, 1995). After *Slackers* and *Dazed and Confused*, this quintessential Gen X director made this wonderfully verbose romance in which American student Ethan Hawke, on his last day in Europe, falls in love with bright French beauty Julie Delpy over the course of a long Viennese night. No film captures the sound and feel of young courtship more acutely.

49. *When We Were Kings* (Leon Gast, 1996). An exuberant look back at the legendary 1974 Rumble in the Jungle in Zaire between Muhammad Ali and George Foreman.

Both a tribute to Ali, who redefined the public role of the athlete, and an evocation of a bygone era, this music-filled documentary is about the transformative moment when black America, flexing its newborn pride, encountered black Africa.

50. *Saving Private Ryan* (Steven Spielberg, 1998). This devastating movie earns its place on the list for the Normandy-invasion sequence alone—20 gut-wrenching minutes that should be required viewing for anyone who gets the fanciful notion that waging war is a good idea.

—DAVID ANSEN

V
i
c
e
s

"I WOULD kill everyone in this room for a drop of sweet beer." Homer Simpson said that, and most of us, at one time or another, have understood exactly how he felt. You think about the beer, the Scotch, the cigarette, the cigar, the whatever-else-you-might-be-into, and simply put, you've got to have it. Maybe it's something a little more illicit, like the strip club with the brunet lap dancer who knows your name, or maybe it's an impulse gambling trip to Vegas. The results are predictable: You spend a lot of money and generally regret your behavior in the morning. Why did that gin and tonic seem like such a good idea when the bartender shouted last call at 4 A.M.? It's not altogether clear why we do this to ourselves, but the sad fact is, we *do*, so we might as well know what we're getting into. In other words, a man should know his vices.

There is an old saying in the South that you should never count how many you've had, only how many you've got left. This is perhaps not the best advice, but beyond the number of whatever-is-in-the-cooler, we should all pay more attention to what we're drinking, and smoking, and doing when the lights go out. This is not about common sense—your wife or girlfriend will probably take care of those for you—it's simply about having more fun. While it's certainly enjoyable to smoke a good cigar, for example, it's so much better when you know where they grew the tobacco, how they wrapped it, and how to get the perfect draw; if you're going to do some damage to yourself with a bottle of single-malt Scotch, you might as well know how to describe the taste; and if you're always wondering how many beers are left, maybe it's time you brewed your own. For some reason it always tastes better than anything you could buy at the store.

# Brew Your Own Beer

MANY PEOPLE would probably question the motivation of someone who chooses, as a hobby, to produce 10 gallons of alcohol in his kitchen. But for those who have embraced home-brewing, the end product isn't the primary motivation. It's what comes with it: the mad-scientist aspect of recipe formulation, the gadgets acquired as your skill level advances, the endless hours of comparing your beer with a fellow home-brewer's, and—oh yeah—when you're done, you have 126 bottles of beer in your fridge.

Many home-brewers will tell you that beer making isn't just a hobby, it's an obsession. Or as Ross Murray of the *Montreal Gazette* so eloquently put it, "Listening to someone who brews [his] own beer is like listening to a religious fanatic talk about the day he saw the light."

*You can't be a real country unless you have a beer and an airline—it helps if you have some kind of a football team, or some nuclear weapons, but at the very least you need a beer.*

**—FRANK ZAPPA**

## What's in It

Making your own beer is a wonderful cross between Albert Einstein and Betty Crocker—science meets cooking. Before going into the specifics, take a look at the basics of beer making. According to the Reinheitsgebot, the German beer purity law, beer consists of four ingredients: malt, hops, yeast, and water.

**MALT** is really more of a process than a substance. While generally barley, malt can be made up from any one of a number of grains such as barley, wheat, or rye that have been "malted"—a procedure in which the grain is soaked until it sprouts. The sprouted grains are then dried in an intricate fashion, during which time the starches in the grain transform. This transformation allows the starches in the grain to be converted into fermentable sugars by a process called *mashing*. During the mashing process, the malted grain is soaked in hot water, where the fermentable sugars are extracted from the grain.

**HOPS** is a cone-like flower in the cannabis family (yes, the *same* cannabis family) that contains small oil sacks called *lupulin*, which, when exposed to heat, contribute bitterness and aroma to the beer. The level of bitterness and aroma is

GENTL AND HYERS

A Beer to
Call Your Own

**ALL-GRAIN** brewing is practically identical to commercial brewing. The brewer begins with the whole grain and mashes it to produce the sweet sugar water, called *wort* (pronounced "wert"), to produce beer.

**EXTRACT BREWING** is the process by which commercial malt producers mash the grain, draw off the wort, and boil it down until it turns into a thick syrup. This concentrated malt syrup is packaged in cans for sale at home-brew shops. Home-brewers can then simply add water to this malt syrup, or extract, to produce a fermentable batch of wort. (Think of it as a beer version of frozen concentrated orange juice.) Since most home-brewers begin with extract brewing, we'll limit our scope to extract only.

## What You'll Need

The minimum equipment list you'll need for five gallons of beer is as follows:

- 1 12-quart pot
- 1 5-gallon plastic bucket
- 1 5-gallon carboy (glass water bottle)
- 1 bottle capper
- 1 8-foot racking hose
- 1 3-foot blow-off hose
- 1 fermentation lock
- 1 drilled rubber stopper
- 1 plastic funnel
- 1 beer hydrometer
- 1 bottle washer (optional but HIGHLY recommended)
- 1 bottle capper
- 60 12-ounce, pop-top bottles (not twist-off)
- 60 bottle caps

## How You Do It

1. Choose a recipe. Different types and proportions of beer's four basic ingredients (plus a few specialty ingredients, such as oats, honey, molasses, and even chocolate) make different styles of beer. Most home-brewing supply

controlled by a number of factors, but more on that later.

**YEAST** is the magic ingredient: This single-cell organism eats the sugar produced in the mashing process. The waste that yeast expels produces two things that turn sweet malt water into beer—alcohol and carbon dioxide. Long story short, the magnificence of beer is in fact yeast . . . uh, dung.

**WATER** is, well, water. Water treatment is the most scientific aspect of brewing. Different mineral levels and acidity levels (pH) contribute to the taste of the beer, and in many cases, such as Scottish or German beers, define a style.

## The Options

Unlike commercial brewing, home-brewing is divided into two categories: all-grain and extract. Each version requires its own equipment and process.

shops can sell you a kit for your favorite beer style, complete with malt, hops, and yeast for completing one batch of a particular beer.

2. The extract-brewing process begins by bringing a minimum of 1½ gallons of water to a boil in your brewpot. The more water you can accommodate, that is, the bigger your brewpot, the better. In fact, most home-brewers eventually upgrade to a large enough pot to accommodate their entire batch in order to achieve the benefits of a "full wort boil."

3. When the water reaches a boil, turn off the heat and add your malt syrup. Stir until the syrup is dissolved completely to prevent it from scorching and producing off-flavors in your finished product. Turn the heat back on and bring the mixture to a full, rapid boil. Most beers require one to two hours at a full boil.

4. Next, hops should be added at least once during the boil, and at specific intervals throughout the process: Add a "bittering" hop at the beginning of the boil, a "flavor" hop 30 minutes into the boil, and an "aroma" hop during the last 10 minutes. You can use hops of the same variety or of multiple varieties. Some beers also benefit from "dry-hopping," a dose of hops added in the fermentation phase.

5. While your wort is boiling, sterilize your fermentation vessel (a plastic bucket or glass carboy) and other equipment. Yeast will eat bacteria and produce horrid, tainted beer if given the opportunity. So it is essential that all utensils, hoses, vessels, and hands be sterilized from this point on. (Two tablespoons of bleach in five gallons of water makes an effective solution, and home-brew shops carry a variety of more sophisticated chemicals.)

6. When your wort has finished its boil, turn off the heat and allow it to cool before transferring it for fermentation. Cooling your wort is one of the most important aspects of brewing—at this heated stage it's most susceptible to attracting wild yeast and bacteria—so a wort chiller is perhaps the most important gadget you can buy. (Wort chillers are available from all home-brew shops, but instructions for making your own, much cheaper versions can be found in home-brewing books and on the Internet.)

This contraption is a long piece of copper coil bent into a cylindrical shape (a two-liter soda bottle can be used) with a hose attachment at either end. Submerge the copper coil into the hot wort and then run cold water through the coils to cool the wort. If you have not done a full wort boil, add three gallons of sterilized or bottled water to the fermentation vessel. (Do not use deionized distilled water—your yeast needs those minerals to grab on to in order to work properly.) Then, transfer your cooled wort to your fermentation vessel using your racking hose. If needed, add more water until you achieve a quantity of five gallons.

7. Use a thermometor to check the temperature of your wort, which should be between 68 and 70 degrees. This is a very important step in the brewing process and guessing can ruin your beer, so be patient and be careful. If your wort is still above 70 degrees, place the lid on the fermentation vessel and wait until the temperature drops.

8. When the wort has reached the proper temperature, add the yeast. Once the yeast is added, aerate your wort well. Oxygen is the most essential element in facilitating yeast propagation. A small aquarium pump is ideal for oxygenation of your wort, so if you've got another 10 bucks to spend, pick one up. Otherwise give the fermentation vessel a good shake for two or three minutes. Then add your blow-off hose and put the end in a one-gallon bucket filled with water.

## Sweet, Sweet Beer

Now, let the wort sit: This is the time when biology is at its best, making sugar water into beer. Within a couple of days you'll see the beer begin to ferment. A thick white foam of yeast will form on the top, and the excess will be expelled out of the blow-off hose.

After two or three days, when the most intense activity has subsided, use your racking hose to transfer your beer to your secondary fermenter (your glass carboy). Add your fermentation lock to the top of the carboy.

Let the beer continue to ferment for an additional five to seven days. How do you know when it's done? For beginners, watch your fermentation lock—when the interval between bubbles is more than one minute, the beer if fully fermented. Then it's time to bottle.

## Capping

Prepare by santitizing 60 12-ounce bottles and 60 bottle caps. Rinse well using your bottle washer.

Boil ¾ cup of corn sugar with 1 cup of water and add it into your plastic fermenting bucket (which has been thoroughly cleaned and sanitized!). Siphon the beer into the bucket. Then siphon the beer into the sanitized bottles and cap using your bottle capper.

Once you've bottled your beer, place the bottles in a cool, dark place for 10 to 14 days, during which time the additional corn sugar will work with the residual yeast to carbonate the beer.

What next? What else—decant your beer and enjoy. What begins as a hobby will surely lead to an obsession. This isn't conjecture, it is simply a statement of fact. Happy brewing.

For beginners, and those looking to move on to more complex beers and techniques, the best book to start with is *The Complete Joy of Homebrewing* by Charlie Papazian. In home-brew circles it is known simply as "the bible."

**–PATRICK HIGGINS AND**
**MAURA KATE KILGORE**

# A Very Fine Year

IT'S A FACT that perfectly matched food and wine bring out the best in each other. The reason is, quite simply, chemical. Gary Dexter, the wine buyer for La Case Sena, a renowned restaurant in Santa Fe, New Mexico, with a cellar of over 1,000 different wines, admitted that in a simple, perfect world, the old adage about whites with fish and reds with meat "might hold water . . . but with today's fusion cuisines and spicy ingredients, there are no rules anymore. For instance, here in New Mexico where chilies and other strong spices are used in the cuisine, you have to stay away from wines like Bordeaux or Cabernet Sauvignons—wine with big alcohol content—since it'd be like throwing gasoline on a fire."

Dexter said that as chefs become increasingly creative with cuisine, it becomes a challenge for wine buyers to match the right wine. He cited an appetizer on the previous night's menu: "The chef came up with lobster nori rolls with a wasabi cream sauce. Wines I might've recommended for the lobster wouldn't work because of the spiciness of the wasabi. We finally settled on several dry, sparkling wines.

"A lot of it is common sense," says Dexter. "You'll never go wrong matching cuisine and wine from the same region. Over generations, the cuisine was tailored, consciously or unconsciously, to the wines from the local vineyards. For instance, on the island of Madeira, they drink Madeira with turtle soup . . . one of the local specialties. They're made for each other."

When ordering at a restaurant, you should never hesitate to ask your waiter and wine steward a few simple questions: In what region of Italy is this risotto rapini a specialty? What are the wines of that region? Of those wines, which will go best with this dish?

Dexter says that aside from fusion dishes, there are a few guidelines that will at least help in picking wine for your own table. "Generally, lighter meats, such as chicken or rabbit and lean pork, go best with lighter reds, such as a pinot noir, a Barbera, or a Beaujolais. Game meats, such as pheasant or quail, go better with a more medium bodied red, such as a Rhone. For heavy meats, such as venison or steaks, you want wine with enough tannin to neutralize the heavier chemicals in the meat. This is when you'd go for a Cabernet or a Spanish Rioja or a wine from St. Emilion."

Unless you're eating a very simple rendition of Dover sole, you needn't confine yourself to a dry white wine like a Meursault from Burgundy.

Champagne and dry, sparkling wines tend to go very well with simply prepared shellfish, such as oysters, mussels, or crab, but everything changes in the way the shellfish is prepared. For instance, if the mussels are Provençal or the shellfish comes in a bouillabaisse, you might want to consider a fuller-bodied white like a Chenin Blanc from the Loire or an Alsace Riesling; even a lighter-bodied red might do well. Likewise, fish in cream or butter sauces need a wine from Alsace, Loire, a Chardonnay from California, or a pinot gris from Oregon that have enough body to take on the weight of the sauces.

One rule that Dexter says has not changed over the years is that wines should always be served sequentially. "You want to start with the lighter wines and finish with the big reds. Usually, this is logical, since you start with lighter dishes and finish with heavier ones. . . . It really doesn't work to do it any other way."

Finally, the only sure way to learn to pick the right wines is, in the opinion of one of my local wine gurus, to "learn to taste, taste, taste. . . ." The only sure way to know which wines will go with which cuisine is to log lots of tactile experience onto your taste buds. I know. It's a helluva thing to ask, so you better get started.

–KENT BLACK

# The Whisky Trail

THE CUSTOMS OFFICIAL at the Glasgow airport asked me why I was visiting Scotland, and I made the mistake of telling him the truth. "I'm here to travel the Whisky Trail." In a split second he signaled another customs agent over, and before I knew it, the two were lecturing me about their preferred malts.

That's the problem with single-malt Scotch. Once you've sampled the aqua vitae you become a missionary for the cause. Forget blended Scotches; no matter how refined or expensive, there's no comparison. Single malts have all the merits and complexity one requires of a longtime companion.

Scotland, or the Holy Land, is loosely divided into four areas of distillation: Highland malts, Islay malts, Lowland malts, and Speyside malts. These areas encompass, roughly, over 100 different distilleries. In the midst of this land of casked treasure, the Scottish Tourist Board promotes something called the Whisky Trail. It's an actual route, marked by road signs, that weaves its way through Speyside (in the northeast) through the heart of single-malt country. Half the country's distilleries can be found here, drawn to the area by the glut of pure water sources. For someone wishing to sample single malts, the rolling hills surrounding the river Spey are nothing short of paradise.

Now, one could argue that one doesn't need to traverse the Whisky Trail to drink a wide variety of single malts. One could easily sit in a well-stocked Edinburgh pub and accomplish the same thing. But really, where is the romance in that? At best you'd be little more than a barfly. The visitor to Speyside, on the other hand, is an explorer like Magellan.

For a minimal fee, many of the distilleries along the Whisky Trail offer tours of their facilities. On such a tour, you'll see how a single malt is born: Sprouted barley (malt) is dried in a kiln, milled into grist, washed with hot water—oh, screw it, you don't really care. Sure, the visual of the onion-shaped copper stills is impressive, as are the heat and the beer-like smell that wafts through these places, but what you really want is to get to the "wee dram." That's the product sample awaiting you at the end of each tour.

For those unaccustomed to "weeing," a dram is an inexact measure of single malt, which is reliant on the generosity of the pourer. On one splendid Scottish day of still-hopping, I had my first dram by 10 A.M. and hit four more religious sites during the afternoon.

You've probably noticed I haven't inundated you with brand names so far: "So-and-so is a silk slipper; such and such is bilge water." You know why? It all boils down to personal taste. Is a blonde more beautiful than a brunette? I don't know. Does the blonde have any money? The best way to resolve this issue is to drink.

If you're going to be scientific about this exploration, there are established criteria. Connoisseurs have exacting standards. First, they talk about "nose." What is the fragrance of the whisky? Adjectives like smoky, sherry, honey, flowery, and peaty are frequently used. Color is important, as is "body." Is it firm? Smooth? Then comes the palate, how it actually tastes. And finally the "finish," or the lingering effect, which is described with great poetry: "warming, enveloping, long."

You can buy authoritative tasting guides if you're so inclined. But the only way to really handle these issues is to go to Scotland and taste the way the sea and peat are present in the island of Islay malts. You also need to know what it is to eat a five-course Scottish breakfast. You should experience a sunset at eleven o'clock at night. And most important, you must see how a man can wear a skirt with dignity. Only then will you begin to fathom the profound solace of this divine drink.

—JOHN McCORMICK

# Get Ripped, Sauced, Blind

SOMETIMES AMERICA is plagued by puritans. The Puritans, for example—within a year of landing at Plymouth Rock, they had dragged the poor Wampanoag Indians to one of those family Thanksgivings full of religious aunts, Rotarian uncles, and Hillary Clinton–type girl cousins all eating overdone turkey, with no booze in the log shelter and nothing worth popping in the bathroom medicine cabinet. And I'll bet the meal was timed so that the Wampanoag tribe missed the

> ## *You're not drunk if you can lie on the floor without holding on.*
>
> **— DEAN MARTIN**

Michigan–Michigan State kick-off. Then there was the eighteenth-century Great Awakening, the nineteenth-century Revival Movement, twentieth-century Prohibition, and, now, cable TV advertisements for *Buns of Steel.*

These puritans are ruining my essay on how to get hit by a whiskey truck with grace, style, and wit. I meant to address important questions such as: When is it appropriate to get drunk? (When you're sober.) When is it appropriate to sober up? (When you come to and find your dog is wearing a negligee.) Are there things you shouldn't say after letting go of the water wagon with both hands? ("I do.") Then there were the myriad matters of technique: When making a dry martini, you can use, as an emergency vermouth substitute, more gin. And so forth.

Alas, health, fitness, and self-respect are in vogue. A man who drinks in a healthy, fit, and self-respecting manner will mix vodka with yogurt and get tangled in the Nautilus machine trying to kiss his own ass. Thus I am compelled to skip

the do's and don't-you-dare's, the how-to's and here's how's. Instead I must explain why you should tear the MADD bumper sticker off the De Soto of your superego, make John Barleycorn your designated driver, and weave across both lanes of life with nothing on but your fog lights. (Metaphorically speaking, of course.)

Do it for the sake of humanity. Lushes are morally superior to uninebriated people. Beer-jerkers, mugg blotts, and potwallopers are careless and bad-tempered, it's true. But consider the greatest evils of history. Is *careless* the word you'd use to describe Hiroshima? Was the Gulag Archipelago something Stalin did instead of kicking the cat? It's smoking in bed versus the fire-bombing of Dresden. Real evil requires the kind of thoughtful planning that is hard to do when you're wearing a soup tureen on your head and trying not

---

### DUCK A HANGOVER

According to Peter Doherty, a bartender at New York City's White Horse Tavern—the Greenwich Village pub where Dylan Thomas drank himself to death—the best way to avoid a hangover is to toss back an ounce or three of prevention. Avoid bingeing on an empty stomach; chase each round with an equal or greater amount of water; and choke down a couple of coated aspirin before bed, to get a step ahead of your headache and muscle aches. Doherty also suggests you skip the Old Rotgut on the bottom shelf—pricier brands of liquor emerge from distillation with fewer impurities. "'It's pay now or pay later,' I tell folks. Even if you can't taste the difference between a premium vodka and a well vodka, you'll feel it the next day." One more thing. Repeat after us: I am too old for body shots.

**—ALEX BHATTACHARJI**

to let your wife notice you're taking a leak in the potted palm. The worst people always have an abstemious streak. Hitler was a teetotaler. What if he'd been a soak? What if Himmler and Goering had emerged from the Reich Chancellery asking each other, "How do we persecute the gnus?" Real evil also requires lying, and in vino ("Adolf, you really oughta shave that booger broom") veritas. A drinking man couldn't have written *Mein Kampf*. Give Schicklgruber a couple of silly milks, and you'd get *Turn Your Head and Kampf*. And think of all the suffering mankind would have been spared if *The Communist Manifesto* had said, "Workers of the world: It's Miller Time."

—P.J. O'ROURKE

# Make Your Own Moonshine

**M**OONSHINE—a.k.a. white lightning, redeye, Carolina corn, Texas tea, rotgut, stinksweat, radiator wine, pine juice, boar's breath, and bush whiskey—is admittedly America's darker side of baseball, July Fourth, and Mom's apple pie. The production and consumption of homemade grain alcohol may bring revenue and ATF agencies down on you (they're well known for their lack of delicacy) and even earn you a stretch in federal prison. Consumption of an ill-fated batch can cause blindness, insanity, and impotence and most definitely will give you a gruesome hangover you will not soon forget. But the legacy of Al Capone, the backcountry lifestyle, and *The Beverly Hillbillies* have lured many a spirits lover to the time-honored, albeit illicit, art of making moonshine—a tradition that predates liquor stores by several thousand years. Just about the time man could stand erect, he figured out a way to make home brew. Prior to the mid-nineteenth century, when the world population was largely engaged in agricultural pursuits, wine, beer, and harder spirits were locally made and locally consumed. It wasn't a political statement; it was just simple economics and pride in creating a good buzz with your own hands. Calvados, marc, grappa, and poteen are all great spirits born of this pride and tradition.

So although we don't encourage anyone to make a longtime habit out of making or drinking the stuff, it is devilishly fun to indulge in a great American pastime. So, follow these basic guidelines given by Camino Doug, who lives in a small rural town and learned the trade in East Texas from his uncles, originally hailing from Kentucky.

In the United States, corn is the most commonly

used ingredient, though potatoes are used in regions where they're plentiful. The basic "mash" is thus made with corn, water, sugar, yeast, and malt. Doug says that back home, mash is usually mixed in old oil drums or wood washtubs but that an old oak wine barrel is ideal. In a 50-gallon barrel, mix up about 50 pounds of corn meal, 25 pounds of sugar, a couple of pounds of yeast and malt, and enough water to fill the barrel. The barrel should be kept in a warm place to aid in fermentation. The mash can take up to a week to "ripen." Doug advises keeping your operation well away from the house: "As the mash gets ripe, it makes popping sounds like little firecrackers and stinks to high heaven. It's not somethin' you want in your basement."

The basic idea behind making any spirit is to heat the mash until the alcohol vaporizes and then cool the vapor so it reaches a liquid form. Doug says this can take a dozen different forms depending on how much liquor is being made, but it can be as simple as "just a big ol' pressure cooker used for canning with the valve drilled out and a piece of threaded copper tubing threaded in . . . to the other end weld a good run of coiled tubing . . . about five or six feet. The coil got run through a horse trough of cool water. When the liquor drips out the end, it drops into a filter filled with hickory charcoal to take out some of the impurities and add a little flavor. If you're real particular, you drip the whole batch into one barrel and let it set a spell for aging."

Doug says the best-tasting are usually the second or third batches, when additional ingredients (except for yeast) are added to the original batch. The first batch is called "sweet mash," while the subsequent batches are "sour mashes." Doug advises against remixing more than five or six times. The first part of the batch is going to be the highest proof, sometimes as much as 180 proof, while the last part of the run might be two-thirds of the first. Therefore, a batch, or even a couple of batches, need to be mixed together. Even so, says Doug, his uncles rarely produced a bottle of less than 100 proof.

Despite having "a hankering now and then for a taste," Doug thinks moonshine should certainly not be your "usual" at cocktail hour. But as George Jones sang in the popular country song, "White Lightnin'," "I took a little sip and right away I knew/When my eyes bugged out and my face turned blue. . . ."

—KENT BLACK

# Know Your Sake

YOU APPROACH a basement stairway off a narrow sidewalk in downtown Manhattan. Take a few steps down, knock on the door. You're looked over and buzzed in, speakeasy style, and the city street seems a mile away. You're in Decibel, a semisecret sanctuary of sake drinking and dislocation, which in this case amount to the same thing. The cavelike atmosphere is dressed up with paper lanterns and cloth banners that look as if they've gone off-duty from a sushi bar and gotten funky. Behind both of the low, dark-wood bars are dozens of gourmet sakes: full-bore and subtle, tangy and mellow, mildly sweet and tonsil-parchingly dry—but none of the bland, American-made restaurant-freebie stuff.

Japanese sake is finally being appreciated in America, with consumption now at more than 2 million gallons per year, about double what it was in the mid-'80s. And Americans who love Japanese food might be soul-prepared to savor even more of the mood—except for one thing: the quality of what they're currently drinking. "When sake was introduced to America through Japanese restaurants in the 1960s, the distributors couldn't ship it right or store it right," says Bon Yagi, the principal partner of Decibel. "It has no sulfites or preservatives; it's more delicate than wine, and it has to be served within a year of bottling. Plus, it was served hot, which makes some of the flavors and aromas disappear."

Today quality-conscious importers are shipping sake in refrigerated containers, and savvy bars and restaurants are serving it cool so that all its nuances can be tasted.

There are more than 2,300 sake producers in Japan, with output in an array of regional and house styles that easily rival those of single-malt Scotch for subtle connoisseurship. The Japanese have more words to describe the full compass of these sakes than the Inuits do for *snow*—more than 90 of them, according to Hiroshi Kondo's *The Book of Sake* (Kodansha)—from *kudoi* ("garrulous") to *sabishii* ("lonely and sad").

All are brewed (in a process somewhat like that for beer) from rice, but the end results can get pretty exotic. A wood-aged *taru* brand, such as Kiku-Masamune, smells like fresh-rasped cedar; the rough-filtered Nigori is milky; while the big-bodied, Gobi-arid Yukino Matsushime tastes like the mother of all dry beers. Or you can take your cup *hire-zake* style, meaning with a dried blowfish fin bobbing in it. But never mind about that.

The sakes you'll find at better Japanese restaurants and at most liquor stores will probably include some American-produced brands, such as Gekkeikan and the more flavorful Ozeki and Hakusan. These have the virtue of being available, simple, and affordable. But it is the imports that open the door to the drink's evening-energizing pleasures.

Choosing an imported brand from its esoteric label description can, at first, seem impossible. As when ordering sashimi, you have to experiment and mix-and-match. Knowing the four basic sake types will help: *Junmai* is a traditional style, often with a full body; *bon jozo* is alcohol-fortified, rich but smooth; *ginjo* is a refined and filtered version, second only to the super-refined *dai ginjo*. In addition, sakes are rated for dryness (+20 is very dry, –20 very sweet); good restaurant lists will note this. There is no dominant, Heineken-like import, but some high-quality producers to look for include Kamotsuru, Daishichi Kaiden, Ikkashin, Harushika, and Momokawa.

Heated up, the simplest brews of these imports or their American-made cousins provide a fine nightcap or a literal warm welcome for guests. (Pour the drink into a coffee mug or other stout container and place it in a pot of hot—but not boiling—water for a few minutes.) Warm or chilled, most sakes work well with an amazing variety of foods, from marinated beef to fried scallops to cold mushrooms. Though there are delicate types that probably won't taste like the celestial essence of plum blossoms when paired with a T-bone, the concentrated character and alcohol strength (usually 15 percent to 17 percent) of these drinks make them deceptively sturdy.

"I can't think of too many foods it *doesn't* go with," claims Fred Eckhardt, a Portland, Oregon–based writer who publishes *The Sake Connection* newsletter. "I served sake at Thanksgiving one year, and it goes very well with turkey and gravy." Just don't forget to pass the blowfish fin.

—**RICHARD NALLEY**

**CIGARS**

# Blowing Smoke

WINSTON CHURCHILL helped win World War II while smoking them. George Burns lived to the ripe old age of 100 while puffing them. Sure, they're supposed to be bad for you, but the cigar's distinctive smell and hardy taste lure you every time. Of course, we're not advocating cigar smoking (puff, puff), but we do suggest that if you're going to indulge, make sure you're enjoying the best.

Choose a good cigar with care. There are some eight categories of cigar tobacco, from the mild Claro claro to the dark, aromatic Colorado Maduro, and some two dozen styles, from long, fat double Coronas to sleek, little panatellas; it's necessary to smoke a few cigars before you find the ones that are right for you.

The first step, though, is learning how to smoke it. First, test a cigar by rolling it between your thumb and forefinger. If it crackles, it's too dry, and if you feel hollow spots, it won't burn evenly. The tobacco should be firm but have a little give. Next, remove the band, unless you need to show off the brand name.

Next, you need to cut the closed end. How much you cut will determine how much smoke you draw in. If you're not experienced, it's best to start small and recut if you don't feel you're getting a good draw. As the cigar burns down, the harshness of the smoke will increase. If you've started out with too big a hole, it'll probably be necessary to abandon the cigar before you've even smoked half. I recommend a special cutting or poking tool to create the hole. Tearing off the end with teeth or fingernails almost invariably results in a ragged end, which will become even more ragged during the course of the smoke. I find the best result comes from wetting the end slightly with your lips and then snipping off the end with a cutter.

Before lighting up, it's advisable to warm the end (or foot) of the cigar with a match by turning it slowly over the flame. This will make it very easy to light the cigar on your second match. Don't light a cigar cold. It usually results in the smoker overdrawing, which, in turn, creates a hot foot. This, in turn, increases the intensity of the tar and the harshness of the smoke.

Wet the end of the cigar with your lips so that it turns easily as you light up. The flame of the match should be held at least an inch away so that you don't taste any sulfur. The cigar should be rolled slightly over the flame so that it lights evenly. Correct any slight unevenness by blowing lightly on the end of the cigar after your match is extinguished.

A cigar should not be puffed repeatedly, and the glowing should never be longer than the tip of your thumb. Avoid tapping ash whenever possible. A good ash keeps the end of the cigar cooler and will prolong the length of the smoke.

Sadly, one of the final lessons in smoking is not to overdo it no matter how delicious and expensive the cigar. Because of the accumulation of tars, it's not really recommended to smoke a cigar to the nub or even more than halfway. Still, it's a matter of personal preference. As one of my smoking buddies says, "Smoke it 'til you don't enjoy it anymore."

—KENT BLACK

# Stack the Deck

NOW THAT nearly every state in America with a wide river, an Indian reservation, or a budget deficit has legalized, full-strength gambling, casinos—like coffee bars and the information superhighway—are fast becoming ubiquitous. Unfortunately for most, that means you can now lose money closer to home, not just at the annual Vegas convention. No matter what the charlatan system-sellers claim, the odds are against you. You *will* lose. And the more you play, the less chance there is that freakish good luck will bail you out.

Unless you play blackjack. Expertly.

By adhering to what's known as the basic strategy—which incorporates the highest percentage plays—you can reduce the house edge on a six-deck shoe game to approximately 0.5 percent and to virtually zero on single-deck games. Here are the fundamentals of the strategy, some of which must be slightly modified, depending on variations of casino rules:

1. You hold 13 through 16; dealer shows 2 through 6: Stand.
2. You hold 12 through 16; dealer shows 7 through ace: Hit.
3. You hold 17 or above; Stand unless it's a "soft" 17 (ace and 6).
4. Always double down (double your bet and get one more card) on a 10 or 11 against dealer's 2 through 9.
5. Always split aces and eights.
6. Never take insurance—a side bet in which you put up half again your original bet when the dealer is showing an ace. If he has a blackjack, you don't lose your original amount; if he doesn't, you lose the insurance.

But playing "basic," alas, does not turn a loser into a winner. To make a profit, you'll need to master what professional gamblers call "advantage plays." These are clever, perfectly legal maneuvers that exploit the game's—and the casino's—weaknesses, transferring the edge from house to gambler.

## Card Counting Made Easy

This is the original advantage play. Though you can study an array of methods, they all track the ratio of good cards to bad cards. Counters do not, Rain Man–like, memorize every card. They merely assign a value to each *type* of card and keep track on the relative richness (or poorness) of the deck. When it's rich, they bet big; when it's poor, they bet the minimum.

For example, in the popular "hi-lo" count, twos, threes, fours, fives, and sixes are worth +1. Tens, face cards, and aces count –1. Sevens, eights, and nines don't count. A freshly shuffled deck starts at zero. If the first eight cards out are four face cards, two sevens, a deuce, and an ace, the count would be –4. The negative count indicates a disadvantage to the player: Bet the minimum. When the count turns positive, indicating a richness of big cards, the player has the edge because he gets paid 3-to-2 for a blackjack but pays the house even money— a 50 percent advantage. The higher the count and the fewer cards remaining, the greater your edge.

Approximate player advantage: 1 percent to 1.5 percent (when played optimally)

Degree of difficulty (1 to 10 scale): 3

## Dealer Tells All

A "tell" is part of the subconscious body language commonly associated with poker—the subtle mannerisms that expose the value of a hand. Astute players can recognize dealers who unwittingly tip their hand through a vocabulary of physical and verbal signs. This is usually done when a dealer peeks at his hole card, checking for aces underneath 10s and face cards.

Does the dealer pull back from the table when he has a bad hand or lean into the action when he's pat? Observe the dealer's body language as he goes around the table: Does he seem to "include" players in the game with an open hand gesture when his cards are strong and almost skim over the table

when he's weak? Or vice versa, which can happen when the dealer is unconsciously rooting for a player, perhaps in expectation of extra tips? Some experts even recommend "priming the pump" with a few well-placed tips immediately after sitting down. Though only a handful of Nevada casinos require their dealers to peek, readable dealers can be found in Iowa, Washington, Colorado, Illinois, and Louisiana.

Approximate player advantage: 1 percent to 2 percent

Degree of difficulty: 6

## Getting the Bends

Like dealer tells, playing the "warps," or "bends," is effective only if the dealer peeks under his 10s to check for blackjacks. If he does, and if the cards have been in play for close to an hour and have been handled roughly, the deck will often develop readable warps. Generally, the 10s and face cards, which the dealer has bent up, will have a slight arch to them when facedown; the other cards will have a slight cup. With a warped deck, the big cards will create distinct bows, or "breaths," between cards. Perceptive players can use this information to make insurance decisions (an exception to the rule), cut themselves a big card after the shuffle, and determine the value of the dealer's hand. Players who "help" put warps in the card are cheating; dealers who warp the cards create an advantage available to anyone who's paying attention.

Approximate player advantage: 0 percent to 9 percent (varies with application)

Degree of difficulty: 7

## Tracking the Rich Clumps

Most casual players assume that the casino's shuffling procedure produces random results. In fact, not only are most casino shuffles not random; the vast majority are "trackable," allowing expert players to predict where key cards (aces) and rich clumps of high cards will be located after the shuffle. To make sequences random, the casinos would need to shuffle their decks at least seven times. Most shuffle only three times, because the more time spent shuffling, the less time spent dealing cards.

Shuffle trackers analyze casino shuffles, "map" the distribution of cards throughout the deck or decks, and bet big when they know they'll be receiving good cards. Adjacent cards, when shuffled purely, move one card apart from the first card after the first riffle, four apart after the second riffle, and eight apart after the third riffle. (Turn two cards faceup, shuffle, and see for yourself.) By memorizing three-card sequences—usually two "key" cards preceding or surrounding the "target" card (an ace)—trackers can collect enough data to follow desired cards through the casino's surprisingly vulnerable shuffling procedure. Knowing where all four aces per deck will fall is an enormous advantage. Knowing where even *one* ace will fall can turn a losing game into a winner.

Approximate player advantage: 1.5 percent to 2 percent

Degree of difficulty: 9

A fuller explanation of basic strategy can be found in most reputable books on blackjack, such as Steve Forte's *Read the Dealer*, Arnold Snyder's *Blackbelt in Blackjack*, and Stanford Wong's *Basic Blackjack*.

—MICHAEL KONIK

# Deal With the Big Dogs

## 52 WAYS TO LEAVE THE POKER PITS OF VEGAS WITHOUT GETTING BIT

A LOT OF poker players go to Vegas on a lark—drinking for free, eating prime rib and lobster, smoking cigars, and wondering if they'll get lucky. What they don't realize is that some people make a living off the game. These are the Big Dogs of poker, and they are so good that they can crush you without even looking at their cards.

The best poker in the world is played at the Bellagio card room, a beautiful space with tasteful frescoes on the walls, an efficient staff, and 24-hour games. The stakes run from a few dollars to hundreds of thousands. At the midlevel games you can see Johnny Bond, charismatic raconteur and the editor of *Real Poker,* a compilation of columns by the legendary Roy Cooke. You'll recognize him by his multi-pocket vest and wraparound sunglasses. He'll tell you that Texas Hold'em is the Lexus of poker, the game of champions. It is simple to learn but hard to play. Hold'em is a fast game that consists of four betting rounds. A dealer gives each player two cards facedown. You look at these cards and bet. Then comes the flop: The dealer turns three cards face-up in the center of the table. You mentally add the flop to your facedown cards and bet some more. At this point the stakes double. You get two more cards to bet on, and with a couple of bad beats, you will find yourself sucked in so fast you won't know what happened until you're standing in line at the ATM for the fifth time in a day—or maybe at the pawnshop.

Here's how to avoid this scenario: Use your brain. Poker is a game of wits, skill, and paying attention. Learn that, and you will stack your chips in giant towers. Cash out a winner, tip the dealer, see a show, and go home happy.

*Patience, and shuffle the cards.*

—MIGUEL DE CERVANTES, *DON QUIXOTE*

1. Poker is not what happens at the table, but what other people think happens.

2. If you play properly, you'll lose only with your good hands, since you'll be throwing away bad cards. So losing with good cards means that you're playing well.

3. Johnny Bond says: "The only answer to a question about poker is 'It depends.'"

4. Wars are won not by the most organized army but by the least disorganized army. It's the same with cards. Poker is won not by the person who makes the most good decisions, but by the person who makes the fewest errors.

5. Scared money never wins.

6. Don't waste your chips by calling bets simply because you're bored. If you're bored in Vegas, you either have a deep-seated problem or you're a missionary (in which case you have no business being in a card game).

7. Poker is about information—obtaining true while conveying false.

8. Picking the right table is very important. Drunken businessmen make for a good game. A game with dealers in it is considered good because dealers are notorious for being fast, loose players. Or you may prefer a table with an attractive young woman because she'll distract the other players. Unless, of course, you're easily distracted by attractive young women.

9. Where to sit: to the left of tight players, to the right of loose players.

10. Most people bluff at the wrong time and way too often. The easiest players to bluff are solid players, who know enough to believe you. The best way to bluff is to make the other players think you never bluff. Once you have mastered these two skills, leave poker and enter politics.

11. If you flop the mortal nuts, you should slow-play the wheels off them until the turn, then hammer the river and snap their bullets like sticks. Leave them stuck and steaming. If you don't understand what this means, stick to the nickel slots (or see "Poker Talk," p. 323).

12. Johnny Bond says: "If you can't raise, you should fold."

13. Never play loose to recover losses, and never play tight to minimize losses.

14. A bad beat is when someone with a lousy hand outdraws your great hand. Many players will get mad and lose a stack on the next hand out of anger. A better idea is to buy

a buck's worth of dimes and feed them to a slot machine one at a time. You'll feel better, and it will only cost you one dollar instead of a hundred.

15. Johnny Bond says: "Poker brings out the worst side of the best people, and you wouldn't believe what it does to the worst people."

16. Your poker wardrobe deserves careful attention. Comfort is crucial, since you'll be sitting for long hours in a heavily air-conditioned room. Just as you would for getting a massage or attending an execution, you need to wear loose clothes and bring a jacket. The current card-room uniform is an expensive gym suit with no belt, zipper, or snaps to bite into your gut. If you want to look like a pro, waste some of your stake on fancy workout clothes.

17. You can also impersonate a tourist. Wear golf clothes and say you're in from Iowa for a convention but really just want to hit the links and thought you'd try poker since you played it when you were a kid. Sit back and watch the locals' eyes light up. Then proceed to clean them out.

18. A related technique is to dress like a cowboy and act like a bonehead, or to wear garish shirts and talk like a nut. One guy, a Greek Canadian, takes the disguise further by shaving his head, chain-smoking, wearing sleeveless shirts, talking French, and cussing like a sailor when he takes a loss. He's such a gambler that he proposed to his wife overseas by mail—and included $20,000 for her to buy a house.

19. Johnny Bond says: "Feel a hunch, bet a bunch. Throw caution to the wind and chips into the pot."

20. You have to play good to run bad, and you have to run bad to play good.

21. Never draw to an inside straight. The worst thing that can happen is that you might hit it, and if you do that you'll spend the rest of your life burning off stacks of chips in hopes of hitting the next one.

22. For a terrible player, having fun is important. For a bad player, winning the pot is important. For a good player, playing the cards correctly is important. For a great player, winning the World Series of Poker is important.

23. Johnny Bond says: "Playing craps is a sin because Einstein said that God doesn't throw dice. If He don't, I don't."

24. If you're in every hand, you're a loser. This is the same as with sex but the opposite of love.

25. Poker players wear a lot of jewelry on their hands and wrists because that's what you see the most of. The more flash you wear, the more people call your bets. They figure you've got money to burn. Wear your jewelry loud, large, and a lot.

26. The local pros are there to separate you from your money, and it is important to discern who they are early on.

## DOUBLE YOUR RAISE

It's not really *gambling* if all you do is bet favorites in horse racing. Fortunately, the secrets to finding a winning nag at a nice, fat price, says *Washington Post* racing writer Andrew Beyer, are available to anyone who picks up a *Daily Racing Form*. The legendary handicapper devised a system for rating horses so effective that the Beyer Speed Figure, a measure of a horse's speed that's designed to factor out the variations between tracks and races, is now a standard tool of the pony-picking trade.

 • First, check the horses' past perform-ances to see if there's a higher-odds competitor with a Beyer Speed Figure comparable to some of the favored horses in the field. In spite of the odds, the speed figure could indicate real talent.

 • Next, check out the horses' trainers. You want to see a winning percentage of 20 percent or better over time. Finding a horse that has changed from a weak trainer to a strong one is another potent betting angle.

 • Finally, check the running line, which gives each horse's position at four intervals during past races. "If there's a horse with a lot of early speed, consider it," says Beyer. "You're betting that it will open up a lead early and hold on for the upset." *Run, Windfall, run!*

—ALEX BHATTACHARJI

Pros tip 50¢ pieces from a roll they bring to the table. They wear dark glasses and headphones, a billed cap, and a loose jacket. They play solitaire on miniature video-game machines. They eat, nap, and receive phone calls at the table. They're also the ones who ask new players where they're from.

27. Johnny Bond says: "If you're unsure whether someone is tourist or a local, look at his shirt and ask yourself, 'Did he pack that for Vegas?'"

28. Pros are easily distinguished by the way they buy chips. Tourists open their wallet, but the locals carry a roll of cash in their front pocket. The rubber band holding the wad together has usually been tied and retied in knots where it broke. They are reluctant to replace it since it's their lucky rubber band. And the absolute stone-cold way to tell a local is with your ears. The more they whine, the longer they've lived in Vegas.

29. A *fish* is a sucker, a donator. If you're in a game and you can't tell who the fish is, it's you.

30. Don't play poker with a guy wearing a beat-up shirt with frogs on it. It's the lucky shirt of Ted Forrest, who in 1994 won three World Series of Poker events—Razz, Seven Stud, and Omaha. He's so good that he knows what you're going to do before you do.

31. Be careful if a player casually asks about your SAT scores. Be very careful if he offers to take the test with you for money. Forget about it altogether if he offers to spot you some time or some points. You're talking to David Sklansky, a top authority on poker, who incidentally scored a perfect 800 on the math SAT. What you should do is leave the table immediately, go buy his books, and read them. Then read them again.

32. Stay away from Chinese poker if you meet a young man from Pittsburgh in the game, particularly if he's cheerful, dapper, and polite. It's Greg Grivas, the 1996 world champ of the $1,500 game and a floor supervisor at the Bellagio.

33. Never play poker with a Chinese man from Texas. Especially if he's wearing a Versace shirt. Especially if his nickname is the "Oriental Express." Especially if the game is at the highest stakes in the country. Especially if you don't want to lose to Johnny Chan, two-time World Series of Poker champion and the biggest money-winner of all time in WSP events. Go find yourself an easier game.

34. Avoid playing with a jovial older gentleman with a white Amish-style beard, a walking stick, an ever-present cigar, and a sly drawl. This is none other than former world champion Puggy Pearson. Don't let his manners fool you—

Puggy will gut you at the table, then tell your wife to see the outhouse because you just lost your ass.

35. Johnny Bond says: "Never play poker with a pregnant woman. It's bad luck to beat her."

36. The best time to play poker in Vegas is during big sports events such as the Super Bowl, the Kentucky Derby, the Final Four, the NBA playoffs, and any heavyweight boxing match. Card rooms are often near the sports book and will draw sports bettors. Then you can take advantage of some buckethead whose mind is on the point spread instead of on his cards. By the same token, you can always impersonate a sports nut and take advantage of the poker pro trying to take advantage of you. Unless, of course, he's onto you. Or you're onto him.

37. The absolute best poker in the world is played during the four weeks of the World Series of Poker—at Binion's Horseshoe casino from mid-April to mid-May. Afterward, go to California and play, because everyone is just back from Vegas and they're weak, tired, and vulnerable.

38. The first of the month is always better than the end of the month because people have more money. The worst time to play is in July and August; due to the heat, it's the slowest time in Vegas. This means you're up against more locals.

39. The true measure of a poker player is how well he plays when he's losing.

40. Johnny Bond says: "Watch the bad players. Sometimes they do something so stupid, it's brilliant."

41. A *tell* is a mannerism that gives away a player's hand. Nearly everyone has tells, and learning to read them is an important part of the game. The easiest tell is the guy who tries to hurry the dealer. You can bet your case money he's sitting on pocket rockets. Get out quick.

42. The opposite tell is the guy who slams his chips into the pot in an exaggerated way—he's got nothing in the

## POKER TALK

# PARLEZ-VOUS CUTTHROAT?

**Bad beat:** Losing to a lousy hand that got there.

**Broadway:** An ace high straight.

**Bullets:** Aces, also known as *pocket rockets.*

**Case money:** A player's last chips.

**Drawing dead:** A hand that's beat even if it gets there.

**The flop:** The first three community cards.

**Flopping the nuts:** Getting the best possible hand on the flop.

**Free rolling:** Having a chance to win without a chance to lose.

**Getting there:** Hitting your draw cards to make a good hand.

**Gutshot:** A card that makes an inside straight draw; also known as a belly buster.

**Make a move:** Betting out against weak players (a form of bluffing).

**The mortal nuts:** An absolutely unbeatable hand.

**Nutcrackers:** A hand that if it gets there will beat the best hand.

**On tilt:** When your emotions affect your play.

**Rainbow:** A flop with three different suits.

**The river:** The fifth and last community card.

**Rock:** A player who only plays good cards.

**Set:** Three of a kind.

**Slow-play:** Calling with the mortal nuts in order to get more players.

**Snapped:** Losing with good cards.

**Stuck:** Losing.

**Toke:** Vegas slang for tipping the dealer.

**The turn:** The fourth community card.

**Two-outer:** A hand that can only get there by hitting two cards.

**Up:** Winning.

– C.O.

hole. He's a big bluffosaurus. Raise his ass out of the chair and send him limping home to Momma.

43. Then there's the player who tries to entice you to bet by holding his cards as if he's going to throw them away. This means he's got a good hand. The same guy will lean forward holding chips in his hand before you act, implying that he will call your bet. What that really means is that his cards are terrible and he wants you to check. He's a bully. You're not allowed to shoot him, but at the poker table you can look him in the eye and take his money.

44. Johnny Bond says: "Confidence is the most important quality. No matter how low you get, always feel like you can kick a snake in the ass."

45. When you go on a rush and win a few big pots, it's natural to begin thinking about turning pro—quitting your job, leaving your wife, moving to Vegas, and playing cards for a living. If you're successful at the Bellagio, your future is only 30 feet away, at the higher-stakes games. Take a good look. It's the same game in the same room with the same dealers. Only the players are better. A lot better.

46. The pros are not gamblers, they're entrepreneurs, in business for themselves. Their bankroll is their inventory.

47. Keep your thinking straight. Beware the poker player's trap: When you're lucky, you believe it's due to skill, and when you're playing badly, you blame it on bad luck.

48. Don't play drunk, stoned, angry, tired, or hung over.

49. Away from the table, poker players tend to be kind, generous, polite, and warm. At the table, the only honor lies in getting the chips. Take advantage of everything. If a player is drunk, buy him a drink. If he's a moron, compliment his intelligence. When he loses, tell him it was just bad luck. When he gets lucky, tell him how great a player he is.

50. Most people think you need a big bankroll to play, but that's not true. You don't need money to play poker. You need to win. You need to have courage, and you must be ruthless. You must be willing to check-raise your mother out of her mortgage payment.

51. Poker is a game of the long run, but the short run can be awfully long.

52. Johnny Bond says: "I don't lie, cheat, or steal. Who else can say that and make the money I do independently? Where else could I pick my hours, look at beautiful women, drink all I want, and eat for free? It's a hard way to make an easy living."

—CHRIS OFFUTT

## SEX

# Going to a Bordello

YOU'RE IN a foreign city, and curiosity takes over—you're going to a bordello. Ethical questions swarm your brain, but you don't have to worry. You may think this is about sex for money—you're wrong. Under the surface lies what may be the greatest coverup for champagne promotion ever conceived.

Everyone in Amsterdam knows Yab Yum, the most exclusive brothel in the city. Taxi drivers, bartenders, and hotel clerks are paid to know about it, but the locals will tell you for free: In a country where prostitution is out in the open, it's the most elegant place to visit. Yab Yum's manager is Mitch—just Mitch. He is impeccably dressed and well poised; a mischievous grin is all that separates him from a man running a four-star restaurant. And if you're visiting a high-class bordello, he insists you treat it no differently than just that. "There is no dress code," says Mitch, "but anyone who looks too weird will be turned away." If you want to gain admittance, do not show up drunk, stoned, or out of control. Coming by yourself or in a small group is also preferred; they want you meeting women, not talking to your friends.

After paying a $75 admission fee, you are taken to the bar, where beautiful women abound and you may drink for free—except champagne. Mitch points out that the bartenders do more than serve martinis. They are your allies in helping you find the woman you desire. Discuss your tastes with them and they will know who to point your way.

Never feel any pressure to select the first woman who comes to you or decide that someone you've been talking to isn't your type. "Everything changes when we come through that door," says one young blonde, "so we don't take it personally."

The patrons at Yab Yum extol its relaxed atmosphere compared to other bordellos, where a higher entrance fee includes an hour of sex but where refunds are not an option if there is no one to your liking. One man even shuddered when talking about bordellos in Nevada, where a "police lineup" of prostitutes are brought in the

*When choosing between two evils, I always like to take the one I've never tried before.*

**—MAE WEST**

moment you enter and a decision is expected immediately.

Yab Yum doesn't require you to go upstairs. But if you wish to stay at the bar and enjoy the female company, you are expected to open some champagne. Bottles cost from $100 to $1,000, while going upstairs with a woman is only $250 for an hour. Remember—movie theaters make their real money from the popcorn.

Upstairs you are taken to a plush room and led past the bed and Jacuzzi and over to the couch for some conversation. There are two reasons for this. First, your companion now receives a 20 percent commission on champagne sales. While not required, you will make her very happy if you order something. Second, they ideally want to have sex only once every hour, and the couch-Jacuzzi-bed circuit stretches out the time.

When the management suspects that you don't have a lot of money, they will advise the woman that everything should be finished in one hour. Otherwise, things are timed so that when someone downstairs calls to see if you'd like to stay longer, she will be doing things to ensure that your answer is a quick yes.

Condoms are mandatory for all activities upstairs—no exceptions. Women who work at Yab Yum are examined by a doctor twice a week and tested for HIV every six weeks, but no place can offer an absolute guarantee in this line of work. Always use protection.

Many customers are celebrities, and Mitch says there is a "gentleman's agreement" not to discuss who you've met inside. Everyone is treated the same, and there are no special entrances or secret routes upstairs for those wishing total privacy. If you wish to keep your own visit undercover, it might be best to pay in cash. Credit cards are charged under an innocuous business name, though, as Mitch will warn you with a smile, "accountants all over the world are very familiar with that company." Play it safe and leave Visa out of it—after all, you only went there for drinks.

—ADAM MORGANSTERN

# CONTRIBUTORS

Formerly the assistant editor of Rolling Stone Press, **ANN ABEL** is a copy editor at *GQ*.

**ANTHONY ACERRANO** lives in western Montana and often writes about outdoor subjects for *Men's Journal* and other national magazines.

*Men's Journal* staff photographer **ANDY ANDERSON** has worked as a fly-fishing guide in Alaska, a mechanic at Sears, and a firefighter in the U.S. Air Force. Anderson has taken pictures across the globe, from Alberta to Saudi Arabia. He lives in Mountain Home, Idaho.

**DAVID ANSEN** is a senior editor and movie critic for *Newsweek* magazine.

A former radio talk show host and journalist, **COY BAREFOOT** has recently written books on e-commerce and Virginia history. He lives in upstate New York.

**ROBERT A. BARNETT,** features editor of Miavita.com, is the author of *Tonics: More Than 100 Recipes That Improve the Body and the Mind* (Harper-Collins, 1997).

**DAN BENSIMHON** is a former contributing editor at *Men's Journal* and is currently a resident of internal medicine at Duke University Medical Center.

*Men's Journal* associate editor **ALEX BHATTACHARJI** often contemplates how, if he ever were to play pro sports, his name would fit on the back of his jersey. His work has appeared in *Sports Illustrated*, *Sports Illustrated for Kids*, *NBA Inside Stuff*, *Rolling Stone*, and *Men's Journal*.

**MARK BITTMAN** is the author of the award-winning *How to Cook Everything* (Macmillan 1998) and the *New York Times* column "The Minimalist."

**KENT BLACK** is a *Men's Journal* contributing editor as well as a contributor to *Outside*, *Smithsonian*, and *The New York Times Magazine*. He lives in Madrid, New Mexico.

**JON BOWERMASTER,** the author of six books, has made first descents of rivers from Chile to China. Most recently, he has led *National Geographic*–sponsored expeditions by sea kayak to the Aleutian Islands and the coast of Vietnam.

**ANTHONY BRANDT** has written for many national publications and is working on a book about the rise and fall of literary reputations.

**EUGENE BUCHANAN** is publisher and editor in chief of *Paddler* magazine. A former kayak instructor and guide, he freelances for *Men's Journal*, the *New York Times, Sports Afield, Outside,* and *National Geographic,* among other publications.

**MICHAEL CASTLEMAN**'s ten books have more than 2 million copies in print, notably *Sexual Solutions: For Men and the Women Who Love Them,* a self-help guide to men's sex problems, and *Blended Medicine,* a home medical guide that combines mainstream and alternative therapies.

**SUZAN COLON** is currently *Jane* magazine's editor-at-large.

**PATRICK COOKE,** currently the executive editor of *Forbes FYI,* is a former editor at *Men's Journal.* He has written for *The New York Times Magazine, Rolling Stone, Vogue,* and the *Washington Post.* He is also the author of *Sentenced to Live,* which is currently in production as a motion picture at Warner Bros.

**GREGORY CROUCH,** a regular contributor to *Rock & Ice* and *Climbing,* is the author of *Route Finding: Navigating With Map and Compass.* Based in Santa Barbara, California, he is currently working on his second book, *Enduring Patagonia.*

**JEFFREY C. CSATARI,** a former deputy editor of *Men's Journal,* is currently the editor of *MH-18,* the *Men's Health* magazine for teens.

**LYNN DARLING** is a writer based in New York City. Her first book, *The Slut Museum,* will be published by Little, Brown in 2001.

When freelance health and fitness writer **JOHN DELVES** was training for his dozens of marathons and 10Ks, high mileage and long hours were king. He wishes he'd known then what he knows now.

**DAVID DiBENEDETTO,** an associate editor of *Men's Journal,* has also written for *Rolling Stone,*

*Outdoor Life,* and *Boating.* He lives in New York City, where he has little time to gear up for wilderness trips or work on his jump-rope technique but has become expert at finding ingenious ways to pry off beer-bottle tops while sitting on his couch.

Oakland-based **JOEL DRUCKER** writes about sports and popular culture for *Men's Journal, Cigar Aficionado, HBO Sports,* and *Tennis* magazine.

**STEVEN EDWARDS,** a Los Angeles–based journalist, writes for numerous magazines and newspapers.

**SID EVANS** is a deputy editor at *Men's Journal.* He was the editor of the *Deer Hunter's Almanac* and the *Trout Fisher's Almanac,* both published by Atlantic Monthly Press. He has also written for *Men's Journal, Sports Afield* and the *Oxford American.*

**BILL FLANAGAN** is the editorial director of VH1 and author of the novel *A&R,* as well as the books *Written in My Soul* and *U2 at the End of the World.* He has written for *Rolling Stone, Vanity Fair, Esquire,* and *GQ,* among other magazines.

**RICHARD FORD** is the author of several novels, including *The Sportswriter* and *Wildlife,* and short-story collections *Women With Men* and *Rock Springs.* His 1996 novel *Independence Day* was the first book to receive both the Pulitzer Prize and the PEN/Faulkner Award. Ford lives in New Orleans with his wife, Kristina.

**BRETT FORREST,** a New York City–based freelance writer, has written for *Rolling Stone, The New York Times Magazine,* and *Sports Illustrated.*

**CHARLES GAINES** is the author of 13 books, including *The Next Valley Over: An Angler's Progress,* a collection of fishing stories published by

Crown. He is a contributing editor of *Men's Journal* and *Sports Afield* magazines.

**HOLLY GEORGE-WARREN** has cowritten and contributed to numerous books, including *The Working Woman's Guide to Managing Stress* (Prentice Hall, 1994). She has also written for *Men's Journal*, *Rolling Stone*, and the *New York Times*. She is editor of Rolling Stone Press.

**JON GLUCK** is a magazine consultant and a former senior deputy editor at *Men's Journal*.

**LAURENCE GONZALES** is the author of nine books, including *One Zero Charlie: Adventures in Grass Roots Aviation*.

**JIM GORANT** is a New Jersey–based freelance writer who covers travel, health, fitness, and outdoor sports. He was deputy editor of the *1999 Men's Journal Gear Guide*, and his work has appeared in *GQ*, *Men's Journal*, *Sports Afield*, *American Way*, and *Maximum Golf*, among others.

**LAMAR GRAHAM** is a contributing editor and columnist of *Parade* magazine and an associate professor of journalism at New York University, where he specializes in new media. He lives in Brooklyn.

**MIKE GRUDOWSKI** has written for *Outside*, *Men's Journal*, *The New York Times Magazine*, and other publications. He lives in California.

**PATRICK HIGGINS** and **MAURA KATE KILGORE** coauthored with Paul Hertlein the *Homebrewer's Recipe Guide* (Fireside, 1996), named one of the outstanding beer books of the year by *Food & Wine* magazine.

**CARL HOFFMAN** is a writer based in Washington, D.C.

**JOSEPH HOOPER** is a freelance writer who writes regularly about sports medicine and fitness for *Men's Journal* and about culture and music for the *New York Observer*.

**MARK JANNOT,** former deputy editor of *Men's Journal*, is the executive editor of *National Geographic Adventure* magazine.

**PETER JARET,** who won the James Beard Award for food writing in 1997, is a contributing editor at *Health* magazine and WebMD. His work has appeared in many magazines, including *Men's Journal*, *National Geographic*, *Vogue*, *Newsweek*, *Harper's Bazaar*, *Reader's Digest*, and *Glamour*. He tends a small garden and vineyard in Sonoma County, California.

**STEVE JERMANOK** writes frequently on mountain biking for such publications as *Men's Journal*, *Outside*, *National Geographic Adventure*, and *Sports Afield*.

**ROBERT F. JONES** is the author of eight novels and five works of nonfiction. His articles and essays, which have appeared in *Audubon*, *Time*, *Life*, *Sports Illustrated*, *People*, *Harper's*, and the *New York Times*, have been included in 22 anthologies.

**SEBASTIAN JUNGER** is the author of the number-one bestseller *The Perfect Storm: A True Story of Men Against the Sea*.

**MICHAEL KONIK,** the West Coast editor and golf columnist of *Delta SKY* magazine, is the author of *The Man With the $100,000 Breasts and Other Gambling Stories* (Broadway).

**STEVEN KOTLER** is a frequent contributor to *Men's Journal*, *GQ*, *Details*, and other publications. His novel, *The Angle Quickest for Flight*, was published in 1999 by Four Walls Eight Windows. He is currently at work on a second book.

**ERIK LARSON** is the author of *Isaac's Storm*. He lives in Seattle with his wife, three children, and three guinea pigs.

**TED LEESON** is the equipment editor for *Fly Rod & Reel* magazine and is a contributing editor to *Field & Stream*. His books include *The Habit of Rivers: Reflections on Trout Streams and Flyfishing* and *The Fly Tier's Benchside Reference to Techniques and Dressing Styles*. He teaches writing at Oregon State University.

**GARY LEGWOLD** is a Minneapolis-based author and writer who has written extensively on health and fitness topics.

**MARK LEVINE** is a contributing editor to *Men's Journal* and teaches poetry at the Iowa Writers' Workshop.

**LYDIA LUNCH** is a confrontationalist who uses music, film, photography, and the written word as the landscape upon which she dissects the human condition and its multiple obsessions.

**ALEX MARKELS** is a frequent *Men's Journal* contributor and former staff reporter for the *Wall Street Journal*.

**JOHN McCORMICK** is a screenwriter living in Los Angeles whose film credits include *Living on Tokyo Time*, Russ Meyer's *The Bra of God*, and John Woo's *King's Ransom*.

**EVAN McGLINN** is the executive editor of LuxuryFinder.com, a luxury e-commerce site. His writing has appeared in *The New York Times, Town & Country, Forbes, Men's Journal*, and *Rolling Stone*.

**THOMAS McINTYRE** is an outdoor writer who has traveled through Europe, Africa, Australia, South America, the Arctic, and China. He lives in Wyoming.

**BUCKY McMAHON**'s great life includes writing about the outdoors, especially about marine adventures. He lives with his wife on a dog farm near Tallahassee, Florida.

**ADAM MORGANSTERN** is a filmmaker and freelance writer living in Manhattan. He only visits bordellos when paid to do so by major magazines.

New York–based writer **RICHARD NALLEY** is a contributing editor to *Men's Journal*.

**T. EDWARD NICKENS** has been a freelance journalist for more than a decade and has written about adventure travel and natural history across North America. He lives in Raleigh, North Carolina.

**CHRIS OFFUTT** is the author of the short-story collections *Kentucky Straight* and *Out of the Woods*, the novel *The Good Brother*, and the memoir *The Same River Twice*. Offutt lives in Kentucky.

**BILL OLSEN** is a freelance writer based in Michigan's Upper Peninsula. He has written about log building for the *New York Times* and *Log Home Living*.

**P.J. O'ROURKE** is the foreign affairs desk chief of *Rolling Stone* and a contributing editor to *Men's Journal*. He is the author of nine books, including the bestselling *Eat the Rich* (Grove/ Atlantic).

**STEVE PEZMAN,** who started surfing at 16, began writing for surf magazines in 1968 and two years later became the publisher of *Surfer* magazine, a position he held until 1991. He is currently copublisher of the *Surfer's Journal* with his wife.

**LARRY PLATT,** author of *Keepin' It Real: A Turbulent Season at the Crossroads With the NBA* (Avon Books, 1999), has written for *GQ, Details, Men's Journal,* and *The New York Times Magazine*.

**GEORGE PLIMPTON** is the founder and editor of the *Paris Review* and the author editor of 26 books, most recently, *Truman Capote: In Which Various Friends, Enemies, Acquaintances, and Detractors Recall His Turbulent Career* (Doubleday, 1997).

**STEPHEN RAE** is a New York–based writer.

**TED G. RAND,** a journalist and new-media producer, is the author of *Athletic Forever* (Contemporary Books) and has written extensively about technology, medicine, and fitness.

**DOUG ROBINSON,** former president of the American Guides Association, is the owner and chief guide for the rock-climbing school Moving Over Stone. He has a bestselling instructional video, *Moving Over Stone,* and has published a collection of essays, *A Night on the Ground, a Day in the Open.*

New York writer **JULIAN RUBINSTEIN** is a contributing editor to *US Weekly* and *Gear.* His work has also appeared in *Sports Illustrated, The New York Times Magazine, Men's Journal, Outside,* and *Salon.*

**ALLEN ST. JOHN,** a father of two, has written for *Parenting* and has changed, at last count, 6,793 diapers, St. John has also covered three World Series for *The Village Voice.*

**DAN SANTOW** has written for *People, Metropolitan Home, Redbook, Good Housekeeping,* and *Men's Health,* among other publications. He is also the author of *Frommer's Irreverent Guide to Chicago* and children's biographies of Eleanor Roosevelt, Jacqueline Kennedy, and Mary Todd Lincoln. He lives in Chicago.

**PAMELA REDMOND SATRAN,** a former fashion editor at *Glamour,* is a columnist for *TV Guide* and *Ladies Home Journal.*

**PAUL SCOTT,** who lives in Bangor, Maine, has written on a variety of topics for *Men's Journal* since 1997. Though he tended bar in Minneapolis and New York for 10 years, he has never been in a bar fight. He likes it that way.

**JEFF SIEGEL** lives in Dallas, where nothing makes him happier than a fine bottle of wine. He has written for *American Way, Southwest Spirit, Sports Illustrated, Men's Health, Gourmet,* and *Travel & Leisure.*

**STEVE SLON** has written widely about health, fitness, sports, and sex. A former managing editor of *Men's Health,* Slon later became editor in chief of *Success* magazine and is currently editor in chief of www.FitLinxx.com.

**MARISSA SPRING** is a frequent contributor to technical journals for the software industry.

**G.S. STEVENS** has written extensively for several men's magazines. He teaches journalism at a small Pennsylvania college.

**ROB STORY** won the Trailwood Elementary School Spelling Bee in 1975. He writes about adventure sports for a variety of halfway decent magazines.

San Francisco–based journalist **JAY STULLER** is the author of *How to Love a PMSing Woman—When Timing Is Everything.*

**JOHN TAYMAN** is an editor-at-large of *Men's Journal.* He was the founding editor of *Rocky Mountain* magazine, a senior editor at *Life* magazine, and deputy editor of *Outside* magazine. He lives in Colorado and serves as editor-in-chief of StreetAdvisor.com, a financial site for investors.

**JIM THORNTON** won the 1998 National Magazine Award for a series of health articles pub-in *Men's Journal*, for which he is a contributing editor. He is the author of three books: *White Wolf: Living With an Arctic Legend* (NorthWord Press, 1988), *Chore Wars: How Households Can Share the Work and Keep the Peace* (Conari Press, 1997), and *The Arginine Solution: The First Guide to America's New Cardio-Enhancing Supplement* (Warner Books, 1999).

**ANDREW TILIN** has been writing about fitness for more than a dozen years. He has also written for the *New York Times*, *Outside*, and *Wired*. He lives in Santa Fe, New Mexico.

**REBECCA VOELKER** is a Chicago-based freelance writer and a contributing editor to the *Journal of the American Medical Association*. She has been writing about health and medical issues for more than ten years.

**DONOVAN WEBSTER,** a longtime contributor to *Men's Journal*, lives with his family in central Virginia.

# ACKNOWLEDGMENTS

As the first *Men's Journal* book, *The Great Life* is in many ways a product of eight years of writing, editing, and thinking about the subjects men care about most. That said, thanks should go to Jann Wenner, who founded the magazine and established its vision; John Rasmus and Terry McDonell, the magazine's former editors; Mark Bryant, its current editor; Kevin O'Malley, its former publisher; Kent Brownridge, the chairman of Wenner Media; and Wenner Media vice president John Lagana.

Enormous thanks goes to Kathryn Huck, whose hard work, determination, and thoroughness made this book possible. It was also a great pleasure to work with Holly George-Warren, Ann Abel, and Andrew Simon; literary agent Sarah Lazin and her staff; and Janet Goldstein and Alex Babanskyj at Viking Penguin.

The *Men's Journal* editorial staff is the best a person could ask to work with, and their efforts, ideas, and talents are reflected in these pages. Thanks to: Thomas Alberty, Chad Anderson, Alex Bhattacharji, Mark Cohen, Jenny Comita, Ben Court, Jeff Csatari, David DiBenedetto, Tanya DiBello, Dan Ferrara, Tom Foster, Maura Fritz, Jon Gluck, John Haney, John Mather, Greg Melville, Naomi Nista, Matt D'Amico, Will Palmer, Carin Pearce, Christine Penberthy, Robert Perino, Taylor Plimpton, Jenny Rubinfeld, Corey Seymour, Casey Tierney, Sarah Tuff, David Willey, Beverly Xua, and Bob Yeager. I would also like to specially thank Andy Anderson, Rob Howard, Michael Lawton, P.S. Mueller, and P.J. O'Rourke. In addition, thanks to the many talented writers, photographers, and illustrators whose work appears here.

Others who made important contributions are Evelyn Bernal, Emily Bodenberg, Janice Borowicz, Todd Meier, Mia Risberg, Rachael Shook, Dennis Wheeler, and Agata Zak. — S.E.

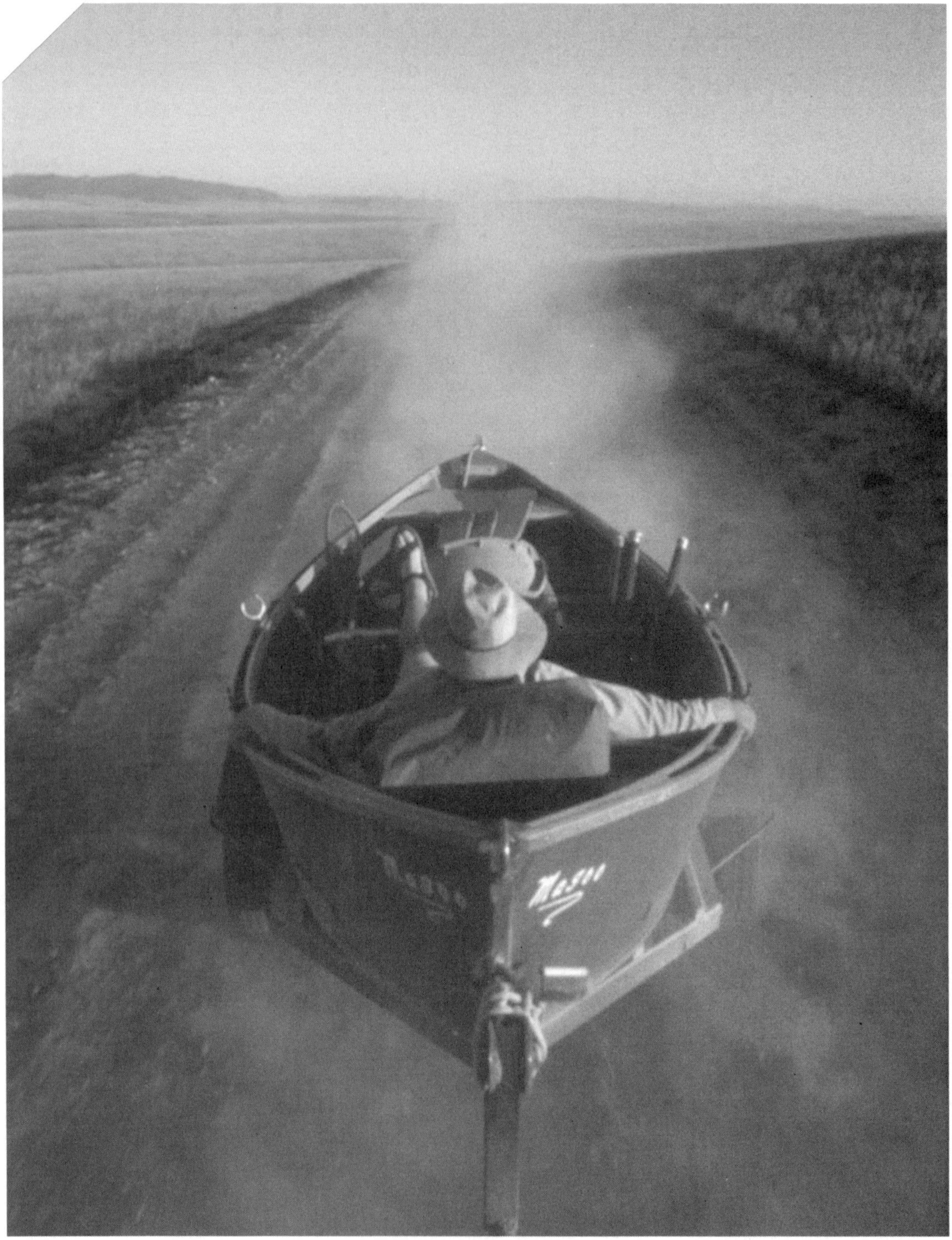

ANDY ANDERSON

# INDEX

## FOR THE BEST IN PAPERBACKS, LOOK FOR THE

In every corner of the world, on every subject under the sun, Penguin represents quality and variety—the very best in publishing today.

For complete information about books available from Penguin—including Puffins, Penguin Classics, and Arkana—and how to order them, write to us at the appropriate address below. Please note that for copyright reasons the selection of books varies from country to country.

**In the United Kingdom:** Please write to *Dept. EP, Penguin Books Ltd, Bath Road, Harmondsworth, West Drayton, Middlesex UB7 0DA.*

**In the United States:** Please write to *Penguin Putnam Inc., P.O. Box 12289 Dept. B, Newark, New Jersey 07101-5289* or call 1-800-788-6262.

**In Canada:** Please write to *Penguin Books Canada Ltd, 10 Alcorn Avenue, Suite 300, Toronto, Ontario M4V 3B2.*

**In Australia:** Please write to *Penguin Books Australia Ltd, P.O. Box 257, Ringwood, Victoria 3134.*

**In New Zealand:** Please write to *Penguin Books (NZ) Ltd, Private Bag 102902, North Shore Mail Centre, Auckland 10.*

**In India:** Please write to *Penguin Books India Pvt Ltd, 11 Panchsheel Shopping Centre, Panchsheel Park, New Delhi 110 017.*

**In the Netherlands:** Please write to *Penguin Books Netherlands bv, Postbus 3507, NL-1001 AH Amsterdam.*

**In Germany:** Please write to *Penguin Books Deutschland GmbH, Metzlerstrasse 26, 60594 Frankfurt am Main.*

**In Spain:** Please write to *Penguin Books S. A., Bravo Murillo 19, 1° B, 28015 Madrid.*

**In Italy:** Please write to *Penguin Italia s.r.l., Via Benedetto Croce 2, 20094 Corsico, Milano.*

**In France:** Please write to *Penguin France, Le Carré Wilson, 62 rue Benjamin Baillaud, 31500 Toulouse.*

**In Japan:** Please write to *Penguin Books Japan Ltd, Kaneko Building, 2-3-25 Koraku, Bunkyo-Ku, Tokyo 112.*

**In South Africa:** Please write to *Penguin Books South Africa (Pty) Ltd, Private Bag X14, Parkview, 2122 Johannesburg.*